D0852839

The Outlaw State

The Outlaw State

Saddam Hussein's Quest for Power
and the Gulf Crisis

Elaine Sciolino

JOHN WILEY & SONS, INC.

New York • Chichester • Brisbane • Toronto • Singapore

~ Author's note on transliteration

Transliterating terms from Arabic, Persian, and Turkish into English is never easy. In Arabic, for example, the name Hussein can be spelled more than a dozen different ways. Therefore, I have used English versions that commonly appear in American newspapers and newsmagazines.

E.S.

In recognition of the importance of preserving what has been written, it is a policy of John Wiley & Sons, Inc. to have books of enduring value published in the United States printed on acid-free paper, and we exert our best efforts to that end.

Copyright © 1991 by Elaine Sciolino

Published by John Wiley & Sons, Inc.

All rights reserved. Published simultaneously in Canada.

Library of Congress Cataloging in Publication Data

Sciolino, Elaine.
  The outlaw state : Saddam Hussein's quest for power and the gulf crisis / Elaine Sciolino.   p.   cm.
  Includes bibliographical references.
  ISBN 0-471-54299-7
  1. Iraq--Politics and government. 2. Hussein, Saddam, 1937– .
3. Persian Gulf War, 1991. I. Title.
DS79.7.S25   1991
956.704'3--dc20   91–12940
                                                                   CIP

Printed in the United States of America

10 9 8 7 6 5 4 3 2 1

To Andy, who made this book possible

Contents

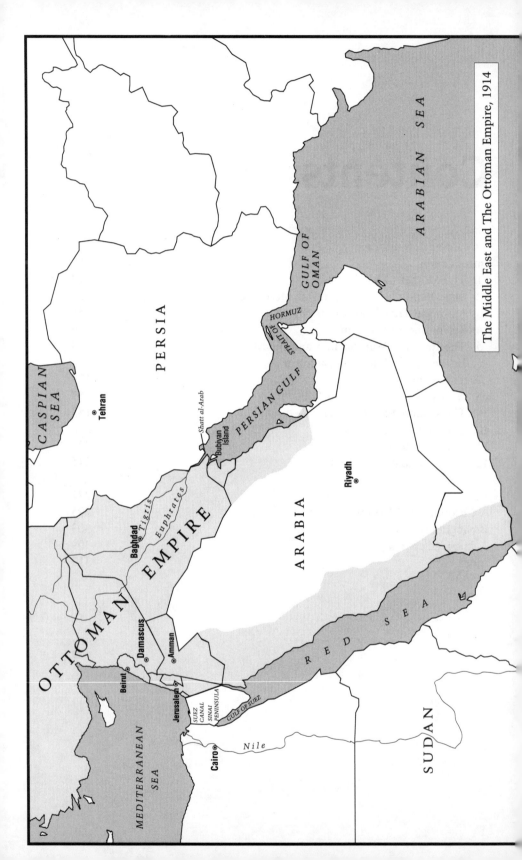

The Middle East and The Ottoman Empire, 1914

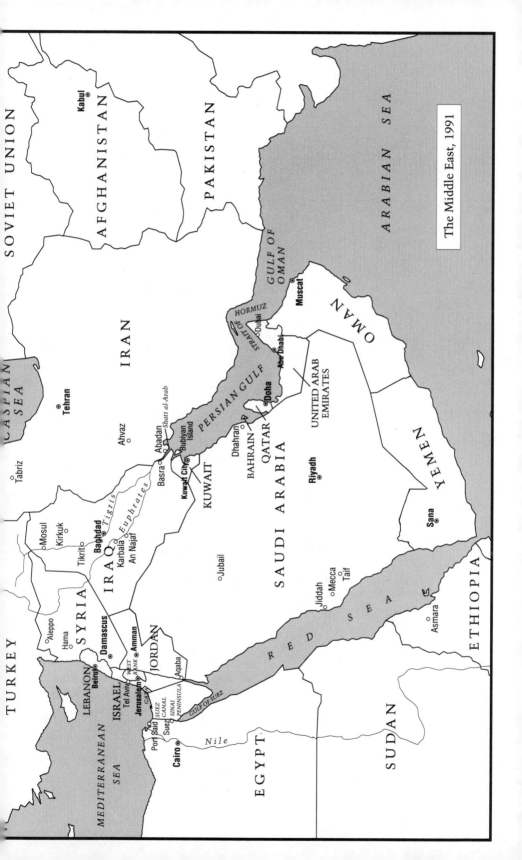

The Middle East, 1991

Introduction

Of all the countries in the Middle East, I have always found Iraq the toughest to penetrate and the hardest to like. Throughout most of the region, hospitality flowed freely. But Iraq under Saddam Hussein virtually eliminated its Western-educated elite and produced a generation of people who knew nothing but the peculiar propaganda of the Baath Party and the rule of fear. Hospitality was dangerous, and the foreigner, particularly the probing journalist, was regarded as an unwelcome intruder.

Even at the height of the American hostage crisis in Iran in 1979 and 1980, I covered the story by day and spent pleasant hours with Iranian friends by night. In Saudi Arabia, I was welcomed at the tables of princesses and in the huts of Bedouins. In Syria, whose regime rivaled that of Iraq for brutality and repression, one could talk—albeit softly—about politics in the private clubs in Aleppo and the salons of Damascus. Not so in Iraq. Iraqi friends from Rome or Paris asked me not to call them when I came to Baghdad and never allowed themselves to be quoted by name. Those who did mingle with foreigners could be called in for questioning or even jailed for fraternizing.

In a Baath Party document published in 1977, Saddam Hussein instructed teachers to teach children to "beware of the foreigner, for the latter is a pair of eyes for his country, and some of them are saboteurs of the revolution." During my first trip to Iraq, in August 1983, I asked Tariq Aziz, Iraq's foreign minister and the benign face Iraq was to show the West, about the inhospitality of the Iraqi people. His reply was simple and straightforward: "Iraqis keep away from mingling with foreigners and frankly, this is encouraged by the leadership." Soon after Iraq and the United States reestablished full diplomatic relations in November 1984, I asked him the same question. This time, the answer was different. If people didn't invite me to their homes, it was not because of policy, he suggested, but rather because I had failed to form genuine friendships with Iraqis. "If you have friends," he said, "they will invite you."

I went back to Baghdad two weeks before the war between the American-led coalition and Iraq broke out in January 1991. During a stopover in Jordan, security at Amman's Queen Alia International Airport was tighter than usual—a total of eight security and passport checks. I assumed that the Iraqi Airways Boeing 707 would be empty; instead, it was overbooked, filled with Egyptian workers, Palestinian families, Jordanian businessmen, foreign television crews, American diplomats, United Nations peacekeepers, representatives of a German peace movement, and Iraqis and other Arabs en route to piecing back their lives. I started a conversation with my seatmate, a woman about 30 years old covered in black from head to foot. She was traveling with three children, a girl of ten and two boys—one six, the other two. Why was she going back to Iraq now? I asked.

"I'm not going to Iraq," she said. "I'm going to Kuwait." She was a Kuwaiti and had fled to Bahrain with her husband and children only six days after the Iraqis invaded her country. But she had an aging mother and father, and she felt she had to go back to them. She still carried blue passports stamped STATE OF KUWAIT for herself and her children, and she assumed the documents would be confiscated as soon as she arrived. On the embarkation card, she defiantly wrote "Kuwaiti" on the line that asked for her nationality.

When the plane touched down in Baghdad in the early evening, Saddam International Airport was eerily empty. Of the airport's 35 gates, only two had planes parked at them. Every country except for Jordan had canceled flights to Iraq because of the global embargo imposed by the United Nations Security Council shortly after Iraq's August 2 invasion of Kuwait. The customs agent asked me to turn in my shortwave radio and computer modem, but I distracted him and he let me pass with an abrupt tilt of his head. In the old days, I might have been in for an hour's search. But he, like the country, was tired, tired of the rules that had lost their meaning as the country drifted toward war.

Outside the terminal, Saddam looked down at me from an enormous poster, his face lit by the full moon.

~

Once in Baghdad, I found a city where the fear of war had slightly, but perceptibly, diminished fear of foreigners. Baghdadis I had known over the years and ones I had never met sought me out. They spoke about their longing for peace after eight years of war with Iran, their frustration with deprivation and sacrifice as a result of the embargo, their worries that their children might not live to enjoy a better life. They did not blame their president, at least not publicly, but they did not praise him, either. One Iraqi, a Christian who had spent nine years in the military and was called up for active duty just before the war, even invited me to his parents' home for dinner.

The Gulf war proved that Saddam put pride and ambition above the interests of his people—despite his constant claims to the contrary and despite the lingering belief in his deceptive rhetoric in many quarters of the Arab world. Before he invaded Kuwait and plunged his country into war, he had emerged as the Arab world's most influential, and feared, political leader. Widely perceived as the winner of the war with Iran, he was expected to focus on the reconstruction of his country and to pursue a pragmatic foreign policy. Publicly, he claimed to be doing just that. But such a moderate and beneficial approach did not fit into his schemes. The war with Iran had helped him build the largest military machine in the Arab world, and sooner or later he would have felt compelled to use it. He coveted Kuwait, with its long Gulf coastline and its vast oil resources, and it became his first target. His willingness to sacrifice his people and his country in a war he could not win stripped away the image he had tried to cultivate as a state-builder and a leader of the Arab world.

With his single, swift, military move into Kuwait and his war against the international coalition, Saddam put the state he had built on a course of degradation and destruction, exposed his countrymen to ruin, divided and betrayed his Arab brothers, plunged the world's oil markets into chaos, and destroyed the regional balance of power. He also shattered the illusion that the end of the Cold War would bring peace and stability to the world. After the sacrifices made by his own people in the war with Iran, he promised them a fat peace dividend and the attainment of what he called their rightful place in the world. But in trying to achieve these ends, he reached for something far beyond his power to keep—the annexation of a sovereign state and a lock on vital natural resources that challenged world order and superpower interests. On August 2, 1990, when his troops rolled into Kuwait, Saddam became the custodian of nearly 20 percent of the world's oil reserves. On January 17, 1991, when the allies invaded and Saddam fought back, he buried, once and for all, any hope that his country would retain a place of importance in regional affairs. By the end of February, he was defeated and his country lay in ruins.

As soon as the war was over, the Iraqi people began to share stories of their suffering and vent their rage. The Shiite Muslims in the southern cities and the Kurds in the north rose up in protest and the regime ruthlessly suppressed them. By mid-April, more than 2 million Kurdish refugees were fleeing the retribution of Saddam Hussein—one of the largest refugee emergencies in recent history.

~

Saddam's consolidation of power in Iraq over more than two decades was in a sense a preparation for his adventure into Kuwait and his decision to wage war against much of the world. Iraq under Saddam had become a world unto itself, a world of untruth and illusion fostered by the Baath Party. Despite the pan-Arab rhetoric, the Party employed techniques borrowed from such masters of illusion as Stalin and Hitler, and Saddam was a Stalin-like figure in Middle Eastern garb. His attempt to shape Iraq's identity led him to articulate an expansionist vision beyond his reach. He manipulated the history of ancient Mesopotamia and grafted bits and pieces of its symbols onto modern-day Iraq. He invented his own mythology, creating a personality cult to make himself all things to all Iraqis.

Just as he rewrote Iraq's history to fit his needs, creating legends to help build his power along the way, he did the same to Kuwait. Just as he invaded Iran, hoping to seize territory and perhaps to overthrow the Khomeini regime in the process, so he sent his troops into Kuwait, going even further by annexing it and trying to blot out its national identity. Just as he expelled Shiites and gassed and resettled Kurds to root out potential sources of opposition, so he encouraged Kuwaitis to flee their country. Just as he executed his own enemies—some of them publicly to teach an indelible lesson to his people—so his troops indiscriminately tortured and executed Kuwaiti civilians as a way to pacify the population.

Much of the world ignored the process when it was applied only to Iraq; with the invasion of Kuwait and the outbreak of war, Saddam's totalitarian style was publicly exposed and had to be confronted. As soon as the allied forces entered Kuwait City in February 1991, the world began to receive confirmation of reports of Iraqi atrocities that had filtered out during the first days of the occupation. They offered stark evidence that Saddam had tried to remold the emirate into the nineteenth province of Iraq with the same tools of terror that he had used to establish absolute power at home. Annexation of the country was not just a matter of closing embassies and pulling down the flags; rather, it was a mythologizing operation fought with brutality and lies, an Orwellian attempt to erase the history, personality, and collective memory of an entire society.

With the Gulf crisis, Saddam assumed a number of different roles, although in the end, none of them fit. He cast himself as the inheritor of the mantle of the much-loved Egyptian leader, Gamal Abdel Nasser. Over a period of 18 years, the revolutionary fervor that Nasser evoked had expelled the French from Algeria and the British from Egypt and provoked the overthrow of pro-Western monarchies in Iraq and Yemen. His confrontation with the West opened the door to Soviet influence in the Middle East, inspired the emergence of the Palestine Liberation Organization (PLO), and stirred the Arab masses. In the end, Nasser was defeated by Israel in 1967 and although he survived, he never recovered his stature. Arab land was put under

Israeli control, Egypt's role as the leader of the Arab world ended, and the seeds of future conflict were sown.

In the first flush of his invasion of Kuwait, the message of Saddam the Arab savior took root in Jordan, in Yemen, in the Palestinian refugee camps of the Israeli-occupied territories, in some circles in Tunisia, Algeria, and Morocco. The enthusiasm was muted after Palestinians and other Arab workers returned home from Kuwait with stories of mistreatment and terror. The poor Arabs loved the message of Arab unity but hated the messenger who pitted Arab against Arab, brother against brother. After the bombing began in January 1991, the televised images of the burned bodies of Iraqi civilians and the destruction of the bridges and buildings in Baghdad—once a great Arab city and the locus of Arab culture—deeply pained many Arabs. They railed against the relentless American-led assaults, but they railed even louder against Saddam. In the eyes of most Arabs, Saddam was getting his due. He and the military machine he built would finally be crushed.

Saddam wrapped himself in the cloak and turban of his onetime nemesis, the late Ayatollah Ruhollah Khomeini of Iran. After fighting the religious leader for nearly a decade, Saddam paid him a bizarre compliment: He borrowed the arguments and rhetoric of Islam. When the American troops went to Saudi Arabia, Saddam, the son of Islam, called the faithful to rise up against the infidel and to expel the foreigners from holy soil. He conveniently forgot that his regime was based on a secular ideology, and that he had purged his country of many of its independent religious leaders and co-opted the rest.

Saddam also suddenly discovered the role of the man who took from the effete rich Arabs and gave to the poor. He decried the unequal distribution of wealth in the Arab world, and in particular the fabulous wealth of the tight oligarchies that ruled the oil-producing Gulf states. The fact that he had squandered his own country's wealth on armaments and war didn't seem to matter to him.

Saddam portrayed himself as a twentieth-century Saladin, a crusader-warrior who had fought the Iran-Iraq war for all Arabs and would take on the greatest power in the world. As such, he was an Islamic knight, one whose role was to protect Arab womankind against the emirs and the "procurers" who had sold the daughters of Islam into what he called "whoredom." He did not mention that his own country had the most active prostitution industry in the Gulf.

In reality, Saddam fit none of his adopted roles. He was not a great Arab nationalist or a man of religion, or a protector of the poor or a modern-day crusader. He was not even a good Arab brother.

Nor did Saddam have a mercantile nature, and it is the merchant who has always dominated Middle Eastern culture and politics. The merchant may posture, bluster, and say outrageous things, but in the end, he plays by three rules: Profit and loss determine the outcome; everything has a price; the price is always negotiable. But bargaining didn't come naturally to Saddam, and he didn't know the rules of the bazaar. For example, he didn't negotiate himself out of the Iran-Iraq war. Instead, he unilaterally withdrew. When he saw that he was losing the war in the Gulf in 1991, he retreated and gave up all his claims, including his annexation of Kuwait and his demand that withdrawal be linked to a resolution of the Palestinian crisis.

Saddam was an outlaw who built an outlaw state. Unskilled in the art of negotiation, he resorted to force as the only way to get what he wanted. He broke the rules of international convention over and over—when he used chemical weapons against Iranian soldiers and against his own civilian population, when he invaded and annexed another sovereign state, when he raped and murdered Kuwaitis and looted their country. Saddam was like the bank robber who is able to grab the cash but gets trapped inside the vault as the alarm bells go off and the doors slam shut behind him. Does he turn himself in or shoot his way out? For Saddam, who liked to remind visitors of his past as a tough underground guerrilla, the only way out was to shoot.

President Hafez al-Assad of Syria, whose brutality at home and abroad rivaled that of Saddam, was much better in the bazaar. The outlaw in Assad knew how to use force when it suited his purpose: in killing between 10,000 and 25,000 of his people when they rose up against him in Hama in 1982, and in seizing huge chunks of Lebanon. But the merchant in him knew how to get away with it, and after Saddam's invasion of Kuwait, he was courted by U.S. President George Bush, who welcomed him with open arms into the anti-Saddam coalition. If Saddam had had the patient cunning of Assad, he might have gotten much of what he wanted from Kuwait without ever having to send troops over the border.

Saddam made four mistakes in invading Kuwait. The first was poor timing, invading in the year of the new international order, when the world's great powers were uninterested in capitalizing on what once might have been regarded as a local dispute. His second mistake was that he swallowed Kuwait whole, rather than just nibbling at its edges. If it had remained a border dispute, there would never have been an international coalition or an American-led war. Saddam's third mistake was to move troops toward the Saudi border, an action that gave the impression that his aggression was unbounded.

Saddam's most serious mistake was that he miscalculated the world's response. He gambled—incorrectly—that the Arab states would never allow foreign forces into the region or fight on the side of the United States. He further assumed that when put to the test, the global coalition built against him would crumble. He based his assumption on the Arab view of history, which was largely cast in terms of a Manichaean struggle between light and darkness. If that history were a guide, then he had every reason to believe that his Arab brothers would take his side. But Saddam was blind to the fact that despite its enormous weapons arsenal, Iraq remained a small player on the world stage. He overestimated the strength of Arab "brotherhood" and failed to realize that the rest of the world would join to stop him. He refused to bend, and in the process, his country and his people were broken. His adventure into Kuwait and the war that followed brought the destruction, not the fulfillment, of his people's dreams. Certainly it did not restore Mesopotamia's glory.

~ 1 ~

The Mother of
All Battles

I will send foreigners to Babylon to winnow her and devastate her
land; they will oppose her on every side in the day of her disaster. Let
not the archer string his bow, nor let him put on his armor. Do not
spare her young men. Completely destroy her Army. They will fall
down slain in Babylon, fatally wounded in her streets.

—Jeremiah 51:2–4

~ Calm Before the Storm

It was New Year's Eve, December 31, 1990, and on the streets of Baghdad
there was little talk of war. Thousands of revelers, dressed in their holiday
finest, strolled idly along Saadoun Street, one of the capital's main thoroughfares. Army reservists on two-day leave from active duty popped in and
out of the gaudy discotheques along the way. One group of bored young men
stopped to watch a street brawl a block away from an Iraqi Airways office
that had been car-bombed a few years earlier. Horns honked and people
waved along the traffic-clogged street. Women in taffeta and ostrich feathers
and furs, men in ill-fitting double-breasted suits, children in glittery costumes
milled through the reception rooms of the al-Rasheed Hotel for a private
party.

The lobby was still decorated with a scrawny Christmas tree and alu-
minum-foil garlands, and the public-address system played jazz renditions
of well-worn Christmas carols. On the dance floor, couples swayed to popular
Egyptian ballads. Liberation Square, where Jews and other "conspirators"

were hanged as spies in 1969, was lit up with red and white lights like New York's Little Italy. Even the palm trees were strung with white and yellow lights. One façade of the Mansour Melia Hotel, which had been a way station for hundreds of foreign hostages until Saddam sent them all home a few weeks earlier, was festooned with blinking lights that greeted all of Baghdad with the words, HAPPY NEW YEAR 1991.

At the home of André Janier, the French chargé d'affaires, diplomats and foreign journalists gathered for the most elegant dinner party in town. Flouting the global embargo against Saddam, the Janiers had smuggled in from Paris six suitcases of delicacies—foie gras, white sausages, smoked salmon, turkeys, and the ingredients for nine desserts—accompanied by French champagne and wines. A French television crew filmed the evening's highlights for broadcast back home. Joseph C. Wilson IV, the American chargé d'affaires, danced with the Italian correspondent from *La Repubblica*. There were no Iraqis at the party. At the Foreign Ministry, meanwhile, Nizar Hamdoon, a deputy foreign minister and former ambassador to Washington, sat in his office and watched a recap of the events of 1990 on Cable News Network (CNN). Eventually, even he left for a party at a private club.

Saddam spent New Year's Eve with his commanders in Kuwait, or so the official Iraqi news media said. Dressed in a military overcoat and beret, a green silk scarf around his neck, the Iraqi leader was shown on television praying with his troops and kissing his officers on both cheeks. A commentator announced that Saddam had gone to the front to prepare dinner for his troops. With Bach's Brandenburg Concertos on the soundtrack, the television footage showed a flat, open field at an undisclosed location, where Saddam, under moonlight, stirred a huge pot of stew on a campfire. He poured liberal amounts of salt into the bubbling pot and showed some of his commanders how to stir it. After sampling the meal, he smiled broadly and shook the hands of Republican Guards who lined up for a brief—perhaps their last—encounter with their leader.

"We asked ourselves where we should go this night," he said to them. "The best place is with our armed forces." Then he launched into a 30-minute lecture, using the Islamic imagery that he adopted after his invasion of Kuwait, telling his men that the New Year would mark the "beginning of the hot confrontation between the alliance of believers . . . and the alliance of infidels, deviationists, and hypocrites." Saddam did not intend to miss an opportunity to remind his troops of their ancient greatness. They might be facing great adversity, he told them, but they must not forget that Iraq was civilized 6,000 years ago, "when others were living in caves like beasts." They would triumph over the so-called superior Western technology, which was, after all, based "on Arab knowledge," he added.

On the surface, Baghdad was deceptively normal. Physically, the capital was not prepared for war. Although some shopkeepers taped their windows to prevent flying glass, few antiaircraft guns and no sandbags were visible. But beneath the calm was quiet desperation. On the morning of New Year's Day, the nation was suffering a collective hangover as the countdown to war began. The streets of Baghdad were empty, the storefronts shut tight. Iraqis wealthy enough to have basements had filled them with at least a month's supply of food and water. Thousands of others put their belongings on the roofs of their cars and fled the capital for indefinite visits to relatives in the countryside. Others settled in Najaf and Karbala, assuming that the American-led coalition would not bomb the holiest sites of Shiite Islam. A ban on all foreign travel left the Iraqi people no other choice.

Ordinary citizens vacillated between a confident belief that both sides were bluffing to a grim fatalism that the country would be plunged into another senseless war. They did not describe the crisis as a struggle for the liberation of Palestine or Arab glory. Yes, they said, they believed that Kuwait was a part of Iraq, but they spoke about it as an abstract fact that they had memorized in geography class as children, not as a burning political issue. Like their president, they were caught between the gloomy predictions emanating from Washington and their own wishful thinking. The United States wouldn't attack them, they said, a question in their voices. There would be a compromise at the last moment, wouldn't there? And even if there were an attack, how could it be worse than the eight years of suffering in the war with Iran? The city's mood seemed to shift with each bit of news. When Iraqi Foreign Minister Tariq Aziz agreed on January 4, 1991 to meet with U.S. Secretary of State James A. Baker III in Geneva five days later, the spirits of ordinary Baghdadis seemed to rise. In what might have been interpreted as a sign of confidence among the business community, the prices of luxury goods in the bazaar in central Baghdad rose as well. When the talks collapsed, so did the spirit of the people and the bargaining power of the merchants.

Most disheartened were Iraq's young men, many of them reservists who had fought in the war against Iran and wanted to get on with their lives. In the stalled Iraqi economy, many of them had become taxi drivers, and they hung around the hotels of Baghdad like vultures, waiting for a foreigner to hire them for the day. One day in December, Baghdad Radio announced that all healthy males born in 1957 had to report to military registration centers, to be given a date to report to duty. A 33-year-old Iraqi driver whom I knew had been born in that year. He had served nine and a half years in the Army as a communications expert, most of them during the war with Iran, then had become a sales manager for an export construction firm. The only problem was that his firm did business in Kuwait, and when the Iraqis invaded, his job disappeared. He had no wife, no children, no prospects. Now he would have to go to war again.

In one sense, Iraq's looting of Kuwait after the invasion gave Baghdad the look of abundance. The Iraqis took spanking-new blue Mercedes buses looted from Kuwait and put them to use on the bus routes of Baghdad. The shops along Saadoun Street were clogged with booty: canned fruits and vegetables, processed meats and cheeses, British chocolates, Rolex watches, Giorgio Armani sportcoats and Bruno Magli shoes, Japanese VCRs, bottles of Coke that said, KEEP KUWAIT TIDY. But these items were hopelessly beyond the budgets of the average Iraqi consumer. The overflowing shops were painful reminders of what Iraqis could not afford.

On another level, Iraq began to take on the look and feel of a once-rich country that had come on hard times. The global embargo, imposed shortly after Iraq's invasion of Kuwait, ground down the spirit of the people. Beggars, who had always been swept off the streets with the morning garbage, were allowed to sit at intersections and ask—aggressively—for money. The price of two automobile tires jumped from 35 dinars in the summer of 1989 to 500 dinars by New Year's Day. When tires became scarce at any price, their theft from cars left on the street became common, a shock to Baghdadis who were accustomed to the strict law and order that accompanied the country's repression.

Cars and trucks were sidelined because of a shortage of spare parts. Hundreds of factories were closed. Baghdadis waited in line for two hours to buy bread at subsidized rates. By New Year's Day, the country was suffering from severe food shortages, particularly of rice, sugar, milk, and flour. Food-rationing coupons bought 25 to 50 percent less merchandise than they did when the rationing system was introduced the previous September. The week before I arrived, government agents had moved through private foodstalls in Baghdad to confiscate scarce staples and put them on sale in the government-owned shops.

The Iraqi Museum, always a calm refuge from the turmoil outside, was closed, its 200,000-piece collection packed into metal crates and stored in bunkers, along with the "Great Mesopotamian Exhibition," a selection of the best of the collection, originally scheduled to tour six American cities as part of a blossoming cultural exchange.

One by one, the better restaurants, even the ones in hotels, began to run out of certain items and then to close. Stores filled with furniture and toys and kitchenware—goods from pre-embargo days—were open but empty of customers. It was hard to believe that this was the country that possessed the second-largest oil reserves in the world, a rich, fertile country watered by the Tigris and the Euphrates. The luxury hotels in Baghdad, where Western and Japanese dealmakers once did business, were now filled with an odd mixture of foreign intermediaries and journalists, delegations of offbeat Muslim groups, and, to my surprise, Kuwaitis. At the al-Rasheed Hotel, a woman who said she was a Hungarian princess wandered the corridors wearing a diamond tiara and a diaphanous dress. Three neo-Nazi pilots in uniforms decorated with swastikas and portraits of Saddam professed their intention to go to the front to die for him. Salah Khalaf, the second-in-command of the Palestine Liberation Organization, lived there until he went back to the PLO headquarters in Tunis, where he was gunned down—possibly on Saddam's orders—on January 14.

The regime did its utmost to nurture antiwar sentiment and raise support in the Islamic world. Foreign peace activists volunteered to become human shields at the front lines to prevent the onslaught of allied troops. Their "peace camp" was a desert spot in Iraq hundreds of miles from the border between the opposing armies, but for them it was a symbol of their protest. "The more people who are here, the less chance there will be that Westerners will make war," insisted Hedwig Raskob, a psychotherapist from Munich. Instead, they became part of Saddam's propaganda machine. When one group of activists was taken to visit a farm outside Baghdad, the farmers burst into song—a war song. "Saddam, you are our leader," they sang, "and we are your willing soldiers." At a peace ceremony not far from Iraq's border with Saudi Arabia, two women were assigned to water a newly planted olive tree. But Iraqi authorities decided that an Iraqi soldier, his rifle on his shoulder, should do the watering. It was not what the peace activists had in mind.

Most intriguing was the status of the Kuwaitis. While thousands of them were imprisoned or executed by the Iraqis, others were left alone, for no apparent reason. They either drove nine hours from Kuwait City to Baghdad in their Mercedeses and minivans or flew north on nonstop Iraqi Airways flights. Some came to use the international phones that were cut off back home or to find relatives who were arrested in Kuwait and transported to Baghdad prisons. Other Kuwaitis took refuge in Baghdad hotel suites. Baghdad was cheaper than Riyadh, Bahrain, even Cairo, and it was easy to come and go to Kuwait when they pleased. Still others went on shopping sprees, filling up their vans with food, toys, clothes, and other consumer goods unavailable in Kuwait. Even though the Iraqi authorities had decreed that the Kuwaiti dinar was worth only one Iraqi dinar, a fraction of its former value, there was a strong black market in Kuwaiti currency in Baghdad. Kuwaiti money was worth ten times more in Baghdad than it was in Kuwait City.

At the American Embassy, Wilson taped on his office door a picture of John Lennon flashing the peace symbol in front of the Statue of Liberty, and he sent a bottle of wine from his home state of California to Foreign Minister Tariq Aziz, a Christian, for the New Year. Every day the Baath Party bused in hundreds of Iraqi women to chant slogans of peace outside the embassy. The demonstrations were timed to coincide with Wilson's briefings for the news media. To show that there were no bad feelings, Saddam sent the embassy a Yule-log cake and a bouquet of purple flowers.

Only when the last-minute Baker-Aziz talks failed in Geneva did Iraqis begin to realize that the country was on the brink of a catastrophic war. Even then, there was denial, and hopes were raised anew when Saddam announced that the National Assembly would convene on the evening of January 13, two days before the United Nations deadline. But the rubber-stamp body voted 220–1 in favor of a resolution affirming Iraq's annexation of Kuwait and authorizing the use of force to defend it. The diplomatic community packed up and departed, leaving the Iraqi people to face the consequences of war alone. The British ambassador, Harold Walker, took his staff to Jordan in a caravan of Range Rovers. Richard Ellerkmann, the German ambassador, left without saying goodbye to either Iraqi officials or fellow diplomats. At the British Club, a haven for Westerners for more than 70 years, there was no longer anyone to play darts or billiards. At the Netherlands Embassy, the chief security guard hurriedly burned huge bales of classified documents in oil drums before the embassy finally closed its doors.

On the eve of war, there was a tense calm among the functionaries in Iraq's Ministry of Information. These were "new Iraqi men" who conformed to Saddam's vision of greatness; they were the ultimate loyalists and also the most closely watched, because they acted as guides, and watchdogs, for foreign journalists. Yet they were uneasy when they talked about war.

Abbas was one of these new Iraqi men. A man in his early thirties whose shirts were too tight for his broad belly, he was my guide during two trips to Iraq in 1983 and 1984. Married, with two young sons, he had been an English major at Baghdad University, where he graduated at the top of his class. He had served in the Iran-Iraq war but never had to use his gun. Like his country and his president, Abbas was isolated, turned inward. Although he had never studied English abroad, he was required to interpret for non-Arabic-speaking journalists. He didn't know words like *slum* or *synagogue*, but could speak for hours about the "Zionist entity" and "imperialist enslavement." We had never been friends. In fact, on my previous trips, we had had violent arguments over what I could and could not do.

I saw Abbas again in Baghdad in early 1991, a few days before war broke out. He had spent five years as a press attaché in Europe and had lost 30 pounds. He was now earning about $1,500 a month at the official conversion rate, a salary worth only $100 a month because of inflation and the rampant black market. He now owned a car and an apartment in a new residential neighborhood of Baghdad. Life could not have been better, but he was gloomy and quiet in the face of the impending war. He asked, hypothetically, about the possibility of studying English in the United States. In a small but telling indication that sanctions were working, he wrote down a long list of medicines he needed for his family and asked if I could smuggle them in. "Look at all this," he said, pointing to the opulence of the al-Rasheed Hotel, in frustration. We're not a Third World country. We could lose it all." A few days later, Abbas and his countrymen were plunged into war.

~ The Spectacle of War

Operation Desert Storm began on schedule, unleashing a hail of bombs and missiles and dashing hopes for a peaceful solution of the Gulf crisis. From the allied side, the war seemed effortless, remote, antiseptic, surreal, a war not of blood and guts but of high-tech glitter and gadgetry. But it was real on the ground in Iraq.

The first explosions awoke Baghdad just before 3 A.M. on January 17, 1991, a pitch-black, moonless night. F-117 Stealth fighters flew over the city, one of them targeting and destroying the headquarters of the Iraqi Air Force. A Tomahawk cruise missile, launched by a battleship in the Gulf, followed a computerized map to its target 700 miles away: Saddam's presidential palace. By early the next day, the American-led forces had launched a hundred more missiles, each capable of reducing a warehouse-size building to rubble.

Saddam said over and over that he welcomed the fight—"the mother of all battles," as he called it. But he came to the battlefield alone. On the other side, the United States had assembled a coalition of 28 members that grew to 37 members by the time the war was over. The coalition included a deployment of more than half a million American soldiers and 205,000 allied troops. Saudi Arabia allowed foreign forces on its soil for the first time in its history, transforming its territory into a major staging area for the attack. Egypt sent 40,000 troops, placing them under Saudi command. The other Arab Gulf states scraped together a 10,000-troop brigade, while Kuwait organized 7,000 of its battered forces and Morocco sent 1,300 ground troops. Syria, a bitter foe of Iraq, contributed 15,000 troops, but participated warily, agreeing to fight on Kuwaiti—but not Iraqi—soil only days before the war.

Britain sent 43,000 troops and equipment from its Army, Navy and Air Force, France 16,000 troops. Argentina declared war on Iraq and sent a frigate and a corvette. Czechoslovakia dispatched chemical decontamination units. Sweden set up a field hospital, while Hungary, the Philippines, Sierra Leone, and Singapore sent additional medical personnel. Australia, Bangladesh, Belgium, Canada, Denmark, Greece, Italy, the Netherlands, New Zealand, Niger, Norway, Pakistan, Poland, Romania, Spain, Senegal, South Korea, even the Afghan mujaheddin guerillas participated.

Turkey did not send soldiers, but quietly provided bases for American fighter-bombers and massed troops on its border with Iraq. The Soviet Union went along with U.N. Security Council resolutions against Iraq but refused to contribute to the military effort. Germany and Japan did little militarily but pledged billions of dollars to help pay for the war effort.

By the time war came, the fate of Kuwait seemed almost incidental to many Americans. The Bush administration had succeeded in diverting attention from Kuwait's shortcomings and in demonizing Saddam. Most Americans believed their country was fully justified in fighting an old-fashioned, black-and-white battle against evil. Just after the fighting began, one poll showed that Bush's approval rate had soared to an overwhelming 83 percent, at that point, the highest of his presidency.

Still, Bush knew that he could not afford to lose the public to the "Vietnam syndrome," and that knowledge guided the structure of the war devised by Bush's generals, all of them Vietnam veterans. The pinpoint accuracy of the Stealth aircraft and cruise missiles meant they could deliver their bombs with a minimum of civilian casualties. "The agony of Vietnam is still with us," Bush acknowledged on December 18. "People remember a protracted war. They remember a war where individuals were asked to fight with one hand tied behind their back, in essence. This will not be, in my view, that kind of a confrontation." There would be nothing reminiscent of Vietnam in the American plan: no fractured world opinion, no body counts, no press roaming freely among the troops, no 50,000 American dead, no long and ambiguous struggle.

The highest priority for the American-led coalition was to bring the fourth-largest army in the world to its knees. The allies concentrated much of their firepower on military command-and-control targets: headquarters, radio towers, communications centers, troop concentrations in Kuwait, missile sites, chemical and biological weapons factories, airbases, barracks. But it also systematically destroyed the political symbols of the state that Saddam created: the Baath Party headquarters, the ministries, Saddam's palaces, buildings and installations in his hometown of Tikrit. Even the economic infrastructure of the country, painstakingly built up over the previous two decades with oil revenues, was dismantled. Refineries, roads, power plants, bridges, and factories simply collapsed. The allies justified hitting these targets for what they called important military value. But their destruction brought another message as well: They provided concrete proof for the Iraqi people that their leader and the modern Iraqi state built in his name might not survive.

The timing of the attack should have come as no surprise to Saddam. The United Nations, in authorizing the American-led coalition to use military force if necessary, set midnight, January 15, New York time, as the deadline for Iraq's withdrawal from Kuwait.

Bush decided to give Saddam one day of grace to withdraw before going to war. The delay allowed the allied commanders to wait for the darkness of the dead of night, after Iraq's capital fell into an uneasy sleep, before launching the air war. By coincidence, this decision meant that the attack was watched live on television around the world. The first news came from downtown Baghdad's al-Rasheed Hotel, where Western correspondents reported that they heard air-raid sirens and saw tracer bullets and antiaircraft bursts light up the sky. John Holliman of CNN began his broadcast slowly, then got caught up in what he saw and heard as the allies attacked and Iraqi antiaircraft tracers streamed skyward. He wasn't quite as eloquent as Edward R. Murrow in his radio broadcasts from London during the World War II blitz, but he was just as powerful. "It looks like a Fourth of July display at the Washington Monument," he said. "The sky is just brightly lighted with all these tracer rounds. Some are red. Some are white. We can see explosions, you know, air-burst explosions from these weapons. Oh-oh! Ope! Now there's a huge fire that we've seen that is due west of our position. And we just heard-whoa! Holy cow! That was a large air burst that we saw. It was filling the sky."

After the first bomb blast was heard on television at about 3 A.M. Baghdad time, President Bush sent his press secretary, Marlin Fitzwater, to the briefing room with the news: "The liberation of Kuwait has begun," he announced.

~

The weapons and the styles of combat on both sides illustrated the different characters of the two adversaries. Saddam had tried to fill his arsenal with the high-technology weapons usually enjoyed by only the most advanced military powers, including his two largest arms suppliers, France and the Soviet Union. He bought not only Soviet MiG and French Mirage fighter planes, but also command aircraft to supervise them. He took a modest Soviet ballistic missile, the Scud, and improved it until it was a respectable, if not terribly accurate, weapon with a reach long enough to range from Baghdad to Tehran and Tel Aviv. And he assiduously tried to develop the kinds of warheads that could turn the Scud into a weapon of mass destruction: chemical weapons, biological weapons, nuclear arms.

He came to the battlefield with other significant strengths: a million-man Army including a loyal, elite Republican Guard of eight divisions, chemical weapons, heavy defensive fortifications, thousands of tanks and artillery pieces, and, if all else failed, the threat of terrorist reprisals.

Saddam's military, however, was the ideal adversary for the allied coalition. It was a stolid, Stalinist war machine, unable to maneuver, rigidly commanded, using Soviet equipment, and trained to a great extent on the Soviet model. Its troops were mainly conscripts, stationed in trenches and bunkers out in the desert at the far reaches of exposed supply lines, powerless to defend themselves against relentless air attacks. For decades the Americans had built up a military machine custom-made for taking on the Soviet Army. American soldiers—all volunteers—had been trained in exercises to fight a Soviet foe. Many of the exercises were conducted in the desert conditions of Fort Irwin, California.

While the Iraqi force deployed in the desert was cut off from resupplies, malnourished, and demoralized, the American-led force was probably the most highly trained, best-equipped, best-educated, best-fed force ever to go into combat. Once these troops arrived in Saudi Arabia, they had nothing to do but build up their physical condition and train for the assault.

It was not by luck that the Americans confronted a Soviet-style force in the Arabian sands. For years they had prepared to do just that. The United States had assumed that in a global war, the Soviets would strike across Iran toward Saudi Arabia in an effort to seize the oil fields that were the lifeline of Western economies. The United States had developed a special force, called Central Command, to deal with such an emergency, and had readied plans for rapidly building up a force in the region—the exact plans that were put into use in Operation Desert Shield before the war itself began.

When it became evident that the Soviet Union was no longer a likely foe in the region, the war plans were adjusted to deal with regional instability. At the time of Iraq's invasion, military strategists were in the process of putting the new plan into place. Five days before the invasion, General H. Norman Schwarzkopf, commander of the allied coalition, and his commanders ran an exercise at their Florida headquarters to examine how they might respond to just such a move by Iraq. There was no time to draw up plans for a counterattack, so Schwarzkopf put one together in his months in the desert.

In those first days of battle, it seemed as if high technology could defeat any foe, no matter how heavily armed; that the trillions of dollars the Pentagon had spent in the previous decade were finally going to pay off in the quick defeat of an adversary who, despite his extraordinary military machine, was still no match for the Americans. The disproportionality of the two sides was staggering. Allied commanders wondered how it could be so easy, and whether Saddam had a secret plan. As it turned out, they believed Saddam's mythmaking and overestimated the strength of the Iraqi forces. In a February interview with C. D. B. Bryan, a journalist who had known him since Vietnam, Schwarzkopf acknowledged his foe's weakness. "The reality that has surprised us probably more than any other is that they're nowhere near as tough as we gave them credit," the general said.

～ An Iraqi Response

Saddam's reaction to the initial bombardments seemed not unlike Hitler's. "Hitler appeared stunned when England and France declared war on him...," wrote Verna Volz Small in her 1983 volume, *Hitler's Psychopathology*. "Believing the West feeble, he simply denied that real war had come and held back his forces to let 'the whole business evaporate.' "

Saddam's war strategy baffled the allied commanders. He refused to send his Air Force aloft into combat, except in a few token engagements. Saddam had always protected his Soviet- and French-supplied Air Force; during much of the Iran-Iraq war, his pilots had dropped their payloads from tens of thousands of feet, preferring safety to accuracy. Now, he sent more than 120 of his best fighter planes, bombers, and transports to Iran. The country that was once his mortal enemy had become a necessary sanctuary that was claiming to be as neutral as Switzerland. Other planes were dispersed as far away as India and Algeria. At first, the allies thought that Saddam was trying to draw Iran into the war; then they speculated that perhaps he was trying to preserve as much of the force as possible, in case the government in Baghdad survived this war, and he wanted them back.

Within a few days, the allied air commanders claimed air superiority, then air supremacy. They flew almost at will wherever they wanted over Kuwaiti and Iraqi territory, bombed their targets, and returned without facing any fire from enemy aircraft. "A leisurely drive through Baghdad," was the way the pilot of a Stealth fighter described his first bombing run.

Saddam's reluctance to fight the enemy in the air did not mean that he did nothing during the first weeks of war. Instead of taking on the coalition according to the rules of conventional combat, Saddam struck back in his own way. He tried to broaden the war by attacking Israel with improved Scud missiles. Refashioned from shorter-range Soviet models, and renamed the al-Abbas and al-Hussein, after two revered Shiite leaders, the Scuds were mobile and therefore easily hidden. He shot them without precision into the skies over Saudi Arabia and Israel. He did not distinguish between military and civilian targets.

Despite the success of American-made Patriot missiles in neutralizing many of the Scuds, the missiles remained a threat because the allies did not know whether Saddam could arm them with chemical warheads. The allies did discover that many of the Scud launchers were duds, decoys that gave the illusion of a much more potent threat. Saddam boasted that he would turn Israel into a "crematorium," terrifying that country's civilian population, which donned gas masks whenever a siren sounded. Instead, he failed to wreak much destruction on Israel. He also failed in his attempt to lure Israel into the war, which he hoped would split the allied coalition and draw the Arab world to his side. But Israel heeded pleas from Washington not to retaliate for the Scud attacks. His attacks on Saudi territory, meanwhile, did little damage until the last days of the war, when one landed on an American barracks, killing 28 and wounding at least 89 American soldiers who had arrived in Saudi Arabia just the week before.

Soon after his invasion of Kuwait, Saddam's propaganda machine charged that the United States planned to dump nuclear waste in the Saudi desert; instead, it was Saddam who unleashed an environmental weapon. When he opened up the pumping stations at Sea Island terminal, some ten miles off Kuwait, he spilled nearly ten million barrels of crude oil, possibly the largest spill in history. It was a tactic he had first used in his war with Iran, repeatedly attacking a number of Iranian offshore wells, spilling more than two million barrels of oil in 1983 alone. Perhaps in his war against the American-led coalition he hoped to complicate an amphibious landing off Kuwait by disrupting naval operations, to set the oil on fire during any attempt to storm the beaches, to cloud the atmosphere and make it harder to precisely aim laser- or television-guided bombs, or to disrupt water supplies in Saudi Arabia by forcing the closure of desalination plants.

Saddam also tried to weaken the coalition's resolve with another tactic— parading prisoners of war on Iraqi television. Bruised and dazed, they stared straight ahead, eyes glazed and faces puffy. "I condemn the aggression against peaceful Iraq," Guy Hunter, Jr., a Marine warrant officer, said. "Our leaders and our people have wrongfully attacked the peaceful people of Iraq," said Jeffrey Zaun, a Navy lieutenant. The world had not paid any attention when Saddam had done the same thing with Iranian POWs. Now there was global outrage and Saddam was branded an outlaw. "It is perfectly clear that this man is amoral," said British Prime Minister John Major. "He takes hostages. He attacks population centers. He threatens prisoners. He is a man without pity, and whatever his fate may be, I for one will not weep for him."

During the air war, allied warplanes flew about 100,000 sorties in the heaviest sustained bombardment in military history. The allies accomplished most of their military objectives for this phase of the operation: They destroyed half of Saddam's tanks, armor, and artillery. They so badly demoralized his Army that units as large as 500-man battalions were surrendering. They forced the Iraqi government to bargain over the terms of withdrawal but they rejected any concessions. They proved the effectiveness of an overwhelming air campaign and were ready to begin occupying territory. The Iraqi economy was in ruins. Phase one of "the mother of all battles" was over.

~ Saddam's Mindset

Behind Saddam's dramatic and almost immediate military losses was a complicated answer to a simple question: How could he have so badly miscalculated the political will and the military power of his enemy? In their public and private diplomacy since the August 1990 invasion of Kuwait, the coalition members warned Saddam over and over that if he chose to stay and fight, he risked the destruction of his military, his political future, and his country, but somehow the message did not get through to him. And once the war started, even the prospect of the devastation of his country's military, political, and industrial infrastructure did not move him to give in.

Saddam's military strategy was a black box. Since his invasion of Kuwait, he had been in an improvisational mode, taking steps that proved he was both unpredictable and capable of fulfilling his deadliest promises. Just as he unnerved his own people, who did not know whether he would go to war, so he unnerved his enemies. In choosing to fight, Saddam Hussein was motivated by overlapping, sometimes contradictory impulses, some suggesting that he knew he would lose, others indicating that he believed he could win.

In the months before the war, Saddam saw war as inevitable. Instead of listening to the signals as they grew more ominous, he ignored them. He told a number of emissaries that when faced with either a political or a military defeat, he chose to lose militarily, and it became more and more apparent to a bewildered world that Saddam was not going to back down.

Yevgeny M. Primakov, one of Moscow's best Arabists, who had known Saddam for two decades, concluded in October that Saddam would fight. " 'If the choice is to fight or surrender, I'll fight,' " Primakov quoted Saddam as telling him. Primakov interpreted that statement to mean that Saddam had embarked on the road to political suicide. "Saddam Hussein has what I would call a Masada complex," Primakov said in an interview in November with the weekly *Literaturnaya Gazeta*, referring to the Dead Sea fortress where Jews committed mass suicide rather than surrender to a besieging Roman Army in A.D. 73. "The defenders, understanding the hopelessness of their position, announced their willingness to die, but not to surrender," Primakov added. "As far as I could understand, Saddam Hussein is concerned about such questions as: Will not a blow fall on Iraq even if he withdraws his troops from Kuwait? Will economic sanctions be abolished if he withdraws his forces?" But even Primakov was confounded by Saddam's behavior. "He'll never back down," the Soviet envoy told President Bush in a meeting in Washington on October 19. In almost the same breath, however, Primakov predicted that Saddam might back down, but that he would need something in return.

In more than four hours of talks on January 3 with Michel Vauzelle, a confidant of French President François Mitterrand and president of the National Assembly's Foreign Affairs Committee, Saddam sounded fatalistic. "I know I am going to lose," he told Vauzelle. "At least I will have the death of a hero." In a meeting with some Palestinians a few days before the January 15 deadline, Saddam said that he knew he was in a lose-lose position. He would eventually lose a military confrontation against the American-led coalition, and would also lose if he capitulated and withdrew from Kuwait. "Shall I lose militarily or politically?" he asked, then proceeded to answer the question himself: "I shall lose militarily."

Even as Saddam sensed that war was inevitable, he also believed that Iraq's unique place in world history had grown, not diminished. Over and over, he expressed the importance of dignity—*haiba* in Arabic—for himself and the Iraqi people. The United States; his closest non-Arab allies, France and the Soviet Union; the United Nations; even his Arab brothers had deeply humiliated him when they imposed sanctions, publicly condemned him, and threatened him with war, he believed. Dignity was more important than peace. "We gave rivers of blood in a war that lasted eight years, yet we did not relinquish our humanity, meaning Iraq's right to live with dignity," Saddam told April C. Glaspie, the American ambassador to Baghdad, in a meeting eight days before he invaded Kuwait, according to a flawed, but largely correct transcript of their meeting released by the Iraqi foreign ministry. He repeated that sentiment over and over in the months leading up to war. "Accordingly, we categorically reject that anyone should injure the dignity of the Iraqi people or compromise their right to a happy, prosperous, and fulfilling life."

Another key to Saddam's strategy was that he had none. Saddam held the rank of field marshal, but he had never been a military man. He believed that the war against the coalition would replicate the Iran-Iraq war, and that he could fight it and win it with the same strategy. He used a three-tier defense with some of his poorest troops dug in along the Kuwaiti border, mechanized forces in reserve, and elite Republican Guards behind them, as he had done in the later, successful stages of the eight-year border war with Iran. He firmly believed that the troops aligned against him could never bomb his nation into submission. His strategy was to draw them into a costly land battle that he believed they could not win.

America had the technology, he conceded in a speech to an Islamic conference in Baghdad on January 11, 1991, but he had the experience. "They will tell you that America is developed in terms of missiles, developed in aircraft, and developed in its ability to jam the Iraqis. . . ," Saddam said. "They have weapons that strike from afar. Under all circumstances, one who wants to evict a fighter from the land will eventually depend on a soldier who walks on the ground and comes with a hand grenade, rifle, and bayonet to fight the soldier in the battle trench. . . . All this technological superiority, which is on paper, will eventually be tested in the theater of operations. We are not people who speak on the basis of books; we are people with experience in fighting."

Saddam also had the men. After the Iran-Iraq war, he had demobilized only about 25 percent of his million-man Army. Even if he lost 80 percent of it in a war against the allies, he would still be left with a military about the same size as it was on the eve of the Iran-Iraq war in 1980. He may have calculated that such a force would be large enough to threaten most of his neighbors and probably to require a substantial American military presence in the region. His military would remain greater than that of Jordan, Iran, or Saudi Arabia and the smaller Gulf states together. Only Syria and Egypt would have stronger armies in the Arab world.

On one level, Saddam believed that even if he lost Kuwait, he could still emerge as a formidable neighbor who could never be tampered with. He might be able to survive, perhaps even emerge triumphant as the Arab leader who fought against the United States, the greatest military power in the world, and the coalition aligned with it. He could win the war simply by not losing it, he thought, just as he had in the Iran-Iraq war. Only days before the war began, Nizar Hamdoon, Iraq's deputy foreign minister, compared Saddam to Egypt's Nasser, even though the analogy didn't fit. Hamdoon noted that Nasser was defeated militarily in the 1967 Six-Day war but held on politically, summoned back to power by the Egyptian masses who took to the streets in his support. "We could lose the war," said the official, "but the people of Iraq will still support the president." What Hamdoon did not mention was that although Nasser hung on, he was humiliated throughout the Arab world and never recovered politically or militarily from his defeat.

But on another level, Saddam fantasized that he could outlast the United States and its allies in any war. When he thought of America's staying power, he thought of Vietnam and Beirut, not World War II. He told Ambassador Glaspie that if the Iranians had overrun the Gulf region during the Iran-Iraq war, the American military could not have stopped them without using nuclear weapons. America was too far away and the American public had no stomach for war, he believed. "That is not to belittle you," he said, "but it is a reflection of the facts of geography and the nature of American society, which has made the U.S. unable to bear the possibility of ten thousand dead in one battle." He boasted that his troops would again spill rivers of blood, portraying the conflict—just as George Bush did—as one of good against evil, darkness against light. He dismissed the infidel invaders as drunken, pork-eating whoremongers infected with AIDS.

Saddam was portrayed as having a bunker mentality. A Düsseldorf manufacturer gave a spate of interviews describing a fairyland bunker that he built for the Iraqi president below the guest house of the presidential palace in Baghdad: a 12-room complex 50 feet below ground that could withstand a ten-megaton blast from a nuclear bomb. Sensational accounts in German tabloids reported that the bunker had six-foot-thick, lead-lined concrete walls, air-vent shafts that filtered all gases and chemicals, a swimming pool, a private mosque, a year's supply of food, a sauna and toilets that could test for radiation levels, family quarters furnished with plush carpeting and crystal chandeliers. The bunker supposedly was accessible by elevator and included a war room where Saddam could follow battlefield action on 24 television screens and address his people from an adjacent broadcasting studio. Prince Bandar bin Sultan, the Saudi ambassador to Washington, talked about how Saddam traveled to meetings with other Arab leaders not only with a food-taster but also with a bed-tester, in case someone planted a hypodermic needle or a snake in his bed.

In the end, Saddam misread the will of the American people to go to war. He viewed the debate within Western democracies as evidence of weakness and believed that he could outlast American will in any war. According to Egypt's President Hosni Mubarak in an address to Parliament on January 24, 1991, much of Saddam's view of the United States came from watching television, including CNN. The Iraqi president misinterpreted the network's coverage of the congressional debate over American policy on the Gulf as evidence that such a divided country would never go to war. "He didn't realize that there could be democratic debate, but when a decision was taken, it would be over" the Egyptian leader said. "He didn't believe that there could be a war." Mubarak added that when he tried to warn Saddam, "I was barking at the moon."

That sentiment was echoed by Syria's President Hafez al-Assad, Saddam's longtime foe, who told Egyptian officials, "This man is crazy. He thinks because he fought the Iranians he can threaten the Israelis and the Americans. He has never fought the Israelis. He doesn't know what real military power is."

~ Mesmerizing a People

As the terrible consequences of a war against the allied coalition were felt in Iraq, the world wondered: How had Saddam held onto power for so long, and would his people rise up to overthrow him? In the wake of the revolutions in the name of democracy that swept Eastern Europe in 1989, it was hard for outsiders to understand why the Iraqi people didn't take to the streets in open revolt against the man who had brought them misery and destruction. They had no electricity, no running water, no sanitation facilities, no medical care, no industry, and little food and gasoline. Schools and factories were closed. People spent their nights in bunkers, in shock and paralysis. Could the people of Iraq be more afraid of Saddam than they were of the relentless allied assault?

Saddam built a political tradition by projecting a fantasy world of greatness and fear that both captivated and terrorized his audience. He mesmerized his people into thinking that he was all-seeing and all-knowing. Saddam could have been the model for Machiavelli's Prince. It was best to be both loved and feared, said Machiavelli, but if one had to choose, it was better to be feared. Saddam was feared, but was he also loved?

Despite the first shock of the reality of war, the people of Iraq clearly felt—at least during the war—that they had no alternative except to submit to Saddam's punishing paternalism. Saddam had told his people that stability was more important than freedom, and as inheritors of a history of violence and political uncertainty, they had believed him. Slowly, however, some Iraqis awakened to the fact that theirs was a stubborn leader who was unaware of his own limitations. There was wishful thinking in the West that the Iraqi people would rise up against him as Romanians had done against Nicolae

Ceausescu, and speculation continued about a coup from within his inner circle or his military.

But in his years in power, Saddam had made sure that no political leader, no military commander, no opposition party, and no exile movement emerged strong enough to threaten him. How had he so thoroughly central-ized power and developed a system of rule that had for so many years ensured the failure of any plot against him? And could he continue to do it?

~ 2 ~

State-Building on the Ruins of Mesopotamia

On this spot where the Tigris meets the Euphrates the holy tree of our father Adam grew symbolizing the garden of Eden on earth.
>   —Bronze plaque at the site of an apple tree in Qurna, Iraq

Even if he controls the four quarters of earth, no military leader can become the master of the world unless he controls Babylon.
>   —Saddam Hussein quoting an ancient proverb, November 19, 1990

~ The Search for an Identity

Behind a pale brick fence in a small garden on the outskirts of Qurna sat a small, gnarled apple tree with a double trunk. According to Iraqi scholars, this tree marked the site of the Garden of Eden. Set at the point in southeastern Iraq where the Tigris and Euphrates rivers meet, the town boasted a pleasant rest house with verandas that overlooked the rivers, a modest restaurant, even a bar. The unassuming shrine to the Creation on the edge of town was a comfortable patch of green for weekend picnickers, but it was little more than that. Despite the inscription on the plaque at Qurna, the Tigris and Euphrates rivers never even met in ancient times, when they ran separately to the sea.

After a visit to the apple tree in Qurna, I asked an archaeologist in Baghdad about its authenticity. After all, Sir William Willcocks, the British irrigation expert, thought he found Eden at another spot on the Euphrates. The Syrians have long claimed that the home of Adam and Eve belongs to them in a place called Ghutah, and the Yemenis cite a semi-wooded area in the south of their country. The archaeologist laughed and called the place a tourist trap. Neither the Koran nor the Bible nor the Torah said where the Garden of Eden was, he explained. But when I started to take notes, a serious tone edged his voice. It was dangerous to question authority in Iraq, or the official interpretation of the country's mythology. The archaeologist did not know how far he could go. "Many Iraqi scholars believe that Qurna is the Garden of Eden," he said hastily. "It could be true."

The existence of the apple tree in Qurna and the claims made for it reveal the force that shaped and drove the outlaw state created by Saddam Hussein: the yearning for greatness amid uncertainty about the very identity of the country and its people.

The ancient Greeks called the land between the rivers Mesopotamia; much of what is modern-day Iraq was located in the flat cradle between the Tigris as it flows south from Turkey and the Euphrates as it flows southeast from Syria. The rivers merge in the Shatt al-Arab, a slow-moving waterway that divides the southern borders of Iraq and Iran and then flows into the Gulf. It was this waterway that Saddam seized when he invaded Iran, seeking in part to expand his access to the sea. Except for a 26-mile coastline on the Gulf, Iraq is landlocked, cursed by geography never to become a seafaring power.

The modern Iraqi state is a British invention, an artificial mosaic that reflects the interests of the great powers after World War I rather than the aspirations of its strikingly heterogeneous people. The country was pieced together from three provinces that had been part of the Ottoman Empire: Basra in the south, Baghdad in the middle, and Mosul in the north. The arrangement made little sense. Iraq as a country had no ethnic, sectarian, or geographic ties to bind its people.

About 75 percent of Iraq's population of 18 million are Muslim Arabs, but another 20 percent are Kurds, an ancient Indo-European people with its own language, culture, and traditions. Although the Kurds form the fourth-largest ethnic and linguistic group in the region after the Arabs, Turks, and Persians, the British paid them scant attention when they drew the borders of the modern Middle East. The Kurds, who are predominantly Sunni Muslim, are spread out across Iraq, Iran, Syria, Turkey, and the Soviet Union; they have periodically revolted in vain pursuit of their dream of an independent, or at least an autonomous, Kurdish state. The remaining 5 percent of Iraqis are the remnants of ancient invasions and long-past civilizations: Turkomans, Christian Armenians, Persians, and Assyrian and Chaldean Christians. Until 1951, there was a Jewish population of about 120,000, but of these only a few hundred remain.

Iraq's Arab population is further split along religious lines. Although the Sunni sect of Islam represents 90 percent of the world's Muslim population, about 55 percent of the people of Iraq are Shiite. Most of the Kurds and the rest of the Arabs are Sunnis, an unlucky formula that further inflamed Iraq's lingering ethnic divisions. Sunnis and Shiites largely adhere to the same beliefs, but over the last 1,400 years, they have fought some of their most bitter battles on Iraqi soil.

The origin of this religious schism is fairly straightforward: Who was the Prophet's successor? Shortly after Mohammad's death in the seventh century, the Muslims began to argue over who should become the caliph, or Mohammad's spiritual and political heir. The Sunnis, whose name comes from the Arabic word for "tradition," argued that the process should be decided in the accepted tribal way: The elders of the community would elect a leader, as they had done in the age before Islam. The Shiites, the underprivileged minority, whose name in Arabic means "partisans," insisted that only the descendants of the Prophet and his family could succeed him. They demanded that his first cousin and son-in-law, Ali, be made the Prophet's "replacement" as the next leader of the Muslim community; they were Ali's "partisans." Ali was stabbed to death as he prayed in the doorway of his newly completed mosque at Kufa, in present-day Iraq, in A.D. 661. His followers called on his son, Hussein, the grandson of the Prophet, to take over. But Hussein, outnumbered by the Syrian cavalry and archers of his enemies, died in Karbala—also in Iraq—with a sword in one hand and the Koran in the other. The Sunnis prevailed, and the Shiites carry the burden of that ancient oppression and the sense that they are still wrongly governed.

Geography also divides the Iraqi people. The Kurds live in the mountains and highlands of the far north; most Sunnis live north of Baghdad in the flat, fertile plain between the Tigris and the Euphrates; the Shiites live in the river plain south of Baghdad and the marshes of the southeast; some Bedouin tribesmen roam the sparsely populated Syrian Desert, which extends into western Iraq, eastern Jordan, northern Saudi Arabia and central Syria. Meanwhile, Iraq has always been surrounded by stronger, more powerful neighbors—Turkey to the north and Iran to the east—with different cultures and peoples that conquered and dominated Iraq over the centuries. The country also has no strategic depth. The Iranian border is 70 miles away from Baghdad, and only 13 miles from Basra, Iraq's second-largest city.

In the ancient glory of Mesopotamia, Saddam found an epoxy that he believed could hold together a country that seemed to have little reason to reach for unity. Over and over, he reminded the Iraqi people of their ancient greatness and called upon them to restore it. He invented myths that he apparently believed and that he tried to force his countrymen to believe. Because he did not separate the national interest from his own grandiose ambitions, he believed that the mythmaking was justified. He manipulated, twisted, and shaped history both to fit his own worldview and to lend religious and cultural legitimacy to his rule.

Other leaders in the region also tried to manipulate their cultural heritages and incorporate them into modern-day politics, but without much success. Kemal Atatürk, the nationalist leader of Turkey for much of the 1920s and 1930s, reached back to the Sumerians and Hittites in an attempt to convince his people that the culture and civilization of all nations flowed from the Turkish homeland. Shah Mohammad Reza Pahlevi of Iran presented himself as a modern-day Cyrus the Great. The most dramatic attempt to link himself to the ancient conqueror who created the Persian Empire was an outlandish celebration of its 2,500th anniversary in 1971 at Persepolis, catered by Maxim's of Paris. The Shah stood in front of the simple stone tomb of Cyrus and called out, "O Cyrus, great King, King of Kings, Achaemenian King, King of the land of Iran, I, the Shahanshah of Iran, offer thee salutations from myself and from my nation."

The attempts to tap the power of ancient myth by both Atatürk and the Shah were not taken seriously by their people. As for Iraq, it was impossible to gauge the extent to which its population believed the myths created by Saddam. In Iraq's repressive regime, no citizen dared laugh at his use of ancient symbols. Some of the stories may have even seeped into the Iraqi consciousness, especially among the young. Schoolchildren and university students alike were steeped in Mesopotamian history, and even educated Iraqis who lived abroad declared their firm belief that their land was the cradle of civilization.

But even before the war against the allies, there was a startling discontinuity between the glories of the ancient past and the privations of the present. As historian Phebe Marr explained, "There is a discrepancy between the ancient glories of Babylonia and the Arabian nights that Iraqis read about in their textbooks and the grim reality of the present day. They know they were once at the center of the universe and that knowledge has compelled them to aspire to greatness, but the greatness hasn't arrived."

~ Historic Greatness

It is difficult for the casual visitor to Iraq to comprehend that this is where the world's most advanced civilization once flourished. It was in what is now Iraq, well over 6,000 years ago, that the Sumerians became the world's first agriculturalists. Mesopotamia was the grain belt of the Middle East, full of cereals and date palms and rich, green fields where sheepherders first domesticated abundant flocks. Even today, dates are a staple of the Iraqi diet; Iraqis believe that their dates are the best in the world. When the global embargo imposed on Iraq after the invasion of Kuwait began to affect the availability of some foodstuffs, Manal Younis, the head of the Federation of

Iraqi Women, praised the lowly date as the ancient staple of the Iraqi diet. Iraqis could live on dates if they had to, she seemed to say, adding that a team of specialists had compiled a book of date recipes. But the past did not carry its abundance into the present: Despite its fertile plains, in recent years Iraq imported 80 percent of its food. The war with Iran destroyed many of the vast date-palm groves along the Shatt al-Arab waterway, and for the first time, Iraq stopped most of its date exports.

It was also in Mesopotamia, some 5,000 years ago, that the Sumerians developed the first form of cuneiform writing—pictograms—or simplified pictures on clay tablets. They made the first wheeled chariot and discovered along the way that smelted tin and copper made the most durable bronze. The Sumerians knew square roots and cubes and quadratic equations. They created the first accurate calendars and the system of telling time that we use today. The world's first cities were founded in what is now Iraq, rich cultural and political centers where the first loyalty was to the community as a whole and not to the tribe or clan.

Some 3,800 years ago, in the city of Babylon, King Hammurabi devised the world's most comprehensive—and the strictest—legal code, which included laws dealing with marriage, divorce, rent, wages, farming, the responsibilities of professional men, and the buying and selling of slaves. The code was intended, he said, "to cause justice to prevail in the country, to destroy the wicked and the evil, that the strong may not oppress the weak." Herodotus wrote that it was in Babylon in the sixth century B.C. that King Nebuchadnezzar built the hanging gardens, one of the seven wonders of the ancient world, for his princess. Nebuchadnezzar, a warrior-king, gave Babylon one of its few periods of conquest by seizing Jerusalem, destroying the Jewish temple, and carrying tens of thousands of Jews and the king of Judah into captivity. But the kingdom of Babylon flourished for only about 70 years. Persian imperialists captured it in the sixth century B.C. and made it a colony. The great Mesopotamian cities were destroyed, buried under sand; the tribes rebelled; the Mesopotamian languages disappeared. The Persians moved traditional trade routes away from Babylon, and the dams and dikes that controlled the Tigris and Euphrates crumbled. Instead of being a focal point of a great civilization, the land between the rivers became a target of outside conquests.

There are few traces of Mesopotamia's ancient greatness left in modern-day Iraq. Unlike the Egyptians and other ancient empire-builders, the people of Mesopotamia had no stone, and their palaces and mud-brick ziggurats— the graceful temple-towers in the form of terraced pyramids—were buried by floods and shifting sands. One of the only traces of Babylon are bricks once buried some 60 feet under the earth. As Georges Roux wrote in his splendid study, *Ancient Iraq*, "The dissolving rain, the sand-bearing winds, the earth-splitting sun conspired to obliterate all material remains, and the desolate mounds which since concealed the ruins of Babylon and Nineveh offer perhaps the best lesson in modesty that we shall ever receive from history."

Much of what lasted was plundered by Westerners. The Hammurabi obelisk that sits in Baghdad's Qahtan Square is a copy. The splendid glazed-ceramic tiles that once covered the Ishtar Gate of Babylon were moved to Berlin; a nine-foot shaft of black basalt inscribed with Hammurabi's legal code was installed in the Louvre; other remnants were scattered around the world in places such as the British Museum and the University of Pennsylvania. The pillage of Iraq's cultural heritage never sat well with Iraq's Baath leadership, which launched a major campaign in the mid-1970s to force the world's museums and universities to return the treasures. The Iraqis even managed in 1975 to push a resolution through the United Nations General Assembly calling for the return of antiquities to their countries of origin. In his 1991 book, *Culture, History and Ideology in the Formation of Ba'thist Iraq*, the Israeli scholar Amatzia Baram relates an incident from 1979, when French Prime Minister Raymond Barre visited Baghdad to talk about an oil deal and Saddam apparently asked him about returning Hammurabi's law code. The Iraqi newspaper *al-Jumhuriyah* called Barre "the heir of the antiquities robbers," adding that he was astounded when Saddam "demanded of him that the Louvre return the stele of Hammurabi."

~ The Legacy of Violence

Despite the periods of stability during which civilizations flourished in what became Iraq, the country's history was dominated by force and rooted in violence—perhaps more so than any other country in the Middle East. Because of its coveted location at the juncture of the Tigris and Euphrates, Iraq was tempting prey for conquering armies. It needed a central authority to manage the unpredictable river systems. The divisions within the country, the absence of any unifying hero or ideology, the successive invasions and conquests by foreigners over the centuries also contributed to Iraq's violent history. In a country like Egypt, by contrast, the political culture was traditionally based on a social contract between the ruler and the ruled. But Iraq was a land governed by what Freya Stark, the British travel writer, called the "pendulum-swing of murder, ancient and long-familiar, which has made the pattern from the day when the first Ali was stabbed in Kufa and probably long before." Politics was a life-and-death matter, and a leader had only two choices. He could either rule, and rule forcefully, or perish. During his years in power, Saddam was not a usurper; rather, he was a product of the Iraqi soil, inheriting the legacy of violence that had conditioned the people who lived on that territory for centuries.

Mesopotamia, like Syria and Egypt, was not originally an Arab land. It was not until the seventh century A.D. that Arab tribesmen, newly converted to Islam, came from all over the Arabian peninsula and took "the land between the rivers" from the Persians, who occupied the territory at the time. That conquest ushered in one of the most violent episodes in the region's history. In the battle of Qadisiyah, an outpost on the Euphrates, the Arabs, outnumbered by more than six to one, slaughtered the Persian forces in A.D. 636. The tribesmen put an Arab and Islamic stamp on Mesopotamia. It was not until centuries later that the plain between the Tigris and Euphrates, from Tikrit in the central north to the southern marshes—became known as Iraq. For Saddam, the Qadisiyah was the opening round of a permanent war with the Persians. He called his war with Iran—the modern-day Persia—"Saddam's Qadisiyah," or the "Second Qadisiyah." Even the invasion of Kuwait, which pitted Arab against Arab, not Arab against Persian, was briefly labeled the "Third Qadisiyah."

The Islamic era also ushered in the Abbasid caliphate, one of the greatest periods in Islamic history. Iraq in the eighth century A.D. blossomed into a prosperous empire and a brilliant civilization that drew on the best traditions of both the Greeks and the Persians. Baghdad, founded in A.D. 762, became the center of one of the largest stable societies in the world, stretching from Spain to what is now Pakistan. By the tenth century, Baghdad had a population of a million and a half people, a trade that reached from China to the Baltic Sea, and a rich intellectual and cultural life that produced scientists, poets, jurists, and philosophers. The Abbasid dynasty also produced one of the most brutal despots in Islamic history, Abul-Abbas al-Saffah, the first Abbasid caliph who ruled from 750 to 754 and was a descendant of the Prophet Mohammad's uncle. His name, which he invented himself, meant "The Bloodletter." He seized power by murdering members of the ruling Umayyad dynasty and surrounded himself with a vast network of spies. By executing leaders of the Shiite sect of Islam who supported him, he ensured that there was no challenge to his rule. The executioner was a member of his royal court.

The invaders arrived again in 1258, when the Mongols, led by Hulagu Khan, grandson of Genghis Khan, killed the last caliph. They looted Baghdad, beheaded its intellectuals, destroyed what was left of Iraq's canal networks, and blotted out all traces of Abbasid culture. Life in the cities deteriorated, swamps and marshes overtook the irrigated lands, trade routes moved elsewhere. The power of marauding nomadic tribes increased and Baghdad lost central control of the region, a trend that continued into the twentieth century. The Ottoman Turks expanded their empire into the region in the sixteenth century, and for the next 200 years, Iraq became a military playing field for Turks and Persians. The country lost its political center during the Ottoman rule as Baghdad fell prey to almost any power that laid claim to it.

By the eighteenth century, the western side of the Euphrates was no longer cultivated. Wars with the Persians, who by now were predominantly Shiite, made the Ottomans suspicious of Iraq's Shiites. The Ottomans began to rely on the only group they thought they could trust—the urban Sunnis—who gradually came to dominate Iraqi politics. Even in the late nineteenth century, when Ottoman reformers introduced newspapers and founded new military and civilian centers of learning, only the Sunnis benefited.

~ British Rule and Revolution

In 1914, when the British discovered that the Turks were fighting on the German side, they landed troops from India in Basra. In a secret accord reached even before the war was over, Sir Mark Sykes, a British lieutenant colonel, and François Georges-Picot, a French diplomat, divided the choicest cuts of the Ottoman Empire between Britain and France. For many Arabs, the deal still lies at the root of all of the region's troubles today. Never in the history of the Middle East has a document been so cursed. Saddam's persistent theme after his invasion of Kuwait—and one that touched the soul of the entire Arab world—was that he was undoing the crimes of British imperialism. In the Palestinian camps of Jordan, there were voices that called Saddam the savior of the Arabs who would abolish Sykes-Picot, redistribute the wealth of the oil-rich kings and princes and emirs, and lead a new, united Arab world.

The Iraqi people got a new master after World War I. In March 1917, the British occupied Baghdad, promising reforms and limited self-rule that would pave the way to an independent Arab kingdom. But the allied powers had no intention of relinquishing control of the Middle East. When the Great Powers met in the Italian city of San Remo in April 1920 to complete the postwar arrangements for the Middle East, Britain took a wide band of territory from southern Syria across Iraq, while France gave itself Syria and Lebanon. Iraq was made a Class A British mandate, a temporary status that was intended to lead to independence. It took this artificial creation by the British to make Iraq a nation-state.

In August 1921, the British made the Hashemite Prince Faisal Iraq's first king in a British-style coronation ceremony. To lend the proceedings an air of democracy, the British staged a referendum that asked one straightforward question: Do you or do you not want Faisal as king? Using a combination of intimidation and the dispatch of potential contenders into exile, the British made sure that the reply would be in the affirmative. The British claimed that 96 percent of the Iraqis who voted chose Faisal. But Faisal, an Arabian prince, was a foreigner. He had also fought with the hated British against the

Ottomans. In the eyes of Iraqi nationalists, he was illegitimate, although other Iraqis respected him as a descendant of the Prophet and an early fighter for Arab independence against the Ottomans.

The British modeled the new administration on their imperial structure in India, introduced the Indian rupee as the local currency, stuffed the Army and police force with Indians, and were slow to appoint local Arabs to positions of responsibility. They even briefly replaced the old Turkish laws with a new civil and criminal code based on Anglo-Indian laws.

British rule covered over the old and new rivalries that rent Iraq's population. The fate of the northern Mosul province illustrated just how arbitrary the imposed boundaries were. Mosul was important for two reasons: Much of the province—though not the city itself—was populated by Kurdish tribesmen who wanted no part of rule by an Arab Iraq. The city was also sitting on oil. At first, the British and French agreed that Mosul would fall under French control. Then the French reluctantly traded Mosul to the British for a share in British-controlled oil operations in Iraq. The 1920 Treaty of Sèvres between the allies and the Ottoman sultan promised the Kurds "a scheme of local autonomy" and recognized their right to form an independent Kurdish state in the eastern portion of what later became Turkey. But when Atatürk, with his fierce nationalism and policy of ethnic assimilation, came to power in Turkey three years later, the treaty was never implemented. The British decided to keep Mosul as an integral part of Iraq, and in the process, the Iraqi monarchy gained formal title to, although not actual control over, Mosul's oil. No matter that the Kurds wanted no part of a country of Arabs.

The central administration imposed by the British on Iraq joined the three ethnically and religiously distinct provinces: Kurdish-dominated Mosul, Sunni Muslim Baghdad, and Shiite Basra. Throughout the 1920s and 1930s, the Shiites and the Kurds revolted, over and over. The British sometimes had to call in the Air Force to put them down, simply bombing villages out of existence. Saddam learned this lesson well. He used the same strategy as the British but with far greater ferocity when he destroyed Kurdish villages and gassed their inhabitants in an effort to control them in 1988. When Shiites and Kurds rebelled in the aftermath of the 1991 Gulf war, he again moved ruthlessly to suppress them.

In October 1932, Iraq finally became independent and was unanimously admitted to the League of Nations. But the internal splits were so deep, the national boundaries so artificial, that King Faisal wrote a confidential memo on the eve of his death in September 1933 that sounded a ring of despair. "I say, and my heart is full of sadness," he wrote, "that there is not yet in Iraq an Iraqi people, but unimaginable masses of human beings, devoid of any patriotic idea, imbued with religious traditions and absurdities, connected by no common tie, giving ear to evil, prone to anarchy, and perpetually ready to rise against any government whatever."

The Iraqi royal line limped along, doing little to establish real authority over a country that was ripe for revolution. Faisal was succeeded by his son Ghazi, young, handsome, and Western-educated, but inexperienced and not very bright—the kind of king who spent long hours drinking with palace servants and young Army officers and driving sports cars. He also became an outspoken critic of British influence. Using a radio transmitter said to be a gift from the Nazi government that he installed in his own palace, Ghazi denounced the British presence in the Gulf, Zionist claims in Palestine, and French rule in Syria. In 1937, he called upon the Kuwaitis to overthrow their corrupt leaders and join the "Iraqi family"—the first of many attempts by Iraq to take over the neighboring sheikdom. The British, firmly in control both in Iraq and in Kuwait, tolerated the bizarre broadcasts. Ghazi held on until he was killed one night in 1939, when, blind drunk, he drove his sports car into a pole. Faisal II, the infant son who succeeded him, was seen as so vulnerable that his English nanny took to preparing and tasting all his food.

During those years, Iraq earned the dubious distinction of being the first Arab country to experience a military coup. In fact, between 1936 and 1941, Iraqi Army officers, aided by civilian politicians, launched seven military coups—not against the king, but against one another and against the civilian population. The violent atmosphere was captured in a letter that Freya Stark wrote in the spring of 1941. It seemed that one afternoon, a well-known visiting Palestinian was late for a lunch at the British ambassador's residence. It turned out that a man on a bicycle had murdered the guest as he stepped out of his hotel. Stark described the reaction of Vyvyan Holt, then the British counselor at the embassy, when he was told why the guest would not be coming: "It appears that after twenty years of Iraqi politics, when he heard the news over the telephone, he merely said, 'I suppose we needn't wait lunch any longer.'"

Iraq's lust for strong leaders who could defeat their enemies was so strong that during World War II, some Iraqis embraced Hitler, a fact that seemed to have eluded President Bush. Bush called Saddam a modern-day Hitler in verbal assaults that were intended for Western consumption. But among some Arabs, particularly some Iraqis, Hitler was not the incarnation of evil. He was a convenient nationalist model, and many Iraqis hailed him as a hero for attacking both the British and the Jews. In 1941, a government sympathetic to Nazi Germany and Fascist Italy briefly seized power in Baghdad and waited for the Nazis to come to its aid. But the rebel officers were defeated by the British Army and their leaders were hanged by the civilian pro-British faction in Baghdad, headed by the elderly politician and prime minister, Nuri al-Said, and the Regent, Abd al-Ilah. Their crushing defeat created deep resentment in the Army and planted the seeds of revolt against the monarchy. At that time, wrote Stark in a letter, the Iraqi Army was "largely Nazi at heart." The Nazis were so popular, she added, that "by July, 1942, the country was seething with disguised Nazis and swastikas were appearing everywhere—even on the back of my car." As the Iraqis saw it, Hitler's only fault was that he lost the war.

The monarchy suffered through more than two decades of uprisings and decentralized government until July 14, 1958, when Brigadier General Abd al-Karim Qassim and a group of nationalist military officers overthrew Faisal II—and foreign rule—in a bloody predawn uprising. The royal family was gunned down in the palace. Nuri al-Said disguised himself as a woman but was caught as he tried to escape. He was shot on the spot and his body was dragged through the streets. One mob stormed a hotel and killed several Western businessmen and supporters of the monarchy. Nevertheless, the rebels did not quite throw off all the trappings of Western influence. When they took control of the radio station, they played "The Marseillaise."

The revolution placed political power firmly in the Army's hands. It improved the lot of urban workers, peasants, and the middle class and cut down the landed aristocracy. But it also unleashed centuries-old sectarian, tribal, and ethnic feuds, pitting Kurds against Arabs and Sunnis against Shiites. In the next decade, three more military seizures of power followed, including a brief victory by the Arab Baath Socialist Party in 1963, the party to which Saddam belonged and whose ultimate victory would bring him into his country's ruling elite.

~ The Rise of the Baath

The Baath, which means "resurrection" or "renaissance" in Arabic, was founded in Damascus in the 1940s by three French-educated intellectuals: Michel Aflaq, a Greek Orthodox Christian; Salah al-Din Bitar, a Sunni Muslim; and Zaki al-Arsuzi, an Alawite—an offshoot of Shiite Islam. To overcome the split among Arabic-speaking Christians, Muslim Sunnis and Shiites, Aflaq and his colleagues turned to secular models to help shape the Arab identity. The Baath Party saw its task as the creation of a new Arab man, and it sought to revitalize Arab culture and Arab greatness. Beginning in the 1940s, Baathist ideology gradually spread from Syria to Iraq, Jordan, Lebanon, Sudan, Morocco, Saudi Arabia, Yemen, and Libya.

Baath ideology advanced a romantic, mystical vision of Arab nationalism and sought the elimination of the artificial boundaries drawn by the French and British. The only way to revitalize Arab society was to reunify all Arabs in a single Arab state under a single leadership. Once Arabs were united, and therefore liberated, class conflicts would disappear, development and modernization could occur, and the Arabs would recapture the glory of their past. In 1952, the Baath merged with the Arab Socialist Party, little more than a group of antifeudal, landless peasants. The term *Socialist* was added to the party name, and Baathism increased in influence and popularity. Freedom, unity, and socialism became its pillars—freedom from imperial colonialists, unity of the Arab world with equal participation of all religious sects, and a tame socialism that was more nationalistic than Marxist.

The Middle East has long wallowed in conspiracy theories that blamed the outsider, discovering plots everywhere, and the Baath was no exception. In its paranoid view of history, it saw all oppression in the Arab world as a consequence of outside forces, alternately blaming division in the Arab world on the Ottomans, the Western mandates, the oil-rich Gulf states, the superpowers, and Israel.

Aflaq emerged as the chief ideologist of the Baath and became so self-important that he occasionally likened himself to the Prophet Mohammad. Although Mohammad was the carrier of Islam in the seventh century, Aflaq would say that we—the Baath and I—are the carrier of a similar grand ideology: Arab nationalism for modern times.

Baathism was slow to catch on in Iraq. Unlike Syria, where the Party had gone public, in Iraq it chose to remain a clandestine organization. It was not until the mid- to late 1950s that Baathist doctrine began to take root in Baghdad, and even the 1958 revolution included only a few Baathists. By the time Qassim catapulted himself into the presidency, he focused more on Iraq and the Gulf than on pan-Arabism. On February 8, 1963, the Baathists succeeded in overthrowing Qassim, but they were unable to manage the government bureaucracy and were overthrown nine months later.

The Baath Party came to power in Syria on February 23, 1966, but the Syrian and Iraqi branches of the Party soon split bitterly—ostensibly over ideology and dogma but in reality over power and control. Over the years, there were repeated efforts to merge Syria and Iraq, but Saddam and Syria's President Hafez al-Assad both claimed to be the true leaders of the Baath. The two men had nothing but contempt for each other.

The Baath was a violent party in Iraq, beginning as a revolutionary underground guerrilla organization that equated violence with heroism. As late as 1980, Tariq Aziz, the articulate Baath Party ideologue who became Iraq's information minister and later its foreign minister and deputy prime minister, described the party members as "experts in secret organization. They are organizers of demonstrations, strikes and armed revolutions."

The Baathists assumed power in Iraq with the help of non-Baathist Army officers in a military coup on July 17, 1968. The coup was organized by several key disaffected members of the Republican Guards, an elite officer corps originally handpicked by then-President Abdel Rahman Arif. The officers, led by Colonel Abdel-Razzaq Nayif and Colonel Ibrahim al-Daud, had formed the Arab Revolutionary Movement, and, together with the Baath Party, under the leadership of Major General Ahmad Hasan al-Bakr, carried out the coup. The military plotters used garbage trucks to augment their small fleet of tanks. Arif, a weak leader, was ousted.

The Baath of 1968 was not the same organization it had been in 1963. It had learned never to share power with non-Baathists. Ruthless, seasoned, and practical, the Party leaders simply began to maneuver potential rivals out of the way.

What happened in the next two weeks after the 1968 coup illustrated the method by which the Baath regime—and Saddam Hussein—consolidated power in the following two decades. The Baath needed to get rid of Colonels Nayif and al-Daud, who were naïve but ambitious. And Saddam Hussein, a rising star in the new regime, played a key role in their ouster.

Nayif, who was made prime minister in the new government, was not a Baath Party member. Neither was al-Daud, who became defense minister. It wasn't that they were enemies of the new regime, but they were potential rivals who enjoyed an independent power base in the military. In his official biography of Saddam, Fuad Matar openly acknowledged that Saddam felt that Nayif's participation in the new regime "was an obstacle in the Party's path." On July 30, 1968, Saddam arranged for the colonel to lunch with Bakr, the new president, in the presidential palace. After the lunch, Nayif was ushered into a waiting room. Saddam burst into the room, "drew his revolver and ordered Nayif to raise his hands," Matar continued. "Nayif tried to play on Saddam's feelings by appealing to him to spare him for the sake of his four children. Saddam Hussein was adamant; he told Nayif that he and his children would be safe only if he left Iraq." Nayif was forcibly put on a plane and sent off as ambassador to Morocco. Nayif's partner, al-Daud, was also sent into exile that day.

Nayif later went into exile in London, where the Iraqi regime tried unsuccessfully to assassinate him in 1973. Five years later, it tried again, and succeeded. Al-Daud survived, remaining in exile in Saudi Arabia, where he opened a carpet shop. After the 1991 Gulf war, he emerged as a leader of the Saudi-backed Iraqi opposition.

By the end of 1968, the Baath was firmly in charge. Al-Bakr held all the cards and all the titles: He was president, commander-in-chief, chairman of the ruling Revolutionary Command Council, and secretary-general of the Baath Party. Al-Bakr made Saddam his chief aide and deputy, and he became the executor of the president's policy decisions. Responsible for internal security, Saddam used the position, as he had in the past, to eliminate potential opponents. Just as important, he had the blessing of Aflaq, by then a figurehead but still the Party leader.

~ Greatness Through Stability

In struggling to find an identity for the formless Iraqi nation, the Baath emphasized Iraq's greatness, even its superiority. The theme was seized on and amplified after Saddam Hussein assumed the presidency in 1979. He manipulated and glorified Iraq's ancient past, likening himself to a pantheon of ancient heroes, selectively pulling together individual strands of history, and stockpiling images of ancient civilizations. Saddam created an Arab history for Iraq. No matter that the Sumerians, the Assyrians, and the Babylonians—the peoples on whose ancient glories Saddam relied so heavily— were not Arabs. In the mid-1970s, he proclaimed that they were Arabs, and their civilizations were called the basis for Iraq's greatness. In Saddam's mind, he and Iraq's heroes and Iraq itself became one and the same. He used himself as a symbol of unity for the country, both for his own self-aggrandizement and to knit the diverse country together.

Official propaganda compared Saddam to Nebuchadnezzar, Hammurabi, and Saladin and revised their histories to fit his vision. Saladin, for example, was a medieval Muslim warrior who fought back the Christian crusaders, made himself ruler of Egypt and Syria, captured Jerusalem, and at his peak controlled the Islamic world from North Africa to Nineveh, now the northern Iraqi city of Mosul. Even though Saladin was a Kurd whose family emigrated from Armenia, Saddam invoked his memory over and over after his invasion of Kuwait. In a fiery speech on July 17, 1990, Saddam likened to the Crusades what he called an imperialist and Zionist plot against Iraq and an economic plot by some of his Arab brothers. "But the Crusades also remind us of that well-known historic fact that victory in the end was for the Arabs as a result of joint action," he declared. "Saladin was the commander who led the Arabs to victory." He called Saladin "one of the examples and symbols which we turn to in studying chivalry and leadership." In an interview on Japanese television on October 22, 1990, Saddam singled out Saladin and Gamal Abdel Nasser as Arab leaders for whom he had "particular respect." He described the war between Iraq and the American-led alliance as "a second Crusade." The message was clear: Saddam was the new Arab Saladin. Saladin and Saddam did have one thing in common: They both came from Tikrit.

~

Saddam resurrected the important archaeological sites of ancient Iraq. By far the most ambitious project was the reconstruction of Babylon—more a Disney-like fantasy than a faithful re-creation—with its replica of the Ishtar Gate, the Great Ziggurat, the Greek amphitheater, the southern palace and its temples. Sparing no expense, Saddam offered a prize of $1.5 million to anyone who could develop a workable plan to reconstruct the fabled Hanging Gardens, which may never even have existed.

For Saddam, rebuilding Babylon became a vehicle to assert his own greatness, allowing him to compare himself to Nebuchadnezzar. In contemporary Iraq, Nebuchadnezzar was crudely portrayed as a great Iraqi and Arab patriot who dealt effectively with the Zionist problem. The few ancient bricks discovered at the Ishtar Gate of Babylon, which Nebuchadnezzar built, bore his royal seal. As Egyptian, Sudanese, and Iraqi workers reconstructed the site, Saddam ordered written on some of the 60 million newly baked yellow bricks needed to build the 40-foot walls: "The Babylon of Nebuchadnezzar was reconstructed in the era of Saddam Hussein."

Despite his lip service to the Baath Party's egalitarian rhetoric, Saddam really wanted to be king. Following the end of the war with Iran in 1988, he took a number of steps to rehabilitate the notion of monarchy in Iraq. The official Iraqi publishing company released several books praising the patriotic role of the monarchy. Iraq spent $3 million renovating Baghdad's royal cemetery, and when Jordan's King Hussein visited Baghdad in June 1989, he and Saddam visited the graves of King Faisal I and King Ghazi. A black metal statue of Faisal I was put in the center of Gamal Abdel Nasser Square in Baghdad, although no one could explain why it was there. A Ministry of Information guide told me that the king had been "an Iraqi patriot."

"But didn't the colonialist British install Faisal after they drew the boundaries of Iraq?" I asked.

"Yes," the guide acknowledged, "but he was a good man."

There was nothing subtle about Saddam's manipulation of the memory of the ancient Babylonian emperor. The emblem of the 1988 Babylon International Festival showed the profile of Saddam overlapping the profile of Nebuchadnezzar. Saddam's peasant nose was refined and elongated to make him better resemble the ancient king. The festival adopted the slogan: "From Nebuchadnezzar to Saddam Hussein, Babylon arises anew."

The Mesopotamian motif seeped into modern Iraqi architecture, art, and everyday life. The regime sponsored local festivals based on ancient pagan rites. Iraqi poetry and literature began to be filled with a bizarre blend of images from the Arabian Nights and figures from ancient Babylon. Buildings and sculptures liberally adapted Assyrian reliefs, eagles, and Mesopotamian sun emblems. The deer carved on the Agricultural College of Baghdad were reminiscent of those on the Ishtar Gate at Babylon. The walls of al-Zawra Park in Baghdad, appropriately named "the hanging gardens," combined the gate of Ishtar, a garden, and a ziggurat. Government-sponsored fashion shows dressed women in Assyrian-inspired ball gowns. The Tomb of the Unknown Soldier, a graceless monument in the center of Baghdad, mixed the Ziggurat of Ur and the spiral minaret of Samarra with an iron dome that represented the shield of the dying soldier. The entrance of Baghdad's Ishtar Sheraton Hotel was a miniature Ishtar Gate.

Sometimes the distinction between Saddam and the ancient greats got garbled in the minds of the Iraqis themselves. Daniel Williams, a correspondent for the *Los Angeles Times*, described a visit to Babylon a month after the invasion of Kuwait that captured the extent to which the myth of Saddam's greatness penetrated the Iraqi psyche. "The tour guide at a reconstructed palace in Babylon described the restored monuments of the ancient city—the lion sculpture, the brick reliefs of bulls and griffins, the newly painted hanging gardens," he wrote. "Then she got to the throne room and, with a sweep of her hand, pointed to the empty platform. 'This is where the leader Saddam Hussein had his throne. This is where Saddam Hussein sat,' she said, her voice rising in pride. The short, stout woman looked around at the quizzical faces, then caught herself with a nervous laugh. 'I mean Nebuchadnezzar. Nebuchadnezzar. Nebuchadnezzar had his throne here.' "

Building of the new Babylon ended abruptly when Saddam invaded Kuwait. Even during the war with Iran, the project continued, as hundreds of Iraqi craftsmen were granted exemptions from military service to work there. But after the invasion of the emirate, the cash crunch from the world embargo of Iraqi oil, the call-up of construction workers to report for military duty in Kuwait, and the repatriation of many foreign workers stalled the project. The fast-food restaurants on the edge of an artificial lake fed by a canal to the slow-moving Euphrates were shut down. The enormous palace that many Iraqis suspect was being built for Saddam stood unfinished on a hill above the ruins.

Although Saddam exalted the ancient sites, when war came, he proved that he was also willing to sacrifice them. He parked two Soviet-made MiG fighter planes next to the Ziggurat of Ur, a 5,000-year-old massive spiral mudbrick tower erected in the ancient Sumerian birthplace of Abraham. In the end, the legacy of Mesopotamia meant nothing to him.

~ The New Iraqi Man

The tension between the glories of Iraq's ancient past—real or invented—and the reality of the present was made palpable in an official coffee-table book available at Iraq's Ministry of Information. Published in 1980, just before Iraq's adventure into Iran, the book was intended as a subtle challenge to Egypt's domination of the Arab world. Filled with dramatically shadowed pictures of winged bulls, Babylonian walls, and eerie sculptures from Iraq's ancient pantheon of heroes, it dismissed the Egyptians and asserted that the charm of the sacred cities of the Nile "has not survived." The book claimed a kind of cultural continuity for Iraq, with its manufactured ancient sites alternating with symbols of modernity (oil installations, bulldozers, universities) and of prosperity (fertile valleys of barley, palm-lined rivers).

"From the arid lands of the North, to the permanently watered tree plantations of the South, Iraqi civilization has spread its wings like the divine king of Nimrod which we see here, offering the pomegranate of everlasting love. The palm trees of Basra remember that they were once worshipped as the tree of life. . . . It is the flow of water which makes the most extreme form of modernization possible. . . ."

But the book left out a lot. There were no photographs of the thousands of tiny villages of one-story crumbling mud-brick huts that dot the Iraqi landscape. Such villages did not testify to Iraq's greatness. They would give outsiders the wrong message. While journalists in many countries were strictly limited in what they could photograph near military bases and other sensitive installations, in Iraq I was also told not to take pictures of farm animals. "We are instructed to show Iraq as a modern country," said Abbas, my guide from the Ministry of Information, when I tried to take a picture of a man and his donkey during a visit to Iraq in 1983. "Such pictures show us as backward. It's forbidden." Much of his job was to tell me what I couldn't do. No, I couldn't go to Kurdistan. "We don't have the proper papers," he said. No, I couldn't take pictures of beggars or bootblacks. Abbas never used the word *censored*. Rather, one of his favorite words was *forbidden*. He could lose his job if he did forbidden things, he said, and I believed him.

So just as the coffee-table book showed only images of prosperity, the donkey carts in Baghdad, the sheep tied to the lampposts in Najaf, the cow running past the kebab stand on the road to Basra did not exist. It was this kind of censorship that Kremlin dictatorships used in their attempts to persuade the rest of the world that the Soviet Union was a modern, prosperous country. It worked no better in Iraq than in the Soviet Union. Illusion flourished and passed for reality only as long as the governments controlled the media and the societies remained isolated.

After the invasion of Kuwait, the farm animal was elevated to a new status. Officials acknowledged that government vehicles used for food distribution broke down because of the lack of spare parts, but it made no difference, they added, because the goods could be moved by donkey. When war broke out and the supply of gasoline dried up, the only ordinary Iraqis who could get around easily were those who owned a donkey.

～

Just as Saddam rewrote his own country's history, after the invasion of Kuwait he redrew geography. Newly printed maps hung on the walls of some ministries in Baghdad, showing Kuwait as Iraq's nineteenth province. And a tourist guide published in 1982 by Iraq's State Organization for Tourism and distributed by Iraq's Information Office in Washington was hastily revised. Bits of paper were securely glued over maps on the first page of each chapter. After scraping one off with soap and water, I discovered why the books were outdated: They contained maps of Iraq, crudely drawn and out of scale. But they did not include Kuwait, so they were simply papered over.

~ 3 ~

From the Tribesman to the Mythmaker

The perfume of Iraq, its dates, its estuary of the two rivers, its coast and waters, its sword, its shield, the eagle whose grandeur dazzles the heavens. Since there was an Iraq, you were its awaited and promised one.

—Poem about Saddam Hussein

We're dealing with Hitler revisited, a totalitarianism and brutality that is naked and unprecedented in modern times.

—George Bush, speaking at a campaign rally in Manchester, New Hampshire, on October 23, 1990

~ Humble Beginnings

To write about Saddam Hussein is to enter the labyrinth. The truth is, there have always been many Saddams: the imaginary Saddam of his own invention, the heroic Saddam of the semiofficial biographies, the ambiguous Saddam of diplomatic cables, the relentlessly brutal Saddam of his enemies, the maniacal Saddam of world opinion since the invasion of Kuwait. As American-led forces in the Gulf waged war against Saddam, the outcome hinged on how he would react. Was he a cunning strategist capable of holding the world by the throat or a blundering bully trapped by his own isolation? Many thought of him as a survivor who knew when to blink. Others saw him as a Samson who would engulf the Middle East in flames on the way to his self-destruction. For the Bush administration, he was not a merchant who could be bargained with, but rather an outlaw who would have to be defeated by force.

Although Saddam had been president of Iraq for eleven years, and the power behind the presidency for eleven years before that, most of the world probably never heard his name before the invasion of Kuwait. There was little to distinguish him from any other authoritarian Middle Eastern leader in the public mind. He possessed neither the burning piety of an ayatollah, nor the revolutionary flamboyance of a Qaddafi, nor the aura of a Saudi king.

Saddam—the name means "the one who confronts"—was born into a landless peasant family on April 28, 1937, in a tiny village of a few dozen families called al-Uja on the outskirts of Tikrit, a town about 100 miles northwest of Baghdad. His birth "was not a joyful occasion," wrote one of his official biographers, Amir Iskander, "and no roses or aromatic plants bedecked his cradle." The biography included a blurred photograph of the house in which he was born: a mud hut with a roof of reeds.

Al-Uja was undistinguishable from hundreds of villages throughout the plain, where unpaved roads were washed away by seasonal floods, where cow dung was burned for fuel, and where the electricity and running water of Baghdad did not reach. People were so poor that most went barefoot, Saddam told Diane Sawyer of ABC in an interview in June 1990. "Some peasants," he said, "would not put on their shoes until they had reached their destination . . . to protect them from the sand and from wear and tear."

Tikrit was a primitive area of semisettled tribes in the heart of Sunni country on the Tigris River. In the nineteenth century the town was famous for its *kalaks*, round rafts of inflated goat bladders that it sold to other towns for moving goods up and down the rivers. But the market for *kalaks* declined as overland routes improved, and by the beginning of the twentieth century, many villagers abandoned home for Baghdad; the ones who stayed behind tried to find work on the Baghdad-Mosul Railway or on the first oil pipeline to Turkey.

By the 1930s, there was another way out of the poverty of the area: the Army. Tikrit's native sons were able to gain entry into the elite, tuition-free Royal Military Academy and into the officer ranks because of one of Tikrit's inhabitants, the Mosul-born landowner, Mawlud Mukhlis. A vice-president of the Senate under the monarchy and a protégé of King Faisal, Mukhlis lobbied so well for his kinsmen that a disproportionate number of Tikritis entered the officer corps, a tradition that has survived to this day. Many of the commanders who fought the eight-year war against Iran and the subsequent war in the Gulf came from Tikrit, and when the Gulf war broke out in 1991, men whose families were Tikriti held more senior positions in the Iraqi military than people from any other city or town in Iraq, including Baghdad.

Tikrit was considered the big city in the area—at least it boasted one paved road. Saddam subsequently built Tikrit into a modern city, with a highway, modern houses, a new mayoralty, a hospital, a museum, and a university. Still, in his 1980 travel book on Iraq, Gavin Young called Tikrit "the sort of place you might drive through without giving it a thought; it seems very ordinary and so it is."

Tikritis trusted family first and fellow Tikritis second. After the Baath Party came to power, it was an honor for a young Iraqi to be publicly linked with Tikrit, because it meant proximity to the locus of power. Iraqis who came from villages near Tikrit often added al-Tikriti to their names to enhance their status. Tikritis eventually dominated not only the Army but also the intelligence agencies and the Baath Party. The networks of family and village ties became important to the regime, and many of Saddam's closest political and military aides had a Tikriti or a family connection—or both.

Intermarriage became a vehicle to strengthen alliances rooted in the Iraqi provincial soil. A few examples make the point. Saddam himself was a distant cousin of Ahmad Hasan al-Bakr, a Tikriti, who became president when the Baath Party took over in July 1968. Bakr treated Saddam, 23 years younger than he, like a son, and in the early years of Bakr's presidency, Saddam spent much of his day with him at the presidential palace, often serving tea to visitors. Saddam married Sajida Tulfah, a maternal first cousin from Tikrit. Even before Saddam became president, he appointed her brother, Adnan Khairallah, to the position of defense minister. Saddam also married off one daughter, Raghad, to a paternal first cousin, Hussein Kamel al-Majid, the head of Iraq's Ministry of Industry and Military Industrialization and probably the second most powerful man in Iraq at the time of the invasion of Kuwait and the Gulf war. Saddam married off his other daughter, Rima, to Hussein Kamel's brother, Saddam Kamel, a colonel in the missile brigade.

The rough, dirt-poor, lawless atmosphere of Saddam's village shaped his character and outlook. His willingness to use force as an instrument of his domestic consolidation of power was rooted in the peasant environment in which he was raised. Families invented their own rules—tribal rules. They settled feuds among themselves—quickly and decisively. They only turned to outsiders for help when it was absolutely necessary, and they followed the age-old Middle Eastern rationale that "the enemy of my enemy is my friend." They categorized outsiders in a series of concentric rings: those outside the immediate family, those outside the extended family, those who came from outside their village, everyone else in the world. They had no use for symbols of authority, such as local police.

The Tikrit connection became so strong that Saddam eventually was forced to downplay its importance in order to minimize the tribelike quality of the ruling elite. To build Iraq into a modern nation-state, he needed to give the country a leadership that seemed more nationalistic in character. So Saddam changed his name. He was born Saddam Hussein al-Tikriti, after his birthplace. But the Tikritis became so powerful and conspicuous that in 1976, Saddam decided to drop the place of origin from his name and decreed that all Iraqis do the same.

Saddam never knew his father, Hussein Abdel Majid, who died shortly before his birth. Saddam's mother, Subha, then married her husband's brother, Ibrahim Hassan, forcing him to divorce his wife first. Saddam was passed back and forth among relatives as a child, and Hassan, a rough, illiterate peasant, had only one use for him: He put him to work tending the family's sheep.

When Saddam's first cousin Adnan Khairallah went to school, Saddam wanted to do the same. Whether he desperately wanted to learn to read and write, as his two official biographers claim, or simply wanted to escape from the rigors of sheepherding, is not known. According to the local mythology, some villagers encouraged him to run away to relatives in Tikrit, and even gave him a pistol. So in 1947, at the age of ten, Saddam left home one night to live with his maternal uncle, Khairallah Tulfah, Adnan's father, in Tikrit, where he went to school.

In 1941, Tulfah, an Army officer who would later become governor of Baghdad province, supported an anti-British coup. He was dismissed from the Army by the British and served five years in prison for his actions. Tulfah told the young Saddam of his humiliation by the British and taught him to distrust foreigners. He also told Saddam stories of the greatness and heroism of Egypt's president, Gamal Abdel Nasser, who became a role model to a generation of Arabs.

Saddam attended school in Tikrit until 1955, when he followed his uncle to Baghdad—in those days a political center seething with nationalist plots against the monarchy. But Saddam was not interested in the nuances of ideology and politics. Even then, his approach to power was to acquire it by force. He swaggered around Baghdad with a pistol hidden under his shirt. He wanted to become an Army officer like his uncle but was rejected by the elite Baghdad Military Academy because of poor grades. In 1956, he participated in violent mass demonstrations by a group of nationalists and some members of the fledgling Baath Party. Taking their inspiration from Nasser, they protested against the monarchy in Iraq and in support of his nationalization of the Suez Canal that year. In 1957, at the age of 20, Saddam became a junior member of the Baath Party.

Saddam was arrested for the first time and served a six-month prison sentence in 1958—not for a heroic deed of revolution but as a result of a violent family argument, according to one version of the story. Saddam was accused—with his Uncle Khairallah—of killing his brother-in-law, Saadoun al-Alousi, a teacher from Tikrit and a Communist. The story came from a former comrade of Saddam's who was in the same prison at the time. "Saddam told me his uncle gave him a gun and asked him to kill the relative because he was a Communist," recalled Hani al-Fekaiki, an Iraqi who later became a leading Baathist and senior official in the brief 1963 Baath regime before he went into exile in London. "He was a professional killer. But I also have to admit in those days that I admired him. He was brave, courageous, and killed for what he believed in."

The story may be true. But Saddam may also have invented it to impress his comrades and create the beginnings of a terrifying myth. In any case, the 1950s in Iraq were a time of minimal governmental control, when family and tribal disputes meant little to the authorities. Saddam was soon released.

Saddam's formal education was sidetracked by the 1958 revolution. In 1959, at the age of 22, he was one of ten young Baath Party guerrillas assigned to assassinate Abd al-Karim Qassim, the dictator who had overthrown the monarchy the year before. The would-be assassins botched the plan. One of them was supposed to move his car to block the street so that Qassim's car could not get through. But the driver lost his car keys. The assassins sprayed the dictator's station wagon with machine-gun fire as it approached a narrow point on Rashid Street but failed to kill him.

"The Party wanted people who didn't mind killing," said al-Fekaiki. "Saddam had already killed one of his relatives, so he was a proven killer. But the plan was stupid. The people who planned it weren't military men. They put the assassins on both sides of the street. Saddam was not injured by one of Qassim's guards. He was shot by one of his own comrades in the crossfire."

Saddam escaped, and a myth was spun around the episode.

There are many versions of the story, but all agree that during the assassination attempt, Saddam was shot in the leg. The most heroic version was that Saddam was badly wounded and cut the bullet out of his thigh with his own knife as he fled across the desert on a donkey to Syria. In her interview with Saddam, Diane Sawyer asked whether the story was true. "It is essentially true," he told her. Nizar Hamdoon, the former Iraqi ambassador to Washington, once told me that Saddam "was shot by a bullet and during his escape he used his knife to bring the bullet out. He has always dealt with events in an unconventional way. He's a tough guy." Even Hanna Batatu, the eminent Iraqi historian, accepted the version. "Wounded during the incident by the fire of his comrades," he wrote, "he extracted, in the car that sped away from the scene, a bullet from his leg with his own knife."

Amir Iskander, one of Saddam's official biographers, told the story somewhat differently. In a chapter entitled "The Voyage of the Wounded Cavalier,"

Iskander wrote that Saddam, seriously wounded, asked a comrade, Ahmad Tahal Azzouz, to dig out the bullet. "Do you have the courage to do the operation or do I have to do it myself?" Saddam asked Azzouz bluntly, according to Iskander. When Azzouz hesitated, Saddam issued an order. "Bring me a new razor blade and a pair of scissors," he said. "Begin by cutting in the shape of a cross the flesh around the bullet; then sterilize the scissors, put it into the wound and take out the slug. That's all." According to this version, Azzouz took out the bullet; Saddam fainted from the pain. Later he disguised himself as a Bedouin tribesman, swam across the Tigris, stole a donkey, and rode across the desert to safe exile in Syria. Because of this adventure, the tale continues, Nasser summoned the young revolutionary to Cairo, where he began the underground life of intrigue that would ultimately bring him to power.

A third version of this story is told by Saddam's former comrades-turned-opponents, although it may be tainted by their deep sense of betrayal at his hands. According to them, Saddam suffered a superficial wound that was treated by a sympathetic doctor, Tahseen Muallah, who was a member of the Baath Party leadership at the time. By the time Saddam was brought to Muallah, there was no bullet, recalled the doctor, who now lives in London, only a minor wound. "I cleaned and dressed the simple superficial wound, then I gave him an injection of anti-tetanus serum," said Muallah. This version was confirmed by al-Fekaiki. "I was in Syria in a small village, living there on the border smuggling arms into Iraq for our party," he recalled. "I was the first person to meet Saddam when he came over the Syrian border, and he stayed in my house. I can assure you, the injury was very minor. He tried to exaggerate things after he came to power. To impress people. To impress the new generations."

Saddam spent the next four years in Cairo. In Iraq, he was tried in absentia and sentenced to 15 years in prison. In 1961, at the age of 24, he finally finished high school, then enrolled in Cairo University Law College with an Egyptian government scholarship. He spent little time in class, and it was generally known in political circles that he was under Nasser's personal protection. In 1961, he was arrested and charged with threatening to kill an Iraqi, but he was released after Nasser intervened.

Saddam's hangout in those days was the Andiana Restaurant on Cairo's bustling Dokki Street. Hussein Abdel Meguid, the Andiana's owner, portrayed Saddam as a loner who hardly ever went to class, borrowed money from the waiters, and enjoyed picking fights with the Syrian and Yemeni patrons. "He would come and just sit all day," said Meguid. "He would eat his three meals here, and when he wasn't eating he would just sit. He never studied. He would read newspapers, drink Turkish coffee, and watch the old men play chess. But he never played chess himself. He was really quite lonely. He didn't have any friends." Meguid recalled one incident in which Saddam, armed with a pocketknife, picked a fight so serious that a number of people were injured and the police were summoned. But the police refused to arrest Saddam because of his connection to Nasser.

Years later, when Saddam became president of Iraq, Meguid was surprised. "I couldn't believe," he said recently, "that such a bully who was picking fights all the time could grow up to be president of Iraq."

$\sim$

When a group of Baathist Army officers and Arab nationalists succeeded in killing Abd al-Karim Qassim in 1963 and briefly installed a Baathist regime, Saddam hurried home to Iraq. He was given a minor position—membership in the Party's Central Bureau for Peasants. He still owed several hundred dollars to the Andiana, which he paid—with generous interest—several years later. He never got his law degree from Cairo University but later enrolled in Baghdad University. In 1970, when he showed up at the bar exam with his bodyguard, he was handed his degree.

Saddam eventually turned against Nasser, accusing him of sentimentality toward the Israelis and weakness regarding Arab unity. But he remained loyal to his uncle Khairallah Tulfah. Their relationship was solidified in 1963 when Saddam married his daughter, Sajida, then a primary-school teacher in Baghdad. The uncle's corruption was so egregious that it eventually cost him his job as governor of Baghdad province, and Saddam forced him to retire. But in 1981, as a special tribute, Saddam arranged to have the official government printing house republish one of his uncle's political pamphlets. Titled *Three Whom God Should Not Have Created: Persians, Jews and Flies*, it called Persians "animals that God created in the shape of humans," Jews a "blend of the dirt and leftovers of various peoples," and flies useless entities "whom we do not understand God's purpose in creating."

∼ The Rise to Power

The Baath Party lasted in power for only nine months after its 1963 takeover, outmaneuvered and ousted by the military. The Party went underground again. Saddam was arrested for participating in another coup attempt in 1964 and spent two years in prison. "In prison, he was known by his comrades as a strong-willed freedom-fighter who stood firmly in the face of his jailers, rejected submission, refusing to relinquish the bold principles he believed in," said a biography of Saddam published in 1983 in the English-language newspaper, the *Baghdad Observer*, to commemorate Saddam's birthday. According to Saddam's own version, he did not play cards, as most prisoners did, nor did he smoke. Rather, he began to plot what he called "a scheme" to avoid repetition of the mistakes that had prevented the Baath Party from holding onto power. "Saddam learned three lessons from 1963," the historian

Phebe Marr said. "First, never share power with another group. Second, put the Army in its barracks and keep it there. And third, prevent splits in the leadership at all costs." Throughout his rule, these lessons remained his desiderata.

Saddam escaped from prison in 1966. During an official appointment outside the prison, he and two fellow prisoners talked their guard into letting them go out for a good meal in a restaurant before they returned to their cells. One of them stayed behind at the table and Saddam and a third prisoner fled through a back door in the washroom, escaping in a waiting getaway car.

Saddam swiftly moved up the ranks of the Baath Party, which elected him as secretary-general of the new regional command in 1966. But the Baath at that time was less a party than an underground terrorist organization, and promoting Party unity did not mean campaign promises and backroom negotiations. The 1960s were a time of complicated conspiratorial coup attempts, when plotters of various factions aligned themselves with disgruntled military officers, most of whom moved in and out of prison. The priority was to build power bases, not develop ideology. Between 1966 and 1968, Saddam was not the Party strategist; rather, he was the hit man assigned the most difficult jobs. One of these was to raid safe houses controlled by the pro-Syrian faction of the Party and to steal their weapons and printing presses.

Saddam was also assigned to create the Jihaz Haneen, or Instrument of Yearning, a secret organization of armed cells of Party members who specialized in intelligence and terrorist activities. It became the basis for the Party's watchdog militia. How important Saddam was in those days depends on who is telling the story. One Iraqi opposition leader remembers him as a minor player in the Party decisions that led to the 1968 takeover. "It was 1967 or 1968 and we were meeting in my office," recalled Saad al-Jabr, an Iraqi who leads an opposition group from London. "We were plotting a takeover. It was lunchtime and we had let the coffee boy go home. So one of the guys pulled out a dinar and told Saddam to bring back five bottles of Ferida beer. That was his role, to buy the beer."

Other Iraqis who participated in those conspiratorial days recall events differently, saying that it was al-Jabr who was never the big-time plotter.

Saddam was not, as he claimed, the man in a military uniform who "led the tank assault on the presidential palace" when the Baath Party came to power with military help on July 17, 1968. A civilian, he played a key role behind the scenes. He kept a low profile for the next year, moving to consolidate power—slowly and patiently—in case the new regime did not last. By November 1969, Saddam surfaced as the second most important personality in the regime when he was appointed to the position of deputy chairman of the ruling Revolutionary Command Council.

As Saddam built his power base, he began to covet the presidency. Aware that Ahmad Hasan al-Bakr had the full support of the military, he ruthlessly purged anyone suspected of posing a threat to his own leadership. He restructured the secret police organizations, putting them under the authority of the Revolutionary Command Council—and, therefore, under his control. He firmly believed in the rationalization that Freya Stark said dominated Iraqi political life in the 1940s: "Build, and let the abuses die in their own time and of their own accord." The abuses never died; they were expanded to adjust to Saddam's mounting ambition.

One of his instruments of power was the Palace of the End—the Qasr al-Nihayyah—a much-feared torture chamber that the Party established after its 1963 coup. Saddam was responsible for the prison and conducted some of the interrogations himself, usually after the victims were beaten or tortured. "He was the man who gave the orders," recalled Sami Faraj Ali, an Iraqi journalist now living in exile in London who was imprisoned briefly in 1969. "He had the authority, with one word, to decide if you stayed alive or died. I was brought into a big room with Saddam and about twelve people who worked for him. By the time he interrogated me, I had already been beaten by others. Torture wasn't his job. I was lucky. He said to me: 'This time we scared you. But next time you will not survive. We will hang you.' As soon as I was released, I left the country."

According to Phebe Marr, it was Saddam's underground, conspiratorial activities that determined his approach to power. "His secretiveness, his cautiousness, and his distrust of outsiders sprang from years of being hunted, and from his own considerable talents in organizing conspiracy," she wrote in her history of modern Iraq. "At the same time, his courage and fearlessness contributed to his image as a *shaqawah*, a local term denoting a kind of tough or bully—a man to be feared. These experiences also inclined him toward the Stalinist model of political control. He has admitted to admiring the man who, in his early years, captured and controlled the civilian Soviet Communist Party and so firmly entrenched it in power that it could not be dislodged, even by the Army."

Until the mid-1970s, Saddam functioned as a sort of junior partner to Bakr, the first person in modern Iraqi history who enjoyed complete control over the military establishment. Saddam gradually took over most of the day-to-day operations of government, including the resolution of internal political problems. In 1970, it was Saddam who was assigned to conclude an autonomy agreement with the Kurds. He also took on some of the important foreign-policy functions of government, negotiating a Treaty of Friendship and Cooperation with Moscow in 1972 and an arms relationship with Paris in 1975. By then, Saddam had emerged as the real political authority in Iraq: The regional Party offices, the intelligence services, and many of the ministries began to report directly to him. Bakr, in ill health and mourning the deaths of his first wife and oldest son, ceded more and more power to Saddam.

On July 16, 1979, Bakr announced his resignation. Saddam assumed the presidency the next day. The official version was that President Bakr, suffering from diabetes and recurrent heart trouble, was too ill to continue. The other version was that Saddam simply bullied him out of office.

~ The Mythmaking Begins

In the 1970s, Saddam still retained the aura of a terrorist guerrilla, an image he tried to shed by wearing expensive double-breasted pin-striped suits and a diamond-studded platinum wristwatch with matching diamond cufflinks. He smoked Havana cigars and a pipe, choosing from a rack of Dunhill's finest that he kept near his desk. But just as Saddam would pick threads from ancient Mesopotamia to weave a tapestry of Iraq's greatness, he invented a mythology for himself when he assumed the presidency.

By 1980, a year after he became president, he began to cultivate the image of the benign "Father-Leader," as he liked to be called. One widely circulated photo showed Saddam smiling broadly with the youngest of his five children in his lap, a cigar in one hand.

Saddam never served in the Army, but even before he assumed the presidency, he began to make himself into a military man. In 1976, he arranged to be named a lieutenant general, with the rank equivalent to chief of staff. In 1979, after becoming president, he promoted himself to field marshal. During the Iran-Iraq war, and again after his invasion of Kuwait and the outbreak of war with the allied coalition, he often appeared on television visiting his troops and holding interminable meetings with his military commanders. But he kept his commanders in the background so that no other hero could emerge, and he took personal credit for technological advancements and battlefield victories. For example, a book published after the decisive Iraqi offensive that drove the Iranians from Iraq's Fao Peninsula in 1988 explained that the operation "was planned and conducted by the President himself who was present in the battlefield."

During his war with Iran, Saddam, a diehard secularist, made himself a man of religion. In his fervent drive to curry favor with Iraq's majority Shiite population, Saddam had no difficulty tampering with history to achieve his end. Three months after his mother died in 1983, Saddam revealed a "secret": He claimed that she had been a Shiite. In fact, she had been a pure-blooded Sunni. When Michel Aflaq, the Baath Party founder, died in 1989, Saddam declared that Aflaq had secretly converted to Islam sometime before his death. Saddam obviously felt uncomfortable with a Greek Orthodox Syrian Christian as his political mentor. Pillars in the courtyards of Shiite mosques across Iraq displayed photographs of Saddam dressed in the white shroud of a pilgrim in Mecca—an effort, one assumed, to portray himself as beloved by the Shiites. Not even Iran's ayatollahs dared to compete with the Prophet and his spiritual successors by hanging their own portraits in mosques.

In what many Muslims viewed as an act of heresy, Saddam once had an elaborate family tree invented that traced his ancestry to Mohammad's daughter Fatima, his son-in-law Ali, and their son Hussein, the spiritual patrons of Shiites. It was posted near the tomb of Ali in Najaf and at the lecture hall adjacent to Hussein's tomb in Karbala. On one level, the family tree could have been seen as an effort to appeal to the religious sensibilities of the people. On another level, according to *Republic of Fear*, a relentless account of repression in Iraq by the pseudonymous Samir al-Khalil, "This gesture . . . signified total contempt for the populace, large numbers of whom he knew would accept this proof of ancestry."

After his August 1990 invasion of Kuwait, Saddam emphasized this religious side even more. In an ingenious way, he adapted the language of Islam to his totalitarian dictatorship in preparing his people for war with the American–led coalition. At one point during his meeting with the Reverend Jesse Jackson shortly after the invasion, Saddam abruptly left the room, saying that he had to pray. In another illustration that shows he began to believe in the myth he had created, Saddam referred to himself as a descendant of the Prophet in a biting open letter to Egypt's President Hosni Mubarak on August 23. An Iraqi-run newspaper in occupied Kuwait published an article a month after the invasion that tried to show that the country's ruling family descended from the Christian crusaders who fought the Muslims from the eleventh to thirteenth centuries. On another occasion, the same newspaper reported that the Saudi royal family was of Jewish descent. Just before the 1991 Gulf war, Saddam more firmly embraced the language and imagery of Islam. He ordered that the Islamic battle cry, *Allahu Akbar* ("God is great"), be added to the red, white, green, and black flag of Iraq.

~

Over the years, Saddam became an actor, donning a costume for every occasion. Images of Saddam were ubiquitous and reinforced the myth that he was all-seeing and all-knowing. "Saddam Hussein exists in every corner, every place, every eyebrow, and every heart in Iraq," he boasted to a group of foreign reporters in 1982. Eight years later, he reiterated the importance of his personality cult by explaining how every Iraqi is dependent on him, telling ABC's Diane Sawyer in 1990, "Saddam Hussein is present in any quantity of milk given to a child, and is present in any clean or new jacket that an Iraqi may wear."

In the thousands of 20-foot-high paintings spread throughout the country, Saddam became all things to all Iraqis in an unceasing attempt to create a mythology to bind his people. He lacked the personal charisma of a Nasser; perhaps these portraits were intended to compensate. At Baghdad University, Saddam was depicted as a young graduate in cap and gown; at the racetrack, a desert horseman; at the entrance to Basra, a peasant cutting wheat with a sickle; on a neon lollipop on the Baghdad-Babylon highway, a Bedouin. He was a sheik, a commander-in-chief in uniform and aviator glasses, a waving soldier, a president in a suit and tie, a construction worker carrying a bowl of wet cement on his shoulder. After the invasion of Kuwait, he appeared in the traditional long white robe and headdress worn by the Kuwaitis. Saddam had named a city after himself, and an airport, and an irrigation project, and a dam, and a school, and a Party branch—a practice that was extended to Kuwait when he turned it into Iraq's nineteenth province.

Saddam's portraits appeared on almost any flat surface—hotel lobbies, bazaar stalls, immigration booths, bus windows, and construction fences; on gold-trimmed cake plates, calendars, schoolchildren's notebooks. A bank in Baghdad even gave out Saddam Hussein keychains to customers who purchased life insurance policies. Twenty years' service in the Baath Party was rewarded with an octagonal, gold-plated Saddam Hussein pin. I knew a foreign diplomat's wife who was convinced she received better service at the supermarket after she began to wear one.

Even the monuments of Baghdad were intended to glorify Saddam. In the early 1980s, Saddam spent more than $100 million to build the Tomb of the Unknown Soldier in the center of Baghdad. The soldier might have been unknown, but the leader was not. I counted 106 photographs of Saddam hanging on the walls of the tomb when I first visited in 1984—Saddam being kissed on his chest by Kurdish women, Saddam pinching the cheeks of Kurdish children, Saddam kissing the Koran, Saddam examining cucumbers in a government greenhouse. I visited the tomb again just days before the allied war against Iraq. The photographs had changed, but their subject had not. The Ministry of Information guide who accompanied me had never been there and didn't even know where the entrance was. The tomb had not gained in popularity among ordinary Baghdadis, and except for two honor guards and four cleaning women, the tomb was empty.

Saddam began to use state-run television to sell himself to his people as soon as he became president. No aspect of Iraqi life was too insignificant for his attention. Whether it meant attending a ritual circumcision, lecturing to engineers on how to raise cattle, swinging a sickle with peasants in a wheat field, pulling on a fisherman's line, sitting cross-legged with Bedouins sipping cardamon-laced coffee from thimble-sized cups, inspecting melons and radishes in a greengrocers' market—Saddam was there. The visits often included gifts—the announcement of a road to be built, the arrival of refrigerators or television sets. An Iraqi woman once told me that her children insisted on having tea and cakes ready at all times just in case Saddam stopped by. As a reminder of Saddam's omnipresence, even the official television spokesman who often read his speeches in front of a map of the world resembled a young Saddam.

Television also became a vehicle to drum into the Iraqi people—over and over—their duties as citizens and the way in which loyalty to the state was enforced. When Saddam was running out of money to fund his war with Iran in the summer of 1983, he came up with an ingenious way to raise capital through the Federation of Iraqi Women. It started as an impromptu gesture and became a nationwide voluntary campaign. Except that it was compulsory. One day, Saddam's soldiers went door to door asking people for their gold. Local Party headquarters and government offices throughout the country were transformed overnight into collection centers for gold and cash donations. People sat lined up in the corridors waiting to be received. Each piece of gold was weighed and the donors were given receipts. Some were even pressured into relinquishing their wedding rings. One Iraqi agricultural expert brought in his new Mercedes. His wife donated a kilo of gold worth more than $100,000, because, she said, "I love the president, Saddam Hussein, too much."

Every night for days, Saddam appeared on television to greet people who made donations, and an anonymous newscaster read off long lists of names and the amounts of their gifts. In one speech, Saddam warned what would happen to those Iraqis who didn't give enough, telling the story of a millionaire from his hometown of Tikrit who gave only $3,000 and a dagger. "How much faith does this man have in the homeland and in the revolution?" he asked. Then he struck a more ominous note that was meant to be heard by all television viewers: "I'm sure he will hear me."

Within a few weeks, the gold campaign was over. The government announced the collection of 30 tons of gold. Saddam promised to build the women of Iraq a monument for their "glorious deed." But Iraq couldn't afford it, and a few days later, the finance minister, Thamir Razzouki, gently corrected the president, saying that the gold would not be used to build a monument. Rather, it would be kept in the Central Bank and used as a "strategic cover" for Iraq's currency. The gold was never returned.

In his television appearances, Saddam was less the radical on the road of permanent revolution than the politician on a permanent campaign. Sometimes there was a moralistic message to his forays. On a visit to a bridge construction site, he asked the builders why some of the bricks were not straight. "They must be straight, just as the road of your life must be straight," he told them. He reminded traffic officers that they must strictly enforce traffic regulations, because obedience to these regulations was the beginning of civil obedience everywhere. For a visit to a penal farm in Iraq, Saddam dressed up like a peasant, putting on a sheepskin vest and carrying a shepherd's staff. He commuted the sentences of two prisoners. It was the height of the Iran-Iraq war, and Saddam needed more soldiers. "You have mustaches, and so you must fight," he told them. "You are free—to go to the front." The crowd cheered. But the all-seeing Saddam would be there with them. "I will be watching you and asking your superiors about your performance," he warned, a message that was intended for Iraqi television viewers as well. "You will be punished if you do not perform."

Saddam also collected titles: Hero of Arab Liberation, Sword of the Arabs, Knight of the Nation, Beloved of the People, Leader of the Victory. His speeches were published in hundreds of slim volumes and translated into dozens of languages, from Swedish to Serbo-Croatian, and recorded on cassettes. But the president's portraits eventually became a joke in Iraq. It started about 1983 and was the only joke I ever heard in that country. Question: "What's the population of Iraq?" Answer: "Twenty-eight million: Fourteen million Iraqis and 14 million pictures of Saddam." As the joke was retold over the years and the population increased, so did the number of portraits.

The trouble with telling such jokes was that insulting Saddam or his government was a crime. A diplomat who served in Iraq a number of years ago tells a story of a handful of Australian businessmen who one evening staged a musical review in the garden of their Baghdad villa. When they began singing a song about Saddam and his Army to the tune of "Old Macdonald Had a Farm," three Iraqi soldiers jumped over the fence and arrested them. "You are insulting my president," one said, as he led them away. "They spent a week in prison and were subjected to electric shock, that sort of thing," the diplomat recalled. "I think they were deported in the end. But that was the standard sort of thing that happened."

In 1981, Peter Worth, a British civil engineer working in Iraq, leaned against a wall at a construction project and caused a picture of Saddam to come crashing to the ground. He later told a British reporter that he was arrested, beaten, and tortured by electric shock. After he signed a false confession admitting espionage, he was deported.

In both incidents, the perpetrators were Westerners and their sentences were light. For Iraqis, insulting the president was punishable by life imprisonment and the expropriation of all of the offender's property, according to a 1986 decree. If the insult was done "in a blatant fashion," or was "designed to provoke public opinion against the authorities," the punishment was death. Saddam seemed stunned when ABC's Diane Sawyer told him during her 1990 interview that it was not a crime in the United States to insult the president.

SADDAM: In your country, the law does not punish whoever tries to insult the president?

SAWYER: No, it certainly does not. Half of the country would be in prison—three-quarters of the country.

SADDAM: And no measures would be taken against anybody insulting the president?

SAWYER: To the contrary; they get their own television show.

The joke was lost on Saddam, and, not surprisingly, this exchange was omitted when the interview was aired on Iraqi television. Saddam was not a man who found it easy to banter with foreign visitors. Richard W. Murphy, the assistant secretary of state responsible for the Middle East during most of the Reagan administration, recalled an incident during one meeting in the mid-1980s when Saddam tried to crack a joke. "He said that America treats the Third World like an Iraqi peasant treats his bride," Murphy said. "The honeymoon was wonderful for three days, then it was off to the fields. He thought that was wonderfully funny. I guess I laughed."

~

There was one instance when the cult of Iran's Ayatollah Khomeini outdid the cult of Saddam. I call it "the cult of the watch." In the souks of Baghdad, there were watches with a portrait of a smiling Saddam on them. The photo of Saddam was muddy, the leather strap cheaply sewn, and the watch overpriced at more than $100 at the official exchange rate. Not so in Iran. The Swiss watch in honor of Khomeini that was sold at the beginning of Iran's revolution had a built-in light filter. Khomeini's stern face eerily appeared and disappeared twice a minute. Maybe it was supposed to be a sign that Khomeini was the "vanishing imam" who would someday, as the Shiites believe, bring heaven on earth. The watch was labeled SOUVENIR OF THE ISLAMIC REPUBLIC. Its second hand was a red splotch—symbolizing a drop of martyr's blood. The watch cost $25 in Tehran's main bazaar. It still keeps perfect time.

~ Isolation at the Top

One of the hallmarks of most Middle East leaders is their isolation. Libya's Colonel Muammar Qaddafi, Syria's President Hafez al-Assad, and the mullahs of Tehran, like Saddam, traveled little outside the Middle East. Their worldviews often were limited by their lack of firsthand exposure to a variety of political systems and cultures. In the four months that Khomeini spent in France before returning in triumph to Tehran in February 1979, he never saw Paris. His wife, dressed in a black chador, slipped into the French capital to sightsee and window-shop, but Khomeini did not venture from his cottage headquarters in nearby Neauphle-le-Château.

Qaddafi knew little about the United States when I interviewed him in 1981. He knew there was desert country out West and professed to admire George Washington and "Ibrahim" Lincoln, praising the American Civil War president in particular as "a strong, steadfast man who became an excellent lawyer by teaching himself, better than those who had gone to universities." Qaddafi couldn't understand why Ronald Reagan didn't like him. "We are not Communists," he said. "We are a country that could be very much like

Yugoslavia, and a nonaligned country is better for the United States than a country that is aligned against you."

Similarly, I remember sitting down for an early breakfast with Yemen's president, Ali Abdullah Saleh, in the dining room at Blair House, the U.S. president's official guest residence across the street from the White House. It was Saleh's first state visit, and he arrived not only with his top aides but also with representatives of his American public relations firm, Hill & Knowlton (the same firm that later represented the government-in-exile of Kuwait). Hill & Knowlton had written Saleh's speeches and prepared a glossy press kit, but the firm could not eradicate his biases. Halfway through the breakfast with a dozen American journalists, the Yemeni president turned the tables. Why, he asked, didn't the American media write about the Palestinian uprising in the occupied territories? Nothing we said could persuade him that the American media had indeed covered the story. As far as he was concerned, there was a conspiracy in the American media to prevent the truth from coming out.

Saddam Hussein had even less sense of the outside world. Unlike the Saudi and Kuwaiti royal families, he did not vacation on the Riviera, visit medical specialists in Geneva and London, shop in Paris, or send his offspring to American colleges. He made infrequent forays out of the Middle East— official visits to Paris and Moscow. His only sustained contact with non-Arabs had been with Soviet military advisers. The outside world had little sense of Saddam—so little that after the invasion of Kuwait in 1990, the Israeli military intelligence was reported to have sent a sample of his script to a handwriting analyst to get a better sense of his personality.

Occasionally, specific events exposed the degree of Saddam's isolation— and the absurdity of some of his positions. Shortly after his invasion of Kuwait, his clumsy attempt to show the world his compassion by appearing on Iraqi television with a group of British hostages backfired. In a tense, 40-minute encounter that for most of the Western world was the first close-up look at the Iraqi leader, Saddam gave a tortured explanation of the nuances of Arabic that was lost on his audience of hostages. He explained that they were not "human shields" to be used in a war, but "heroes of peace" who were "preventing danger." The image of Saddam ruffling the hair of five-year-old British hostage Stuart Lockwood was nothing unusual for Iraqi viewers, who were accustomed to seeing their leader in staged television appearances. But both Britain and the United States condemned the performance as shameful theatrics. It took a personal appeal from King Hussein of Jordan to convince Saddam that his approach had played poorly in the West, and that he should at least release the women and children he was holding.

Saddam revealed his isolation once again a few weeks later in an interview with the Reverend Jesse Jackson. In 1984, Jackson had persuaded Syria's president, Hafez al-Assad, to release Lieutenant Robert Goodman, an American Navy pilot who had been shot down by Syria, and Jackson thought he might repeat the coup. So he went to Baghdad, officially as a television journalist for King World Productions, seeking to win the release of American hostages. Jackson later recalled that he tried to convince Saddam to carry out his promise to allow foreign women and children to leave. Jackson reported to Saddam in the absence of a concrete evacuation plan, many of them were reluctant to come out of hiding, fearing capture by the Iraqi Army.

Saddam didn't seem to grasp what Jackson was saying. He insisted that he had decreed that women and children were free to leave the country, so why were some women and children still there? "If people stay and I say they can go, they must be spies," Jackson quoted Saddam as saying. And they would be treated as spies, Saddam added for good measure. Saddam made the statement during an informal conversation over tea and then repeated it on camera. But Jackson was not allowed to use his own television crew for the interview, and when Iraqi officials turned over the official videocassette taped by the Iraqi cameramen, one of the president's men must have realized how silly Saddam sounded. The line about the spies was deleted.

~ Saddam's Men

The years following Saddam Hussein's takeover as president in 1979 produced no heir apparent, no viable domestic opposition, no democratic tradition, no charismatic military commander, and no popular leader-in-exile waiting to return. When it came to political maneuvering or military strategy, Saddam was his own best—or worst—adviser. Although he was regularly shown on Iraqi television conducting meetings of his Revolutionary Command Council or visiting his commanders at the war front, the Iraqi leader surrounded himself with like-minded aides who were bound to him by blood, either through family ties or shared responsibility for killing. They told him to varying degrees what he expected to hear, depending on their level of confidence, although none of them dissented outright. He made sure his close aides knew the price of disloyalty. "If I die, you will not find a finger left of me, and you will all die with me," he once warned members of his Revolutionary Command Council during a meeting with King Fahd of Saudi Arabia a number of years ago, according to a Saudi official who was present. "The only way you will survive is with your loyalty."

Saddam's men fell into three categories. First came his relatives. Then came the diehard political advisers, most of them loyal, look-alike companions-in-arms from the days before the Baath Party assumed power. Finally, there were the military commanders, who proved their bravery in battle in the eight-year war with Iran and were rewarded with positions of leadership and punished when they became either too popular or too independent.

Since Saddam conducted all official meetings in secret, it was impossible to know for certain which aides he trusted and how much he listened to any of them. But those who dealt with him said that a conversation with Saddam was not the same as a dialogue. His style was to state a fixed position and then ask rhetorical questions that he proceeded to answer himself, focusing obsessively on certain points he wanted to make. He ran meetings with his commanders much like a tribal leader or arrogant chairman of the board, and those who murmured about his decisions, or who were perceived to have failed in their duty, were either retired or executed.

From the late 1980s, the rising star in the Iraqi government was Hussein Kamel al-Majid. Kamel was doubly bound by blood to Saddam as his cousin and son-in-law, and Saddam treated him like a son. For his part, Kamel swaggered around Baghdad with "the confidence that comes from sleeping with the president's daughter," a Western diplomat told me on the eve of the Gulf war.

During the latter stages of the Iran-Iraq war, when Kamel was still in his thirties, he rose quickly through the ranks of the military-industrial establishment. As minister of Industry and Military Industrialization, he was responsible for the rapid and extraordinary acquisition and development of Iraq's missile technology, conventional weaponry, and secret nuclear program. It was Kamel, for example, who oversaw the Iraqi modification of Scud missiles that were fired at Israel and Saudi Arabia, and he attended Revolutionary Command Council meetings in the months before the war, even though he was not a council member.

Like Saddam, Kamel—who held the title of general—moved up through the ranks of the intelligence services rather than the military hierarchy. His ministry was the only office in Baghdad that could bankroll its projects independent of the presidential palace. When Saddam had to retreat from a botched policy of gasoline rationing only days after it was instituted in October 1990, he unceremoniously fired his veteran oil minister, Isham Abdel-Rahim al-Chalabi, and temporarily turned over the oil portfolio to Kamel. It mattered little that Kamel had no background or experience in economics or oil. He was one of Saddam's most-trusted henchmen, and a show of strength, not expertise, was what was called for. Al-Chalabi promptly disappeared from sight.

A family tie didn't necessarily guarantee political longevity, however. The political fortunes of Saddam's three younger half-brothers, Barzan, Sabawi, and Watban al-Tikriti, for example, rose and fell over the years with the inner workings of the president's clan. In 1983, all of them were ousted from their government positions and temporarily disappeared.

One version had it that Saddam and Barzan, who had held the powerful job of chief of the intelligence services, had fought over the choice of a husband for Barzan's daughter. Saddam had to wait until their mother died before he could punish his younger half-brother, according to that version.

A second version was that Barzan had political ambitions of his own. He had recently published a 190-page book documenting the various assassination attempts against Saddam. The "plots" covered all possible sources of opposition—the Shiites, the Army, the U.S. Central Intelligence Agency, the Israeli secret service, the Kurds, the Syrians—and in 1983 the book became an instant best-seller. The lesson to would-be plotters was obvious: The regime is all-knowing, so don't even think about attempting assassination. But the book could also have been interpreted as proof that Saddam was not universally loved.

There was a third, more mundane explanation as well: Barzan's drinking and womanizing began to embarrass Saddam and he wanted Barzan out of sight. In any case, six years later, the three brothers were at least partially rehabilitated. Barzan was made ambassador to Iraq's United Nations delegation in Geneva. One of his responsibilities was to participate in the annual proceedings of the United Nations Commission on Human Rights. But Barzan was regarded more as a thug than a diplomat attuned to the nuances of multilateral diplomacy. The diplomatic community in Geneva often repeated the tale of Barzan beating up a tardy chauffeur at a diplomatic reception. More ominous, Barzan was believed to have used his post as a base to secure sophisticated military technology, including equipment for making chemical weapons and parts for nuclear weapons and a long-range artillery "supergun."

Sabawi, meanwhile, became head of the Baath Party intelligence service, and Watban was believed to have held a job in the presidential palace. Putting them in government served a dual purpose: They could keep an eye on potential plots and Saddam could keep an eye on them.

Outside the family circle were the diehard loyalists, the Baath Party veterans who grew up together in the bloody early days of the Party underground and who sat together on the tightly knit Revolutionary Command Council. The man whose thinking most closely matched that of Saddam was Latif Nassif Jassim, the minister of information and culture. Born in the early 1940s in a suburb of al-Rashidiyah outside of Baghdad, Jassim wore a pistol on his hip and held a vast portfolio. He controlled the domestic media, the radio, television, and government-controlled newspapers, all cultural events, popular festivals, and government publications. Accessible to foreign journalists, Jassim was totally trusted, a replica of Saddam, and he faithfully parroted his master's words. "I want to tell you as a member of the leadership, we will never go out of Kuwait, ever," he told foreign journalists over and over in the months after the invasion. Soon after the invasion, he was quoted as saying that if war came, captured American troops would be eaten. Later, the ministry clarified his remarks, explaining that the minister meant to say that the Americans would be eaten by dogs, not by humans.

Taha Yassin Ramadan, first deputy prime minister, was once a potential political rival with a following of his own. But as Saddam consolidated power for himself, Ramadan loyally moved in behind him. Ramadan was even more rigid in his views of government than Saddam. For example, when Saddam was moving toward a more free-enterprise economy in the late 1980s, Ramadan was said to have favored even more governmental control of the economy.

The son of an Arab gardener of Kurdish origin from Mosul, Ramadan commanded Iraq's 500,000-member Popular Army from the time of its creation in 1970. A former bank clerk, Ramadan served as a fairly competent minister of labor and minister of industry. During the long war with Iran, he was put in charge of Iraq's economy, maneuvering to keep store shelves well stocked as the war bill mounted. In his public statements, Ramadan often voiced a harder line than Saddam. Suspicious of the United States even when relations were warming in the mid-1980s, and a bitter opponent of Israel, he once called the U.S. Congress an extension of Israel's Knesset. A fierce defender of Iraq's harsh system of justice, he praised executions of Iraqi officials on bribery charges as necessary examples for the common good.

If Ramadan was Saddam's brass knuckle, Tariq Aziz was his velvet glove. If there was a good face that Iraq wanted to show to the West, then Aziz was the man to do it. The silver-haired, cigar-smoking foreign minister was not only a culture-bridger who spoke good English, but also a master negotiator who tried to move Iraq into the mainstream of world diplomacy. He visited Egypt in the summer of 1983 in the first formal contact between the two countries since the 1978 Camp David accords, and he oversaw the restoration of diplomatic relations with Cairo nine years later. He broadened Iraq's diplomatic and military ties to the West, personally negotiating with France the loan of Super Etendard planes capable of firing sophisticated Exocet missiles that were crucial during the Iran-Iraq war.

When the war was going badly for Iraq and it needed Western help, Aziz was crucial in moving the regime toward restoring full diplomatic relations with the United States in November 1984, driving home the point that Iraq was no longer a rejectionist regime that demanded an armed struggle to overthrow the "Zionist entity."

Aziz was born in 1936 into a poor family near the northern city of Mosul, but an accident of birth kept him from rising too high in the ranks. Unlike Saddam and many in his clique, Aziz was not a Sunni Muslim but a Chaldean Christian. His given name was believed to have been Mikhail Yuhanna, but at some point he changed it to the more Muslim-sounding Tariq Aziz. While Saddam earned his stripes as a gunman, Aziz, armed with a degree in English literature from Baghdad University, became a Party organizer and propagandist, and eventually rose to become editor of the Party daily, *al-Thawra*. After the Baathists seized power in 1968, he became one of the Party's leading ideologues. His years as a journalist and propagandist taught him the importance of image. During the war with Iran, he often wore fatigues and an ivory-handled pistol in his office; on foreign television and trips abroad, a Western business suit was the preferred style.

There were other survivors who remained close to Saddam over the years. Izzat Ibrahim, the vice-president of the Revolutionary Command Council, was officially Saddam's second-in-command, a devoted and completely obedient servant. Another longtime loyalist was Saadoun Hammadi, an articulate economist with a Ph.D. from the University of Wisconsin, who had served as both oil minister and foreign minister. Hammadi had conducted most of the negotiations with the Kuwaitis over money and territory since the end of the Iran-Iraq war. Even though he was a true Baath Party ideologue, he was never completely trusted because of three strikes against him: He was a Shiite; he was Western-educated; and he was an intellectual. In a largely cosmetic cabinet shuffle designed to placate his Shiite and Kurdish populations, on March 23, 1991, Hammadi was named prime minister. Jassim lost his post as minister of information and culture, Aziz retained his title of deputy prime minister but lost the foreign ministry portfolio, and Ramadan became vice-president. A few weeks later, Kamel was made minister of defense.

There had been someone else close to Saddam, probably closer than anyone else in the world: Adnan Khairallah, the cousin who persuaded Saddam to go to school when they were children. Khairallah and Saddam fought together in the Baath underground. They were brothers-in-law. They looked a bit alike and shared the same worldview. In 1977, even before Saddam assumed the Presidency, he made his cousin, then still a colonel, minister of defense. In 1979, Khairallah was also made deputy prime minister and deputy commander-in-chief of the armed forces, even though he had never been an exceptional soldier. In return, he kept the Army loyal through continual purges and won its support by constant rewards, prosecuted the war with Iran just the way Saddam wanted him to, and parroted the leader's line in news conferences with foreign journalists.

In May 1989, Khairallah died in a mysterious helicopter crash while en route from Mosul to Baghdad. According to one version of the story, Saddam arranged to have him killed because of a family squabble. Foreign diplomats and even some senior Iraqi officials agreed that Saddam was known to have affairs over the years, but in the late 1980s, he apparently took a permanent mistress. The woman's identity became publicly known and Saddam even appeared with her at private functions. She was Samira Shahbandar, a member of a prominent merchant family from Baghdad who was married to an Iraqi Airways official when Saddam fell for her. The husband agreed to step aside and later was promoted to director of the airline.

Stories filled Baghdad that Saddam married Samira without first divorcing his wife—acceptable practice in Islam but a degradation of the principles of modernity, progress, and secularism for which the Baath Party stood.

There were even rumors that Saddam fathered a son named Ali by his mistress, rumors that became so strong that people in Basra hailed Saddam in public as "the father of Ali." The rumors hurt the image that Saddam cultivated so assiduously—that he was a good family man—as word of a family squabble burst into the political realm.

It was said that Khairallah never forgave Saddam for humiliating his sister and that Saddam never forgave his brother-in-law for taking sides in the feud. There were also stories that Saddam had verbally attacked Khairallah for not coping properly with an alleged coup attempt in 1989, had stopped his involvement in military purchasing and intelligence, and had stripped him of his authority over the Republican Guards. According to this version, Saddam arranged to have Khairallah killed in a helicopter crash. In an interview with CBS's "60 Minutes" on January 20, 1991, a man named Karim, identified as one of Saddam's former bodyguards, said that he planted a bomb on Khairallah's helicopter. But in a country where the gap between illusion and reality was unbridgeable, others questioned his story.

There was a more benign explanation, according to which Khairallah died in an authentic accident. The later version was based on the assumption that since coming to power, Saddam has never executed members of his family, only banished or fired them.

It was true that there was a bad sandstorm near Mosul on the day Khairallah died—so bad that the sky suddenly turned pitch-black and blew people off their feet, according to a group of Westerners who were trapped in a tower in Mosul. Khairallah's helicopter touched down until the storm passed, but went up again and crashed during a second storm. Nonetheless, the more ominous version was the one told most frequently in Baghdad—and, like all stories in that city, whether it was true or not was less important than the fact that people found it easy to believe. And they feared Saddam, and his wrath, all the more.

Saddam also had two sons, neither of whom was considered competent enough to hold serious positions in government. Qusay, the younger son, stayed out of the limelight and held down a position with the Federation of Iraqi Sports. Uday, the elder, was more infamous. Spoiled, corrupt, hard-drinking, and violent, he was politically protected and became wealthy as the owner of a number of businesses, even though he himself did not work. At the time of the invasion of Kuwait, Uday was building three monstrous palaces for himself in the heart of Baghdad. The project was so ambitious that hundreds of workmen not only worked days, but also nights, under enormous floodlights, according to a diplomat who lived near the construction site.

In October 1988, Uday clubbed to death Kamal Hana Gegeo, his father's bodyguard, valet, and food-taster, at a party in honor of Suzanne Mubarak, the wife of Egypt's president. Gegeo was said to have introduced Saddam to his mistress. Enraged at the loss of his trusted servant, Saddam imprisoned Uday and publicly pledged to try him on murder charges. But Saddam's wife was said to have interceded on her son's behalf. He was sent off to exile in Geneva to work for Saddam's brother Barzan. The Swiss government ordered Uday expelled after he assaulted a policeman who objected to his carrying a gun.

Like father, like son. After all, Saddam routinely used a show of strength to solve his problems. Sahab al-Hakim, an Iraqi exile who lost 22 members of his family to Saddam's executioners, recalled an encounter that one of his friends—Abdel Razzak al-Haboubi, the former governor of Najaf province—once had with Saddam. "There was a time in the 1970s when the governor needed money for some projects in Najaf," said al-Hakim. "So he went to see Saddam. They sat on opposite ends of a long table. He asked for help. When he was finished, Saddam asked him, 'You need money?' He answered, 'Yes, I need money.' So Saddam motioned to his bodyguard and asked for the bodyguard's gun. He shoved the gun to the other end of the table and said, 'Take it. And solve your problem yourself.'"

Years later, Saddam had a similar encounter with Ahmad Bahaa-eldine, a columnist for the Egyptian daily *al-Ahram* and one of the leading intellectuals in the Arab world. Bahaa-eldine and Saddam were acquaintances from Saddam's days in Cairo. During a visit to Baghdad several years later, Bahaa-eldine spent a lively evening discussing politics with Saddam, as they had done over coffee many times in Cairo. "I had argued that power is best held by persuasion," Bahaa-eldine told *New York Times* correspondent Youssef Ibrahim. "He would kid me that we intellectuals know nothing about building nations." Without the gun to force progress, Saddam argued that evening, there would be no progress. At his hotel later that night, Bahaa-eldine said, an Iraqi guard appeared at the door with a velvet box. Inside was a revolver on which was engraved the inscription WITH THE COMPLIMENTS OF SADDAM.

Saddam even advised other heads of state to resolve their problems by force. Prince Bandar bin Sultan, the Saudi ambassador to Washington, recalled a conversation between Saddam and King Fahd, who was then crown prince, after Muslim fanatics seized the Grand Mosque in Mecca in 1979. Saddam, said Bandar, had these words of advice for the king: "Kill them. Kill everybody who went into the mosque. And kill everyone who identifies with them." King Fahd replied that he hoped the matter could be resolved peacefully. But Saddam insisted. "No," he replied, in words that precisely echoed Machiavelli's advice to would-be tyrants in *The Prince*. "Don't waste your time. Kill all the male relatives, too. That way, there will be no one to take revenge."

~ 4 ~

Terror and Enticement

I see heads before me that are ripe and ready for the plucking, and I am the one to pluck them, and I see blood glistening between the turbans and the beards. By God, O people of Iraq, people of discord and dissembling and evil character! . . . By God, I shall strip you like bark, I shall truss you like a bundle of twigs, I shall beat you like stray camels . . . . I swear by God that you will keep strictly to the true path, or I shall punish every man of you in his body.

—speech by Hajjaj ibn Yusuf (seventh-century Umayyad governor of Iraq) that every Iraqi learns as a child

If they keep quiet, go about their business, avoid arousing suspicion, and show the proper degree of enthusiasm for the regime and its leader, they can expect to live in peace, benefit from the rewards that the regime dispenses, and perhaps even prosper.

—*Human Rights in Iraq*, 1990 Middle East Watch report discussing how Iraqis survive their country's repression

~ The Blank Stare

Ever since I've known the country, Iraq has had the smell of fear. The fear was barely detectable, like a pinprick gas leak in the basement that only slowly contaminated—something that the outsider sensed but didn't necessarily see or hear. It was felt most strongly in a reflex of self-protection that Iraqis had mastered: the blank stare.

I once knew a carpet dealer in the main souk of Baghdad. He didn't sell the intricate silk Persian carpets of the Tehran souk; the only "carpets" he had in his closet of a shop were dusty, faded, moth-eaten rugs that had lined the tents of Bedouins or Kurds. But he was a sweet, small, shy man who spoke moderately good English and liked to talk about his one trip to the West—to Switzerland—on a vacation years ago. He had pinned up a postcard of a Swiss mountain underneath a portrait of Saddam Hussein. Every time I went to Baghdad, I went to see the carpet man. He made me sugary tea and sat me down and showed me his carpets. He told me about his sons who had fought in, and survived, the war with Iran. One day in 1983, I was led through the souk by my "minder," a young guide from the Ministry of Information. We passed by the carpet dealer and I stopped to chat. He looked at the guide and then at me as if he were seeing me for the first time. He was polite, if cool, and asked my guide if he could show me a carpet. He never let on that he knew me. The next time I went to see him on my own, he did not invite me for tea.

I saw the blank stare again on a trip to the Shiite city of Najaf in the spring of 1984. The visit was shortly after the regime secretly executed six members of a prominent Shiite clan, the al-Hakim family, some of whose members were openly plotting an Islamic revolution in Iraq with the help of Iran's Ayatollah Khomeini. Rumors of the execution filled the receiving rooms of foreign embassies in Baghdad, and in a news conference, Tariq Aziz, Iraq's foreign minister, confirmed the executions. So I did what any street reporter would do: I stopped people on the street in Najaf and asked them questions. Had they heard about Aziz's press conference and the executions? They answered with the blank stare. Who are the al-Hakims? the stare seemed to say. My official minder took me aside to inform me that the benign atmosphere of the city was a fiction. There were security officers everywhere, he said, with much more power than he had. They were there to prevent any demonstrations like the ones that took place shortly after Khomeini came to power in Iran, any excessive displays of public mourning for Iraqi youth killed in the war with Iran, and any unauthorized conversations with outsiders. "You can't see them, but they are there," he said. "They might be dressed as Bedouins or sheiks, or they might be in Western dress. They might be anyone. They might be those people over there," he added, pointing to old men with pushcarts selling boiled turnips and chick-peas in paper cones.

The blank stare came from years of terror. Iraq had always been wracked by violence and instability, but it took the rise of the Baath Party to institutionalize violence as an instrument of policy. As Fuad Matar, one of Saddam Hussein's official biographers explained it, "As a result of their experiences at the hands of Abd al-Karim Qassim's regime, the Baathists revised their policies and decided to adopt violence as a mode of action."

Before Iran's 1979 revolution, dissidents and students, especially those living abroad, widely disseminated tales of torture and execution by the Shah's dreaded secret police, SAVAK. But the terror in Iraq ran deeper. Although its security apparatus was much larger than SAVAK ever had been, Iraqis—with a few exceptions—were afraid to report abuses to international human-rights organizations.

Iraq became a self-policing state, and the Iraqi people, longing for a ruler who would guarantee stability and bring them national pride, accepted Saddam. He and his people developed a peculiar bond, one based on a paternalistic use of cruelty that subdued them and seemed to break their spirit. Saddam was a Middle East version of the totalitarian, conforming remarkably well to the pattern established by Stalin. Both men were products of isolated, largely pre-industrial societies, and both were determined to catapult their societies quickly and dramatically into modern nation-states. A regime of terror and violence was justified as long as it fulfilled that goal.

Iraq became a country that weakened the family structure and replaced it with fear of the state. It became a place where a father could not demand that his daughter stay at home if she wanted to go to a Baath Party meeting, where sons were encouraged to turn in fathers whose loyalty to the regime was suspect. In a Party document published in 1977, Saddam instructed teachers to teach children to "criticize their mothers and fathers respectfully if they hear them talking about organizational and party secrets," and to object if they discovered that either of their parents were "wasting the state's wealth." That duty cut both ways. At the height of the Iran-Iraq war, Saddam was seen on television pinning a medal on the chest of a father who reported that his son was a deserter. The son was executed.

∼ The Instruments of Repression

Saddam's Iraq was based on three pillars: the secret police, the Baath Party and the Army. The secret police controlled Iraq through separate but overlapping agencies, all of which reported independently to the ruling Revolutionary Command Council, which reported directly to Saddam. The Ministry of the Interior was believed to be the largest organ of government, and the secret police employed tens of thousands of people. They spent much of their time spying on each other.

There were four principal agencies of the secret police. The first was the State Internal Security, or Amn al-Amm, which primarily handled internal operations and was believed to have had close links with Moscow's KGB.

The second was the Military Intelligence Agency, or Istikhbarat, which controlled most operations against Iraqi or other nationals living on foreign soil. It operated primarily from the military attaché's offices of Iraqi embassies, and while it conducted normal military intelligence-gathering, it was also believed to be responsible for foreign undercover operations and assassinations and the surveillance of students and other Iraqis working abroad.

The third was the Intelligence Department, or Mukhabarat, the security arm of the Baath Party. An outgrowth of the first Baath Party security apparatus created by Saddam in the mid-1960s, it handled both domestic and foreign operations. It was the most powerful of the security organizations, because it oversaw the other secret police organizations, corporations and state organizations such as the Army, the ministries and popular institutions such as youth and women's groups.

The fourth agency of the police was the Special Security, or Amn al-Khass, Saddam's personal security police, which was operated from the presidential palace. It was believed to have assumed many of the functions of the Mukhabarat in overseeing senior Party and government officials in recent years.

The second pillar of Saddam's repression was the Baath Party. Built on the Stalinist model, the Baath had turned Iraq into a one-party police state. Over the years, Saddam had made the Party an instrument of his personal rule, transforming it into a mass organization to mobilize, indoctrinate, and control the people. When the Party seized power for the first time in Iraq in 1963, it was a small, tight, revolutionary organization with no more than a few hundred full members. When it took power again in 1968, it launched an ambitious recruitment program.

The Party persuaded, threatened, and forced Iraqis into joining. Recruiters targeted the country's youth, before their loyalties were shaped. Theoretically, anyone could join, but the recruit had to pass through several stages before becoming a full Party member. According to Christine Moss Helms, in her 1984 book, *Iraq: Eastern Flank of the Arab World,* 17-year-olds were eligible for the first stage, as "sympathizers." They then passed through the subsequent stages—"supporters," "candidates," "trainees"—before becoming "working members." The process took a minimum of seven and a half years.

By 1990, the Baath Party boasted an estimated 25,000 to 50,000 full members and 1.5 million lower-level members. The Party or its supporters infiltrated every Iraqi military unit, every school, every office, every factory, every street. To tighten the networks of control, the Party had its own security apparatus and its own militia.

I recall an example of the Baath Party at work during a visit to Baghdad University, where I sat in on a lecture on Hammurabi given by Ahmad Samii. Samii, a charming professor of history, had received his masters degree from the University of Chicago and his Ph.D. from the University of Michigan. The lecture was about Hammurabi's wars to unify Iraq—the conspiracies, murders, escapes to foreign kingdoms, extensions of the boundaries, invasions and victories, political marriages. It didn't sound a lot different from the Iraqi regime under Saddam. At the end of the lecture, Samii gave me permission to ask his students some questions. It was December 1984, and the United States and Iraq had reestablished diplomatic relations the previous month.

So I asked the students about their attitudes toward the United States. Just as Samii was about to call on one of them, a serious young man in the front row, the Party spy for that classroom, interrupted. "No political questions," he announced. "It is not permitted to talk about politics in a history class."

The classroom clearly did not belong to Samii. He apologized, but he did not reprimand the student. Even my Ministry of Information minder got into a heated argument with the young man, who introduced himself as a Student Council representative. "I have instructions," the student said over and over. His voice was apologetic, but he too was afraid. "I will be held responsible for the answers of all the students," he explained. "They are students of history and not politicians, so they cannot answer questions of a political nature. Even the professor cannot answer questions because I will be held responsible. It is forbidden."

Indoctrination into Baath ideology started at a young age. I witnessed the process during visits to the Dijla Elementary School in Baghdad, where every Thursday morning at 8 o'clock, the 500 students donned blue camouflage uniforms, patterned with maps of the Arab world, and gathered in the schoolyard for "Pioneer" training. After chanting slogans to Saddam and singing a song in his honor, they were called on to answer questions. "What are your aims?" the teacher asked the group. "To be soldiers and grow up to be the soldiers of our country," the children replied. Two privileged boys goose-stepped to the flagpole, raised the Iraqi flag, and quoted some of Saddam's most famous sayings.

The convoluted quotes were often memorized without understanding, and they sometimes came out garbled. One 12-year-old girl defined the organization of the 101 countries professing nonalignment this way: "The non-legitimate movement was established in our modern age of the strong genuine needs of the people of the world who have suffered long periods. National health, national character, and national—I forgot it—donate firms of blunder, impulsive blackmail." When I later asked her about the weekly ritual, she replied honestly, "It's homework. You must do it."

The third instrument of Saddam's rule was the armed forces. The Army was used to fulfill Saddam's regional ambitions, to put down minority rebellions, and to keep order at home. The pacification of both the Shiite and the Kurdish populations was the job of the Army, and it carried out its task with a level of brutality out of proportion to the threat.

But Saddam never lost his suspicion of the military, which he eventually transformed into a creature of the Party. He purged potential rivals, required membership in the Party or its organizations for advancement, and allowed the Party to emerge as a competing source of authority within the ranks. Party commissars were installed throughout the military, down to the battalion level. Although there were regular reports over the years of coup attempts against Saddam from within the Army, the "Baathization" of the

Army helped ensure that none of them succeeded. Between 1968, when the Baath took over, and 1980, when Saddam invaded Iran, the Iraqi Army nearly tripled in size, to about 200,000 men. By 1990, Saddam had one million men under arms.

The Popular Army, a national militia formally established in 1970, was another means by which the Baath extended influence. On one level, it helped protect strategic installations, guarded the borders, and served as a military reserve force. But it was also an instrument of political consolidation and a watchdog organization that worked through the Party to prevent any upstart military commmander from building his own power base and trying to take over.

In the early 1980s, Saddam became convinced that he needed his own Army corpus in the event that Khomeini attacked Baghdad. So he tasked his son-in-law, Hussein Kamel al-Majid, and General Hussein Rashid, who in 1990 became the Iraqi chief of staff, to build him a private Army out of the Republican Guards, an elite corps dominated by men from Tikrit. The two men took the Guards—then consisting of fewer than two brigades—and built it into two, and later eight, divisions. The best-trained and most heavily armed element of the Iraqi Army, it scored decisive victories in the final battles of the war against Iran and was the key force that the allies had to defeat in the 1991 war.

~ Methods of Repression

In most countries, treason is limited and well defined: an attempt to assassinate a head of state, a plot to overthrow a government, the sale of state secrets to another government. Not so in Saddam's Iraq. There, treason was vague and all-encompassing: It included any action that could be construed as hurting the state. Anyone who was judged a traitor had to be eliminated, and Iraqi officials spoke openly of the need to use force to ensure stability.

Shortly after Iraq invaded Iran in 1980, Tariq Aziz boasted matter-of-factly to journalist Georgie Anne Geyer that Iraq had hanged Shiite leaders—he called them agents of Iran—who were preaching revolution in the name of Islam. "The Iranians sent hundreds of religious agents," he said. "Most were hanged. Iraq is a very well-organized society." Aziz and other officials routinely defended their system of justice—not because it was just, but because it was effective. "In the liberal world, there is a prejudice that if a country isn't 100 percent liberal, it is repressive," Aziz once told me. "We are satisfied that we have a stable, popular government." Taha Yassin Ramadan, first deputy prime minister, put it more bluntly. "There is no such thing as degrees or levels of treason," he told me. "It's treason. That's all."

Many countries like to hide their brutality because it gives them deniability. This was not so in Iraq, where the regime was eager to flaunt the various degrees of repression.

The first level of repression was arrest, interrogation, and imprisonment—actions that often were taken without cause, with no other purpose than to instill terror and keep the population docile. Sometimes suspects were hustled away secretly, in the dead of night, leaving their family and friends to make desperate pilgrimages to government bureaucracies to find them. "The knowledge that the knock on the door could come at any hour is enough to inspire terror in most people," said Middle East Watch's 1990 human-rights report on Iraq. "But it is only one, and in fact the most gentle, of those [methods] that the Iraqi regime is known to employ."

One British diplomat who served in Baghdad spent much of his time responding to calls from British companies reporting that their employees hadn't turned up for a few days. "I used to make the rounds of all the prisons until I found them," the diplomat said. "There was one chap who had gotten himself put into prison for making a U-turn. He was given five days and then expelled." Nothing unusual, the diplomat continued, adding, "Those were standard things, you know."

The next level of punishment was torture. In a report of human-rights abuses from 1982 to 1984, Amnesty International recounted the story of Robert Spurling, an American citizen who had been the technical director of the Baghdad Novotel Hotel. Spurling disappeared as he was about to board a flight for Paris with his Belgian wife and children in June 1983. Security agents simply diverted him down a ramp, blindfolded him, and drove him to what he assumed was the headquarters of the Baghdad security forces. He later told Amnesty that he was repeatedly interrogated and tortured, first to confess to spying, then to inform on others. His Iraqi captors beat his feet with a rubber hose, kicked his ears with their boots, and used electric shocks on his hands, feet, genitals, kidneys, and especially his ears. They fed him irregularly, sometimes with tainted or heavily salted food; they made his cell either too cold or too hot; they refused to allow him to clean his cell. They threatened to mutilate him and told him they had arrested his wife and she would be punished if he didn't cooperate. He could also hear the screams of other prisoners, he said, adding that his treatment was "nothing" compared to what happened to Iraqi, Iranian, and other Arab prisoners. One hundred ten days after his arrest, Spurling was released. He was never told what he had done wrong.

Spurling was also fortunate compared to the countless victims who died under torture in Iraq. Some were individuals of little political significance whose death may not even have been planned, except that the torturer got carried away. The stories were gruesome, but so numerous that they tended to blend together. Their drama sometimes got lost in the recounting of the details, much like the atrocities committed by Iraqi troops in Kuwait after the 1990 invasion. One story told to Amnesty International has never lost its impact. It was the testimony of an Iraqi mother who found her son's body with nine others at the morgue in Baghdad in September 1982. He had been arrested the previous December. "He had blood all over him and his body was very eaten away and bleeding . . . ," she said. "Another's body carried the marks of a hot domestic iron all over his head to his feet. . . . One of them had his chest cut lengthwise into three sections. . . . Another had his legs axed with an axe. . . . His arms were also axed. One of them had his eyes gouged out and his nose and ears cut off. . . . One of them looked hanged. . . . His tongue was hanging out and the fresh blood was oozing out of his mouth."

Finally, there were the executions. Among them were the stage-managed executions of individuals or groups defined as political enemies. At various times throughout the rule of the Baath, the regime "uncovered" discreet political "plots" against it and used the instrument of execution to weed out real and imagined opponents and to discourage would-be dissenters.

~

In *The Prince*, Machiavelli described the "good use" of cruelty, an occasional "spectacular execution" that both terrified and satisfied the people. That was what happened in Iraq in 1968. Within days of seizing power, the Baathist regime targeted a convenient scapegoat to prove just how far it was prepared to go to establish stability and root out potential opposition. It went after the Jews. The Arab world was still reeling from 1967, when Israel destroyed the armies of Syria, Jordan, and Egypt and eliminated Iraqi units that rushed to help Jordan. At that time, there were about 3,500 Jews left in Iraq. The new regime announced that it had broken up a major Zionist spy ring. One by one, it arrested Jews, along with former government officials and members of Iraq's old intelligentsia. More arrests followed, along with public confessions by the "plotters" on television.

Max Sawdayee, an Iraqi Jew who escaped from Iraq with the help of the Kurds in 1970, kept a moving diary that documented those days of mounting insecurity and terror as the new regime consolidated its power. To read his diary is to discover a rolling process of terror that at first was not fixed—so its horror was not yet known. The published diary helps to explain how that terror came to permeate everyday life.

"I read a terrorizing item in the newspaper: an Iraqi military transport plane loaded with seventeen Jews left Basra last night and landed in a military base in Baghdad," Sawdayee wrote on October 9, 1968. "The newspaper alleges, 'They are all Zionist spies.' This piece of news is very disturbing indeed, as a serious accusation must have been framed against those seventeen helpless victims. I quickly show the paper to a friend living just across the street. He is astounded, and remarks that that means a big trouble ahead for us Jews. In the afternoon the news spread like fire among the Jewish community members, every one of whom is deeply concerned. What does the Iraqi government mean? Nobody knows. My parents come to see me at night. They're highly disturbed. Tonight I'm tense and worried. My wife keeps telling me to take it easy and urges me to practice some yoga before sleep."

On December 5, 1968, Iraq's President Ahmad Hasan al-Bakr appeared on television from the balcony of the presidential palace, where he vowed to "strike mercilessly at the agents of the United States and Israel and at the fifth columnists," Sawdayee wrote. The speech, he added, "is interrupted more than twenty times by the speaker shouting into the microphone, 'What do you want?' and the mob answers, 'Death to the spies, execution of the spies, all the spies, without delay.' "

After a trial on January 4, 1969, the first "spies" were hanged in Liberation Square on January 27, 1969. More than 150,000 people crowded the square to watch the spectacle. Eight Jews and one Christian were hanged, he said, their bodies spaced throughout the large square and labeled with large sheets of paper identifying them by religion and crime. "It is a perfect, masterly, cold-blooded, wicked, diabolical way of distribution indeed," wrote Sawdayee. "It is certainly the best way for everybody in the square to see each one and all of the victims. . . . The sight of the nine, their heads twisted and drooping, their bodies dangling from the gallows and swinging high in the air, with all these vengeful mobs, all excited, agitated, cheering, dancing, chanting, singing, cursing the dead, spitting and throwing stones on them, or jumping high to catch their feet or their toes—it shakes one to the bones. It shakes even one's faith in humanity."

The first hangings, and the ones that followed, were condemned around the world. Even Egypt's Nasser broke ranks with his Arab brothers and expressed revulsion. But the Baath Party leadership was immune to such criticism. Far from hiding the hangings, the Iraqi regime proudly flaunted them. They became a sign of its strength and stability, a linchpin of its foreign and domestic policy. A Baath Party report justified the hangings as "imperative, despite the internal furor and harsh criticism leveled at our revolution." It called them "a big national demonstration . . . that a real and patriotic, firm and competent authority ruled the country."

Nine years later, in 1978, the Baath regime moved against the Communists. The Iraqi Communist Party, initially founded in secrecy in 1934, had become a major political factor in Iraqi politics, boasting a membership of nearly 25,000 by 1959. The Communists were considered so threatening that the Baathists and the nationalist National Democratic Party—the other two major political forces within Iraq at the time—formed underground groups to attack them. By 1961, nearly 300 Communist Party members had been murdered.

When the Baath Party seized power in 1968, the Communists were the main opposition group, although they did not pose a serious threat to the regime. According to the authoritative work *Iraq Since 1958* by Peter Sluglett and Marion Farouk-Sluglett, the Communist Party paper in early 1978 criticized the regime's policies on the Kurds and the economy and implied that it was moving too close to the West. The Baath was concerned about Soviet meddling in Iraq's internal affairs, particularly after the Soviets supported a coup in Afghanistan in April 1978. Fearing internal subversion from the Soviet-supported Iraqi Communists, the Baath wanted to prove that the action in Afghanistan would not be repeated in Iraq. In June of that year, Iraqi officials acknowledged that they had executed 21 Communists, charging that they had set up secret cells inside the Army.

The Iraqi announcement did not say that the soldiers had been in prison since 1975, and that most of them were noncommissioned officers. "In the summer and the autumn there were further reports of executions of Communists and of widespread arrests of party members," the Slugletts wrote. "The regime tortured many hundreds of its victims to death in prison over the next months and years; people were dragged out of their houses and never seen again; in some cases their bodies were thrown in front of their families' houses dreadfully mutilated; in others, relatives were forced to collect corpses from police stations and jeered, abused or assaulted while doing so." In an interview with Arnaud de Borchgrave in *Newsweek* magazine in July 1978, Saddam openly admitted that the executions had been a warning to Moscow against interfering in Iraq's internal affairs.

Saddam believed, he once said, that "the revolution chooses its enemies." So it was not surprising that less than two weeks after he took over the presidency from Bakr in July 1979, he announced the discovery of a plot to overthrow the regime. Saddam was convinced that some of his closest associates had questions about the way he maneuvered Bakr out of power. So he arrested one of them, Muhyi Abd al-Hussein al-Mashadi, a member of both the Revolutionary Command Council and the Party leadership. Under duress or perhaps under torture, al-Hussein agreed to confess that he was plotting to topple Saddam with the help of other members of the leadership and the support of Syria.

On July 22, Saddam convened an extraordinary meeting of the Party Regional Congress to hear al-Hussein's confession. But this was to be no ordinary purge. The meeting was videotaped and the film was distributed to Baath Party branches across Iraq; pirated copies made their way to Beirut and the Iraqi exile community in London. Saddam also delivered copies to other Middle Eastern heads of state, accompanied by notes explaining that the tape would help them understand the need for the purge. Years before Iraq's invasion of Kuwait, Sheik Ali al-Khalifa al-Sabah, who had served as both oil and finance minister in the emirate, sometimes showed the videotape to dinner guests as documentary proof of Saddam's use of terror.

Of all the evidence concerning Saddam's repression, the videotape was by far the clearest and most dramatic window into the nature of his rule.

The black-and-white film is grainy, many of the frames are blurred, and some of the dialogue is inaudible from being copied so many times.

In the film, Saddam marched onstage as the audience of several hundred high-ranking Baath Party officials gave him a standing ovation. Flashbulbs popped as he waved confidently to the faces in the vast auditorium and stepped up to a microphone-filled podium. Taha Yassin Ramadan, who later became Iraq's first deputy prime minister, and Tariq Aziz, later the foreign minister, were seated in the front row. "I wish that we could meet in happier circumstances...," Saddam said in an emotionless voice. "This is a sad meeting. This will be a shock for you. We have treason among us.... in the Party." Like a patient schoolteacher, Saddam described in flowery, almost classical Arabic the plot to make Iraq "a vassal of Syria." Not only was there a plot, but the traitor himself "is sitting down in your ranks." Saddam paused dramatically. Then he revealed the name of the traitor.

Al-Hussein the traitor stepped up to the podium. The audience sat transfixed, in stunned silence. They had no idea who would be implicated in the plot. Al-Hussein read through a detailed confession, often pausing to steal a glance at Saddam, who sat at a large table on the stage, calmly lighting and relighting a cigar and sipping a glass of water. At times Saddam smiled broadly. As al-Hussein accused each of his coconspirators, they were forced to stand. A guard moved up and down the aisles and dragged each man from the chamber.

One of the accused stood up to protest. "Allow me, please," he shouted to Saddam. "Get out, get out," Saddam replied, and the man was pulled from the room. When a second accused man protested, Saddam puffed silently on his cigar. During the film, more than 20 Party members were taken out of the hall through swinging glass doors. It was not by accident that they included Saddam's main rivals, the four other members of Iraq's Revolutionary Command Council.

At one point during the confession, Ramadan began to cry. Then other Party members began to cry. At the end of the confession, Saddam spoke about the dangers of sabotage and the strength of the revolution. To prove their loyalty, the survivors cheered him, shouting over and over, "Long live Saddam. Long live the Party."

But Saddam needed to implicate the Party in the executions that were to come, as he would do repeatedly throughout his rule. He asked the audience what he should do. Some called for more purges; others complained of too much leniency. Still others praised Saddam's leadership.

The five main conspirators and 17 others, many of them Saddam's closest associates, were found guilty and sentenced to death. To legitimize his actions and involve others in the crime, Saddam demanded that other senior ministers and Party officials from all over Iraq participate in the executions—which, it was widely said, they carried out themselves with machine guns.

"Neither Stalin nor Hitler would have thought up a detail like that," Samir al-Khalil wrote of the purge in *Republic of Fear*. "What Eichmann-like refuge in 'orders from above' could these men dig up in the future if they were ever to marshal the courage to try and depose their leader?"

There were other instances when Saddam made examples of officials who were perceived as enemies. In 1982, just as the war with Iran started to go badly, Iraq's minister of health, Riyadh Ibrahim, was executed. Saddam told foreign reporters that Ibrahim had knowingly distributed contaminated medicines. In a rambling speech to the Revolutionary Command Council, which was also filmed and distributed to Party leaders, Saddam called the minister a dangerous saboteur, a traitor. His crime was not just an inadvertent action, a mistake, but a political crime against the state.

Those who knew Ibrahim and his family told the tale differently. According to an Iraqi doctor who investigated the matter, Saddam became worried when Ayatollah Khomeini began to demand Saddam's ouster as the price of peace. "One day, when the pressure of Iranian military forces was very high and Iraq was under the threat of occupation by the Iranian Army, Saddam called a cabinet meeting," the doctor said. "Saddam was in a critical situation. He asked the cabinet ministers, 'Is there any solution you can find to solve this problem?' They said, 'No, Mr. President, you are the hero of our country. You are defending our territorial integrity.'

"Saddam replied, 'No, tell me the truth. What is the best way to stop the Iranian invasion, even if you believe my resigning is the way to stop the war.' All the ministers said, 'No, we don't agree with you.' Then Saddam said, 'No, I don't mind if you tell me the truth.'

"The health minister said, 'Yes, Mr. President. I have a suggestion. If you resign temporarily, for three or four months, the Iranian Army will go back to their bases and then you can reappear again.' Saddam said, 'Yes, thank you very much. You are very brave. Thank you for your solution.' He asked the other members what they thought and they all said no to the suggestion. After the meeting, Saddam turned to his bodyguards. They captured Ibrahim and led him out of the room.

"The wife of the minister knew the First Lady. She asked the First Lady to intervene and ask the President to release her husband. When Saddam's wife told him about the matter, he called the minister's wife himself and asked if she was asking for her husband's release. She said, 'Yes. You're his friend. You are the leader.' Saddam asked her, 'When do you want your husband?' and she replied, 'As soon as possible.' 'Can I send him tomorrow?' Saddam asked her. She said of course.

"The next day the security forces came to her house. She rushed to the door and asked, 'Where is my husband?' They gave her a big black bag and said, 'This is your husband.' And she found the body of her husband, chopped into pieces.

"It was a lesson for others." There is an even more sinister version of the tale. Other Iraqis said that when Ibrahim made his suggestion, Saddam left the room with him. A shot was heard. Some said that Saddam pulled the trigger himself. The story—like so many others—may or may not be true. In Iraq, the details were less important than the moral of the story.

Whenever the West questioned Iraq's widespread use of terror, Saddam issued broad denials of the reality of the police state he had created. In his interview with ABC's Diane Sawyer in June 1990, for example, Saddam distanced himself from the reputation he had earned over the years as a killer of those who opposed him.

SAWYER: There was a report that you personally killed a cabinet minister who said that you should resign. Did you?

SADDAM: Let me ask you, do you personally believe that this is true?

SAWYER: I'm asking you.

SADDAM: I'm leaving doors open from the interview to go to the Iraqi people and talk to them in private and see anybody you like. It's not part of our way to kill.

SAWYER: Have you ever personally killed someone who opposed you?

SADDAM: Never. It has never happened. I have never killed anybody.

Saddam maintained the ability to terrify even those closest to him. When a group of American senators, led by Senate Minority Leader Robert J. Dole, met with Saddam on April 12, 1990, Saddam's longtime interpreter turned up a few minutes late because there had been no room for him in the elevator. "He was afraid, afraid for his life," Al Lehn, Dole's foreign-policy aide, recalled. "He walked in front of Saddam, saluted and clicked his heels. Saddam dismissed him with a wave of the arm. The interpreter was sweating, literally quaking with fear."

~ The Long Arm of the Regime

In its first decade of power, the Baath Party haphazardly assassinated Iraqi dissidents wherever it found them. In the late 1970s, several Iraqis were murdered in Beirut, Cairo, and London. Then in February 1980, Saddam made assassination part of Iraq's official foreign policy, declaring that "the hand of the revolution can reach out to its enemies wherever they are found." The policy put Iraqis who lived in exile on notice that they were not safe, no matter where they lived. Among the assassinations and attempted plots believed to have been carried out by the regime were: a bombing that injured eight people in Vienna in July 1980, leading to the expulsion of an Iraqi Embassy first secretary and attaché; the assassination of Mohammad al-Salman, an Iraqi Shiite and a member of the Islamic Opposition movement in Dubai in 1981; the attempted assassination of Shlomo Argov, the Israeli ambassador to London, in June 1982; and the wounding of Mohammad Zaki al-Siwaij, an Iraqi Shiite clergyman, while leading prayer services in Thailand in May 1987.

In a widely publicized case in January 1988, Mahdi al-Hakim, a vocal dissident and member of the Shiite al-Hakim family, was gunned down in the lobby of the Hilton Hotel in Khartoum, Sudan, where he was attending an Islamic conference. The car used in the operation was registered to the Iraqi Embassy. Apparently the Iraqi intelligence service had organized the conference, with the aim of luring al-Hakim out of Britain. The Iraqis did not want to assassinate al-Hakim on British soil and thus risk damaging their good relations with the government of Prime Minister Margaret Thatcher. When Sudan announced officially that Iraqi Embassy personnel had taken part in the assassination, Iraq closed its embassy in Khartoum.

Assassination attempts even extended to the United States. An unsuccessful plot against two Iraqi exiles in California in February 1990 was linked to the Iraqi Mission to the United Nations. A federal grand jury indictment said that Andri Khoshaba, an Iraqi who once had worked as a driver at the mission, made two trips to New York to discuss with an official of the Iraqi Mission a plan in which he was to be paid $50,000 to murder opponents of the Iraqi government in the United States. A target of the alleged assassination plot was Sargon Dadesho, chairman of an Assyrian-American organization critical of the Iraqi government. Dadesho told reporters that he was to meet with Jalal Talabani, the Iraqi Kurdish leader, and that FBI agents told him that Khoshaba planned to kill both of them. Khoshaba fled the United States shortly after FBI agents questioned him.

For other Iraqis, threats sufficed, just as they did for opponents of the Iranian and Syrian regimes. Saad al-Jabr, one of the few outspoken Iraqi opponents of Saddam and the leader of a London-based opposition group, related the following story: "A number of years ago, Saad Bazzaz, who was then the Iraqi cultural attaché in London, came to visit me. I knew him from Baghdad and he said he had a message for me from Saddam. He said there were just a few words and that he had nothing to do with the message. The message was, 'If Saad [al-Jabr] hides in a matchbox, I will find him.' It always stayed with me, that message, because of the image of me in a matchbox. Can you imagine that I'd make myself so small as to fit into a matchbox? In other words, there was no escaping Saddam if he wanted to get me. I told Bazzaz that I dared Saddam to do it. Nothing happened. Maybe he thought that I had American or English agents protecting me."

~ The Homogenization of Iraq

In a 1982 interview with *Time* magazine, Saddam expressed the clearest wish of all totalitarian dictators. "Any leader would prefer his people to think from one point of view, to be of one religion, one sect, in one city," he told the interviewers. True to this sentiment, Saddam's domestic policies—his use of history, Party organization, and repression—contributed to the physical and intellectual homogenization of the diverse population of Iraq.

Although minority groups such as Jews and Communists were dealt with easily, the Shiites and the Kurds presented a more serious threat, as they would again after the 1991 Gulf war. Throughout the twentieth century, the populations of predominantly Shiite cities frequently revolted whenever there was a lapse in control by the central administration in Baghdad. When the al-Dawa al-Islamiyah Party, or the Call of Islam, began to stir up trouble against the Baath in the 1970s, it was brutally repressed. Supported by Ayatollah Mohammad Bakr al-Sadr, Iraq's most respected Shiite leader, the underground organization preached a message of a return to Islamic principles in government and social justice for the people. In 1974, following antigovernment demonstrations, the regime secretly executed more than two dozen Shiite leaders on charges of plotting against the state. In 1977, there were serious antigovernment riots in Karbala after the regime closed that holy Shiite city to pilgrims in the midst of a religious ceremony. Several people died in clashes between police and demonstrators. The rioting spread to Najaf and had to be put down by the Army. In 1979, Shiites in Najaf and Karbala and in the slums of the al-Thawra district of Baghdad staged massive riots against the regime after Ayatollah Bakr al-Sadr tried to lead a procession in honor of Khomeini's revolution in Iran. In April 1980, Bakr al-Sadr and his sister, Bint al-Huda, and about 20 of their followers, were executed.

The regime also punished the prominent Shiite al-Hakim family for the sins of its members. After Iran's revolution, Mohammad Bakr al-Hakim, a leading Iraqi cleric, moved to Iran, where he organized a revolutionary movement with Iranian funding. Although the government-in-exile he later organized did not play an active military role during the Iran-Iraq war, it called for the installation of an Iranian-style Islamic republic in Baghdad and regularly broadcast calls from Tehran for Iraqi Shiites to overthrow Saddam. In May 1983, about 90 male members of the al-Hakim family were arrested, including a boy of nine and a man of 80.

"The men were rounded up and taken by bus to Baghdad," recalled Sahab al-Hakim, a dental surgeon who has since organized an Iraqi human-rights organization in London. "Saddam sent a message to Mohammad Bakr al-Hakim warning that if he didn't stop, some family members would be executed. He refused and announced it publicly on Iranian radio in Arabic. Saddam executed six of our family by firing squad and forced Mohammad Hussein al-Hakim, the oldest member of our family, to watch. After the executions, he was ordered to go to Tehran to deliver a message to Mohammad Bakr al-Hakim to stop his activities. The old man was told that if he did not return with a reply, his sons would be executed."

But the old man gave no reply and did not return from Iran. The younger al-Hakim refused to stop his activities against Saddam, and the messenger went mad and died in Tehran. In March 1985, the Iraqi regime executed his three sons and seven other family members. Since then, said Sahab al-Hakim, another six were executed or died in prison, and more than 50 other family members remained in detention. "Saddam wanted to show the people, to say, 'Look, this is a very famous family in the Islamic world and I have humiliated them,' " he said. "He persecuted us to make ordinary Iraqi people afraid, afraid that such a thing could happen to them."

Sahab al-Hakim and his immediate family took refuge in London in 1982 while attending a medical convention in Europe after he received a warning from a friendly Baath Party official that his arrest was imminent. He carries the 24-hour phone number of Scotland Yard in his wallet, along with a card on which he has handwritten: "The Saddam regime of Iraq has killed 22 members of my family (al-Hakim). He may kill me at any time. I will not stop my activities against the Iraqi regime which violets [sic] the human rights of the Iraqi people."

In addition to executions of at least hundreds of Shiites believed to be involved in al-Dawa and other political groups, the regime found other, more creative, ways to punish Shiite dissent. On July 11, 1982, assassins tried to kill Saddam during his visit to the village of al-Dujayl, a stronghold of Shiite militancy about 40 miles northeast of Baghdad. The president and his entourage were trapped by gunfire for several hours before being rescued by the military. The assassins and some of Saddam's bodyguards were killed. To teach the town a lesson, Saddam deported the entire population, and razed the village, only to build it up again.

Saddam was not the only Middle Eastern leader to resort to such extreme measures. Syria's President Hafez al-Assad had used the same tactic in Hama, one of Syria's most beautiful cities, in February of that same year. Assad sent in thousands of troops to put down the uprising of the Muslim Brotherhood, a loosely organized underground group of Sunni fundamentalists. By the time the massacre ended several weeks later, between 10,000 and 25,000 people, most of them civilians, were killed. Bulldozers were brought in to crush entire neighborhoods, and buildings in Muslim Brotherhood neighborhoods were dynamited. When I visited Hama four years later, there was a new, broad highway through the city and construction teams were busy working on a mosque and apartment complexes. The side streets were still filled with rubble from the rebellion.

The Iraqi regime also tried to homogenize its population by simply banishing the unwanted. In 1971 and 1972, as many as 40,000 Shiites suspected of political activity—most of them of Persian origin—were sent across the border to Iran, largely in retaliation for the Shah's seizure of three small islands in the Strait of Hormuz. After Khomeini came to power in Iran in

1979, the Iraqi regime expelled no fewer than 200,000 Shiites, charging that they were an Iranian fifth column threatening the stability of Iraq.

"At times whole families were deported, including children, aged parents and other relatives," wrote Middle East Watch. "Evidently some Iraqis not of Iranian origin or of the Shiite sect were caught up in these deportations, either because they had married into Shiite families or because the regime found it a convenient moment to get rid of them." In one instance, the regime invited a group of prominent Shiite merchants to lunch, put them on trucks, and shipped them across the border to Iran. As Tariq Aziz once explained rather matter-of-factly to me: "We had a fifth column. They were of Persian origin. We said to them, 'You love Khomeini. Go back to his paradise.' We put them on trucks and sent them to the border."

After accepting the cease-fire in the Iran-Iraq war in August 1988, Iran demanded that Iraq take back 200,000 deportees, claiming that they were Iraqi citizens. Iraq refused.

~

If the Shiites fared badly in Saddam's Iraq, the Kurds fared even worse. The Kurds are non-Arabs and never fit well into Iraq under Baath rule, which extolled Arab greatness. Saddam's dogged and ruthless efforts to forge an Iraqi identity for his people only partially succeeded with the Kurds. A wealthy Iraqi Kurdish businessman who now lives abroad explained the dilemma of many Kurds: "We feel like Iraqis except when Iraqis get too Arab with us. Then we feel Kurdish."

In the decade before the Baath came to power, the Kurds were in permanent revolt, and an inability to quash the rebellions contributed to the overthrow of successive Iraqi governments. In March 1970, an agreement was reached with the Kurds that promised them autonomy and a voice in the affairs of the central government, but it was short-lived. In the early 1970s, the Shah, Mohammad Reza Pahlevi of Iran, with the help of the Central Intelligence Agency and Israel, funded and armed Kurdish separatist guerrillas. The foreign-backed Kurds kept the Iraqi Army occupied and killed and wounded tens of thousands of Iraqi soldiers. In Algiers in 1975, Saddam reached an agreement under which the Shah promised to end his support for Iraqi Kurdish rebels. Following the agreement, according to Kurdish leaders, up to 60,000 Kurds were arrested and sent to detention camps in southern Iraq. More arrests and executions followed.

The regime also executed Kurdish civilians in reprisal for guerrilla attacks against it. In the fall of 1985, Iraqi authorities reportedly arrested about 300 Kurdish children and young people in northern Iraq, in an effort to pressure their family members—some of them guerrillas or deserters in the Iran-Iraq war—to turn themselves in. Many of these young people were tortured and as many as 29 were executed. Their bodies were returned to their families, some bearing signs of torture, some with their eyes gouged out, according to a 1985 Amnesty International report on Iraq's repression of children. Some of the families were often asked to pay an "execution fee" to cover the government's expenses for coffins, transportation, and bullets.

The punishment of children for their parents' sins was not at all unusual, according to both Amnesty International and Defense of Children International, another human-rights group. At times infants were detained with their parents and deprived of milk in order to pressure the parents to confess. After his invasion of Kuwait, Saddam cynically charged that the international embargo was depriving Iraq's children of milk.

Then came the resettlements of the Kurds. Since 1987, wrote Middle East Watch, "on the pretext of protecting the Kurdish population and providing them modern amenities, the Iraqi government has expelled several hundred thousand Kurds from their mountain villages and towns, razed their dwellings and obliged them to resettle in 'new towns' in hot dry lowlands where they find little if any way to provide for themselves." Some of them starved to death. According to conservative estimates, the Iraqi government destroyed about 1,200 Kurdish villages and towns-places where Kurds had lived for centuries—and large segments of traditionally Kurdish areas of Iraq were depopulated. The new towns, or "strategic hamlets," could be controlled more easily by the Baghdad government.

In a report to the Senate Foreign Relations Committee written after a visit through Iraq in 1987, Peter Galbraith, a staff member, wrote, "The Iraqi Army has, over the past few months, been dynamiting the evacuated Kurdish villages. In at least one case, the Army requisitioned earth-moving equipment from a foreign engineering firm so as to eliminate any traces of previous habitation. With hundreds of villages leveled, the Kurdish countryside has an eerie, deserted quality to it. Fruit trees, graveyards, and cemeteries stand as reminders of the absent people and livestock. The Iraqi Army conducts itself in Kurdistan as if it were a foreign occupying army."

But even the massive forced relocations in Kurdistan paled in comparison to Iraq's use of chemical weapons in the region. Iraq had begun to use chemical weapons in its war with Iran as early as 1983, in direct violation of the Geneva Protocol of 1925, which it had signed. In 1987, it turned those weapons against the Kurds. In April, the Iraqi Army attacked Kurdish-controlled villages in Suleimanieh and Arbil provinces, leaving more than 300 people dead. But those attacks, and others in later months, received little attention. The world took notice only when journalists filmed and photographed hundreds of decaying bodies of Kurdish villagers, including women and children, in a city called Halabja the following March.

A few days before the chemical-weapons attack, in a large-scale Iranian offensive with the help of Kurdish guerrillas, Iran's Revolutionary Guards had seized a large swath of territory in the Kurdish mountains, including the city of Halabja. Iraq lost between 1,500 and 4,000 men, as well as large numbers of tanks, artillery weapons, and support vehicles. The Iraqi regime treated these towns as little more than treasonous hotbeds. As soon as its forces fled the towns, the government used chemical weapons to teach a lasting lesson to the anti-Iraqi Kurds. Iran invited journalists to witness the aftermath, showing that up to 4,000 civilians had died of attacks of mustard gas, and perhaps phosgene, nerve gas, and cyanide. Later evidence indicated that both Iraq and Iran had fired gas shells into Halabja.

After the attack on Halabja, the Iraqis built another city in its place, 12 miles west of the original site. It was called "the new Saddam city of Halabja." It had no running water.

Even as the war with Iran wound down, the chemical-weapons attacks on the Kurds continued. The cease-fire with Iran on August 20, 1988, brought no respite for the Kurds from these weapons. On the day of the cease-fire, the regime launched what it called its "final offensive" against the Kurds. No longer were such weapons necessary to fight back the Iranian hordes; they were simply an instrument to pacify the Kurds once and for all. Saddam sent troops into Kurdistan, where five days later they dropped chemical weapons from planes and helicopters on more than 40 villages.

The villagers reported that they heard only a faint sound, saw a yellowish cloud dissipating into a thin mist, and smelled an odd odor—something like garlic or rotten apples or spoiled parsley. Kurds who were close to the explosions died almost instantly. Others began to feel the burning of their eyes, skin, and lungs; many suffered temporary blindness; some suffered uncontrollable coughing and sneezing, nausea and vomiting, before painful, burning blisters erupted, causing huge patches of skin to fall off. The fortunate ones saved themselves by jumping into nearby streams to wash off the chemicals, and by covering their faces with wet cloths to block the poison gas. In the three days of attacks, hundreds of Kurds were believed to have perished, most of them unarmed civilians. Some Pentagon analysts later said that the communications intercepts on which the chemical-weapons charges were based were inconclusive. But the State Department remained convinced that the Iraqis had indeed used chemical weapons on their own civilians after the war with Iran was over.

~ Enticement

From the time that he came to power, Saddam proved over and over that he was a survivor. By 1991, his regime had already lasted longer than any other government since Iraq became a state. But he did not rule by terror alone. Saddam was a modernizing bureaucrat who valued stability and knew that his regime needed the loyalty and support that only rewards could bring.

His concept of rule was institutionalized in Iraq and was known by two alliterative words in Arabic: *tarhib*, "terror," and *targhib*, "enticement."

Despite its divisions, Iraq was a society that shared profound hopes and dreams. Saddam created a vision of modernization, of a better material life, personal advancement, and national grandeur. He played on the vision in a particularly manipulative way, motivating his people with promises of wealth and pride and coaxing loyalty from them with grants of status and power. From the start, there were special rewards for loyalty to the Baath Party and its leader, special enticements for minorities, and gifts of land, cash, and automobiles for the families of casualties from the war with Iran.

For the country at large, there was the ideological enticement, instilling in every Iraqi a belief in the glories of the past and the promises of the future. Iraq was the center of the Arab nation, Saddam told his people, and, to some extent, they believed him.

At the same time, in his role as benevolent patron, Saddam used his country's extraordinary oil wealth to try to create a generous welfare state. The Baath accelerated a process of modernization that had begun with the overthrow of the monarchy in 1958. Under Saddam, much of Iraq was transformed from a dusty, dirt-poor, agricultural backwater into a developing country with superhighways, glittery hotels, and numbered blocks of modern condominiums with refrigerators. If a road or a bridge was built, it was because of Saddam, the television and radio said, and some of the people who hung his picture in their homes were genuinely grateful.

The Iraqi people also knew that they could count on the regime to last—until the war against the American-led coalition shook that illusion—and this sentiment allowed Saddam to use the stability that the repression brought as an enticement for individual loyalty. If someone joined the Party or the Army or took a job in a government bureaucracy, the position came with a certain security.

Saddam spread the wealth around, with an eye to maximum political effect. Those who cooperated were rewarded: Their sons got into the military schools; they were awarded government contracts or given jobs in the unwieldy bureaucracy; they received cooking oil or bottled gas for their kitchen stoves and space heaters when these items were scarce. Thus, a month after the invasion of Kuwait, when Baath Party officials visited Baghdad shopkeepers to inform them of the rationing of basic commodities, they also gave them lists of the only people in the neighborhood who would be permitted to buy the rationed goods.

Saddam also coopted some of his potential opponents by showering them with financial rewards. As soon as he assumed the presidency in 1979, he began to court the military: He raised their salaries, gave them better housing and access to consumer goods, and increased military spending. The continual purging of his enemies in the Army was a political cleansing that narrowed the base. But it was also a means for creating new positions that could be filled by the men loyal to him.

In his efforts to encourage loyalty from ethnic groups, Saddam was particularly attentive to the Shiite majority. He pumped hundreds of millions of dollars into renovating their shrines and rebuilding their towns—installing air-conditioning, laying acres of Italian marble, and hanging dozens of German-crystal chandeliers in the mosques of Najaf and Karbala. He also built a new highway between those two holy cities and new housing and tourist facilities along the way. During the Iran-Iraq war, Iranian prisoners were often taken there for sightseeing tours. The Najaf governorate building was probably the most opulent structure in the dusty city. Visitors who sought relief from local or family problems were seated in enormous gilt armchairs with fawn-colored upholstery and served tea as they waited to bring their complaints to someone in charge.

The Baath regime also substantially increased Shiite participation in the government and the military. When the Baath Party came to power in 1968, there were no Shiites in senior positions anywhere. At the end of 1990, Shiites filled two of the seven positions in the Revolutionary Command Council and nearly 50 percent of the regional Party leadership posts. Twenty to 25 percent of the country's 400 Army generals and nearly 50 percent of the heads of state-owned enterprises were also Shiite in 1990, according to unpublished research by Israeli scholar Amatzia Baram. Following the invasion of Kuwait, when Saddam needed even more support than usual, he appointed a Kurd, General Hussein Rashid, as chief of staff and a Shiite, General Saadi Tuma Abbas, as minister of defense. The vast majority of Iraqi generals, however, were still Sunni Arabs, many of them Tikritis.

Women enjoyed more freedom in Iraq than almost anywhere else in the Arab world. They drove cars, dressed as they pleased, went to college, voted, and held more than 10 percent of the seats in the showcase National Assembly. During the war with Iran, women took many of the jobs once held by men, and when the war was over, they were reluctant to vacate them. Still, cultural prejudices were slow to die. "There are no favors given to us because we are women," Manal Younis, the longtime head of the Federation of Iraqi Women, admitted to me in an unguarded moment. "Women are considered incompetent until it is proven differently. For men, it is the reverse."

In terms of geography, Saddam did not distribute rewards evenly. Those who were closer to Baghdad or considered more of a potential threat were rewarded more; the more unlikely the threat, the less need for reward. There was a modern asphalt road leading south from Baghdad, but it stopped at Babylon, 55 miles to the south. Why go farther than the seat of the ancient Mesopotamian empire?

In 1983, I became ill while on a bus tour to Basra organized by the Ministry of Information during the Iran-Iraq war. The bus had to drop me off at Kut, a Shiite city. Supporters of Saddam's Iraq in those days were always extolling the regime for building hospitals and roads and schools, and indeed, there was a hospital in Kut. It was filthy and fly-infested and smelled of urine. The waiting room was full of Iraqis but no doctor or nurse was on duty. My Ministry of Information guide was so appalled that he would not let me wait until a doctor arrived or even let me use the hospital restroom. We stayed in an open-air metalworking shop until we found a taxi to drive us back to Baghdad.

When it came to enticements, one group that Saddam's regime ignored was the Jews. The few hundred Jews still left in Iraq could practice their religion and work in private enterprises, but they were not allowed to work for the state or serve in the Army. Baghdad's last functioning synagogue, in al-Badawiin, once the Jewish quarter of Baghdad, was a pale reflection of past glory. Unlike the Shiite mosques, or even the Christian churches, which underwent constant renovation, the synagogue was a crumbling, buff-colored building tucked away in an alley. When I visited it a few years ago, its paint was peeling and water had damaged the 30-foot ceilings. Green floral drapes covered the dirty windows, some of which were boarded up. Six women huddled around a floor heater, awaiting the monthly delivery of kosher meat. Only 20 or so Jews went to the Saturday service, a far cry from the days when the balconies were filled with women and the men prayed downstairs and the children attended Hebrew school nearby. There were no portraits of Saddam in the synagogue. The Jews had nothing to lose by staying outside the system.

Nor were the Kurds offered many enticements—just the hard choice of being transformed into city people. During the war with Iran, the regime made conciliatory moves toward those it could coopt and quiet. It began negotiations with Jalal Talabani's Patriotic Union of Kurdistan, one of the two leading Kurdish organizations, and declared that promotion of the Kurdish identity was an acceptable expression of Iraqi patriotism as long as it did not suggest rebellion. The regime sponsored festivals of Kurdish culture in the major cities and launched a propaganda campaign saying that Kurds were treated better in Iraq than in other countries. They were flushed out of their old villages on the borders with Iran and Turkey and relocated into new towns in well-guarded plains and valleys where they could be governed more easily. The regime claimed they had to be moved to protect them from future attacks by Iran or its collaborators, adding that the Kurds were paid generous compensation and given new homes in new communities that were to have electricity, running water, and Kurdish schools. But the towns had no farms, no place to plant tobacco or raise sheep.

~

The long war with Iran gradually eroded Saddam's ability to employ the tool of enticement. For the first few years, the regime was able to insulate Iraqis totally from any economic hardship. The government successfully minimized the war's economic impact by pouring billions of dollars into public subsidies from its estimated $35 billion in reserves and by obtaining direct payments from Saudi Arabia, Kuwait, and the other rich Gulf states. But no one expected the war to last so long, and the regime was forced to halt its ambitious development program. It slashed imports, froze some major projects, demanded that foreign contractors finance others, and launched a campaign of economic liberalization. It could no longer pay families 10,000 dinars—about $30,000 on the official exchange—if their sons or husbands died on the battlefield.

Contrary to Baath economic principles, the regime began to encourage private investment in manufacturing and agriculture and to discourage investment in trade and real estate. As the war dragged on, the regime relaxed the regulations that had stymied private investment; privatized factories and farms, supermarkets and gas stations; and disbanded peasants' cooperatives. It allowed farmers to sell directly to wholesalers, encouraged joint ventures, and loosened import-export and foreign-exchange restrictions. The war also opened new avenues for private contractors, who became rich from deals with the government. Few Iraqis living in exile were willing to come home to invest their wealth, and many private investors put their money into speculative ventures rather than long-term projects such as hotels or transport companies. But the policy broadened support for the regime—if only slightly— among the middle class and the military. Repression was more tolerable when it was served up with stability and well-being.

But not for everyone. Samir al-Khalil is an Iraqi who has lived in Europe for more than a decade. An intense, slightly built man who wears rumpled clothes and has the air of an impoverished professor, he spent five years writing *Republic of Fear*, a relentless, carefully documented account of repression in Saddam's Iraq. At first, his book received little attention when it was published in 1989 by the University of California Press, after a number of larger publishing houses turned it down. Samir al-Khalil is not his real name, and when he gave interviews on television—as he was asked to do often after Iraq's invasion of Kuwait—his face was obscured in shadows. Those who meet him do not know who he really is. The most poignant expression of repression under Saddam is found in the last sentence of the opening note in his book. "I owe a handful of very dear friends a great deal in the writing of this book," he wrote. "But things being what they are under the Baath, I can no more mention their names than I can write under my own."

~ 5 ~

The Iran-Iraq War: Saladin and the Messiah

When a clash is a patriotic and national duty, we shall wage it in all its forms. . . . Iraq is once again to assume its leading Arab role. Iraq is once again to serve the Arab nation and defend its honor, dignity, and sovereignty. Iraq is destined once again to face the concerted machinations of the forces of darkness. . . . This demands sacrifice, but you are not tired of sacrifice.

—Saddam Hussein, April 15, 1980

I address this Army which is still collaborating with the dirty regime of Saddam to use this opportunity and join your brothers who are ready to help you to throw this regime into hell. It is either the victory of Islam and the victory of justice or the defeat of Islam and a great shame for Muslim nations. Before it is too late, rise up.

—Ayatollah Ruhollah Khomeini, July 1982

~ Scenes from the Front

Many of the bodies still were not buried when I arrived in Beidha. Thick smoke from burning huts rose hundreds of feet into the air, mingling with the stench of bodies still trapped among the marsh reeds. Beidha once was like hundreds of poor, floating communities that dotted the 580-square-mile Howeiza marshes in southeastern Iraq. For centuries, the villagers of the community six miles west of the Iranian border had eked out a living spearing fish, hunting game birds, and raising water buffalo among the bulrushes. They built one-room mud-and-reed huts on manmade islands of earth and plied the watery "streets" in graceful reed canoes.

Now the village was destroyed, the villagers dead or in hiding on safer ground. Overnight, the Iraqi soldiers had put hundreds of war dead into shallow pits and covered them with a thin layer of dirt. They showed me what was once the village school and police station—now piles of mud-bricks and twisted metal. They mounted an artillery gun on the roof of what was left of a one-room mosque, nailed a portrait of Saddam Hussein to a smoke-blackened tree, and hoisted an Iraqi flag on a bamboo pole. A popular Arabic song blared from the loudspeaker of a truck as the soldiers poked through the empty applesauce and powdered-milk cans left behind by the fleeing invaders. One group of soldiers, clearly hoping to impress their American visitor, raised their Kalashnikovs over their heads, gave the V-for-victory sign, and began a bizarre chant: "We'll chop off the hands of the invaders at our borders. We'll chop off the hands of the invaders at our borders."

It was February 1984, and Iraq's war with Iran was more than three years old. The battle of the marshes was part of Iran's Operations Dawn V and Dawn VI, when 250,000 to 350,000 Iranian men and boys massed on the border for some of the bloodiest battles of the war.

A mile away, in the marsh village of Sakra, there was a similarly relaxed victory atmosphere, as the Iraqi soldiers got on with the business of everyday life. Some soldiers shaved, others dressed their wounds or hung laundry to dry on barbed wire. They napped in shallow foxholes made comfortable by the mattresses and blankets they had looted from the homes of their countrymen. Not far from the bloated corpses of Iranian soldiers floating in the marsh, an Iraqi speared an enormous silver fish, which another soldier grilled on a barbecue made from a villager's bedspring. A third soldier took a stick and poked at the body of an Iranian lying face-down in the water to prove that he was dead. When I asked whether it was safe to eat fish caught in water contaminated by human corpses, a local commander told me with appropriate military fervor, "Our fish are getting fat and happy on the bodies of dead Iranians."

The week-long battle for the marshes pitted Iranian zeal against superior Iraqi firepower, reflecting the nature of most of the Iran-Iraq war. Iran's bold offensive began with a nighttime naval invasion that took the Iraqis by surprise. The Iranians moved in hundreds of boats—reed canoes, motorized rowboats, large aluminum craft—seizing floating villages and slaughtering villagers who did not flee. The invading troops also occupied the two Majnoon "islands"—oil installations that were cemented shut by the Iraqis at the beginning of the war. The Majnoons were a coveted strategic prize believed to sit atop billions of barrels of oil.

The Iraqi counterattack was brutally effective. Led by helicopter gunships, more than 30 Soviet-made amphibious armored infantry carriers, tanks, and artillery bore down on the Iranians. Some of the Iranians were armed with machine guns and light weapons; others came armed only with sticks.

It would take four and a half more years before the war was over. In the course of the eight-year war, between 600,000 and one million people died, and between one million and two million were wounded. The economies of both nations were devastated. By some estimates, the war cost the Iraqis as much as $450 billion and the Iranians as much as $650 billion. Even then, neither side achieved its goals. Saddam unleashed chemical weapons for the first time since World War I, but he neither "liberated" the Shatt al-Arab waterway nor overthrew Ayatollah Khomeini. The Iranian cleric neither ousted Saddam nor installed an Islamic republic in Baghdad. No territory was exchanged; the 730-mile border remained virtually the same as it was before. But Saddam did not learn a lesson. "Saddam's Qadisiyah," as he called his war with Iran—after the seventh-century battle when the Arabs rousted the Persians from what is modern-day Iraq—turned out to be a grim prelude to his move into Kuwait and the war in the Gulf that followed.

~

A week before the 1984 Iranian attack in the marshes, Baghdad's Voice of the Masses radio had talked of "a certain insecticide for every insect," adding the ominous words, "We have this insecticide." What was curious about the marshland casualties in early 1984 was that many of the bodies remained intact and showed no evidence of bullet or shrapnel wounds. Some victims were found curled up dead in their foxholes. Others had small streams of blood coming from their noses and mouths.

It was only back in Baghdad that I realized that the Iraqis had used a sulfur-based mustard gas in the battle for the Majnoons. They may also have used a blood agent, a chemical weapon that blocks the supply of oxygen, to turn back the Iranian invaders at Beidha and Sakra. Gravely ill Iranian soldiers began turning up in the hospitals of Western Europe, where they were diagnosed as victims of chemical weapons. The response from Western governments was muted; Saddam's Arab neighbors, not wanting to antagonize a fellow Arab leader and one who was fighting Iran's revolutionary regime, remained silent. The United States publicly accused Iraq of using chemical weapons but did not follow up the protest with anything but words.

Baghdad issued pro forma denials and wondered what all the fuss was about. Iraqi officials were indignant that they should be asked to play by clean rules in a dirty war. "Do you want us to wash our dirty linen in public?" Adnan Khairallah, Iraq's minister of defense and Saddam's first cousin, asked reporters at a press conference in Baghdad. Why was the world picking on

Iraq when other countries had the same weapons? he asked. "We are no different from any country in the world." Major General Hisham al-Fakhri, a commander on the southern front, would not admit that Iraq was using chemical weapons, but did say to me, "You cannot expect us to welcome an invading force with flowers and perfume." Later that year, Saddam blamed "the Zionists" as the source of Western criticism of his conduct of the war.

Like the tides of the Gulf, the Iran-Iraq war ebbed and flowed sluggishly. It had three main phases: the initial Iraqi invasion, in which the Iraqis took Iranian territory but then bogged down and retreated; the long war of attrition, with enormous casualties on both sides; and the cataclysm that finally brought about a cease-fire in 1988. In the first phase, from 1980 to mid-1982, Iraq took the offensive, then Iran liberated its territory and forced Iraq to sue for peace—a plea that Khomeini rejected outright. From 1982 to 1986, Iran pushed ahead with waves of offensives, forcing Iraq to fight a defensive battle. In the third phase, Iraq expanded the war throughout the Gulf and managed to build an army that prevailed against the enemy.

~ The Makings of War

By mid-1980, Saddam's treasury was full. His military machine was considered one of the best in the Middle East, behind only those of Israel and Egypt and on a par with Syria's. Exploiting Iraq's oil wealth, he poured much of the profits from Iraq's $23 billion a year in oil revenues into the country— raising salaries, providing free education and medical care, and launching literacy campaigns. Those were the salad days, when the state-run department stores were filled with consumer goods—toys, refrigerators, televisions, and imported foods—and the people had money to buy them. Saddam embarked on ambitious development schemes that began to bring electricity, purified water, dams, and roads to rural villages throughout the country, as well as housing, schools, hospitals, and petrochemical, steel, and cement plants to the cities. With his development projects, Saddam hoped to ally the Kurds of the north and the Shiites of the south with the regime in Baghdad, and in the process to make them more dependent on central authority.

Even before July 1979, when Saddam assumed the presidency, he was maneuvering Iraq into a position of leadership among the Arabs and among nonaligned countries. After years of dependence on Moscow and a reputation as a radical outcast in the Arab world, Saddam wanted Iraq to become a major power. A secular Messiah, he was ready to inflame the region's Arabs with visions of their greatness. He was well positioned to fill the Middle East power vacuum: Egypt was isolated in the wake of the September 1978 Camp David accords, which established peace between Egypt and Israel; Syria was preoccupied with internal problems and with Lebanon; Iran was distracted by the beginnings of its revolution. Saddam had begun to transform Baghdad into a modern city in preparation for the summit meeting of nonaligned nations that was to be held in Baghdad two years later, in 1982. He built a futuristic conference center, a string of luxury hotels, and a new headquarters for the Baath Party. The summit would have made him the de facto leader of the nonaligned world, the Marshal Tito of the 1980s.

Then came an unexpected event—and Baghdad would neither host the summit nor lead the Arab world. In February 1979, a 79-year-old cleric overthrew the Shah of Iran. Saddam had never liked the Shah Mohammad Reza Pahlevi, but by 1975, the two had found a modus vivendi. The Shah promised to stop arming and funding Iraqi Kurdish guerrillas; Saddam in turn was forced to cede partial control of the Shatt al-Arab, the 120-mile waterway dividing southern Iran and Iraq. For more than three centuries, the Arabs and the Persians had fought over access to the Shatt, since rivers in both Iran and Iraq flow into it. The Shatt was Iraq's only outlet to the Gulf, but Saddam, then deputy chairman of the Revolutionary Command Council, signed the agreement with the Shah in Algiers in 1975 that established the international border on the thalweg, or deep-water line of the waterway. The agreement was a humiliating compromise for Saddam.

When Ayatollah Khomeini landed in Tehran after 14 years of exile and succeeded in his revolution to establish an Islamic republic, Saddam felt threatened. Khomeini's Islamic message proved more potent than Saddam's vague, secular calls to Arab brotherhood. The Iranian cleric stole Saddam's thunder, calling for the liberation of Jerusalem and the expulsion of the imperialists—but in the language of religion that people understood. Almost from the moment of his return to Iran, Khomeini stated clearly that Iraq was his next target: "What we have done in Iran we will do again in Iraq," he declared.

Khomeini provided moral and material support for outlawed Iraqi Shiite groups. He gave refuge to their leaders, including those associated with the underground al-Dawa al-Islamiyah Party, which had organized antigovernment demonstrations and small-scale attacks against police stations and Baath Party headquarters in the 1970s. Khomeini also gave his blessing to a revolutionary movement whose goal was to transform Iraq into a Shiite satellite of Iran. Mohammad Bakr al-Hakim, the Iraqi Shiite religious leader, used Tehran as a base to call for an armed struggle against Saddam—in the name of Islam. When Iraqi Foreign Minister Tariq Aziz was wounded by a hand grenade in an assassination attempt on April 1, 1980, Saddam arrested the al-Dawa leadership and hundreds of Shiite activists.

~ Saddam's Impatience

By September 1980, Saddam had lost his patience with months of Iranian pinpricks into his territory, the clashes along the border, and Khomeini's interference in his domestic affairs. Unlike his invasion of Kuwait, which he kept secret from other Arab rulers, Saddam boasted in advance that he would invade Iran. He told Saudi Arabia's King Fahd, then the crown prince, that the Iranians threatened the Arabs and that Arab dignity must be protected. "We must finish those Persians," Prince Bandar bin Sultan, the Saudi ambassador to Washington, quoted Saddam as telling Fahd. Fahd discouraged Saddam but did not talk him out of it. "Mr. President, my brother, the decision to go to war is yours," he said. "But the decision to disengage is theirs. Don't take your decision lightly."

Fahd advised Saddam not to tamper with the 1975 border agreement even if he did invade, saying, "You never know if you want to go back to it." But Saddam refused, telling Fahd that he had signed the agreement only because he had no choice. "I'm going to march into Tehran and pull the beard off Khomeini's face," he said.

On September 17, 1980, Saddam made a dramatic speech on Iraqi television during which he ripped up a copy of the Algiers accord. He asserted that the Shatt al-Arab belonged to him. Tearing up the treaty was an act of vengeance for Saddam, vengeance for the personal humiliation he felt he had suffered. He summoned a delegation of senior officials from the other Gulf states to Iraq, ostensibly to discuss ways to curb Khomeini's vow to export Islamic revolution to the region. Instead, he announced that he was going to war. Arriving at a scheduled lunch three hours late, he told the group that he had just held a meeting of his senior generals and decided on his battle plan. He would teach Iran a lesson by invading it. Three days later, on September 22, 1980, he did just that.

Saddam's stated aims were by no means solely defensive. He wanted Iraqi control over most of Iran's Khuzestan province, control over the Shatt al-Arab, sovereignty over a border area of about 90 miles, and an end to Iranian interference in Iraqi affairs. In addition, Saddam saw himself as a liberator of Arab lands, demanding that Iran surrender to "the Arab nation" three small islands in the Strait of Hormuz that the Shah himself had secured from the United Arab Emirates in 1971. Saddam also hoped that he could strike such a crushing blow that Khomeini's regime would fall. Saddam assumed that his move into Iran would be easy, a blitzkrieg similar to Israel's Six-Day war in 1967. If he could win quickly, he reasoned, he would enhance the prestige of his regime. He could have gone to the Arab League summit in Amman scheduled for six weeks later as the man who conquered Iran in six days. He could have been the new Nasser. Saddam miscalculated, much as he did a decade later by invading Kuwait.

Launching a massive air and ground assault, he attacked the oil-refining center at Abadan, the port city of Khorramshahr, the military center at Dezful, the provincial capital and industrial center in Ahvaz, and ten military airfields. On the second day, he seized the Shatt al-Arab and occupied a 30-mile-wide strip of Iranian territory, while six Iraqi divisions crossed the border and began to advance deep into Iran. He invited hundreds of journalists from around the world—and footed the bill for most of them—to witness the great Iraqi victory. But the Iraqis moved too slowly and were led by a poor command. They gave the Iranians time to fight back—with revolutionary zeal and patched-up American military hardware. Just as Saddam did immediately after his invasion of Kuwait, he announced he was prepared to cease hostilities and hold direct negotiations to settle the dispute, but not to withdraw.

The world community, enraged by Iran's seizure of the American Embassy in November 1979, and its threats to export revolution, took Saddam's side, as it did through most of the conflict. The United States merely cautioned that it "could not condone" Iraq's seizure of Iran's oil-producing province of Khuzestan. It took the United Nations Security Council more than a week to pass a weak resolution that urged the combatants "to refrain immediately from any further use of force" and accept any "appropriate offer of mediation." The Security Council did not call for a cease-fire or demand that Iraq withdraw immediately to the internationally recognized border. Khomeini had only himself to blame, the Security Council seemed to say. He had violated international law and the rules of civilized behavior when he seized the American Embassy and held diplomats hostage. Iran would not forget that resolution, which it cited over and over in its refusal over the years to allow the United Nations to mediate a settlement.

The response could not have been more different after Iraq's invasion of Kuwait in 1990, when, in a matter of hours, the Security Council passed a strong resolution condemning the invasion, demanding a complete withdrawal to international borders, and threatening global economic sanctions if Iraq did not pull out. Because most of the world took his side in the Iran-Iraq war, perhaps Saddam did not imagine that he would be isolated when he invaded Kuwait. But the invasion of Iran took place in a different era, when Khomeini—a messianic figure who brutally eliminated the remnants of Iran's old regime—was the international outlaw, a pariah on the world stage. Iran was also a dangerous regional power—not a small, militarily weak emirate like Kuwait. The world was secretly pleased that there was a Saddam to make the Ayatollah suffer.

～ More than Boundaries

The Iran-Iraq war was not just a dispute over boundaries. On one level, the war was a continuation of the 13-century struggle between Arabs and Persians. The antipathy toward "the Persian racists"—as Saddam sometimes called Iran's leaders—was evident in a film shown every day at the height of the war on the closed-circuit television in the luxury hotels of Baghdad. It was the story of "Qadisiyah." The Persians were portayed as drunkards, rapists, gluttons, and woman chasers—bejeweled louts who lay on stuffed couches and ate exotic fruits. The Arabs, by contrast, were true believers and battle-toughened warriors who plotted their strategy on the ground next to their swords and horses. "Let's send delegates to the Persians," one of the Arabs said in the film. "Let's reason with them. If they won't reason, at least we'll know how they think." Not surprisingly, the Persians refused to "reason," and the Arabs attacked. That's just what happened when Iraq invaded Iran in 1980, and Kuwait a decade later. In both cases, Saddam concluded that his enemies had refused to "reason" with him. So he took by force what he did not want to bother to get by negotiation. In the film version, however, the Arabs won after only three days.

~

On another level, the war was a bitter personal feud between Saddam and Khomeini. The Shah had expelled Khomeini to Turkey in November 1964 because of his statements against the monarchy. After 11 months, he was allowed to take refuge in Najaf, Iraq, the site of one of Shiite Islam's holiest shrines. It is hard to believe that for 13 years, Iraq gave refuge to Ayatollah Khomeini, with police protection provided by the regime. There he lectured that all Muslims were duty-bound to "overthrow all treacherous, corrupt, oppressive, and criminal regimes" and restore the unity of the world's Muslims.

In 1984, I found Khomeini's former house in Iraq a few blocks away from the tomb of Ali, the founder of Shiite Islam, on a narrow dirt alleyway littered with rotting orange peels and animal bones. Children played amid the rubble as Sudanese workers dug the foundation of a house next door. Khomeini's house was a nondescript two-story beige-brick building with rickety overhanging balconies and a tangle of electrical cables. At the time he lived there, Khomeini was revered as a learned Shiite scholar, perhaps a bit eccentric but certainly not dangerous. Every day, he would walk from his house to pray in the mosque and then return home to lecture a group of fervent students who traveled from Iran and Lebanon to sit at his feet and hear his wisdom. That was until Saddam put Khomeini under a loose house arrest in 1977 for preaching sermons against the Shah of Iran. The following year, when the cleric's message—dispersed to the vast mosque network in Iran via cassette tapes—began to take hold, Saddam expelled Khomeini from Iraq. He settled near Paris, a move that ironically gave him access to the world's news media and propelled him to instant fame.

After Khomeini's rise to power in Iran, some of the citizens of Najaf were eager to spin negative stories about him. He never said hello to people on the street; everyone in the city hated him; he never had any followers and was fed his ideas by the imperialists; he tried to split the Sunnis and the Shiites, when everyone in Iraq knew there was no difference between the sects; he didn't cry at the funeral of his son, Mustapha, who some of his followers said had been assassinated by the Shah; he left Iraq without paying his phone bill. "Look," a guide from the mosque told me, pointing to a second-story window of Khomeini's house. "We even gave him an air-conditioner. What ingratitude."

Not far away, Sheik Ali Khaifai, a plump, full-faced Shiite Iraqi leader with unimpressive religious credentials, sat in his rundown, one-room living quarters furnished only with carpets, pillows, an electric space heater, and a telephone. Flies settled on his great black robe and full beard. Holy books were piled high in the corner and one bare lightbulb lit the dim room. He served his guests Pepsis and Kent cigarettes as he denounced Khomeini and his regime. He had once respected Khomeini, he told me, but he had been wrong. "Khomeini was like any ordinary religious leader here," the sheik said. "He took advantage of us. He forgot our hospitality and our patronage. Khomeini was a severe and savage man. If we knew he had such an ugly face, we never would have accepted him. We should have known better."

∼

Finally, the Iran-Iraq war was a struggle for power between two mutually exclusive despotisms, both lusting for regional supremacy. To Iran, Iraq was a secular regime that propelled its people—sometimes unwillingly—into modernity, with forced literacy campaigns and Western vices such as the drinking of alcohol and the liberation of women. Khomeini called Saddam "the Iraqi Zionist," "the infidel." Iraq's state-controlled media referred to Khomeini as "the turbaned Shah," "the Arab hater," "the senile old fraud," "the mummy," and "a Zoroastrian fire worshipper." Saddam denounced Khomeini's pretensions to the leadership of the Islamic world. The role of regional leader, he declared, was his. "The Koran was written in Arabic," he claimed, "and God destined the Arabs to play a vanguard role in Islam." "He who hates the Arabs," he argued, in an implicit criticism of the non-Arab Persians, "cannot be a true Muslim." Finally, Saddam twisted a Koranic verse that alluded to the Muslims as "the best nation among mankind," replacing "Muslims" with "Arabs."

In war, Saddam saw an opportunity to rid himself of an enemy who appealed to the Iraqi Shiites, and to expand his influence. Iran's revolutionaries executed, purged, or drove into exile the Shah's most senior officers, and Saddam believed that the once-powerful Iranian Army was disintegrating in Khomeini's hands. Saddam and his coterie never admitted that they wanted to overthrow Khomeini, but they hinted at it broadly. "We cannot topple Khomeini," Tariq Aziz frankly told journalist Georgie Anne Geyer when the war was still going Iraq's way. "But maybe the war could be an assisting element."

Iran, on the other hand, was a modern-day theocracy whose leaders were guided by the Koran and determined to spread Islamic revolution throughout the Muslim world. The war became the glue that bound the revolution together and excused the Iranian regime for demanding sacrifices of its people. "If you can kill Saddam before we execute him, stab him in the back," Khomeini told Iraqi Shiites. "Paralyze the economy. Stop paying taxes. This is war between Islam and blasphemy." For Khomeini, Saddam was nothing more than a "pro-American mercenary," an "infidel."

~ The War Drags On

The war took on a permanence and quickly settled into a military stalemate. Saddam's superior military equipment did not topple Khomeini. Over the years, Saddam had ensured the loyalty of his military by filling key posts with men chosen for their loyalty to the regime rather than their military capability. Commanders took orders from "Field Marshal" Saddam, and for most of the war were required to conduct operations according to political, rather than military, needs. For the first year, the war sputtered along inconclusively, as the Iraqis made limited gains at a horrendous price and the Iranians were distracted by power struggles at home. The Iraqis dug miles of elaborate trench networks reminiscent of World War I and prepared for a long stay, just as they did in Kuwait a decade later when they prepared for an attack from the American-led allied forces.

There were times during the Iran-Iraq war when it seemed impossible that the Iraqis wouldn't win. But then the Iraqi troops would make moves that made me wonder how they ever accomplished as much as they did. On one trip back to Baghdad from the southeastern front in a Soviet-made helicopter with a group of foreign journalists, I watched as an Iraqi plane flew close by, then casually launched a missile over an uninhabited patch of Iranian marshland. It was as if we didn't exist. As it sped away, out of range, Iranian antiaircraft guns tried to hit the only flying object in sight—us.

Although the quality of the Iraqi Army differed widely from unit to unit, its initial conduct of the war was appalling. An intelligence report from one embassy in Baghdad whose military worked closely with the Iraqi Army reported back home: "The Iraqis are suffering from no motivation, low morale and extremely poor leadership . . . . The Iraqi Army is not fighting for a cause but out of fear of persecution from Baath Party functionaries." A Western military attaché explained the problem of Iraq's soldiers more bluntly: "They go to sleep at night."

In late 1981, the Iranians went on the offensive, scoring a series of victories with massive human-wave assaults that for a while turned the tide of the war in their favor. The shape of the war changed in March 1982 with the battle for Khorramshahr. In one of the biggest battles since World War

II, Iranian troops recaptured the city after a two-month siege. They drove the Iraqis back across the Shatt al-Arab into Iraq and captured more than 20,000 prisoners. In June, Saddam stunned the world when he declared a unilateral cease-fire, withdrew his forces from most of Iranian territory, and called for peace. It was Khomeini's turn to blunder. He rebuffed Saddam's peace gesture and called for his ouster.

In an important speech in June 1982, Khomeini declared firmly that the war was not over. The goal was now the annexation of Iraq. The Iraqis "will free themselves from the talons of the tyrannical clique and will link themselves with the Iranian nation," he said. Once that happened, all the other small Gulf nations would join them. A month later, Iran took the war into Iraqi territory for the first time in a massive invasion north of Basra. The better-armed, better-trained Iraqi soldiers brutally crushed the Iranian soldiers and smashed their dream of an easy victory. Even Iraq's Shiite majority did not want to be part of an Iranian satellite state.

The threat of the exportation of Iran's revolution struck fear in the hearts of the rich Gulf Arabs. They were only too willing to pay blood money to Iraq so that its soldiers could serve as Arab mercenaries who would protect them all from Khomeini's wrath. The war was not a distant matter like the Arab-Israeli conflict but rather an immediate threat on their doorstep. The sounds of shelling around Basra could be heard as far away as Kuwait City and the coast of northeastern Saudi Arabia. Over the course of the war, Saudi Arabia, Kuwait, and other oil-producing Gulf states contributed as much as $40 billion in cash and in oil sold on Iraq's behalf. Of all the Arab states, only Syria and Libya lined up with Iran. A banker from Kuwait once told me: "The Lebanon war concerns us. The Iran-Iraq war terrifies us."

If Iraq had the weaponry, Iran had the will. Iran's clerics scoured towns and villages, sometimes by motorbike, in search of able-bodied soldiers. The cult of martyrdom prompted Khomeini to send human waves of child-martyrs with little formal military training to die on Iraqi battlefields in the name of Islam. I saw Iranian soldiers ready for battle wearing small gold keys on their uniforms where other soldiers might wear medals. They were the keys that would immediately unlock the gates of heaven if they should die on the road to their destination—Karbala, the holy city where the Shiite hero Hussein had been slaughtered 13 centuries earlier.

Some Iranian soldiers wore blood-red headbands that read WARRIORS OF GOD. In some battles, soldiers in the rear carried their own funeral shrouds. During one tour of the southern Iraqi border after a particularly grisly battle, Iraqi victors showed me the shriveled bodies of a dozen Iranian soldiers, their crude weapons, and their belongings. I found one explanation for Iraq's inability to win a decisive victory near Basra in the contents of a suitcase that an Iraqi soldier dumped unceremoniously on the ground. Out poured religious relics of the dead Iranian soldiers that testified to their religious zeal—icons that were supposed to have staved off danger. There were pocket-size copies of the Koran, stained with blood; pictures of the Prophet Mohammad; and prayer stones inscribed with Koranic verses. The most interesting artifacts were laminated plastic cards like the holy cards that American nuns handed out in Catholic elementary schools in the 1950s. Instead of the Virgin Mary or the saints, however, these holy cards showed Khomeini's portrait on one side and an image of Karbala on the other. Khomeini had promised to liberate Karbala, and the young fighters thought they would march straight to the land of their Prophet. He probably didn't tell his soldiers that Karbala was more than 300 miles from Basra.

The Iraqi soldiers were terrified of the Iranian human-wave commandos. Not only did Iran have more motivation, it potentially had more men. In the early stages of the war, Iran had a disorganized regular army of about 150,000; 30,000 Revolutionary Guards, created by Khomeini in May 1979 as a new force to legitimize the revolution and to eliminate opposition; and a largely untrained militia, the 75,000-man-strong Basij. Iraq had an Army of about 200,000 troops and a Popular Army with a paper strength of about 650,000, little more than a half-trained reserve force. But with a population three times that of Iraq, Iran had an unlimited supply of new recruits. Early in the war, Iraqi soldiers were known to abandon their posts—and their Soviet-made equipment—at the sight of the Iranian hordes marching over the horizon. Iranian television showed footage of entire Iraqi depots captured intact, the tea still brewing on the stoves. It was a foreshadowing of the massive desertions that occurred in the 1991 Gulf war.

In the fall of 1982, a story began to circulate that Saddam had approved the execution of 300 high-ranking officers and a small number of Party officials for grumbling about the war. In one version of the story, Saddam personally executed an officer who had ordered a tactical retreat during one battle. According to that version, when the man was thrown at Saddam's feet, he drew his pistol and shot him in the head.

When a reporter from *Stern* magazine asked Saddam about the executions later that year, Saddam acknowledged that some officers had been executed.

STERN: It is known that Your Excellency is not satisfied with the Iraqi military command. Is it true that in the recent period, 300 high-ranking military officers have been executed?
SADDAM: No. However, two divisional commanders and the commander of a mechanized unit were executed. This is something very normal in all wars.
STERN: For what reason?
SADDAM: They did not undertake their responsibilities in the battle for Muhammara [Khorramshahr].

Similarly, senior and junior officers were executed after the invasion of Kuwait. According to one story, seven high-ranking officers were executed because they argued against the invasion while it was still in the planning stages. Other, lower-ranking officers reportedly were executed when they expressed dismay after realizing that they were not heading to Kuwait to conduct joint exercises, as they had been told, but to invade. In October 1990, the chief of staff, General Nizar al-Khazraji, disappeared. Following the outbreak of war in January, there were reports that some Iraqi soldiers who tried to desert were executed.

$\sim$

Just as Ayatollah Khomeini mistreated Iraqi prisoners of war, Saddam Hussein used captured Iranian child-soldiers as proof of Iran's barbarity. Iraqi officials often showed foreign visitors a film of Saddam meeting with 20 child-prisoners. In the film, the POWs, dressed in open-necked dress shirts and dress pants, sat in oversize armchairs while an avuncular Saddam lectured them gently on the Iraqi war effort. Did they like the city or the country? he asked them. Did they have brothers and sisters? Were they students or workers? Then they gathered together for a group photograph—the same gesture Saddam made toward a group of British hostages after he invaded Kuwait. "We hope that you can go back to your families and that some of you will become lawyers and engineers," Saddam told the young soldiers. "When you pass your exams, let us know, and when the war ends, come back and enjoy our country's hospitality."

Visiting journalists often were escorted by Iraqi authorities to a model POW camp at Ramadi, 60 miles west of Baghdad. During one visit, 50 barefoot teenagers in fatigues stood at attention in their small barracks. Their fear, mingled with grim resignation, made them reluctant to talk about Khomeini, his revolution, or the course of the war. "I can't answer a political question," stated Mahmoud Allami, who said he had been a blacksmith's apprentice before he "volunteered" for the war at the age of 15. "I came to the war for the sake of defending my country. God willing, the war will end soon. And God willing, I'll go home." Sometimes the staged events backfired on the Iraqi authorities, the gap between illusion and reality exposed. I remember at Ramadi a toothless, partially deaf Iranian who called himself Khalaf and said he was 88, who told me about his capture in the early days of the war. "I was sitting at home, sick in bed with eye problems when the Arabs came and took me away for my security," he said. "I never was a soldier and I was never involved in politics. I just want to go home to my country and my children." When asked about his treatment by the Iraqis, he said, "They promised to fix my teeth and they didn't. And I'm in the hospital because of their Iraqi food. It's bad for my stomach."

$\sim$ Guns and Butter

Saddam pursued a domestic guns-and-butter policy to subdue criticism of his war effort. In the early years of the war, he spent vast sums of money keeping food plentiful and consumers happy. Large construction projects continued as if it were peacetime. Families of Iraq's war dead received generous compensation, free plots of land, interest-free loans, even free cars. For veterans, there were pensions and promises of free education.

At the Basra Sheraton, a glittery symbol of Westernization and a refuge for wealthy Basrawis too frightened to stay in their homes, the management drowned out the shelling by turning up the Muzak. There were always freshly planted sunflowers around the fountain in the hotel courtyard, but sandbag walls protected the entrance.

For a number of years, it seemed, Iraqi soldiers did nothing but wait for the Iranian aggressor. During one visit to a border position known among foreign military attachés as a "showpiece front" in the north, near Khanaqin, I was served iced soft drinks and candies in an air-conditioned, carpeted room furnished with plush armchairs and glass and chrome coffee tables. An international ice-skating championship was shown on a color television in the corner. The soldiers had so little to do that they planted sunflowers in the garden. They were pampered at the front with cold beer and hot meals, newspapers from Baghdad, and a full night's sleep. For a while, they even got one week's home leave every month.

But then reality struck. Plans for Baghdad's subway and a nationwide railway system—as well as new housing, highways, and tourist-village projects—were canceled. Iraq began to tell contractors it couldn't pay its debts. Its prewar foreign reserves of $35 billion dwindled to nearly nothing. Foreign workers left Iraq and returned home; limits were set on how much foreign currency they could take with them. Gambling casinos began to reject Iraqi currency for buying chips; only the hard currencies of the West and the rich Gulf Arabs would do. Iraqis began to open banking accounts abroad, even though the penalty for smuggling currency out of the country was death. At one point, there was no butter in all of Baghdad. A boat from New Zealand loaded with butter steamed up and down the Gulf of Aqaba, waiting until the Iraqis paid for their previous shipment.

As war casualties mounted, the regime discouraged public displays of mourning. Elaborate funerals were forbidden, and the mosque became the only sanctuary where public mourning was acceptable. I once donned an *abbaya*—a long, black, shapeless cloak worn by many Iraqi women—and entered the Shiite mosque of al-Kadhimain in Baghdad. Non-Muslims were not allowed inside the mosque—one of the most important shrines of the Muslim world, where two of the 12 imams (leaders) are buried—and I knew well that I was breaking the rules. Inside the mosque, the calm rhetoric and vows to die for Saddam did not exist. Women, most of them mothers, touched and kissed the holy shrine and wailed, over and over, "Oh, God, Oh God, please make this war end. We have lost our sons. We have lost our brothers."

To boost the morale of his commanders, Saddam began to give them identities. At the beginning of the war, Iraqi television regularly showed Saddam pinning medals on his men. They were always anonymous. A strong military hero might develop his own cult of personality and compete with Saddam, whose only military credentials were titles and uniforms. But as the war dragged on, he publicized his commanders' names and permitted them to grant interviews to foreign journalists and the local press. The officers talked of peace initiatives, not battle plans. Their orders were to defend Iraqi territory, not to push into Iran.

"As a military man, I've tried to do my job and finish the war," Brigadier General Hekmat Abdel Qadr told me in 1983 during a visit to Khanaquin. "The enemy is just behind those hills and we can expect an attack at any time." But the general couldn't hide his frustration that so many military decisions were made in Saddam's office and not on the battlefield. He couldn't explain why his troops had to withdraw from Iranian territory rather than fight on. I asked him whether a military victory was possible, and he shrugged his shoulders, answering in a way that conveyed his deep sense of resignation. He asked, "How did you have to solve your war in Vietnam?"

～ A Global Tilt

As it became obvious to Saddam Hussein and his inner circle that they would not win the war, they began to blame everyone else for their predicament. They blamed the industrialized nations for continuing the war by supplying arms to Iran; they accused the various mediators of cutting economic deals with Iran while presumably making peace; they criticized the Saudis, the Kuwaitis, and the smaller Gulf states for not giving them enough money; they even lashed out at the Western press for not writing enough about the war. In the view of the world's news media, Foreign Minister Tariq Aziz once complained to a group of journalists, "we seem on a lower standard, and more importance is given to wars involving developed countries." Saddam and his men stuck to the line that the war was all Iran's fault—that Iranians were expansionist in their rhetoric and provocative in their forays into Iraq before his invasion. Thus, the official Iraqi version was that the war started on September 4, 1980, when Iranian units committed aggression against Iraqi territory. Privately, and very quietly, however, some Iraqi officials began to acknowledge that the war had been a mistake, an unfortunate diversion that derailed the state from its fast track of modernization.

Then Saddam got smart. The Iraqis mounted an extraordinary international campaign to get the world on their side, sending emissaries around the globe to speak of Iraq's historic greatness, its longing for peace, and its role as a force for stability in the region. They largely succeeded. They just couldn't get the war to end. The war became nastier as both sides sought to break the stalemate. In February 1984, Iraq launched its "war of the tankers." With its flashy new French-made Super Etendard planes and Exocet missiles,

Saddam bombed Iranian tankers and attacked Iran's main oil-loading installation at Kharg Island. But the Iraqi pilots did not want to get too close to their targets, so they dropped the missiles from high altitudes and headed for home as quickly as they could, wasting many of the expensive Exocets and even hitting some fishing boats. It was a Mirage F-1EQ plane carrying two Exocet missiles that attacked the American vessel USS *Stark* in May 1987. One missile spewed 300 pounds of flammable propellant into the sailors' sleeping area; the second ripped a 15-foot hole in the ship's side. Thirty-seven American sailors were killed in the attack.

Iraq had attacked oil installations and merchant shipping before, but the tanker campaign was different: It was massive and it was aimed at least in part at drawing in other states, particularly the West. If, for example, Iran could be provoked into closing the Strait of Hormuz—the waterway that carries about 25 percent of the world's supply of oil—the rest of the world might wake up.

Iran, meanwhile, launched a succession of "final offensives," all of them failures. Despite an American initiative to impose a global arms embargo on Iran, the ruling ayatollahs managed to get enough weapons to continue the war. Showing considerable imagination in scouring the world for weapons and spare parts, they handed out weapons wish lists to visiting foreigners and used their diplomats and exiles abroad to procure arms. They bought weapons, spare parts, and other equipment from a score of countries: Chieftain tank parts from Britain, Silkworm missiles from China, ammunition and mortars from Portugal, spare parts for American-made Hawk missiles from Italy, small boats from Japan, Katyusha rockets from Syria, chemical-warfare equipment from Czechoslovakia, tents from India, hand grenades from Brazil, uniforms from South Korea, Scud missiles from Libya, a vast array of weaponry from North Korea, even spare airplane parts from Israel.

After it was revealed that the United States violated its stated policy in an operation that traded American arms for the release of some American hostages held by Iranian-backed groups in Lebanon, Iraq gained more international support for its side.

The Gulf states had managed to confine their involvement in the war to paying Iraq to singlehandedly keep Iran at bay. But in the fall of 1986, Iran dragged Kuwait into the war. Pressured by Iraq's relentless bombing campaign against its tankers and economic targets, Iran attacked ships moving in and out of Kuwait with Chinese-made Silkworm missiles and threatened to launch an "offensive to end all offensives."

Kuwait thought up an ingenious strategy that did what the Iraqis would have liked to do: It drew the superpowers into the war. In January 1987, Kuwait asked both the Soviet Union and the United States to provide military protection for its supertankers entering and leaving the Gulf. Keeping the Soviets out of the Gulf had long been a goal of American policy in the region, and by inviting the Soviet Union into Gulf waters, the Kuwaitis in effect gave Washington no choice but to say yes.

In July 1987, the United States began what came to be known as the "reflagging" operation. Eleven Kuwaiti tankers essentially changed nationality. They were registered under the American flag and assigned American naval vessels to escort them safely through the Gulf. The reflagging operation largely succeeded in keeping Kuwait's oil flowing to its markets thanks to a convergence of factors: Iran's deteriorating military situation, a favorable military environment, and more than a bit of good luck. Unlike its experience in Vietnam, the United States did not have to initiate actions; it simply had to respond to attacks.

The United States operated on another track as well. In January 1987, it initiated a move at the United Nations for a cease-fire and a framework for negotiations. Unlike the resolutions following Iraq's 1990 invasion of Kuwait—which were passed in a matter of days, or even hours—Resolution 598 would take another six months, until July 20, to pass.

~ The War Ends

In December 1986, Iran massed hundreds of thousands of troops across from Basra and launched its last major offensive of the war. Iraq's second-largest city dominated the roads to the south, and Iran may have intended to follow its conquest by setting up a provisional Shiite government there. Because of its importance, Basra was heavily defended with flooded lakes, minefields, barbed wire, earthenworks, and fields of artillery—a massive digging-in operation that Saddam largely duplicated in Kuwait in 1990. By the time the battle was over, there were 40,000 Iranian and 10,000 Iraqi casualties. Iran finally lost its enthusiasm for the human-wave assaults in which thousands of ill-trained and ill-equipped Iranian troops stormed the border to face instant martyrdom. With American and European navies in the Gulf, Iran became increasingly isolated.

After six years of being on the defensive, Saddam allowed his military commanders more initiative on the battlefield, and they launched swift, stunning attacks of their own—starting with the Fao Peninsula. Fao, the southeastern tip of Iraq, guarded Iraq's limited but coveted access to the Persian Gulf, and when Iran seized it in 1986, Iraq was imprisoned in a landlocked cage. When the Iraqis attacked, they mounted an assault unlike any they had initiated before, combining aircraft, armor, artillery, infantry, and their newly built-up crack force, the Republican Guards, to retake the peninsula in April 1988.

By June, Iraq had put a huge tank force east of Basra and recaptured the Majnoon islands, held by Iran since 1984. The battles taught Saddam that he could emerge victorious if he was willing to take huge casualties. He could go 15 rounds against a heavyweight and as long as he was still on his feet—no matter how bloodied and bruised—he would be seen as a champion, at least in his own neighborhood.

On July 3, 1988, the United States missile cruiser *Vincennes* shot down a civilian Iranian plane, after one of its helicopters was fired on by Iranian boats. All 290 passengers were killed. Iran appeared convinced that the United States was determined to get involved in the fighting. The war that had boosted Iran's revolution for so many years was now beginning to destroy it, and Khomeini lost his stomach for battle. On July 18, he accepted the year-old Security Council resolution. "I had promised to fight to the last drop of my blood and to my last breath," Khomeini said in a stunning statement read on Tehran Radio. "Taking this decision was more deadly than taking poison. I submitted myself to God's will and drank this drink for His satisfaction." With those words, Khomeini reversed the course of his revolution. No longer was his goal permanent revolution throughout the Muslim world; it was simply the pursuit of an Islamic republic in one country.

The cease-fire took effect a month later. Iraq should have been relieved. Instead, Saddam, influenced by his Army generals and his personal lust for revenge, stepped up both the fighting and his demands. It took the personal diplomacy of Saudi Arabia's King Fahd to persuade him to stop. But the Iran-Iraq war was over. Less than a year later, Khomeini was dead.

~ Saddam Triumphant

Despite the length and brutality of the war, the Iraqi people remained surprisingly loyal to the state that Saddam had built. Just as Saddam miscalculated when he thought that Iran's population would rise up and embrace Iraq's secular regime, so did Khomeini when he thought that Iraq's majority Shiite population would revolt against Saddam. The Iraqi people viewed the Iran-Iraq war as the only way to repel the Persian invaders who threatened to install an Iranian-style Islamic republic on Iraqi land.

Saddam used the war with Iran to create the illusion that he was a heroic warrior. Military strategies such as the battle to retake the Fao Peninsula were portrayed as the result of his military genius. Having defined the war in 1980 as "Saddam's Qadisiyah," he ignored the defeats but took personal credit for the victories. The war also enabled Saddam to make himself more important than the institution of the Baath Party. He transcended the Party by presenting himself as a great historical leader in direct contact with his people, a sort of republican sheik. As he told provincial Party officials in a stunningly transparent explanation of his aims, "I wanted to get the help of the people against you. I wanted the people to make use of my words and my conduct so that nobody would come and tell them the opposite or act in a contradictory way, claiming that this is the line adopted by the Party."

Saddam also made sure that the Army he built in wartime did not become too powerful in peacetime. Mindful of the threat the military had posed to civilian regimes throughout Iraq's modern history, he did not tolerate potential competitors. No commander was allowed to emerge as too popular, and those who attracted a following did so at their own risk.

The case of Major General Maher Abdel Rashid proved the point. The fearless commander of the respected Third Corps near Basra for much of the war, he was by far the most popular war hero in the mind of the Iraqi people. Unlike most commanders, who remained anonymous throughout the war, Rashid was seen as a liberator and became known as "the Rommel of the Arabs." He will go down in Iraqi history as the man who recaptured the Fao Peninsula. He also had two other factors in his favor: He came from Tikrit and his daughter was married to Saddam's son Qusay. But Rashid fell from grace once the war was over. He tampered with the battle plan for Fao and did not allow Saddam's Republican Guards to shine on the battlefield and take the credit. Rashid's men were awarded only a few medals after they recaptured Fao, while the Republican Guards were heralded as the true heroes and given many more. At the awards ceremony, Saddam made it clear that he would tolerate no competition. "The commander should remain level-headed when he is honored, when he deals with the authorities, when he deals with money and when he is confronted by worldly temptations," he said. Were his words a warning for Rashid?

Sometime afterward, one story goes, Rashid was cheered as the hero of Fao during a visit to Basra. Later, he was summoned to Baghdad, where he was stripped of his uniform and medals and sent back to Tikrit. He then disappeared, and his daughter and Saddam's son were said to have separated.

~

At the end of the war, Saddam erected more than 90 statues along the Shatt al-Arab. The figures, representing Iraqi officers killed in the war, were dark, silent sentinels whose outstretched arms pointed across the waterway toward Iran. For nearly a mile they stood, symbols of the eternal enmity between the two countries. Yet less than two weeks after the invasion of Kuwait in 1990, Saddam suddenly offered to make peace with Iran. The man who had vowed never to stop fighting until he controlled the Shatt al-Arab offered to give up everything and go back to the principles of the 1975 border agreement that he had torn up on Iraqi television on the eve of the Iran-Iraq war. Iran's president, Ali Akbar Hashemi Rafsanjani, readily accepted the offer. Banner headlines in Tehran newspapers declared: WAR, WAR AND NOW VICTORY. Tehran's charge that Saddam was a war criminal who must be brought to justice did not seem so important for the ruling clerics. The Kuwaitis and others began to make the accusation.

~ 6 ~

Inside the Middle East Cauldron

The Iraqi leaders have great ambitions. Their ambition is to dominate all the Middle East. Saddam Hussein dreams to be the successor of Nasser. So far he has been going deliberately and successfully in that direction.
> —Yitzhak Shamir, then foreign minister of Israel, in an interview published in *The New York Times* on September 28, 1980

We Arabs can make peace among ourselves overnight but then relations between us can collapse overnight.
> —Saddam Hussein to Joseph C. Wilson IV on August 6, 1990

~ The Myth of Arab Unity

When Saddam Hussein invaded Kuwait in August 1990, Ibrahim Nafei, the editor of the largest Egyptian daily, *al-Ahram*, called the attack worse than the 1967 Arab-Israeli war. The invasion, he said, brought one of the blackest days in Arab history; it opened up "the doors of hell to the Arab nation."

Saddam's invasion exposed the myth of Arab unity. The Kuwaiti government-in-exile swiftly called for military action against Iraq from its hilltop hotel suite in Taif, Saudi Arabia. Saudi Arabia, Egypt, the smaller rich Gulf sheikdoms, Syria, and Morocco joined the United States and its allies to confront Saddam's aggression. Saddam called for the overthrow of the governments that opposed him, much as Ayatollah Khomeini had urged the overthrow of the Gulf regimes—"the palace dwellers," as he called them—more than 11 years earlier in the name of Islam.

On the other side, Jordan, the Palestine Liberation Organization, Algeria, Tunisia, and other poor Arab states, while not fully embracing Saddam's invasion, opposed the deployment of foreign troops, insisted that Saddam had legitimate grievances, and called for "an Arab solution." When Ahmad Ben Bella, the former president of Algeria, the hero of Algerian independence, returned home in December 1990, after a decade of exile in Switzerland, he gave a speech to 50,000 supporters in which he called on Algerians to volunteer to fight on the side of Saddam.

Reflecting the deep level of acrimony a month and a half after the invasion of Kuwait, Jordan's King Hussein and Prince Bandar bin Sultan, the Saudi ambassador to Washington, exchanged excoriating and uncharacteristically public accusations on American television and in the pages of America's most influential newspapers.

"While Jordan recognizes the sovereign right of Saudi Arabia to seek assistance from friendly states, and the sovereign right of the United States of America to respond to its request, we strongly feel that the presence of United States and allied forces on the land of the state, which is the custodian of the two holiest shrines of Islam, must be terminated within the shortest possible period of time, lest it result in incalculable grave consequences involving Arabs and Muslims the world over for generations to come," King Hussein warned in a letter to the U.S. Congress and the American people that he read on CNN on September 22, 1990. He added, "This is the first time that Islamic history has seen the arrival of non-Arab and non-Muslim forces on the soil of the custodian, and moreover, at a time when the United States' strategic ally, Israel, occupies the third-most holy Islamic shrine in illegally annexed Arab Jerusalem as well as Christendom's holiest sites in Jerusalem and Bethlehem, an occurrence that now inflames the deepest sensitivities of all Arabs and Muslims alike."

The letter enraged the Saudis, and Prince Bandar, a cunning, often irreverent member of the royal family, answered the king in a bitter reply in the *Washington Post* on September 26. He accused the Jordanian leader of failing to protect the holy places in Jerusalem, of depriving the Palestinian people of their rights and statehood, of misreading history, and of not appreciating the Saudi financial and military support given to his kingdom over the years. "Your Majesty," wrote Bandar, "I long had great respect and affection for your people. But I no longer can feel that you are the same man I knew."

For more than a decade, some Arab intellectuals had proclaimed the death of the idea of Arab brotherhood. The romantic pan-Arab goal of one Arab nation with a divine mission, a nation that would stretch from the Atlantic Ocean to the Gulf, based on a common language and a shared history, was a sham, they argued.

Indeed, there was little to bind an Arab nation, just as there had been little to bind the Iraqi people. Some 185 million people live in the 17 countries that make up Arab territory, which spans five time zones and 4.6 million square miles. The distances are so great that Morocco is closer to Pennsylvania than it is to Oman. Bahrain is smaller than New York City, Oman is the size of Kansas, the Sudan is more than three times as large as Texas. Egypt's population is more than double that of any other Arab country.

More than 90 percent of the population in the Arab world is Muslim. Eighty-five percent of the Muslims are Sunni, 15 percent Shiite. There is also an important Christian minority—Iraq's Tariq Aziz is a Christian, for example, and Christians account for 25 percent of Lebanon's population. Thousands of Jews are still scattered—tolerated in varying degrees—in Syria, Yemen, North Africa, and Iraq.

Cultural differences also split the Arab states. In Jordan and Lebanon, more than 70 percent of the people are literate; in Yemen, 85 percent are illiterate. In Saudi Arabia, women must be veiled in public and cannot drive cars; in Egypt, women are allowed to wear Western dress and to hold jobs in most of the professions. Saudi Arabia officially prohibits alcohol, but Westernized Saudis quietly drink scotch in the homes of diplomats, and every weekend Saudis drive across the causeway to Bahrain, where they drink themselves into a frenzy. Iraq and Egypt offer not only whiskey and strong beer, but also belly dancers and prostitutes.

No difference among Arabs is as profound as that of wealth. In 1988, Egyptians had a per capita income of $490 a year; Kuwaitis, $10,410. In recent years, the gap between haves and have-nots has widened. The Arab League resolution on August 10, 1990, to dispatch troops to Saudi Arabia following Iraq's invasion of Kuwait reflected the rich–poor split: The pro-Western, rich oil states—Saudi Arabia, Kuwait, the United Arab Emirates, Qatar, Oman, and Bahrain—were among the 12 Arab countries that voted for the resolution. Exceptions to this economic breakdown were Egypt, a leading member of the anti-Iraq coalition and heavily dependent on the United States for economic aid; Syria, whose president, Hafez al-Assad, was a longtime enemy of Saddam; plus Morocco, Lebanon, Somalia, and Djibouti. The PLO, Iraq, and Libya voted against the resolution; Algeria and Yemen abstained; Jordan, Sudan, Mauritania, and Tunisia didn't show up for the vote.

Yemenis and Egyptians resented the fact that rich Arabs turned more and more to Asian laborers, who didn't understand the language, mingled less with their hosts, and kept quiet about their grievances. "Why should they bring other nations to serve them when the Arabs are nearer, when Arabs are more entitled?" one Yemeni ambassador asked me just days before the war against Iraq broke out. He answered the question himself: "They don't want headaches."

In this vast and disparate region, even language does not always unify. The literary language of the Koran is used in documents and newspapers throughout the Arab world, and radio and television commentators speak a sort of modern standard Arabic. But colloquial Arabic does not lend itself to written form, and the dialects are so different that in North Africa, Arabs sometimes converse in French in order to be understood. A Lebanese journalist who visited Iraq for the first time found Iraqi Arabic so difficult to understand that he had to rely on an official interpreter during interviews.

The Arab world's tolerance for political freedom also varies from country to country, although pluralistic democracy is nonexistent. Iraq's totalitarian repression was well documented. But other countries also impose degrees of control on their citizens. In Saudi Arabia, for example, King Fahd is an absolute monarch who rules by decree, appointing and firing ministers, most of whom are members of his family. Open criticism of the Saudi royal family is forbidden; political parties are banned; Saudi television and radio are state owned and operated; and the press is forbidden to publish anything that might embarrass the royal family, the regime, or the religious leadership.

In Egypt, there is an elected parliament but a weak opposition and a news media that largely reflects the government line. While most of the Egyptian people lined up behind their president, Hosni Mubarak, in support of his decision to fight on the side of the American-led coalition against Iraq, dissenters were dealt with harshly. When a small band of demonstrators assembled in Cairo in February 1991 for a march on the presidential palace, authorities cracked down, breaking up the protest with nightsticks and arresting demonstrators. Even Kuwait, whose government the United States went to war to restore, limited its citizens' freedoms. When the war was over and the Sabah family restored to power, Kuwait resisted calls for political reform and democratization.

By the 1990s, it was clear that the notion of "national interest" had developed in the Middle East and that certain distinctive identities were taking shape in its various countries. The nation state—still a new, rather fragile creation—had become a fact of life in the Arab world. However artificial the national boundaries once were when they were drawn by the British and French colonizers decades earlier, they had largely survived, and a sense of loyalty to one's own country had begun to emerge.

National differences have been exacerbated by more than a score of active, but largely unsuccessful, boundary disputes in the Gulf region since the beginning of the century. Not a single country in the Middle East was immune to these hagglings—which, as the Gulf war proved, could stir deep passions. In 1949, for example, the Saudis decided to expand southward by claiming a substantial part of Abu Dhabi, a claim that was revived in 1970 when a new oil field on the Abu Dhabi side of the border was discovered by Aramco. Few of the boundaries of the seven states that make up the federation known as the United Arab Emirates have ever been determined, although they were often disputed. In one 1972 case, when the ruler of one of the emirates tried to give a date garden to the ruler of a second, the ruler of a third objected on the grounds that the water within the date garden was used by his subjects as well. The date garden covered only one-quarter of an acre, but more than 20 people were reported killed in the battle fought over it.

Yemen has laid claim to three southwestern provinces which have formed part of Saudi Arabia since a 1934 war between the two countries that the Saudis decisively won. Discoveries of new oil reserves in the late 1980s along Yemen's common border with Saudi Arabia have inflamed border tensions. The Saudis demanded sovereignty over the reserves—which were estimated at more than one billion barrels—and put increasing pressure on Yemen to renounce its claims. When Yemen refused to do so, and then abstained or voted against a number of the United Nations' resolutions against Iraq after the invasion of Kuwait, Saudi Arabia reacted by expelling Yemeni guest workers. More than 800,000 Yemenis returned home.

Saudi Arabia and Iraq have a 2,500-square-mile neutral zone between them to ensure that Bedouin tribes do not cross international boundaries during their migrations. Iran has claimed Bahrain from time to time, and in 1979 Ayatollah Khomeini called that tiny city-state "Iran's fourteenth province." The rival ruling families of Bahrain and Qatar both have claimed sovereignty over two small islands. And there were some 20 different disputes between Bahrain, Saudi Arabia, Qatar, Iran, Abu Dhabi, Oman, and the United Arab Emirates concerning oil rights under the sea.

There have been attempts to fuse Arab states, most of them unsuccessful. Egypt and Syria created the United Arab Republic in 1958, but Syria withdrew three years later. At various times, Libya announced mergers with other countries, including Algeria, Chad, Egypt, Niger, Sudan, Syria, Tunisia, and Morocco. Syria and Iraq briefly discussed a merger in the early 1960s, but, according to Patrick Seale in his authoritative book, *Asad: The Struggle for the Middle East*, "It was a hollow exercise. The talks were no more than a smokescreen hiding profound differences from view."

In 1990, North Yemen and South Yemen, which together had been the ancient domain of the Queen of Sheba, merged. The union succeeded because of a favorable confluence of history, culture, and politics. In contrast to the feudal traditions that still prevail in the Gulf sheikdoms, Yemen established a system of pluralistic politics with a multi-party system. After the merger, the new government announced plans to hold a referendum on a new constitution, with parliamentary elections to follow within two years. In the beginning of 1991, Yemen had about 25 newspapers, more than two dozen political parties, and a 139-seat Parliament that gave fair representation to the less-populated south.

Even the rich Gulf Arab states have not necessarily gotten along with each other. The Saudis and the Kuwaitis—who have oil wealth, the desert, tribal heritage, royalty, and the Gulf in common—have little tolerance for each other. The Kuwaitis have long projected an arrogance that has been irksome to the Saudis, whose strict religious establishment has curbed such behavior. For years the Saudis have complained, for example, of Kuwaiti smuggling of prohibited goods, including alcohol, cigarettes, and even people, during the annual pilgrimage to Mecca.

In the year before the invasion, the Saudis became fed up with Kuwait's overproduction of its quota stipulated by the Organization of Petroleum Exporting Countries (OPEC), and they were less than pleased when called upon to shelter the Sabah regime after Saddam Hussein had seized Kuwait. In the lobbies and corridors of the Sheraton Hotel in Taif, where the ruling Kuwaiti family took refuge, the Kuwaitis and the Saudis did not mix. When President George Bush landed in Dhahran, Saudi Arabia, for his 1990 Thanksgiving Day speech, handpicked American, Saudi, and Kuwaiti troops dressed in crisp camouflage uniforms were assembled on the ground in front of him—symbols of the international force ready to confront the Iraqis. But the Arab troops stayed strictly separate, none of them communicating with the other.

Personal enmity has exacerbated Arab disunity. Many Arab leaders hate each other, and these emotions often color their politics and prevent them from pursuing common goals. Nonetheless, before Iraq's invasion of Kuwait, feuds among Arabs were largely kept within the family and quietly resolved. "Airport diplomacy"—the embrace of two Arab enemies at an airport in a foreign capital in the presence of local and international photographers—has long been one of the linchpins of Arab peacemaking. There were also unspoken rules that were never broken. Saddam and Assad were mortal enemies who ruled over rival camps of the Baath Party. Their history has been one of vying for preeminence in Arab affairs. Although Assad supported Iran against Saddam during the eight-year Iran-Iraq war, he did not send troops to fight for the ayatollahs. Not until Saddam's invasion of Kuwait did Assad commit troops against Iraq.

Money has papered over differences between rich and poor Arab states. The rich Middle East countries have made and kept friends more by cunning, guile, and checkbook diplomacy than by shared values or history. The Saudis, who sit on the world's largest proven oil reserves—estimated in 1991 at more than 250 billion barrels—have helped underwrite the PLO and shore up the desperate economies of Syria, Jordan, and Lebanon—insurance policies to ward off terrorist attacks. Kuwait was a staunch supporter of the Palestinians, and its press was an intellectual outlet for the *intifadeh*, the Palestinian uprising that began in Israel in 1987. That support meant little when the Iraqi invasion came, and Jordan and the PLO sided with Saddam. Shortly after the invasion, PLO Chairman Yassir Arafat flew around the Arab world in his Iraqi jet looking for an Arab leader to receive him as a potential mediator in the crisis. The Saudis refused to let him land; the Abu Dhabians allowed him on the ground only for refueling—as long as he stayed aboard the plane.

Although Iraq controlled the world's second-largest oil reserves, in 1988 its people had a per capita income of only $1,950—in part because Saddam squandered his country's wealth on the war with Iran. Unlike his richer Arab brothers, Saddam did not use oil revenues to curb the radical impulses of the poorer Arab states. When he did try to buy his way to influence, it was done clumsily. Forty-eight hours before he invaded Kuwait, Saddam phoned President Mubarak of Egypt to offer $25 million to buy wheat for the Egyptian people and promised another $25 million within a month. Mubarak refused the offer.

Saddam gave 150 Mercedes automobiles to the North Yemen government at its independence celebrations in Sanaa in September 1989 and pledged $150 million in development aid at the unification of the two Yemens in May 1990. He sent Mercedes-Benzes to Jordanian cabinet ministers and Toyota Corollas to sympathetic Jordanian newspaper columnists. A Porsche and a Ferrari went to members of the Jordanian royal family. When Saddam tried to do the same with Egyptian officials and journalists, President Mubarak refused to allow the gifts to go to individuals. Some of the cars went to the government pool, others to the newspapers.

~ On the Margins

Ever since the 1950s, Iraqi leaders believed that their country was destined to be the primary actor in Arab politics. Even before the Baath Party's rise to power, Iraqi nationalism created regional ambitions in the minds of Baghdad's leaders. But Iraq was never able to resolve the basic dilemma of what came first, the Arab nation or the Iraqi state. The tension between these two goals helped explain why the rumored union between Iraq and Egypt in the 1950s never happened. Although Iraq wanted Arab unity, it feared that union with a stronger and more cohesive Egypt would force it into a subservient role. Ideology also helped keep the two countries apart. Egypt under Nasser pursued Socialist, neutralist policies while Iraq under the Hashemite monarchy remained a bastion of British influence. Ironically, after Iraq's revolution in 1958, the new regime became too pro-Soviet for Nasser's taste.

When the Baath came to power in Iraq in 1968, it struggled to realize its grand vision of a united Arab world. The Party said its goals were to eliminate the exploitation of the Arab masses and to end the backwardness of the Arab world. It offered Arab revolution, permanent revolution, in which all the regimes would be replaced with one truly popular socialist and pan-Arab nation—modeled, naturally, on the regime in Baghdad.

However, in seeking to achieve these ends, Iraq's Baath Party sabotaged itself. While other Arab regimes were joining forces and burying their ideological differences, the Iraqis attacked the very regimes they should have wooed, alienating them in the process. Instead of embracing other Arabs and finding common ground, they boasted that they were better than the rest. While Britain was preparing Bahrain, Qatar, the United Arab Emirates, and Oman for full independence in the late 1960s, for instance, Iraq antagonized those governments by supporting underground guerrilla groups opposed to pro-British regimes.

The Baath tried to appropriate the legacy of Arab leadership from the ghost of Egypt's President Nasser, whose dream of creating an Arab nation was crushed in 1967 when Israel trampled on the armies of Egypt, Jordan, and Syria in the Six-Day war. But in trying to fill the vacuum left by Nasser, the Baath needed to destroy him as a heroic figure. The Party attacked the Egyptian leader as "defeatist," and his regime as elitist, bureaucratic, and detached from the masses. "The Baathists were not in line with Nasser," Nizar Hamdoon, Iraq's deputy foreign minister, told me just days before his country went to war against the American-led coalition. "They believed that he deceived the masses. They said that he didn't reflect their sentiments and that he stole the slogans of the Baath. He was also a dictator." The Baath Party also denounced the rich Arab sheikdoms as illegitimate regimes set up by the imperialists to perpetuate their colonial influence. Members of the Saudi royal family were called Arab reactionaries, and the rival Baathists in Syria, opportunists.

Baghdad felt that the only way it could be heard was to talk tougher than the rest of the Arab capitals. Even by Arab standards, its attitude toward Israel was exceptionally hostile. Geographically distant, it was always on the margins of the Arab-Israeli dispute. Jerusalem is only 147 miles from Beirut, 135 miles from Damascus, and 43 miles from Amman, but it is 550 miles from Baghdad. Iraq never had to confront an Israeli military presence on its territory, and thus could afford to talk aggressively because it was not an active player in the most critical issue in the Arab world. "The farther you are from the center, the louder you can shout," said Sir Anthony Parsons, a former British ambassador who spent most of his career in the Middle East.

In reality, Iraq had little say in the Arab-Israeli conflict and little stake in how it was resolved. Iraq sent troops to Jordan in the 1956 Sinai war, but they returned home without fighting. In the 1967 Six-Day war, Iraq sent troops to the Jordanian-Syrian border, but they saw little combat. Two squadrons of Iraqi planes were wiped out by the afternoon of the first day of the war. By the time the Iraqi tank brigades reached their destination, they were no longer fit for battle.

Afterward, Iraq became the leader of the "rejectionists"—which broke with Egypt, Jordan, and Syria by refusing to accept Security Council Resolution 242 on the Arab-Israeli dispute because it called for a political settlement to the Palestinian problem. Iraq continued to insist that the only way to liberate Palestine was through an armed popular struggle. Throughout the

1970s and the early 1980s, Baghdad reinforced this view by offering hijackers a safe haven and giving Palestinian terrorists the same treatment it accorded heads of state.

More than three years after the Six-Day war, Iraq still had a military force of nearly 20,000 troops in Jordan, which it pledged would fight on the side of Palestinians who opposed Israel or any Arab power that threatened them. But Iraq did little to further the cause of the Palestinians. Maintaining these troops far from home was a financial drain, costing Baghdad an estimated 30 percent of its oil revenues. Iraq could ill afford to deploy a large expeditionary force so far away, especially when it faced internal problems with Kurdish rebels. During Black September, when the Jordanian Army crushed radical Palestinians attempting to topple King Hussein in the fall of 1970, the Iraqi Army did not move in to help its beleaguered brothers. It provided the Palestinians with arms, but not soldiers.

Similarly, in the October 1973 Middle East war, Iraq's active support for Syria against Israel was short-lived. The Iraqis were short of tank transporters, so many of their tanks had to travel on their own treads and never reached the battlefront. The Iraqi armored divisions that did fight against Israeli troops on the Golan Heights were badly defeated. Two weeks after the Iraqis arrived, they were on their way home, to confront the Kurds on their own border. When the war ended, other Arab countries agreed to an armistice. Not so Iraq. After the U.N. Security Council called for a cease-fire in late October, the Baath Party regime announced that it did not consider itself "a party to any resolution, procedure or measure or armistice or cease-fire agreements or negotiations or peace with Israel, now or in the future."

On January 24, 1991, in his first public comment after the start of the allied war against Iraq, Egypt's President Hosni Mubarak told his Parliament that Iraq had done nothing to help the Palestinian cause over the years. "Where has Iraq been with regard to the Palestinian issue since 1948?" he asked. "What role did Iraq play in the 1956, 1967, and 1973 wars? . . . Nothing at all."

Despite Iraq's reluctance to commit troops to the Palestinian struggle, Saddam perpetuated the myth of his commitment to Arab unity. In 1975, as deputy chairman of Iraq's ruling Revolutionary Command Council, Saddam called in a group of Iraqi ambassadors and told them, "We don't look on this piece of land here in Iraq as the ultimate limit of our struggle. It is part of a larger area and broader aims: the area of the Arab homeland and the aims of the Arab struggle." Increasingly, "Arab unity" became a rhetorical device for appealing to other Arabs to win their loyalty and enhance the grandiose vision he had for Iraq and for himself.

The Camp David accords, signed in September 1978, gave Saddam an opportunity to assert himself as the leader of the radicals. At first, Iraq waited until the other Arabs reacted. After both Saudi Arabia and Jordan condemned the agreement, Saddam moved to mobilize an Arab consensus against it. Grandstanding, he called Arab leaders to a summit meeting in Baghdad in November 1978 to condemn Egypt for signing a peace treaty with Israel, and he led a successful campaign to expel Egypt from the Arab League. But Iraq's vision of pan-Arabism reflected neither the political reality of the region nor Saddam's ambitions. The Iraqi leader was motivated less by principle than by an illusion of greatness. Increasingly, he revealed that his real goal was to build a strong Iraq first, an imperial Iraq whose glory would spill over onto the rest of the Arab nation.

Saddam articulated this new Iraq-centered view in a speech in February 1979. "The glory of the Arabs stems from the glory of Iraq," he said. "Throughout history, whenever Iraq became mighty and flourished, so did the Arab nation. This is why we are striving to make Iraq mighty, formidable, able and developed, and why we shall spare nothing to improve the welfare and to brighten the glory of Iraq." In an editorial that same year in the Party newspaper *al-Thawra*, Tariq Aziz, then the information minister, acknowledged that there had been "deficiences and mistakes" in the Party's understanding of the relationship between Iraqi and pan-Arab goals. Before 1970, Aziz wrote, Iraq had been pushed into the pan-Arab arena before achieving its nationalist goals. Now, the key to Arab unity was the success of the Baath revolution in Iraq, not the armed struggle in Palestine. Stabilizing the regime and smashing a revolt in Kurdistan had to come first.

In February 1980, Saddam unveiled an ambitious "National Charter for the Arab States" for the decade. It was a remarkable document spelling out Saddam's vision for the region. He rejected any superpower military presence in the Middle East, North Africa, and the Indian Ocean and charted a course of regional nonalignment. He demanded "the rejection of the presence of foreign armies and military forces or any foreign forces and military bases or any facilities in any form, or under any pretext or cover or for any reason whatsoever in the Arab homeland." Transgressors should be punished, he added, saying, "Any Arab regime that fails to abide by this tenet should be isolated and boycotted politically and economically." Economically, the rich Arab countries should "offer all kinds of economic aid" to the poor Arab countries to prevent their dependence on foreign powers. The document made no mention of the united Arab nation, only of individual Arab states.

In retrospect, the most interesting feature of Saddam's charter was that it prohibited one Arab state from using force against another. "All disputes that may arise among Arab states should be settled by peaceful means, and in accordance with the principles of joint national action and the supreme Arab interests," he wrote. The only exceptions were defense of one's national sovereignty, self-defense, and cases where national security was threatened. Initially, all the Gulf states except Oman expressed support for the charter. As Khomeini's promises to export Iran's revolution became louder and more frequent, the conservative Gulf regimes moved closer to Baghdad. When Saddam invaded Kuwait, he became the first Arab leader to violate the charter he himself had written for the region.

~ An Odd Embrace

Saddam Hussein had always been the odd man out in Arab politics. He never had any real friends in the Arab world. Instead, his place in the Middle East was an unsettled one, with a history of alliances based on convenience, fear, and blackmail. In a speech on July 17, 1980, the twelfth anniversary of the Baath Party takeover, Saddam openly showed his contempt for other Arabs. They were corrupt; he was pure. "The main danger threatening the Arab nation and the gravest phenomenon currently evident in Arab life is the widespread corruption in some of the Arab countries, both oil producers and others . . . ," he said. "The continuation of corruption makes the Arab nation incapable of facing the Zionist entity and standing fast against the dangers of foreign intervention."

The war with Iran took Saddam away from his primary objective—cementing Iraq's status so that he could assert his leadership over the rest of the Arab world. The rejectionist who vowed never to recognize the existence of Israel became the pragmatic statesman who needed to build good relations within the region to fight the war.

Saddam received immediate support from the Arab world when he invaded Iran in September 1980. The Gulf states found themselves confronted by an aging ayatollah who called their regimes illegitimate and vowed to throw them into the dustbin of history. Saddam's war became a way of keeping the Iranians at bay. Suspicious of Iraq, but fearful of Iran, the Gulf states were relieved at first when Iraq invaded. The war kept two unlikable regimes occupied. Soon they took Iraq's side in the war, preferring to support another Arab regime and to subscribe to the dubious assertion that Iran had started it.

The Gulf states lined up behind Baghdad, albeit with varying degrees of enthusiasm. Both the United Arab Emirates, whose population included large numbers of Shiites and Persians, and Oman, which was largely insulated from the conflict, went out of their way to maintain strong ties with Iran. Many other Arabs were unrestrained in their allegiance with Iraq. Jordan sent tanks, offered troops and supplies, and made its airfields and its palm-lined harbor of Aqaba available to Baghdad. The conservative Gulf states, particularly Saudi Arabia and Kuwait, pumped an estimated $40 billion into Iraq's war effort. Saudi Arabia allowed Iraq to build a pipeline across its territory to the Red Sea. Kuwait and Saudi Arabia increased oil production and sold the increase on Iraq's behalf.

"We had gone out of our way to help them during the war," said Sheik Ali al-Khalifa al-Sabah, Kuwait's finance minister, after Iraq invaded his country. "Not only financially, but in every other way possible. Our ports were used for their goods and arms. Our country was attacked by Iranian missiles because of our support." Sheik Ali recalled that in the middle of the Iran-Iraq war, he even went on a tour of African capitals to plead Iraq's cause. "We didn't want Iraq to collapse, and our sense of Arab brotherhood drew us," he told me. But in a sign that the bond of Arab "brotherhood" had been broken, Sheik Ali acknowledged, "We even made arguments for Iraq we knew were not completely valid. We said that Iran started the war. Hell, we knew who started the war. But we tried to cover every mistake the Iraqis made."

The Arabs were so supportive of Iraq during its war with Iran that there was no condemnation of Iraq for using chemical weapons against Iran or against Iraq's own Kurdish population. No photos of Kurdish civilian victims appeared in the Arab press. When the United States Senate voted in 1988 to impose sanctions against Iraq for using chemical weapons, the Arab League and most Arab governments and their news media—including the Kuwaiti press—condemned the action, calling the accusations a Zionist plot against Iraq. After Iraq invaded Kuwait, the Arab world revised the story of Iraq's use of chemical weapons during the Iran-Iraq war. "When it happened, the Arab countries said that the chemical-weapons charges were all fabrications by American imperialism and Zionism," said Jalal Talabani, leader of one of Iraq's two main Kurdish opposition groups. "After the invasion of Kuwait, all the newspapers in the Arab world began to publicize the chemical-weapons attacks as if they happened yesterday. They say now that they didn't know. They say that Saddam was telling them lies all along."

Syria and Libya were the only Arab countries that did not support Iraq in its war with Iran. Libya's leader, Colonel Muammar Qaddafi, said that support for Khomeini was "an Islamic duty." Syria also threw in its lot with Tehran, accusing Baghdad of trying to dominate the Gulf and of diverting attention from Israel—the real enemy. Damascus also charged Baghdad with undermining the Palestinian cause by attacking one of its chief supporters, the revolutionary regime of Khomeini. In April 1982, Syria closed its borders with Iraq and cut the pipeline that carried Iraqi oil across Syria to ports on the Mediterranean.

Ironically, the war brought improved relations with both Egypt and Israel. Egypt sold Baghdad $1.5 billion in military equipment, including 4,000 tons of munitions. Egyptian factories worked overtime to produce arms and spare parts for Iraq. Thousands of Egyptian and Sudanese "volunteers" were enlisted in the Iraqi Army, and a work force of one million Egyptians filled the jobs of Iraqis at the front, becoming the largest immigrant group in Iraq. In June 1983, Iraq's Foreign Minister Tariq Aziz visited Cairo in the first formal contact between the two countries since they broke ties over the Camp David accords, and in 1987, Iraq was among the countries leading the campaign to readmit Egypt into the Arab League. Two years later, the two countries formally reestablished diplomatic relations.

The improved relationship with Egypt was not without problems, however. In April 1989, for example, overanxious Iraqi antiaircraft gunners shot down an Egyptian trainer-attack jet over Baghdad after it strayed from its flight path; the two fliers were injured, and at least one person on the ground was killed. But the incident was hushed up. Toward the end of 1989, thousands of Egyptians working in low-paid, menial jobs in Iraq fled the country, and hundreds of Egyptian corpses were flown back to Egypt. Some of the victims were killed in incidents with unemployed Iraqi war veterans who resented their presence, others during a mysterious explosion in August 1989 at a munitions plant. Egypt kept quiet about the incidents, because, as Hosni Mubarak said later, "I didn't want to create problems for them or turn public opinion against them."

Iraq also became more flexible toward Israel during the Iran-Iraq war than did some of its Arab neighbors. Before Iraq invaded Iran in 1980, the Iraqi regime opposed any talk of a negotiated settlement with Israel. Iraq took such a hard line on Israel that it even withheld support from the mainstream PLO, providing financial and military assistance instead to the most extreme factions of Palestinians.

But by 1982, Saddam began publicly to modify his views. In August of that year, he told Congressman Stephen J. Solarz, a New York Democrat, that he believed in the "existence of an independent Palestinian state accepted by the Palestinians. . . . It is also necessary to have a state of security for the Israelis." Saddam added, "No Arab leader has now in his policies the so-called destruction of Israel or wiping it out of existence." No longer was Israel "the Zionist entity," even though it would continue to be called by that name in the news media in Iraq and many other Arab countries. In January 1983, Iraq officially threw its support behind Jordanian-Palestinian-Israeli peace negotiations, stated publicly that negotiations with Israel were acceptable, and allowed Yassir Arafat to reopen an office in Baghdad.

"Of course we don't like this reality," Tariq Aziz told me in 1983 about Israel's right to exist. "But we Arabs are a very practical people." Saddam's supporters insisted that the dramatic change reflected a true shift toward pragmatism in foreign policy. In maturing, the Iraqi leader had moderated his views, they argued. As a final testament to Iraq's more moderate stand toward the Arab-Israeli conflict, Saddam expelled the Palestinian terrorist Abu Nidal, who then set up headquarters in Damascus. A few critics in the U.S. Congress and some Israeli officials insisted it was a feint, a bid to curry favor because the war with Iran was strangling Iraq. But that view was hopelessly out of fashion.

By the second half of the 1980s, the Israeli government and scholarly community was divided into two camps. There were those Israelis, such as then Defense Minister Yitzhak Rabin, who still thought that Israel and Iran, the two non-Arab powers in the Middle East, were destined to be linked, as they had been before Iran's Islamic Revolution. Other Israelis, such as then Foreign Minister and Prime Minister Shimon Peres, argued that Iran under the ayatollahs supported terrorist groups in Lebanon whose goal was Israel's destruction. This group said that Iraq, on the other hand, had moved away from its rejectionist foreign policy and would support the more moderate views of Egypt and Jordan in the Arab-Israeli peace process. By the time the Iran-Iraq war ended, more Israelis, both inside and outside of government, were convinced that while Iraq would probably never sign a peace treaty with Israel, neither would it criticize an agreement reached with the Palestinians.

After the war with Iran was over, Iraq's victory, combined with its formidable military arsenal, began to alarm some Israelis. Iraq began to emerge as a regional power that threatened the strategic balance in the Middle East. Israeli officials tried to warn the West, particularly the United States, of their perception of the threat, including what they called Baghdad's secret crash program to build nuclear warheads for a strategic missile that was under development. But the West could not be moved. Western governments—as well as most Arab leaders—were convinced that Saddam had learned his lesson from the war with Iran and was too weak to launch a new military adventure.

~ The Arab Savior?

With the dream of Arab unity fading, the Arab world still longed for a hero. When Saddam Hussein invaded Kuwait, he played on the passions of the past and defended his aggression as the reunification of an Arab family torn apart by colonialism. He said he had done it for all "zealous Arabs who believe the Arab nation is one nation." For the Kuwaitis and the Saudis, Saddam was the most dangerous man in the world. But in streets and alleyways throughout the Middle East, there were murmurings of support for a leader who had challenged the arrogant Kuwaitis and stood up to the imperialists. For some Arabs, the United States' interest in liberating Kuwait was nothing more than a desire to guarantee its access to oil, and they viewed the willingness of the West to confront Saddam as typical exploitation of their land and people. Saddam was expressing the rage of young, semi-Westernized Tunisians and Algerians, for example, who lived near enough to Europe to know its fruits but who viewed their own countries as dependent and backward.

Saddam took action when many Arabs felt they were being passed over by history. It was not that the Arab masses admired the Iraqi regime. Rather, they were longing for change, any change. As the son of a peasant, Saddam could—more convincingly than some—argue for a more equitable distribution of wealth in a land where dirt-poor Egyptians were compelled to migrate to

Saudi Arabia or Kuwait to clean streets and toilets for their conspicuously wealthy Arab brothers. Although he had squandered many of the billions of dollars earned from Iraq's own oil reserves on the war with Iran and an extraordinary military buildup, Saddam defended his seizure of Kuwait's oil resources and financial assets as a means of restoring Arab wealth to those he called its true owners—the entire Arab people. Within days after the invasion, Jordan's King Hussein underscored the point in an interview with CBS News in which he described the Gulf crisis as "redrawing boundaries between the haves and have-nots" in the region.

In Saddam's desperate attempt to justify his seizure of Kuwait and rally Arab masses to his cause, a connection with the Palestinian-Israeli conflict seemed a natural fit. He demanded that the Gulf crisis be linked to solving all Middle East problems, including the intractable dispute over a Palestinian state and the future of the Israeli-occupied West Bank and Gaza Strip.

Months before the invasion of Kuwait, the United States had made a serious effort to bring Israel and the Palestinians into peace talks. It reversed 13 years of rigid policy to conduct a dialogue with the PLO. But the dialogue fell apart as a result of continued PLO support for terrorist attacks against Israel. By 1990, the world had largely lost interest in the *intifadeh*. When the United States and its allies used the United Nations to validate their actions against Saddam's takeover of Kuwait, Palestinians asked, What about our claims against Israel? To the extent that Saddam tried to give their cause new visibility and new urgency, the Palestinians supported him.

Understandably, that support weakened after Palestinian workers who had fled from Kuwait arrived en masse in other Arab countries, stripped of their livelihoods because of Saddam's adventurism and bursting with tales of Iraqi atrocities. Although demonstrators took to the streets in support of Saddam in Amman and other capitals, there was no sustained Arab opposition to the massive Western military buildup and the war that followed. The Arab street was smarter than that.

~ 7 ~

The Arming of Iraq

America used nuclear weapons against Japan. Israel possesses nuclear
weapons—you and the whole world know about this. Iraq, therefore,
has the right to possess the weapons which its enemy has. . . .
America, moreover, used chemical weapons against the people of
Vietnam. The USSR also used chemical weapons against the people
of Afghanistan. So talk about Iraqi use of chemical weapons is
insincere and hypocritical.

> —Saddam Hussein, in an interview with Spanish television
> on December 22, 1990

~ A Patriotic Duty

On Thanksgiving Day 1990, President George Bush stood atop a camouflaged
truck deep in the Saudi Arabian desert, less than 80 miles from the border
of occupied Kuwait. His face drawn from lack of sleep, he described his
nightmare vision of the late twentieth century: a ruthless totalitarian ruler
threatening the world with a nuclear weapon. Bush declared that unless the
United States stopped Saddam Hussein, he could possess such a weapon in
less than a year. "No one knows precisely when this dictator may acquire
atomic weapons, or exactly who they may be aimed at down the road," Bush
declared, "but we do know this for sure: He has never possessed a weapon
that he didn't use."

As Bush spoke, there was little doubt that this was a public-relations
maneuver, at least in part. First, it was a speech calculated to rally the spirits
of the hundreds of Marines standing before him. They were tired of eating
desert sand with their prefab dinners and eager to do more than wait. The
speech was also designed to provide a fresh, compelling reason for the American military expedition to the Gulf. Opinion polls taken before the Presi-

dent's trip showed that a plurality of Americans was convinced that preventing Iraq from acquiring nuclear weapons was the most persuasive argument for going to war. Finally, the speech was aimed at silencing skeptics who did not believe that American blood should be spilled to restore a desert oligarch, to defend the sanctity of international law, or to protect an ill-defined "new world order."

Bush's warning was based on a secret intelligence report that offered only slim odds that Saddam had the capacity to make a rudimentary nuclear device in such a short time, and there was substantial debate both inside and outside of government about how far the bomb program had progressed. Most of the experts believed that the only bomb that Saddam could have produced in the time Bush outlined would have been so big that it would have to be delivered by air—and so unreliable that it probably would not even explode.

Saddam had tried to develop nuclear capability before, and failed. The project was smashed by Israeli warplanes on June 7, 1981, in a raid on the Osirak nuclear reactor at Tuwaitha, where Saddam would have been able to gather the material needed to build an atomic weapon. Since then, there was overwhelming evidence that the Iraqis were conducting research into nuclear weaponry. Saddam was trying to acquire equipment from abroad that he could use to produce weapons-grade material—highly enriched uranium that would have been just as dangerous as the plutonium that Osirak would have produced. As Saddam explained in an interview with French television on July 8, 1990, getting a nuclear weapon was nothing more than his duty as a great state-builder, just as it had been for one of his few Western heroes, French President Charles de Gaulle. "Why did De Gaulle insist that France possess the nuclear bomb?" Saddam asked. "He insisted on it because the superpowers and some major powers possessed nuclear bombs. Therefore, De Gaulle, out of his patriotism, insisted that France possess the nuclear bomb."

The Iraqi leader had made the massive, steady, and calculated accumulation of arms a top priority of his state, and acquiring a nuclear weapon would have been the logical conclusion of that effort. Saddam had the largest army in the Middle East; he had produced and used poison-gas weapons and was developing biological weapons. A nuclear weapon would have brought him closer to his goal of making the Iraqi state a regional superpower and cementing his position of leadership in the world.

～ Willing Salesmen

Saddam was remarkably successful at acquiring weapons. From 1975 to 1990, Iraq bought $65 billion worth of conventional arms, more than two-thirds of them during the war against Iran, according to military analyst Anthony H. Cordesman. In the five years before Saddam invaded Kuwait, he was one of the world's largest arms buyers—by some estimates purchasing almost 10 percent of the conventional weapons sold around the world in any given year. The shadowy world of arms merchants was peculiarly attractive to the guerrilla warrior in Saddam. It was a world where stealth and cunning were crucial for success, where money was the only qualification for entry. One of the most striking aspects of Iraq's weapons-buying program—the one that most embarrassed the United States and other governments in the West— was the sophistication and long reach of Saddam's supplier pipeline. Throughout Europe and North and South America, Saddam's agents and middlemen created an elaborate network of front companies and twisted money trails, buying both from a wide variety of governments and from private sources.

According to an estimate by the *Armed Forces Journal* in October 1990, Iraq possessed 5,500 tanks, primarily from the Soviet Union and China, and 8,000 armored personnel carriers and infantry fighting vehicles from the Soviet Union, China, Czechoslovakia, France, and Brazil. Iraq received technology and assistance for a solid-fuel missile project from Argentina, Egypt, West Germany, and Britain; concentrated uranium ore from Brazil, Niger, and Portugal.

The list continued: artillery from the Soviet Union, France, Australia, South Africa, and Yugoslavia; rocket launchers from the Soviet Union and Brazil; antiaircraft missiles from the Soviet Union and France; attack helicopters from the Soviet Union, Spain, and France; an impressive fleet of jet fighters from France; at least 70 advanced Soviet MiG-23s (capable of attacking targets on the ground), 25 MiG-29s (among the best in their class at aerial dogfights), and 15 MiG-25 reconnaissance planes. United States intelligence sources reported that the Soviet Union also sold Iraq ten Su-24 bombers capable of bombing the far reaches of the Gulf.

Western governments that did not openly cooperate in Iraq's arms purchases turned a blind eye to all but the most egregious deals for the most basic of reasons: It was good business. Germany, for example, allowed chemical companies to sell whatever they pleased to Baghdad. Many of Saddam's arms purchases were made during the Iran-Iraq war, and when shady deals were exposed in the aftermath of Iraq's invasion of Kuwait, Western governments justified them as the only way to ensure that Ayatollah Khomeini would not win the war and carry his Islamic revolution beyond his borders. In the end, Saddam acquired the means to carry out his imperial ambitions from some of the very countries that later condemned him over and over in the United Nations and ultimately authorized the use of force against him.

The United States had an embargo on selling arms to either Iran or Iraq during their border war. However, between 1985 and the the start of the Gulf war, American companies, with the approval of the Department of Commerce, delivered $500 million worth of high-technology equipment to Iraq. Much of it was destined for Iraq's military-industrial complex, according to records made available by the Commerce Department in March 1991 to a congressional subcommittee investigating patterns of business dealings with Iraq. The range of American equipment bought by the Iraqis illustrated their creativity in circumventing restrictions. They obtained, for example, $2.8 million in computers for the Iraqi Atomic Energy Commission in 1987; $1.4 million in manufacturing equipment for the Iraqi Nasr State Establishment, an arm of the Defense Ministry, for jet engine repair and rocket cases in 1988; and $10,368 worth of photographic equipment useful for research into the behavior of missiles and their warheads in flight. In all, 771 licenses were approved by the Department of Commerce, with the acquiescence of other agencies, including the Pentagon.

The United States also participated in Iraq's missile programs through exports to the Saad 16 complex, an Iraqi military facility in the mountains near Mosul. The military research-and-development center was built by a number of foreign contractors based in Germany, Austria, Brazil, Egypt, and Italy, and in its dozens of laboratories, work was done on advanced technologies, including the development of missiles and warheads. American suppliers sold Iraq equipment that could be used for weapons research, including electronic instruments and computers useful for missile research, graphics, and mapping, according to Senate Foreign Relations Committee investigators. One item was especially controversial: a hybrid computer that the Pentagon believed could be used to monitor wind-tunnel tests for ballistic missiles. In a November 1986 memorandum, Pentagon officials warned that the license should be denied "because of the high likelihood of military end use and the association of the involved companies in sensitive military applications." But the Commerce Department overrode the objections and the sale went through without any conditions. The Saad 16 complex, as well as other Iraqi facilities that bought Western weapons technology, were key targets of allied bombing raids in 1991.

It was not just the blindness, complicity, or sloppiness of governments that allowed Saddam to acquire his huge arsenal. There were also individuals operating in the shadows of the international arms market, an informal army of globe-trotting private entrepreneurs with contacts in high places and access to warehouses of weapons. They included legitimate arms dealers with their own stocks, brokers who never took possession of the weapons they delivered, technical geniuses, and small-time swindlers. Most functioned not only as businessmen but also as freelance diplomats whose actions sometimes affected foreign policy. These individuals worked directly for Hussein Kamel al-Majid, Saddam's son-in-law, who, as minister of Industry and Military Industrialization, was the mastermind of much of the Iraqi weapons program.

One such dealer was Gerald Bull, the inventor of the enormous "supergun" that Saddam coveted as a way to strike Israel. Bull, a Canadian scientist-turned-arms-dealer, was building a 60-meter-long, one-meter-in-diameter gun capable of launching satellites into space or artillery shells thousands of miles into enemy territory. The Iraqis possessed a prototype of his gun, known as "Baby Babylon," and had test-fired it near Mosul, as well as an impressive arsenal of artillery weapons that he had developed. Forty-four of the 52 barrel sections for the supergun had already arrived in Iraq by the time British customs agents seized some of the remaining shipments. The project came to an abrupt end when Bull was gunned down in a Brussels suburb in March 1990, presumably by Mossad, the Israeli secret service.

Financiers also were crucial to Saddam's arms buying. Christopher P. Drogoul, manager of the Atlanta branch of Italy's Banca Nazionale del Lavoro (BNL), for example, helped Saddam Hussein obtain billions of dollars in loans from the United States. From 1983 until 1990, the Department of Agriculture's Commodity Credit Corporation (CCC) provided some $4.5 billion in loan guarantees to Iraq. The guarantees allowed Baghdad to borrow money from private banks with the assurance that if it defaulted, the United States government—in reality, the American taxpayer—would make good on the debt. Saddam turned to BNL, Italy's largest financial institution, which had considerable experience with CCC credits. In the summer of 1989, irregularities in the granting of loans were uncovered, which led to investigations by both the Agriculture and Justice departments. On March 1, 1991, a federal grand jury in Atlanta handed down a 347-count indictment charging three former officials of the BNL branch and four Iraqi officials with fraud. The loans were ostensibly for projects such as agricultural development and civil construction, but the Department of Justice suspected that Iraq diverted considerable amounts of the American funds to weapons purchases.

The money trail was extraordinarily difficult to follow. The bank lent money to companies in the United States and other countries that had contracts with Iraq to supply technology or equipment designated for an ostensibly nonmilitary purpose. XYZ Options, a small Alabama firm, for example, in 1988 received a $14 million line of credit from BNL to ship to Iraq machinery for making carbide tools, according to federal court documents cited in a report prepared in late 1990 by *Middle East Defense News* for the Simon Wiesenthal Center. American officials eventually blocked the sale of a precision grinder to Iraq on the grounds that it could have been used to make parts for nuclear weapons.

Saddam knew that if he were to become a truly great military power, he had to do more than simply buy weapons from foreign suppliers. He also had to make them. Foreign suppliers could cut off the weapons any time relations became strained, as the Soviets did from time to time, or when bills were not paid, as some Western countries did. Certain kinds of weapons—including the most advanced ballistic missiles and the materials needed for the chemical weapons that Saddam wanted—were not available legally and were therefore more difficult to obtain. Finally, making one's own weapons stimulated domestic industry, reduced unemployment, and cost less than buying foreign. Saddam needed someone he trusted to manage Iraq's indigenous weapons industry. So he chose his son-in-law, who took charge and showed an uncanny ability to find legal loopholes in the laws of Western democracies and to obtain material and equipment for weapons production.

Another method of operation in Iraq's arms-buying business was to set up front companies that worked from abroad to avoid arousing suspicion. In September 1990, the United States Customs Service quietly seized the assets of a small Ohio machine-tool distributor called Matrix Churchill, Inc., in which Iraq had purchased a major interest. The Bush administration might never have acted had Saddam not invaded Kuwait. The seizure was conducted only because of Bush's order to freeze all Iraqi assets in the United States after the invasion. In announcing the seizure, U.S. Customs Commissioner Carol B. Hallett said that her agency believed that "Iraqi interests" had purchased the company "for the specific purpose of illegally acquiring critical weapons technology."

Once again, the trail was jagged. Customs officials said that Matrix Churchill was actually a wholly owned subsidiary of Matrix Churchill Ltd. of London, a manufacturer of sophisticated lathes and grinding equipment, which was bought by an Iraqi-owned investment company in 1987. The Iraqi firm was a front for purchases of dual-use technology and of companies manufacturing sensitive weapons-related technology—and the man responsible for setting up the operation was Saddam's son-in-law. By the time the Customs Service seized Matrix Churchill's Ohio plant, Iraq had used $16 million in credits from BNL to buy from that company precision lathes and other equipment that could be used for making weapons.

~ The Paris and Moscow Connections

Iraq would never have become a regional military power had it not been for two countries outside the Arab world: the Soviet Union and France. For both countries, the arms connection helped to make Iraq their closest ally in the Gulf.

The complicated, often tortuous relationship between Moscow and Baghdad evolved after the revolution of 1958 when President Abd al-Karim Qassim overthrew the monarchy in Iraq, abandoned Britain, and embraced the Soviet Union as a weapons source. From then until the global embargo imposed after Saddam's invasion of Kuwait in 1990, Moscow served as Iraq's chief supplier of conventional arms.

The relationship was based on mutual interest more than shared ideology, and its terms were always straightforward: Iraq received arms and technology and the Soviet Union obtained influence in the Arab world and Iraqi oil, which it sold for hard currency. The connection was solidified in the 15-year Treaty of Friendship and Cooperation, which Saddam negotiated during a trip to Moscow in 1972. "In that visit, the Iraqi leader stated that his country and the Soviet Union were prompted to cooperate because they have certain common objectives—opposition to Western imperialism, Zionism and American designs for peace in the Middle East—stressing in particular the ideological grounds for cooperation . . . ," the Iraqi scholar Majid Khadduri wrote in his 1978 book, *Socialist Iraq*. "Soviet support in foreign affairs, and the cooperation between the Communist and Baath parties in domestic affairs, enabled the Baath regime to pursue an independent policy in such matters as nationalization of the oil industry, settlement of the Kurdish question and other matters."

Iraq relied on the Soviets to develop its oil industry in part because the United States and Britain were busy developing the oil resources of the competing Gulf states. Iraq also came to depend almost exclusively on the Soviets for help in building canals and dams for irrigation, manufacturing fertilizer for agriculture, and developing its small-arms industry. The Soviets helped the Baath Party develop its security apparatus using the expertise of the KGB. Among other tasks, the KGB helped reorganize Iraq's internal security, trained Iraqi security agents in the Soviet Union, and provided Iraq with sophisticated surveillance equipment.

Despite the Treaty of Friendship, the two countries were never friends. There were ideological and cultural differences, as well as the Baath's suspicion of Communists. When oil prices quadrupled and the incomes of oil-producing states soared after the Arab oil embargo of 1973, the enhanced revenues gave Iraq the freedom to buy the better-quality goods of Western Europe. Moscow ceased to be Iraq's sole supplier of military equipment, and the Soviet share of Iraq's military imports fell from 95 percent in 1972 to 63 percent in 1979. However, the increase in volume of Iraq's arms purchases more than compensated for Moscow's loss of market share.

For its part, the Baath Party, although technically committed to socialism, never made a secret of its anti-Communist sentiments. When the Soviets tried to reassert their influence in Baghdad through the Iraqi Communist Party, Saddam launched a bloody purge in 1978—a warning to the Soviets, he said, to stay out of Iraqi affairs. Saddam executed at least 21 Communist Party members and imprisoned thousands more. When the Soviets sent tanks into Afghanistan in December 1979, Iraq took a leading role among Arab countries in condemning the invasion. Between 1979 and 1980, the semi-official Iraqi press criticized Soviet activities in the Horn of Africa, particularly Moscow's support for Ethiopia against what it called "Arab" Somalia. In early 1980, Saddam angered Moscow by promising support for rebels fighting the Marxist government of South Yemen, where the Soviets had a naval base.

When the Iran-Iraq war broke out in 1980, the Soviets infuriated Saddam by cutting off all arms shipments as part of a campaign to promote a cease-fire. The shipments resumed in 1982, when Iran moved into Iraqi territory for the first time, but Saddam remained deeply suspicious of Moscow's motives, believing that Moscow eventually wanted to forge a closer relationship with Iran than with his own country.

From 1982 to 1989, the Soviet Union sold $23.5 billion worth of conventional arms to Iraq, slightly less than half of its total weapons purchases. Following the cease-fire in the Iran-Iraq war in August 1988, the Soviets delivered another $2 billion to $3 billion in arms to Baghdad, proving Moscow's willingness to continue to build Iraq's military arsenal, even in the absence of war. At the time of the invasion of Kuwait, nearly 9,000 Soviet military and civilian advisers were working in Iraq, and there were suspicions in Washington that many of them stayed behind to keep Soviet-made weapons operating in the first weeks after the global embargo was imposed.

One of the weapons the Soviets delivered to Iraq over the years was the Scud missile, a workhorse of a weapon that was modeled on a rocket used by the Nazis against London toward the end of World War II. The unwieldy, 37-foot-long ballistic missile, designed to deliver nuclear warheads over a short range, was so inaccurate that it could miss its target by more than a mile. Saddam made the missiles even less accurate by extending their range— up to 390 miles for a version he renamed the al-Hussein, up to 540 miles for one he called the al-Abbas. But inaccuracy was not important when the missiles were pointed at urban centers, and the purpose of Scud attacks was to terrify a population rather than to destroy specific targets. In the latter stages of the Iran-Iraq war, both armies had used Scuds as weapons of terror against each other's capitals during the bloody "war of the cities." Scuds were also the high-profile weapon of the 1991 Gulf war. Saddam lobbed them into Tel Aviv, Haifa, Dhahran, and Riyadh in a futile effort to draw Israel into the war, crack the allied coalition, and cause heavy civilian and military casualties.

The invasion of Kuwait brought the era of Soviet-Iraqi cooperation to an abrupt end. Moscow was suddenly confronted with the fact that Soviet-made warplanes capable of launching chemical-weapons attacks were sitting on Iraqi military bases. Moscow quickly suspended its military shipments to Baghdad, and the Soviet military attaché in Washington gave the Pentagon information, albeit limited, on the types of arms his country had sold Iraq over the years.

Two weeks after the invasion, Mikhail Gorbachev acknowledged Moscow's responsibility in building up Iraq's arsenal and expressed his willingness to break the close relationship with Baghdad. "For us to have acted otherwise would have been unacceptable, since the act of aggression was committed with the help of our weapons, which we agreed to sell to Iraq only to maintain its defense capability rather than to seize foreign territories and whole countries." Commentators in the Soviet news media complained, rather disingenuously, that despite the lengthy relationship, Iraq had not consulted the

Soviet Union about the use of Soviet-made weaponry before the invasion of Iran in 1980 and of Kuwait a decade later.

~

Moscow was not the only large supplier of arms to Iraq during these years. An increase in oil revenues following the 1973 oil embargo gave Iraq the opportunity to adopt a more pragmatic, less suspicious, approach to the West. Baghdad publicly proclaimed its policy shift in January 1974, when it grudgingly acknowledged that the West was not made up "totally of enemies and imperialists." The West could provide not only consumer goods, but also sophisticated armaments that Moscow could not. Britain was rejected because of its colonial past in Iraq; the United States was too closely allied with the Shah's Iran and Saudi Arabia. So Saddam turned to France. He found appealing the legacy of Charles de Gaulle's self-centered, independent brand of nationalism and his pro-Arab sentiments. While most of the world had condemned the first public hangings of Jews and other "Zionist spies" in Baghdad in 1969, for example, De Gaulle had dismissed the hangings as an "inexorable" outgrowth of the Arab-Israeli crisis.

Over the years, France became Iraq's chief military supplier and apologist in the West. France consistently praised Iraq as the most forward-looking Arab country, pointing to its internal stability, its progress toward state-building, its efforts to pour oil money into its infrastructure, and its success in avoiding the widespread corruption that plagued some of the rich Arab Gulf states and Iran under the Shah. French officials predicted that Iraq would some day have a television in every home, a totally literate population, and a female population dressed in Parisian designs. When the French were criticized for strengthening such a repressive state, they claimed that the relationship helped to recycle petrodollars and to ease Baghdad away from the Soviet orbit.

Shortly after Iraq nationalized the Western-owned Iraq Petroleum Company in June 1972, Saddam, who was then Iraq's vice-president, visited France with a technical delegation to conduct delicate negotiations on French participation in Iraq's oil sector. Iraq promised to safeguard French interests in the nationalized oil fields in exchange for French help in running the operations. Three years later, Saddam again traveled to Paris, this time on a technological buying spree. Jacques Chirac, then prime minister of France under President Valéry Giscard d'Estaing, was so enamored of this tough young leader that he spoke of him affectionately as a "personal friend" and invited him to his home. The two governments signed a nuclear cooperation pact under which France agreed to build the Osirak nuclear reactor outside of Baghdad and to train Iraqi scientists and technicians to run it. The following year, construction began. French leaders insisted that there were controls in place to prevent misuse of the facility.

Iraq's 1980 invasion of Iran gave France a new justification for selling advanced weaponry to Baghdad, and François Mitterrand built a lively arms-for-oil relationship with Baghdad when he became president the following year. In 1982 alone, Iraq accounted for nearly 40 percent of France's total arms exports. Over the next few years, France provided Iraq with a Third World country's dream of a military arsenal.

In 1982, Baghdad entered into an agreement with France to buy nearly $600 million worth of powerful mobile howitzers—weapons that were a cross between a cannon and a tank, capable of propelling themselves across the ground and then accurately firing an explosive projectile up to 20 miles. But French delivery was slow, and Iraq was eager to take possession of the guns as quickly as possible for use against Iran. So Saudi Arabia, which already had a number of the howitzers, handed them over to Baghdad while it waited for the order to be completed. Through much of the Iran-Iraq war, Iraq used these weapons with devastating effect against front-line Iranian troops. When the American-led coalition attacked Iraq in January 1991, the howitzers were a priority target, both because of their range and precision and because they were a highly successful method of delivering chemical weapons.

In 1983, the French loaned Iraq Super Etendard aircraft capable of firing advanced Exocet missiles, describing them as deterrent weapons that the Iraqis probably would never use. At the time, the French newspaper *Le Monde* criticized the move, saying, "France today finds itself in the detestable position of being donor to one of the protagonists of the Gulf [Iran-Iraq] war." The Iraqis not only used them; they used them extensively throughout the rest of the war against third-country ships going to and from Iranian ports.

Iraq's arms purchases helped keep much of France's troubled arms industry afloat. Iraq bought more than 130 Mirage fighter planes from Dassault, saving the French airplane manufacturer from bankruptcy. Iraq also bought Magic air-to-air missiles, Super Frelon helicopters, advanced radar systems, laser-guided bombs, 155-millimeter rapid-fire artillery cannons, two military electronics factories, even American-made inertial navigation systems for the Super Etendards that improved their accuracy. But Iraq's economic troubles after the Iran-Iraq war left France with $4.5 billion in unpaid bills. By 1989, France realized that it was best to find other Middle East allies and trading partners, and it began to focus on improving relations with Iran.

After Iraq invaded Kuwait, France contributed 10,000 troops, as well as tanks, combat aircraft, and ships to the allied coalition. Less than three weeks after the invasion, President Mitterrand condemned the Iraqi move and acknowledged in a news conference that the crisis in the Gulf had entered "a logic of war." Later, however, the French president felt the need to justify his country's arms sales to Iraq. He told France's National Assembly in a speech on September 24, 1990, that France had helped Iraq in order to help preserve "the historic balance between the Persians and the Arabs, a balance whose upset would have triggered a chain reaction."

Jacques Andreani, France's ambassador to the United States, went further than his president, saying that in selling weapons, France was fulfilling the wishes of the Gulf Arabs and the United States. "Who was asking us to do not less but more?" Andreani asked at a breakfast for journalists after the invasion of Kuwait. "The Sabahs of Kuwait, King Fahd of Saudi Arabia, and in fact, the U.S. government. So I don't think we should be guilty." Neither Mitterrand nor his ambassador mentioned the fact that France's military relationship with Iraq had begun long before the war with Iran. Nor did either of them say anything about how profitable that relationship had been.

After France joined the coalition, the Iraqis felt betrayed. Saddam told a French television interviewer a few weeks after the invasion of Kuwait that he felt "profoundly deceived" when France turned on him. In an interview with *Le Figaro*, published on August 23, 1990, Iraqi Information Minister Latif Nassif Jassim lamented the French decision to send troops to the Gulf. "What interest does it have in defending these Kuwaiti sheiks whose sole concern in life is to accumulate women and money?" he asked. "Many of these Gulf sheiks are at present gambling in the casinos of Monte Carlo. And you are going to let young soldiers die to defend such people."

~ Chemical and Biological Weapons

Throughout the Middle East, chemical weapons had long been the poor man's nuclear bomb. Israel, Egypt, Syria, Iran, and Libya—in addition to Iraq—had stockpiles of different sizes and varieties. The weapons could be delivered via artillery, ballistic missiles, projectiles, rockets, and bombs. They included mustard gas, which burned the lungs and blistered the skin; vomit gas, a more potent form of tear gas that was used for clearing enemy forces out of fortifications, buildings, and other closed areas; blood agents that killed quickly after they were absorbed through the lungs; and nerve gas, an extremely deadly agent that killed by attacking the central nervous system.

The world was slow to react to Iraq's use of chemical weapons. Between May 1981 and March 1984, Iran charged Iraq with the use of chemical weapons on 40 occasions. But Iran had little credibility in the international community, and there was a reluctance at first to believe or even to investigate the charges. The accusations piled up, most of them ignored, on the racks of press releases on the third floor of the United Nations Secretariat. At the end of 1983, Iranian diplomats at the United Nations began to distribute grisly photographs of soldiers whose faces and bodies were disfigured and swollen with sores. According to the diplomats, the soldiers were victims of Iraqi chemical weapons, and by early 1984, there was widespread agreement in the international community that Iraq was using them in the war. Despite mounting evidence of Iraq's chemical-weapons use, Foreign Minister Tariq

Aziz consistently responded to the charges with straight-faced denials or evasive statements. In 1984, when I asked him about the subject, he laughed, asking, "Have you smelled any chemical gases here?"

At first, Iraq used poison gas defensively in its own territory to prevent Iranian breakthroughs and to disrupt Iranian human-wave attacks and night attacks. As the war dragged on, the Iraqis turned the weapons on Iranian troop concentrations to weaken them before an Iraqi attack. By the end of the war, chemical weapons were used routinely as part of each battle.

The processing of chemical agents into poison-gas weapons was relatively simple. Its technology was similar to that used to produce pesticides, and in Iraq, the production of poison gas was supervised by the euphemistically named State Establishment for Pesticide Production. As early as the mid-1970s, Iraq sought foreign help in building what it said would be a pesticide plant. In reality, the plant was used to make four toxic chemicals similar in structure to nerve gas.

After some false starts, the Iraqis built a pesticide plant in the early 1980s at Samarra, northwest of Baghdad, with equipment provided by a subsidiary of a West German company named Karl Kolb. The Kolb connection illustrated just how hard it was to track the flow of chemicals to Iraq, especially when the supplier was uncooperative and its government was lax in policing such exports. Kolb defended its involvement in the Samarra project, saying that it was built to produce pesticides, not poison-gas weapons. But American intelligence officials asserted that beginning in 1984, the plant produced nerve gas that was used against Iran. By 1991, German officials conceded that it was designed specifically to make chemical weapons.

The difficulty in identifying Iraq's home-grown chemical and biological weapons facilities was dramatically illustrated during the first week of the allied bombing campaign in January 1991. Peter Arnett, a CNN correspondent who won a Pulitzer Prize for his coverage of the Vietnam war, was taken to a heavily damaged building near Baghdad that Iraqi authorities described as a factory that produced infant formula. Indeed, film footage of the plant when it had been in operation showed bottles of formula and tins of formula powder coming off the assembly line. But there was an odd touch in the film. The workers were wearing shirts with the words BABY MILK PLANT prominently displayed in English. General Colin L. Powell, chairman of the U.S. Joint Chiefs of Staff, insisted that the Iraqi facility was "a biological weapons facility. Of that we are sure, and we have taken it out."

To add to the confusion, the French contractor who built the factory in the late 1970s claimed that it was indeed constructed as an infant-formula factory. Technicians from New Zealand who visited the plant in May 1990 said they saw it canning milk powder. Arnett later said that the plant was not heavily fortified and that he remained convinced that it produced milk.

At first, Saddam had to rely on foreign sources for the chemicals needed to make weapons. He was helped by the fact that it was often difficult to distinguish military-oriented operations from more benign ones such as the manufacture of agricultural and industrial chemicals. As Western countries started to enforce trade restrictions on the so-called precursor chemicals, Saddam began to build his own production plants, which allowed him to circumvent international controls and was cheaper than importing the chemicals from abroad.

In 1990, there were reports based on a complicated web of circumstantial evidence that Iraq was seeking financing for a sophisticated petrochemical complex that could have produced chemicals to make "precursors" for mustard gas without any outside help. According to an April 1990 report in *MidEast Markets*, a London-based subsidiary of the *Financial Times*, Iraq had been searching for $2.5 billion worth of loans and credits to build the plant in Musayyib, southwest of Baghdad. The plant was to have been built around an ethylene production facility that was under construction by a New Jersey–based company called Lummus Crest. The ethylene plant would have been able to produce a substance known as ethylene oxide, a step away from thiodiglycol, a chemical agent widely used for dyes and inks. It was also the essential ingredient for making mustard gas when mixed with hydrochloric acid. *MidEast Markets* said that Iraq, which could not find financing for the project even before the invasion of Kuwait, wanted to have the plant in production by 1994. The publication added that the plant would have enabled Iraq to produce an additional 1,000 tons of mustard gas per year. Lummus Crest strongly denied the allegations.

Although estimates of the extent of Iraq's chemical-production capacity varied, most analysts agreed that in 1990 Iraq was capable of producing more than 1,000 tons of chemical agents a year, including mustard-type weapons and the nerve gases Sarin and Tabun. The list of Iraq's chemical arsenal consisted of what arms experts liked to call "short-range delivery systems"— artillery devices dropped from airplanes and a wide variety of air-to-ground rockets. Iraq was trying to develop chemical warheads to place on its extended-range Scud missiles. After the invasion of Kuwait, there was a flurry of speculation, though no hard evidence, that Baghdad might already have succeeded. The American-led coalition expected Saddam to unleash chemical weapons during the 1991 war in the Gulf, and it was protection against that possibility that substantially delayed allied readiness.

~ The Quest for a Nuclear Weapon

Saddam Hussein had begun a nuclear program in the 1970s that was centered on the construction of two nuclear reactors, Osirak (or Tammuz I) and Tammuz II. As with any nuclear program, Saddam's first task was to acquire the fissionable elements needed for the core of a bomb—enriched uranium or plutonium. At least one of these reactors, Osirak, was designed for that purpose.

Osirak was under construction at Tuwaitha, a facility ten miles southeast of Baghdad. Named after Osiris, the Egyptian god of the dead, it sat behind a gigantic earthen wall dozens of yards thick and about four stories high, overwhelming the surrounding flat farmland. It was developed not to produce nuclear-generated electric power but for research purposes, and it would have run on highly enriched uranium fuel, which could be used to build a bomb or converted into plutonium for a different type of nuclear weapon.

Saddam consistently claimed that Osirak was intended for peaceful purposes. In an interview in 1980 with *al-Watan al-Arabi*, a Paris-based Arabic magazine, Saddam said that Iraq's aim was "to possess the expertise and potential to use the atom for peaceful means in a way serving our nation." He also noted that Iraq had signed the 1968 Nuclear Non-Proliferation Treaty, which committed signatories to curb the spread of nuclear weapons and to submit to international safeguards.

But the United States, bending to Israeli pressure, expressed its concern about Osirak to France, which was building the reactor, and to Italy, which was constructing a processing plant that could be used to extract plutonium for weapons from irradiated uranium. Washington asked both European allies to stop supplying Iraq with technology and equipment for the projects. When they refused to back out of their contracts, Israel began a top-secret campaign to destroy the reactor. On April 5, 1979, three days before the reactor core was to be shipped to Iraq, an explosion damaged the device while it was still in the French nuclear-production facility at La Seyne-sur-Mer, near Toulon. The damage delayed delivery for two years. The French blamed Mossad, the Israeli secret service, for the explosion, as well as for the murder of Yahia al-Meshad, an Egyptian nuclear specialist and a key figure in Iraq's nuclear program, who was bludgeoned to death in a Paris hotel on June 14, 1980.

Nearly a year later, on June 7, 1981, American-made Israeli warplanes took less than three minutes to destroy the $250 million Osirak reactor. Iraq's nuclear program lay in ruins. King Fahd, then crown prince of Saudi Arabia, offered to finance the reconstruction of Osirak, but France refused to rebuild it. By then, Saddam had acquired some nuclear fuel; his ambition to become a nuclear power only increased. He began an all-source shopping expedition to buy components that might further his nuclear program. France, Britain, Germany, Brazil, and Pakistan all sold him equipment and material that could help produce nuclear weapons. Although a nuclear device is one of the most difficult weapons to build, Iraq's ambitions had to be taken seriously, especially since Saddam had acquired the ballistic-missile technology that might have made it possible for him to deliver an atomic weapon to Israel or other countries.

This time Saddam used a different strategy. Instead of building a nuclear reactor such as Osirak to "breed" weapons-grade material out of natural uranium, he decided to develop the ability to enrich uranium to weapons-grade, using the gas centrifuge system. The most astonishing aspect of this attempt to acquire nuclear weapons was that the West only haphazardly tried to stop it. When key shipments were discovered, they were sometimes stopped almost by accident. During an appearance before a group of businessmen in the White House in late August 1990, for example, President Bush announced that his administration had blocked the export to Iraq of some American-made furnaces that could be used for building nuclear weapons. Bush proudly told the businessmen that this had occurred even before Iraq's invasion of Kuwait. What he did not tell them was how long it took for the United States government to act against the sale, and how the furnaces almost slipped through American export controls. The episode was only one example—and by no means the most egregious—of Western bureaucratic ineptitude and lax export controls that Iraq was able to use to its benefit.

In early 1989, the Commerce Department received notice from a New Jersey company named Consarc Corporation that it had received a $10 million order from Iraq for three extremely high-temperature furnaces. The Iraqis said they needed the furnaces for research purposes and for the manufacture of prosthetic limbs for veterans of the Iran-Iraq war. On the face of it, the deal seemed benign, but Consarc wanted official guidance regarding the legality of the sale. Raymond J. Roberts, Consarc's president, informed the Commerce Department that although he had no information about Iraq's intent, the furnaces could be used as part of a nuclear-weapons program.

When Iraq's Ministry of Industry and Military Industrialization made a formal purchase offer in March 1989, Consarc once again sought the advice of the Commerce Department, offering to cancel the deal if the U.S. government objected to it. But the Commerce Department approved the sale after obtaining a written pledge from Iraq that the furnaces would be used for their stated purpose. For a time, it seemed that the sale would go through. But then the Pentagon—traditionally much less willing than Commerce to permit sales of technology that could have potential military uses—got involved, by accident.

Stephen Bryen, a former under secretary of defense for trade security, learned of the sale from a newspaper reporter, became suspicious, and contacted friends at the Pentagon. In June 1990, the Pentagon discovered that Iraq had ordered five furnaces, including two from a Scottish subsidiary of Consarc. An Iraqi company that had once been associated with weapons work was to install the furnaces at a site south of Baghdad, far from any medical facility. Concluding that the furnaces could be used to process material for nuclear weapons, missiles, and jet engines, the Pentagon asked the Customs

Service to hold up shipment of one of the furnaces that was already on a dock in Philadelphia. The move sparked a bureaucratic brushfire. The Commerce Department protested the Pentagon's meddling, arguing that there was insufficient documentation that Iraq intended to use the furnaces for weapons production. On July 12, after the *Philadelphia Inquirer* published an article about the suspension of the shipment, eight senators wrote a letter to President Bush urging him to stop the sale. The president asked his National Security Council to investigate. It recommended that the sale be blocked, and Consarc voluntarily backed out of the deal.

∼ A Weapons Empire Destroyed

In a speech to the nation on January 17, 1991, the day the Gulf war began, George Bush made clear that he intended to "knock out Saddam Hussein's nuclear bomb potential." Six days later, the president said that allied bombers had completed the task, adding that the attacks had "put Saddam out of the nuclear bomb-building business for a long time to come." Two weeks after that, General H. Norman Schwarzkopf, the allied commander, announced that the American-led coalition had attacked 31 Iraqi nuclear, biological, and chemical weapons facilities. "We have destroyed all of their nuclear reactor facilities," he said, adding that more than half of all the nuclear, chemical, and biological facilities had been "severely damaged or totally destroyed." When the cease-fire began in February 1991, Iraq's entire weapons-manufacturing system no longer existed, but Saddam still possessed a huge military establishment—at least on paper.

In his briefing on February 28, the first day of the cease-fire, however, Schwarzkopf announced that Saddam no longer posed a potential military threat. "There's not enough left at all for him to be a regional threat to the region, an offensive regional threat," the general said. "As you know, he's got a very large army, but most of the army that is left north of the Tigris and Euphrates Valley is an infantry army. . . . It's not an armor-heavy army. So it doesn't have enough left unless someone chooses to rearm them in the future."

Still, despite the mass of data and claims of success, the military briefers left questions unanswered. No one claimed to have destroyed the entire stockpile of chemical and biological weaponry that Iraq might have already produced. Nor was it known whether the allied bombing had damaged nuclear materials. On January 27, General Schwarzkopf acknowledged that Iraq's capability to manufacture nuclear weapons had been "neutralized." But senior administration officials and independent experts on nuclear proliferation said that it was impossible to determine whether Saddam had salvaged some, if not all, of some 50 pounds of weapons-grade uranium that could form for the core of a bomb. "We don't know where that fuel is today," said Leonard

S. Spector, director of the Nuclear Non-Proliferation Project of the Carnegie Endowment for International Peace at a news conference on February 11. "It has not been confirmed that the fuel was destroyed in the raids. It probably was moved beforehand, since it is so valuable, both strategically and in dollar terms, and we will really have to nail down where this material wound up. Was it, in fact, destroyed? Has it possibly been secreted someplace, and will it wind up on the black market?"

~

What was the price tag of the damage done to Saddam's Hussein's military arsenal? Quoting studies by the Congressional Research Service and the Arms Control and Disarmament Agency, military analyst Anthony H. Cordesman estimated that in the end, the war against Iraq would cost the American-led coalition $100 billion. When the economic costs to Iraq, the region, and the world were factored in, the war would cost more than ten times the amount that Saddam had spent on weapons, he said. "If Iraq serves as nothing else," wrote Cordesman in a 1991 study on arms transfers to Iraq, "it serves as a grim warning about the cost to the world of a flood of continued arms sales to nations that do not initially seem to threaten other states, but build up military capabilities that almost inevitably lead to conflicts that become regional or global in nature. . . . While Iraq is hopefully the worst-case example of the 1990s, no one can afford to underestimate how serious a threat future world arms transfers can be to peace."

~ 8 ~

A Case Study in a Failed Policy

Well, we tried the peaceful route; we tried working with him and changing [him] through contact. . . . The lesson is clear in this case that that didn't work.

> —George Bush in a news conference on February 5, 1991, when asked by a reporter if war might have been avoided if the United States had been tougher with Saddam Hussein

We committed a boner with regard to Iraq and our close friendship with Iraq.

> —Ronald Reagan, in a speech at Brigham Young University on February 15, 1991

~ The Honeymoon Begins

At 10 A.M. on November 26, 1984, two members of the American Embassy staff in Baghdad raised the Stars and Stripes over the river Tigris for the first time in more than 17 years. To mark the restoration of relations, a modest 20-minute reception was held at the nondescript concrete villa that would serve as the American Embassy chancery. The ceremony was staged without fanfare and attended by only 40 people—two midranking officials from the Iraqi Foreign Ministry, American officials assigned to Baghdad, the Belgian ambassador, a few American businessmen, and the embassy's Iraqi gardener. Theodore H. Kattouf, the acting head of the U.S. mission, proposed a toast to "U.S.–Iraqi friendship." There were no Iraqi reporters and the Americans had to hire a photographer to document the historic event.

At the White House that day, Iraqi Foreign Minister Tariq Aziz was ushered in to see President Ronald Reagan, and that night he was feted at a gala reception at the residence of the Iraqi ambassador. "If the Americans call it a honeymoon, I shouldn't discourage them," Aziz remarked afterward. "When you solve old outstanding problems in such a way, it is a success for both sides, of course." He was eager to explain how Iraq had changed, boasting about its *maturity*, which became the catchword to justify the move toward Washington. "We grew up," he said. "We matured as politicians. It's maturity, a matter of maturation. People grow up, mature. That's it."

From the day of the flag-raising in Baghdad, it became official Iraqi policy to be nice to Americans. Iraq's anti-American rhetoric evaporated. Iraqi generals and colonels began to invite American diplomats to lunch at their private clubs. Usually abrasive customs agents greeted American visitors with words of welcome. At an embassy Christmas party for American citizens living in Baghdad in 1984, a gift of cocoa-dusted cookies arrived from Saddam Hussein himself. War-weary shopkeepers, usually reluctant to express an opinion in a country where freedom of expression was forbidden, were eager to know if Washington was going to step in and stop the stalemated war with Iran.

Every day, Iran and Iraq shelled each other's positions at the border, adding new casualties. And every night, "Aloha"—a glittery American floor show of Californians dressed in little more than pom-poms and grass skirts in one of Baghdad's fanciest hotels—brought a touch of Las Vegas to the land of Sinbad and Ali Baba. At the Dijla Elementary School in Baghdad, 12-year-old students began to memorize English sentences that described the glowing new relationship. "Our friendship with America begins now and we are very pleased to get such friendly people as friends," a small, serious boy in eyeglasses explained to me shortly after relations were renewed. "The people of America love the people of Iraq because Iraq is on the side of peace." A more affable youngster was more direct: "The Russians give us our ammunitions; the Americans are our friends."

It was not destiny that drew Iraq toward America, but desperation. Had it not been for its expensive, slow-moving war with Iran, Baghdad probably would have kept Washington at arm's length. Along with a number of other Arab nations, Iraq had broken diplomatic relations with the United States after the 1967 Arab-Israeli war. While the rest of the Arab world had restored relations with the United States over the years, Iraq had stood firm, vowing never to do so until the Americans abandoned their pro-Israel policy. But by late 1984, Iraq already had squandered $35 billion on the war with Iran and there was no sign that the hostilities would end soon. Baghdad needed friends, and even allies of the enemy Israel qualified. A closer relationship with Washington gave Iraq access to loans, food, and agricultural technology; boosted its war effort; opened cooperation with American intelligence agencies; and helped burnish Saddam Hussein's vision of his country as a Middle East superpower. The United States also used its influence to press its allies to stem arms supplies to Iran and to discourage them from buying Iranian oil.

The seduction was not one-sided. America was eager to improve relations with Iraq for four reasons. First, the United States, paranoid about Iran and still smarting from the seizure of the American Embassy in Tehran in November 1979, wanted to ensure that the mullahs did not win the Iran-Iraq war, expand their revolution into Iraq, and destabilize the balance of power in the region. Second, a closer relationship with Baghdad might help woo Iraq away from Moscow, its chief arms supplier, and curb Soviet influence in the Gulf. Third, Iraq was second only to Saudi Arabia in oil reserves, and as such represented a vast, untapped market for American agriculture and industry. Finally, the United States hoped that Saddam Hussein would play a constructive role in the Arab-Israeli peace process.

The American approach was both concrete and practical. Washington would try to moderate the behavior of Iraq by rewarding it with a series of economic and political incentives. But the policy was also characterized by poor intelligence, interagency feuds, an unwillingness to chart a course contrary to Washington's Arab allies, and just plain neglect. When the Iran-Iraq war ended in 1988, the United States missed an opportunity to craft a balanced, nuanced policy that reflected the fact that Iraq had become a military threat to the region. It ignored signs that Iraq was spending extraordinary amounts of money it did not have on building a military arsenal, including a nuclear weapon, and did not make clear to Baghdad that it would not tolerate new foreign adventures. Although the United States saw Saddam's military capability, it failed to recognize that he also might intend to use it.

In addition, both the Reagan and Bush administrations were convinced that imposing sanctions on Iraq would drive it away from Washington and back to its radical pre-Iran-Iraq-war posturing. Even Iraq's use of chemical weapons, its acquisition of high-technology items that could be used to develop nuclear weapons, and its horrendous human-rights record did not alter Washington's mindset. In early 1990, when Saddam began saying and doing things that suggested expansionist designs, the Bush administration was inclined to give him the benefit of the doubt. Although the United States protested his behavior in discreet instances, there was never a comprehensive reassessment of policy.

The Americans were not alone in their thinking, and the story of America's relationship with Iraq is only one case study of a policy gone wrong. More than any other Western country, France had courted Iraq with economic investment and deliveries of expensive military equipment. Most of the other European nations had also embraced Iraq long before, and they largely continued close relationships even when Baghdad defaulted on loan payments. Even more important, key moderate Arab leaders such as Egypt's President Hosni Mubarak, Saudi Arabia's King Fahd, and Jordan's King Hussein had urged Washington to expand the relationship with Saddam and his regime and to excuse his excesses.

~ A Rocky Start

Historically, Washington and Baghdad were not close. Suspicious of Iraq's long-standing relationship with Moscow, the United States had little reason to woo Iraq. It did not border on the Soviet Union, the focal point of U.S. policy, as did Turkey and Iran. Nor did it have the large populations of Turkey, Iran, or Pakistan. Physically remote from Israel, Iraq was not a key player in the Arab-Israeli dispute. Perhaps most important, the United States was never dependent on Iraqi oil.

Attempts by Washington in the 1940s to increase its influence with Baghdad were discouraged by Britain, Iraq's principal ally until its 1958 revolution. At one point in 1944, Britain successfully blocked a United States move to boost its diplomatic representation in Iraq. Britain also managed the Iraq Petroleum Company, even though American oil companies owned 23 percent of the venture. After World War II, the Truman administration accepted the fact that the British government was the dominant Western power in Iraq, and the United States turned its attention elsewhere in the region. With the advent of the Cold War, however, the United States was eager to create regional defense alliances to contain Soviet influence, and in 1954, Secretary of State John Foster Dulles signed one of several loose bilateral regional military arrangements with Iraq. More symbol than substance, the agreement provided only 11 advisers and $9 million in assistance for the first year. But for the first time, it brought Iraq marginally into the American sphere of influence.

Dulles's diplomatic maneuvering produced another collective-security arrangement that led Iraq to sign a pact with Turkey in February 1955 and another with Britain two months later. That fall, Iran and Pakistan joined in. The intertwining alliances came to be known as the Baghdad Pact. But Egyptian President Gamal Abdel Nasser saw the pact as a threat and persuaded the United States to accept observer status rather than become a formal member. After Iraq's 1958 revolution, the relationship between Washington and Baghdad deteriorated. Distrustful of Western regimes and keen on building ties with Moscow, the new Iraqi government pulled out of the Baghdad Pact in March 1959 and canceled its bilateral military assistance agreement with the United States two months later.

The United States was so concerned about Iraq's tilt toward Moscow that in 1960 the CIA approved a special operation to "incapacitate" an Iraqi

Above: Tikrit, near where Saddam was born, as it looked in the 1950s, a painfully poor village with no running water or electricity and one paved street. (Phebe Marr)

Right: This apple tree near Qurna was proudly hailed by many Iraqis as the site of the biblical Garden of Eden. (Elaine Sciolino)

Overleaf: Saddam Hussein—president, commander-in-chief, and self-proclaimed field marshal—built his Army into the fourth-largest military machine in the world in striving to make Iraq a regional superpower. (J. Pavlovsky/SYGMA)

Above: Children, in military uniforms, at the Dijla School in Baghdad. Iraqis were taught what to think from the time they were in kindergarten. (Elaine Sciolino)

Left: In a Middle Eastern version of an Orwellian nightmare, Saddam Hussein, the watchful leader, was present even in the workplace. (Courtesy of the Ministry of Information and Culture, Baghdad)

Iranian soldiers killed in a battle in the southern marshes of Iraq in early 1984. The war dragged on for eight years, left at least 600,000 people dead and at least one million wounded, and cost the two countries as much as $1 trillion. (J. Pavlovsky/SYGMA)

The Shatt al-Arab, which divides much of Iran and Iraq and flows into the Persian Gulf. Control over the strategic waterway was one of Saddam's military objectives when he invaded Iran in September 1980. (Elaine Sciolino)

Both Iraq and Iran used chemical weapons in the Kurdish village of Halabja in March 1988, when more than 5,000 Kurds were killed. (Courtesy of the Kurdish Library)

An avowed secularist, Saddam embraced Islam in part to win the loyalty of the Shiite Muslim majority. In 1988, he made a pilgrimage to Mecca, where he kissed the Black Stone at the Grand Mosque. (SYGMA)

Saddam inaugurated the twin Victory Arches in Baghdad in 1989, riding a white horse and wearing a uniform similar to one worn by King Faisal I. The arms were modeled from casts of Saddam's own forearms and surrounded by the helmets of 5,000 Iranian war dead. (GAMMA/LIAISON)

In a move that stunned the world, Saddam invaded and occupied Kuwait in less than one day in August 1990. (Sharon Fronabarger)

An exile meets his liberator. Sheik Jaber al-Ahmad al-Sabah of Kuwait with President George Bush at the White House on September 28, 1990. (David Valdez/White House)

"Are you getting your milk, Stuart, and with cornflakes too?" Saddam asked five-year-old British hostage Stuart Lockwood on August 31, 1990. Saddam finally released the remaining Western "human shields" shortly before Christmas 1990. (Wide World Photos)

Iraqi TV Taped Broadcast

In preparation for the largest ground offensive since the invasion of Normandy, U.S. troops from the 1st Cavalry Division moved out across the Saudi Arabian desert. (Greg English, Wide World Photos)

On the night of the allied invasion in January 1991, the skies of Baghdad were lit up with antiaircraft fire. By the time Kuwait was liberated in late February, allied pilots had flown 116,000 combat sorties over Iraq. (SYGMA)

colonel believed to be "promoting Soviet-bloc political interests in Iraq," according to 1975 Senate hearings on government intelligence operations. The target was Colonel Fadhil Abbas al-Mahdawi, the brutal, pro-Soviet head of the People's Court who had been targeting pro-American Iraqis, according to Hermann F. Eilts, former ambassador to Saudi Arabia and Egypt, who spent most of his career in the Arab world. "We do not consciously seek subject's permanent removal from the scene; we also do not object should this complication develop," the CIA's Near East desk wrote in a memo that sought endorsement for the plan, which involved mailing to the colonel a monogrammed handkerchief containing an incapacitating agent. The handkerchief was never received, but the CIA testified during the course of the committee hearings that the colonel "suffered a terminal illness before a firing squad in Baghdad (an event we had nothing to do with) not long after our handkerchief proposal was considered."

When the United States and Britain recognized the newly independent state of Kuwait in 1961, Iraq, claiming sovereignty over Kuwait, threatened to break relations. Six years later, Iraq carried out its threat. In the wake of the 1967 Six-Day war, the Baghdad regime joined other Arab states in severing ties with Washington. But Iraq went further than the rest of the Arab world. The only Arab combatant in the 1948 Arab-Israeli war that did not sign an armistice with Israel in 1949, it was also the only Arab country that in 1967 banned the creation of an American Interests Section under the wing of a third country—the lowest level of diplomatic contact in the absence of formal relations.

When Iraq broke off relations in 1967, it also seized what had been the American Embassy compound. The five-acre area—which included the ambassador's residence, a chancery set in a rambling English garden, a staff apartment building, and a house for the Marine guards—was confiscated, along with the embassies of several other countries. They were all incorporated into what eventually became Saddam's headquarters. Washington was never compensated. The property, then worth about $5.5 million, dramatically appreciated in value over the years. It was one of the targets of allied bombs in 1991.

Until interests sections were opened in Baghdad and Washington in 1972, there was no official contact between the two governments. When the Baath Party came to power in 1968, it had neither the desire nor the incentive to improve relations. For its part, the United States saw Iraq as a client of Moscow, a rejectionist state committed to spreading its brand of pan-Arab revolution throughout the Middle East. Baghdad's 1972 Treaty of Friendship with the Soviet Union only enhanced that view. Meanwhile, the United States was building a security relationship with Saudi Arabia and Iran—the so-called two-pillar policy. When President Richard M. Nixon and Henry A. Kissinger, his secretary of state, visited Iran in May 1972, the United States agreed to sell the Shah any nonnuclear weaponry he asked for and to send military advisers to Tehran. That same year, Nixon and Kissinger also agreed to cooperate with Iran and with Israel to destabilize the Iraqi regime by secretly funneling weapons and money to Kurdish rebels and by infiltrating Kurdish guerrillas over the Iranian border into Iraqi Kurdistan. Nixon directed the CIA to send $16 million in aid secretly to Mullah Mustafa Barzani, the Iraqi Kurdish leader who founded the Kurdish Democratic Party in 1946, while the Shah provided much more massive assistance. The interference in Iraq's internal affairs infuriated Baghdad and fueled its suspicion of Washington.

In the aftermath of the 1973 Arab-Israeli war, the Iraqis waged an unsuccessful campaign to convince other Arab states to withdraw all Arab funds from American banks, nationalize all American businesses in the Middle East, and impose a total oil embargo against the United States and other countries that supported Israel. But Saddam did not want to be completely dependent on one foreign power. By the mid-1970s, Iraq had oil money to burn. Why should it settle for second-rate goods from Moscow and its satellite states? Despite the absence of formal diplomatic relations, American exports to Iraq gradually increased as Baghdad selectively chose to ignore the Arab boycott of companies that did business with Israel. The American Interests Section in Baghdad, under the auspices of the Belgian Embassy, kept a low profile but steadily expanded until it became larger than most Western embassies.

Politically, however, Saddam rebuffed diplomatic overtures by the Carter administration and opposed Jimmy Carter's Middle East peace initiatives, especially the 1978 Camp David accords. In December 1979, the United States made Iraq a charter member of its list of countries that supported terrorism because of Iraq's support for radical Palestinian groups. The atmosphere between the two countries was so frosty at this point that in February 1980, Saddam told official biographer Amir Iskander that Americans were "enemies of the Arab nation and enemies of Iraq. . . . So long as the United States is occupying our land through the Zionist entity, we will continue to look upon it as an enemy of the Arabs."

Despite Iraq's unyielding tone, Washington encouraged closer ties. The 1979 Iranian revolution had robbed the United States of its closest ally in the Gulf, and for the United States, Saddam was a natural counterweight to Khomeini, who had vowed to export Islamic revolution throughout the region. This view was stated by Jimmy Carter's national security adviser, Zbigniew Brzezinski, in a much-publicized April 14, 1980, interview on American television that was intended as a signal to Baghdad. "We see no fundamental incompatibility of interests between the United States and Iraq," Brzezinski said. "We feel that Iraq desires to be independent, that Iraq wishes a secure Persian Gulf, and we do not feel that American-Iraq relations need to be frozen in antagonism." When Iraq invaded Iran five months later, Saddam assumed—rightly—that the United States would do nothing to stop him.

~ The Tilt Toward Baghdad

American policy toward Iraq changed dramatically with the Iran-Iraq war. In the first years of the war, the policy in the Gulf remained narrowly focused: to protect Western access to Gulf oil by supporting friendly Arab regimes and to build up American security interests in the region. Shortly after war broke out in 1980, the United States offered to share with the Gulf Arabs military information gathered by American AWACS planes flying surveillance and early warning missions over Saudi Arabia. The only condition was that the Gulf states remain nonbelligerent. But there were no takers. An American military presence was fine as long as it remained over the horizon.

For a long time, it was not contrary to Washington's interest to see the war with Iran drag on. The United States adhered to a policy of neutrality when it came to arms shipments, refusing to sell weapons to either country. But the policy bordered on indifference. Both countries were regarded as brutal, repressive, and belligerent. Former Secretary of State Kissinger was reflecting the prevalent view in the Reagan administration when he said in the early stages of the war, that the ultimate American interest in the war was "that both sides should lose."

But early in the Reagan administration, there were rumblings about exploiting the war to move closer to Baghdad. Reagan's first secretary of state, Alexander Haig, urged the creation of a somewhat-far-fetched strategic "consensus" to counter Soviet expansionism in the Gulf. He spoke of improving relations with Iraq and of somehow bringing the Saudis and the Israelis closer together. In April 1981, Deputy Assistant Secretary of State Morris Draper met with Saadoun Hammadi, then Iraq's foreign minister, in Baghdad to probe the possibility of reestablishing diplomatic relations. The overture was rebuffed.

When Israel bombed Iraq's Osirak nuclear reactor in June 1981, Jeane Kirkpatrick, the chief American representative at the United Nations, and Hammadi worked closely to negotiate a compromise resolution at the United Nations that condemned Israel. But Baghdad remained deeply suspicious of Washington. Senior Iraqi officials implied that Washington had learned of the strike in advance, although, much to its chagrin, the Reagan administration actually knew nothing of Israel's plans.

But as the war dragged on and Iraq felt more threatened by Iran, Saddam reached out to Washington and communications between the two capitals increased. In the first concrete sign that relations were improving, the Reagan administration in March 1982 removed Iraq from the list of states supporting terrorism, opening the way for American subsidies and loan guarantees. The administration argued that Iraq had withdrawn its support for terrorism, but no one had any illusions about the real reason for the switch: helping Iraq in its war effort. The House Foreign Affairs Committee passed a resolution criticizing the action, arguing that Iraq continued to harbor Palestinian terrorists, including Abu Nidal. When Abu Nidal launched a series of terrorist attacks, including the attempted assassination of the Israeli ambassador to London, Shlomo Argov, in June 1982, the administration protested to Iraq but imposed no punishment.

That summer, when Iran crossed over into Iraqi territory for the first time, American policymakers looked even more favorably on Saddam's regime. Iraq not only had a large army, they argued; it was also a secular, Western-oriented state that had used at least some of its oil revenues to modernize the country. While there was little momentum in Washington to stop the war, an Iraqi defeat would have given Iran control over Iraq's vast oil reserves and put the conservative Gulf states in jeopardy. Finally, although Washington did not expect Baghdad to promote American policy in the Arab-Israeli conflict, it concluded that Iraq would not block any initiative that was acceptable to the Palestinians. There was little talk of Saddam Hussein's brutality and the repressive nature of his regime.

Only after considerable congressional pressure did the Reagan administration push Baghdad to expel Abu Nidal. In a press conference in late 1982, Saddam announced that Iraq no longer supported Abu Nidal's movement, either politically or financially. Soon afterward, the terrorist's offices in Baghdad were closed. It was not difficult for Iraq to make the decision. Abu Nidal had begun to freelance; the hired gun became a liability. Worse still, he had flirted with the Syrians. Later, administration officials acknowledged that there was evidence that Abu Nidal had been able to maintain a small office in Iraq, and American counterterrorism officials remained convinced that he retained ownership of a chicken farm outside of Baghdad.

After relations with Washington were restored in 1984, Baghdad's indirect involvement with terrorism remained an irritant but was not a central factor in U.S.-Iraqi relations. For example, when the Palestinian terrorist Abul Abbas took refuge in Baghdad after masterminding the hijacking of the American cruise ship *Achille Lauro* in October 1985 and Iraq refused to expel him, the United States protested but did not restore Iraq to the terrorism list. Abu Ibrahim, a sophisticated bomb maker and the inventor of the altitude-detonated bomb, lived in retirement in Iraq, but when the Americans mentioned his presence, the Iraqis expressed annoyance at what they considered unnecessary meddling. Meanwhile, Washington justified its overall policy by arguing that Iraq was no longer directly involved in acts of international terrorism. In February 1983, when Saadoun Hammadi met for the first time with Secretary of State George P. Shultz in Washington, Hammadi stressed that Iraq could be as reliable a partner as Saudi Arabia. He acknowledged that while Saudi Arabia had wealth and oil, Iraq had power, and that power would be more important in the long run. The United States should look upon its relationship with Iraq, he said, as "a long-term investment."

By that time, Ayatollah Khomeini was vowing to continue the war until Saddam was overthrown, and in 1983, when Tariq Aziz took over as foreign minister, Washington began to praise him as an Arab statesman. There was some American talk of "a new Iraq," one that had shed its rejectionist past in order to enter the community of nations. Saddam did his best to promote that image.

Members of Congress and American businessmen saw dollar signs when they looked into Aziz's eyes. Iraq was an untapped market for American wheat, agricultural products, and industrial goods. Aziz played his role beautifully. In August 1983, he again dispatched to America Ismat Kittani, one of his most senior—and charming—diplomats and a former president of the United Nations General Assembly. Kittani would never go higher. He was a Kurd, not an Arab, and a bit too Westernized for the rough-and-tumble world of Iraqi politics. In New York, he loved to invite guests for lavish dinners prepared by his Armenian chef, and he charmed ambassadors' wives with the best fox-trot on the diplomatic circuit. He was the perfect person to send to the think tanks of Washington and the editorial boards of New York. His message was straightforward: Iraq didn't start the war; Iraq did not want to continue the war. The West had to help. His lively sense of humor served him well in the corridors of the State Department and the warrens of Capitol Hill. When Reagan administration officials and congressmen told him that they were committed to ending the war and preventing an Iranian victory, Kittani told them to put their money—and their weapons—where their mouths were. "Where's the beef?" he'd ask.

Nizar Hamdoon, who became the head of Iraq's Interests Section in Washington in late 1983, and later its ambassador, was even more effective. When Hamdoon arrived, he spoke halting English and wore custom-made white French suits with black shirts. He quickly switched to narrow pinstripes, perfected his English, and set out to sell Iraq to America. He spent much of his four years in Washington on the road, giving speeches and interviews in 33 states to almost anyone who would listen. He reminded audiences that Iraq was not an unknown desert land but "the cradle of civilization." Adept at gauging American dislike for the clerical government in Tehran, he worked hard to convince both official Washington and American public opinion that Iraqis could be responsible partners. While most other Arab ambassadors hosted sedentary dinners where they invited and reinvited each other, Hamdoon invited people such as Kissinger and Katharine Graham, publisher of the *Washington Post*, to his home for working dinners—without spouses. He observed firsthand not only what they were thinking but how they related to each other; he also received free advice. It was at one of those dinners that American foreign-policy specialists helped Iraq evolve the strategy that came to be known as "the tanker war," arguing forcefully for Iraqi attacks on shipping to and from Iran in the Gulf as a way of focusing world attention on the war.

Hamdoon had an extraordinarily practical attitude toward his role. "As long as people don't see war on the evening news, it means nothing to them," he once told me. And in the final sentence of an article entitled "How to Survive in Washington"—written just before he ended his U.S. posting and returned to Baghdad in 1987—he wrote, "Everything and everyone is workable, depending on how you approach them and how much time you spend."

The Iraqi public-relations campaign helped effect an official shift in American policy. In October 1983, a secret National Security Council study concluded that the United States could not allow Baghdad to fall to Iranian invaders. The administration would not sell weapons directly to Iraq, it added, but would encourage other countries to arm and finance Iraq's war effort. In the next few months, Washington policymakers began to acknowledge in anonymous interviews that the administration had "tilted." In Baghdad, senior officials were privately delighted but publicly cautious. In an interview in February 1984, Tariq Aziz made it clear that Iraq had no illusions about the U.S. policy shift. When asked if he found it significant that Washington no longer wanted to see Iraq lose the war, he replied bluntly, "Do you think we Iraqis have suddenly become the beloved of the Americans? I don't. If Iraq lost the war, the whole area would be brought to chaos and destruction."

~ A Good Investment

In 1985, with encouragement from Iraq's embassy in Washington, Marshall Wiley, an attorney and former Foreign Service officer who had spent more than two decades in the Arab world, founded an organization known as the U.S.-Iraq Business Forum, a sort of Chamber of Commerce for American corporations that wanted to do business with Baghdad. All it took was $2,500 to $5,000 to join, depending on the corporation's size. In the next few years, Wiley was to get 70 members, including about a dozen who were on the Fortune 500 list of top companies.

The same year Wiley established his forum, the Iraqi Embassy in Washington hired Edward J. Van Kloberg and Associates—a lobbying firm in the U.S. capital that had other difficult clients, such as Romania and Czechoslovakia—to help improve Baghdad's image. Special targets included pro-Israel members of Congress and the Jewish lobby. According to a letter filed by the firm with the Foreign Agents Registration Unit of the Department of Justice, Hamdoon agreed to pay $1,000 for every interview arranged with an "American distinguished newspaper." The firm earned, for example, $1,000 for arranging a C-SPAN viewer call-in for Hamdoon and another $1,000 for a speech at the National Press Club. According to documents filed with the Justice Department, Van Kloberg also took credit for a number of newspaper articles that the firm had nothing to do with, including one under my byline in *The New York Times.*

In May 1986, the Iraqi Embassy hired Richard M. Fairbanks III, of the Washington law firm Paul, Hastings, Janofsky & Walker, "to provide analysis and counsel" about American foreign policy and "to assist in arranging and preparing for meetings with United States elected and appointed officials," according to the firm's Justice Department registration statement. For those services, Fairbanks, who had recently retired as ambassador-at-large in the Middle East, was paid $5,000 a month. Fairbanks came with both contacts and prestige. He had been the architect of Operation Staunch, the Reagan administration's initiative to prevent America's allies from selling arms to Iran, and was considered to be sympathetic to the Iraqi side. James A. Placke, a former deputy assistant secretary of state for the Middle East, was also called in on the account.

The law firm stuck with its client throughout its chemical-weapons attacks against Iranian troops and Kurdish civilians in 1988, only terminating the account in March 1990 because of Iraq's violations of American export controls on military-related equipment. "I told them that governments have to lie in what they believe to be self-interest, but that they cannot lie to their lawyers," Fairbanks recalled. Admitting that he probably should have given up the account sooner, he put the onus on the U.S. government. "I figured that if there were anything to the chemical-weapons charges, the administration would have gone along with sanctions or put Iraq back on the terrorism list," he said.

~

Economically, Iraq was a sound investment. With its enormous oil reserves and a somewhat-outdated oil and public-works infrastructure built largely by the Soviets, it was a good long-term credit risk and a virgin market for American business. Iraq became the largest importer of American rice and a lively outlet for American wheat, frozen poultry, eggs, dairy cattle, soybean meal, feed grain, corn, beans, vegetable oil, wool, sugar, tallow, and tobacco. American officials and diplomats tried to convince Iraqis to buy American, telling them that irrigation projects operating on the Colorado River would work nicely on the Euphrates, for example, and that Saudi Arabia was delighted with American water-conservation techniques for semiarid farmland.

After Iraq was removed from the State Department's list of countries supporting terrorism, it became eligible once again for loans from the government-backed Export-Import Bank. Under pressure from the Reagan administration, the bank began extending short-term loans to cash-starved Iraq for American-made spare parts and consumer goods. Iraq was also keenly interested in more than credits and rice, but the Reagan administration repeatedly told Iraq not even to ask for weapons. Iraq had more than enough arms from Moscow, Paris, and other capitals to fight Iran, and weapons sales to a country with a history of terrorism and antagonism to Israel would never receive congressional approval.

Baghdad then tried to acquire as much American-made "dual-use" technology as possible. From 1985 to 1990, American companies, with Commerce Department approval, delivered $500 million of sensitive technology to Iraq—with assurances from Baghdad that the items were to be used for nonmilitary projects. The Pentagon objected to many of the sales, arguing in some cases that Iraq's assurances were not credible. Largely because of fierce lobbying by the Commerce and State departments, the sales proceeded. American policymakers justified their actions on the ground that rejection would simply send the Iraqis to other markets for the same items. In some instances, items that could be used for military purposes did go through. In 1985, for example, the United States approved a $200 million sale of 45 Bell helicopters to Iraq, on condition they would be used only for civilian purposes. But administration officials learned later that the Iraqi Army took possession of at least some of the helicopters, painted them in military colors, and used them to ferry VIP delegations and journalists to the war front.

The strategic relationship became so close that in the latter stages of the Iran-Iraq war, the Pentagon and the CIA began to share highly sensitive satellite intelligence with Iraq to help its military pinpoint concentrations of Iranian targets, troops, and military equipment. According to Prince Bandar bin Sultan, the Saudi ambassador to Washington, American officials at first held secret meetings with Hamdoon in Bandar's house. "Then eventually they did it all directly in Baghdad," Prince Bandar recalled. "It was like an alliance. They gave the Iraqis everything they wanted." Hamdoon even met with William J. Casey, when he headed the CIA, and "the two of them became buddy-buddies," said Prince Bandar. Hamdoon remembered the meetings differently. "We were never buddy-buddy," he said of his relationship with Casey. "I met him twice, but they were political meetings, not intelligence briefings. We never met in Bandar's house. We never conducted intelligence meetings in Washington. It was all done in Baghdad."

~ Iran–Contra and the End of the War

As part of its tilt toward Iraq, the United States launched Operation Staunch, identifying arms sales by third countries and protesting to home governments when such sales went through. Many of Iran's arms suppliers found the policy irksome and simply ignored it. Then came the revelations in November 1986 that Washington itself had secretly sold sophisticated arms to Iran in an effort to free American hostages held by Iranian-backed groups in Lebanon. Some of the profits were used to fund American-backed *contra* rebels fighting the Sandinista regime in Nicaragua. The resulting scandal made it much more difficult for the Reagan administration to pressure other countries to curb their own arms sales to Tehran.

A May 1985 memorandum by Graham Fuller, the CIA national intelligence officer on the Middle East, listed a number of steps that could be taken to improve ties to Iran. The memo, which encouraged "friendly states" to sell arms to Tehran, was intended to justify the American arms sales. Another memo written that month revealed that Lieutenant Colonel Oliver North, one of the architects of Iran-*contra*, had told Iranian intermediaries that in Ronald Reagan's view, Saddam was "causing the problem" in continuing the war against Iran. North added that the administration realized that Saddam "must go," one of Iran's main demands for ending the war.

The policy was a cynical aberration from Washington's stated goals. But the revelations jolted Baghdad and rekindled Iraqi suspicions about Washington's geopolitical designs on the Gulf. Iraqi officials who had argued against restoring relations with the United States felt vindicated. The United States now had to win back Iraq's trust and convince the Arab world that it did not want Iran to win the war.

After Iran began to attack Kuwaiti oil tankers, which had been carrying much of Iraq's oil, in January 1987, Kuwait asked both Washington and Moscow to escort its tankers through the Gulf. Largely to avoid giving the Soviets a larger foothold in the Gulf, the United States agreed to the Kuwaiti request.

President Reagan said that the escort operation, known as "reflagging," was necessary to protect free navigation in Gulf waters and the flow of Gulf oil; to bring the Iran-Iraq war to an end; and to curb Iran's "hegemonistic plans for the region," including its intimidation of Kuwait. But the reflagging protected only a fraction of Gulf shipping. While the Iranian attacks on Kuwaiti shipping were a threat, in reality the policy was less a response to an objective military situation than to political perceptions, aimed at reassuring Arab states in the wake of the secret American arms sales to Iran and at countering an expanding Soviet influence in the Gulf. Even the Iraqi missile attack on the USS *Stark* on May 17, 1987, that killed 37 American crew members did not deter Washington's commitment to Iraq. The incident was handled as an unfortunate accident. Nizar Hamdoon and Richard Fairbanks were having dinner when news of the attack came. "What should we do?" Hamdoon asked his lawyer. "Apologize and offer to pay compensation," Fairbanks told him. Fairbanks jotted down some talking points for the apology, which were transmitted back to Baghdad, and an effusive apology was issued by Saddam Hussein himself within 24 hours of the attack. Iraq eventually paid $27.3 million in compensation to relatives of the Americans killed.

Washington was eager to absolve Iraq. A convoluted statement was prepared for the daily State Department briefing saying that Iran was ultimately responsible for the attack because it had escalated attacks on shipping in the Gulf. Reagan called Iran "the villain in the piece." Still, some Reagan administration officials harbor suspicions that the *Stark* incident was not an accident, but a deliberate attempt on the part of the Iraqis to drag the United States into war.

Attempts within the State Department to craft a more balanced policy toward both Iran and Iraq during the Iran-Iraq war failed utterly. In mid-1987, for example, the State Department's Policy Planning Staff argued for a step-by-step approach to a cease-fire that would involve pressuring Iraq to end the tanker war as a first move toward lessening the conflict. These officials calculated that an end to the tanker war could lead to an end to the ground and air fighting, especially during the heat of summer. Such a strategy could provide Iran with a face-saving way of reducing combat without forcing it publicly to abandon its goal of overthrowing Saddam. But Middle East regional specialists opposed such an approach, arguing that any partial cease-fire would benefit Iran by giving it time to regroup. The policy initiative never got off the ground.

After a cease-fire was finally declared in the Gulf war in August 1988, there was another campaign by the Policy Planning Staff for a more balanced regional policy. The effort, drafted by Zalmay Khalilzad in a memorandum to George Shultz, concluded that now with the war over, the time had come to strengthen Iran. The collapse of Iran's armed forces was worrisome, because there was no military force in the region to counter Iraq. The memo argued that the United States should encourage the emergence of a balance of power between the two countries. It also envisioned a formal end to Operation Staunch, arguing that the campaign had lost its relevance since its main objective—the end of the Iran-Iraq war—had been achieved. The memo recommended lifting the total trade embargo against Iran, except for sanctions resulting from Iran's official status as a country that supported terrorism—a designation based on its influence over groups holding American and other Western hostages in Lebanon.

All the plan needed was Shultz's imprimatur. But the plan was leaked to the news media, and Shultz, who knew nothing about it, called an urgent meeting and quickly vetoed it. Concerned that such a policy shift would be widely criticized as moving the administration closer to Iran—a perception he was eager to avoid just six weeks before the presidential election—he decided to stay the course. There were unanswered questions about Bush's role in the Iran-*contra* scandal, and the White House wanted to avoid any sign that it was tilting back toward Iran. It was a simple conflict between geopolitics and domestic politics, and domestic politics won.

~ Sanctions Rejected

When Iraq was using chemical weapons against Iranian combatants, there was little outcry, either in Congress or among the American people. It was only when Iraq used chemical weapons on its own citizens after the cease-fire with Iran that the country took notice.

Then Iraq turned its chemical arsenal against Kurdish civilians in late August and early September 1988; George Shultz was sickened. In a meeting with Saadoun Hammadi, by then a deputy prime minister, in Washington on September 8, Shultz publicly condemned Iraq's actions, calling them "unjustified and abhorrent." His spokesman, Charles E. Redman, made an unusually harsh announcement from the State Department podium that the United States would explore ways to influence Iraq to end these practices, "which are unacceptable to the civilized world."

But the moment of outrage passed. Except for verbal outbursts, the State Department did nothing. Its Middle East specialists urged Shultz to take a less emotional position, and they prevailed. Shultz approved a recommendation that the administration oppose a move in Congress to impose sanctions against Iraq for its use of chemical weapons against the Kurds. As it turned out, the State Department had nothing to worry about. Beginning in early September 1988, in response to the chemical-weapons attacks on the Kurds, the odd couple of Senators Claiborne Pell, a liberal Democrat from Rhode Island, and Jesse Helms, a conservative Republican from North Carolina, had worked together to pass comprehensive financial and trade sanctions against Iraq as well as severe restrictions on the transfer of technology. Pell fought a heroic battle against the administration, the grain companies, and other lawmakers, including Dan Rostenkowski, chairman of the House Ways and Means Committee and an Illinois Democrat. Although the bills and amendments passed the Senate overwhelmingly, they died in the House.

"The special interests got into the act," Pell said in a speech on October 21, 1988. "Agricultural interests objected to the suspension of taxpayer subsidies for agricultural exports to Iraq; the oil industry protested the oil boycott—although alternative supplies are readily available. Even a chemical company called to inquire how its products might be impacted."

The sanctions battle was a dramatic illustration of how profits overcame principle, and of the shortsightedness of American policy, particularly when the cease-fire in the Iran-Iraq war removed one of the main rationales for the tilt toward Baghdad. But the cease-fire came in the final months of the Reagan administration, and it was not the time for a sweeping foreign-policy review. The administration left office without ever addressing Iraq's use of chemical weapons against Iranians and against its own civilians.

~ Automatic Pilot

When George Bush assumed the U.S. presidency in January 1989, the new administration did not see any compelling reason to change American policy toward Iraq. Iraq had emerged as the winner of the war, but the conventional wisdom among Bush and his policymakers was that both Iran and Iraq were so exhausted from the conflict that they would reconstruct their infrastructures, rebuild their economies, and increase oil production—not seek outside adventures. The discussions that were held inside the administration dealt with ways to build on what had been an improving relationship with Baghdad. The State Department, for example, pointed to Saddam's easing of restrictions on foreign travel and his plans to draft a new constitution as evidence that the regime was becoming more confident and therefore more flexible. While there were problematic elements in Iraq's behavior—particularly Saddam's relentless military buildup—the administration pursued what Bush acknowledged after the invasion of Kuwait was a flawed policy toward Iraq, a policy built on the premise that the best way to handle Saddam Hussein and moderate his behavior was by building bridges to Baghdad.

Besides, the Gulf region was never a high priority for the new administration. Secretary Baker decided early on to focus on a few key issues that he considered important: sweeping changes in the Soviet Union and Eastern Europe, German reunification, and, by necessity, the Arab-Israeli conflict. He left second-tier problems to subordinates, which meant that they were dealt with hardly at all. Unlike the open, consultative style of George Shultz, Baker was paranoid about leaks. He kept decision-making among a small group of politically appointed aides in his suite of offices on the seventh floor and cut out most of the State Department bureaucracy. Middle East specialists, particularly the "Arabists" who had spent their careers in the region, had only marginal influence in the department. Most of the Iran specialists inside the bureaucracy had gone. With the absence of diplomatic relations with Tehran for more than a decade, Iran was both an unpopular portfolio and a career graveyard. There were no senior figures inside the administration to look at the entire region and how it had changed in the aftermath of the Iran-Iraq war, or to argue the case for improving relations with Iran. The only hot Middle East policy was the Arab-Israeli conflict, and that portfolio belonged to Dennis B. Ross, the head of the Policy Planning Staff. The policy became so identified with Ross that foreign diplomats came to call it "the Dennis Ross story."

It was not until the fall of 1989, nine months after the Bush administration took office, that a high-level policy review of the Gulf was completed.

National Security Directive 26, the administration's policy doctrine for the region, contained little that was new, despite mounting evidence that Iraq had embarked on a course different from what the administration had assumed. "Access to the Gulf and the key friendly states in the area is vital to U.S. national security," said the secret directive that was signed by Bush in October of that year.

The directive, based on an outdated analysis, assumed that it was Tehran and Moscow, not Baghdad, that potentially threatened security in the region and American interests in the Gulf. "The United States remains committed to defend its vital interests in the region, if necessary and appropriate through the use of U.S. military force, against the Soviet Union or any other regional power with interests inimical to our own," the directive added. No one in the administration envisioned that the "other regional power" would be Iraq. Although the directive acknowledged that the two countries had important differences—over Iraq's continuing military buildup, its interference in Lebanon, and its appalling human-rights record—its conclusion was that the United States should try to moderate Saddam's behavior by rewarding him, not isolating him. To that end, the document recommended that the administration encourage American companies to become more involved in Iraq's postwar reconstruction, particularly its oil industry, despite Iraq's economic problems. In a telling indication of the paucity of high-level concern in the administration about Iraq, from the time the directive was signed until the invasion of Kuwait, the National Security Council never met even once to discuss Iraq.

Just after the directive was signed, the Iraqis made it clear that there were problems in the relationship. In a meeting between Tariq Aziz and Baker in Washington on October 6, 1989, Aziz accused the Bush administration of hostility toward Baghdad that he said he found "disturbing." According to senior officials in Baghdad, he cited unspecific "reports" that American agencies were working to destabilize Iraq, as well as allegations of bribery concerning loans to Iraq. Aziz asked Baker to approve new credit guarantees for commodities' purchases and offered to cooperate with any investigation. Baker denied that the United States was trying to harm Saddam's regime, and in November, the administration extended $500 million in credit guarantees to Baghdad. Despite a move in Congress to halt U.S. Export-Import Bank financing for Iraq, in January 1990, Bush, on the recommendation of the State Department, signed a presidential order stating that it was in the "national interest" to expand trade with Saddam's regime.

By the spring of 1990, the signs of Saddam's confrontational—in some cases irrational—behavior were unmistakable: a call for removal of the American military presence from the Gulf; the execution on spying charges of an Iranian-born journalist with British residency; evidence that Iraq was developing a "supergun"; the acquisition of switches for nuclear devices; a threat by Saddam to burn half of Israel. Some U.S. lawmakers again complained that it was unwise to carry on a policy of détente with Iraq, and they repeated their calls for sanctions.

During this period, the Bush administration did take a number of punitive measures against Iraq, but they were haphazard, uncoordinated and did not alter the oft-stated policy, which was to improve relations with Iraq by moderating Saddam's behavior. The United States confiscated shipments of supergun components and protested the execution of the journalist. The Department of Agriculture did not go forward with a second $500 million installment in Iraq's credit guarantees for agricultural purchases for 1990—not because of Iraqi policies but because of the investigation into possible kickbacks and fraud charges involving the lending bank.

The only people in the administration who seemed to be concerned about Iraqi behavior were stuck at middle levels of the bureaucracy, and their voices were not heard. A paper called "Containing Iraq," written in the State Department's Policy Planning Staff, whose regional experts had long urged a more balanced approach to both Iran and Iraq, argued that Iraq, not Iran, was the primary military threat to the region and must be contained. The idea went nowhere. Even as other officials in the administration and some lawmakers grew uneasy with Saddam's behavior, they saw him as a potential threat to Israel, not to one of his Arab neighbors.

~ Human Rights

Despite the sudden discovery of Iraq's grotesque human-rights record by the Bush administration following the invasion of Kuwait, human rights was generally the lowest priority of U.S. foreign policymaking. Human rights was an irritant, a necessary issue that surfaced once a year when the State Department made public its thick, country-by-country survey as mandated by Congress. Or it became a device that successive administrations used when bilateral relationships deteriorated so much that there was no risk in raising subjects such as executions and torture. In summits and bilateral meetings, human rights usually was the last item on the agenda, even below nuclear proliferation and drug trafficking. Iraq's record was clear: "abysmal," according to the 1989 and 1990 State Department global reports on human rights. But except for the bureaucrats in the Bureau of Human Rights in the State Department, not many people in the administration ever seemed to notice.

So when the Voice of America (VOA) broadcast an editorial on February 15, 1990, entitled "No More Secret Police," it seemed innocuous enough. The editorial hailed the overthrow of repressive regimes in Eastern Europe and urged the democratization of similar regimes in other areas of the world. "The secret police are still widely present in countries like China, North

Korea, Iran, Iraq, Syria, Libya, Cuba, and Albania," it said. Thanks to the democratic revolutions of 1989, it continued, "we believe that the 1990s should belong not to the dictators and secret police, but to the people."

For Saddam Hussein, the editorial was tantamount to war. The classified cables that April C. Glaspie, the American ambassador to Iraq, sent to Secretary Baker, obtained by *New York Times* columnist William Safire under the Freedom of Information Act, testify to the State Department's eagerness to placate Saddam. Nizar Hamdoon, who had become deputy foreign minister, summoned Glaspie to protest a "flagrant violation of the internal affairs of Iraq and the direct official instigation against the legitimate authority," according to her cable after the meeting. In a subsequent cable, she explained that the Iraqis saw the editorial as administration-sanctioned "mudslinging with the intent to incite revolution."

Instead of telling Glaspie to use the incident as a vehicle to raise human-rights concerns with Baghdad, the State Department told her to apologize. On instructions from Washington, she wrote Tariq Aziz, "It is absolutely not United States policy to question the legitimacy of the Government of Iraq nor to interfere in any way in the domestic concerns of the Iraqi people and Government. My Government regrets that the wording of the editorial left it open to incorrect interpretation." The American envoy said later that she was personally outraged by the editorial, telling colleagues that it was a "disgrace, an incitement by a wholly owned government organ to populations of a number of countries to revolt." After the editorial was aired, all VOA editorials dealing with Iraq were subject to State Department review.

Several weeks later, on April 12, 1990, Saddam raised the issue of the editorial with a delegation of five senators visiting Baghdad. The transcript of the meeting, released by the Iraqi Embassy in Washington and which the senators have said is essentially correct, was an illustration of congressional obsequiousness. Senator Robert J. Dole, Republican of Kansas and Senate Minority Leader, assured Saddam—incorrectly—that the Voice of America commentator responsible for the editorial had been fired. Saddam insisted that "an all-out campaign is being waged against us in America and the countries of Europe" to provide Israel with a "psychological, propaganda, and political cover" to attack Iraq. Dole denied the charge, saying, "Please allow me to say that only twelve hours earlier President Bush had assured me that he wanted better relations, and that the U.S. government wants better relations with Iraq." Senator Alan K. Simpson, the Wyoming Republican, went a step further, advising the Iraqi leader to improve his public image by cultivating the media. "I believe that your problems lie with the Western media, and not with the U.S. Government. As long as you are isolated from the media, the press—and it is a haughty and pampered press—they all consider themselves political geniuses. That is, the journalists do. They are very cynical. What I advise is that you invite them to come here and see for themselves." At one point Saddam agreed, telling the senators, "We know the media, just as you know it. Like a spoiled child, if you give it a piece of candy when it cries, it will continue to cry and demand more."

Afterward, Dole tried to explain Saddam to the media. He told a news conference in Jerusalem that the Iraqi leader believed there was a conspiracy behind media reports about his government's alleged plans to develop nuclear and biological weapons. "He indicated to us that he feels very strongly that there's an American-British-Israeli campaign to tarnish the image of his government and his country," Dole said.

A group of senior officials in the administration, meanwhile, met for the first time to consider ways to punish Saddam. On April 16, 1990, Under Secretary of State Robert M. Kimmitt presented a plan of action at a regularly scheduled interagency "deputies" meeting at the White House. The plan laid out a menu of punitive economic measures, including an end to recently restored credits for Iraq from the Export-Import Bank, the cancellation of agricultural credits, and the implementation of measures to prevent Iraq from importing goods that could be used for military purposes. The administration had already imposed some of the restrictions, but a comprehensive plan would have sent a clear public message to Saddam that the United States would no longer conduct business as usual with his regime. The Commerce and Agriculture departments opposed the plan, arguing that it would do nothing except hurt American businessmen and farmers. To defuse the disagreement, Deputy National Security Adviser Robert M. Gates called for further study. But the State Department was caught up with the rush of events in Eastern Europe and the Soviet Union. The plan fell through the cracks and was never pursued. For Commerce and Agriculture, it was a matter of deliberate obfuscation; for the State Department, it was benign neglect.

On June 15, 1990, the State Department sent John H. Kelly, assistant secretary of state for Near Eastern and South Asian Affairs, to Capitol Hill to oppose congressional moves to impose sanctions on Iraq because of its human-rights record. His testimony came after a long and bloody memo war inside the State Department between his bureau and the Bureau of Human Rights, which favored sanctions. Under the existing human-rights statutes, sanctions were to be imposed on any country that was "engaging in a consistent pattern of gross violations of internationally recognized human rights." The Human Rights bureaucrats argued that Iraq fit the definition, branded Iraq a consistent violator of human rights, and informed Congress that the administration would support a resolution imposing sanctions.

Both Bush and Baker opposed any move by Congress to take the initiative on sanctions. Bush in particular reacted viscerally to any attempt by Congress to legislate foreign policy, and both the White House and the Middle East specialists in the State Department argued that sanctions would limit the administration's flexibility to modify Iraq's behavior. Richard Schifter, assistant secretary of state for human rights, protested the decision. He argued—unsuccessfully—in conversations with Baker's aides that there was a point when human-rights considerations could no longer take a back seat to geopolitical and strategic interests. Schifter lost.

Joshua R. Gilder, one of Schifter's deputies, was put in the uncomfortable position of having to acknowledge before Congress that Iraq's record was atrocious, but not atrocious enough to fit the legal definition requiring sanctions. In a May 3, 1990, letter to Dante Fascell, chairman of the House Foreign Affairs Committee, Janet G. Mullins, assistant secretary of state for legislative affairs, explained that the administration could have supported the House resolution only if it omitted the phrase that Iraq was "engaging in a consistent pattern of" human-rights abuses.

~ A Policy of Accommodation

April C. Glaspie was everything a career Foreign Service officer should be: a tough, loyal public servant who never broke the rules. As the United States ambassador to Iraq on the eve of the invasion of Kuwait, she faithfully executed a difficult brief handed to her by the president and the secretary of state.

A Phi Beta Kappa graduate of Mills College in California in history and government, with a master's degree from Johns Hopkins University School for Advanced International Studies, Glaspie battled the Foreign Service bureaucracy to study Arabic when women were not encouraged to make their careers in the Arab world. She was so intense that she would weed the garden of her Georgetown townhouse at night by flashlight, so intrepid that she often made the eight-hour trip from Baghdad to Kuwait City alone to buy groceries, leaving her chauffeur behind. She developed her love for the Arab world from her British mother's family, which served for years in British-mandate Palestine with the British Army. Unmarried, fluent in French and Arabic, a workaholic, the 48-year-old diplomat had held posts in Amman, Kuwait City, Stockholm, Beirut, Cairo, London, New York, Tunis, and Damascus before becoming envoy to Baghdad in March 1988, the first woman to become a U.S. ambassador in the Arab world.

Glaspie was a victim both of circumstance and of American policy. On the morning of Iraq's invasion of Kuwait, she, like the rest of the world, was caught off guard. In London overnight before heading to Washington for a week of consultations, she first learned of the invasion when she switched on the television set in her hotel room. "I wish I had been the only one in the world who was right," she told me a month after the invasion, blaming herself for not predicting Saddam's intentions. "Obviously, I didn't think—and nobody else did—that the Iraqis were going to take all of Kuwait. Every Kuwaiti and every Saudi, every analyst in the Western world, was wrong too.

That does not excuse me. But people who now claim that all was clear were not heard from at the time." The statement was intended to show that no one—not even the Arabs—had understood Saddam. But the suggestion that she and others believed in advance that he might seize some of Kuwait came to symbolize the global appeasement of Saddam.

Glaspie's analysis was virtually the same as that of most other officials in the Bush administration. The conventional wisdom was that Iraq's massive troop buildup was a bluff. There was about a 20 percent chance that Saddam would invade, most analysts thought. If he did, they calculated that it would be only a limited invasion in which Iraq seized strategic bits of territory in order to gain concessions. The United States could probably have lived with that scenario.

In the weeks before Iraq's seizure of Kuwait, the Bush administration, on the advice of Arab leaders, gave Saddam little reason to fear a forceful American response if his troops crossed the border. Largely for budgetary reasons—and against the advice of the State Department—the Pentagon had reduced the American naval presence in the Gulf to its lowest level in a decade. The message, articulated publicly by senior policymakers in Washington and delivered privately to Saddam Hussein by Ambassador Glaspie was this: The United States was concerned about Iraq's military buildup, and believed that Iraq's dispute with Kuwait should be resolved peacefully, but did not intend to get involved in what it perceived as a no-win border dispute between two Arab countries. There was a second part to the message as well: Despite the concerns, Washington wanted better relations with Baghdad. So the administration issued vague warnings about American commitments to protecting its vital interests in the region, but never a blunt, clear warning that the United States would not allow Iraq to invade and seize Kuwait.

For several days in the second half of July 1990, the administration—either in Washington or through the American Embassy in Baghdad—asked Iraqi officials for "clarifications" of increasingly ominous statements and explanations for the military buildup on the Kuwaiti border. The Iraqis were not forthcoming. The administration launched an orchestrated campaign to speak with one voice, in almost the same words, and to speak quietly. In doing so, it was speaking to two audiences: Congress and the moderate Arab states. It did not want to be accused by congressional Democrats of looking to intervene militarily in a Middle East conflict, so it stressed the fact that the United States had no treaty commitments to Kuwait. It also acceded to the wishes of Arab leaders—particularly King Fahd, King Hussein, and Hosni Mubarak—that the United States not do or say anything to antagonize the Iraqi president. With such a weak approach, however, there was one audience the Bush administration did not reach: Saddam Hussein.

On July 24, Washington announced joint military refueling exercises with the United Arab Emirates. At the State Department briefing, spokeswoman

Margaret D. Tutwiler was asked if the United States had a formal commitment to defend Kuwait. "We do not have any defense treaties with Kuwait and there are no special defense or security commitments to Kuwait," she said. Asked if the United States would help Kuwait if it were attacked, she replied, "We also remain strongly committed to supporting the individual and collective self-defense of our friends in the Gulf with whom we have deep and long-standing ties." Although she stated, "There is no place for coercion and intimidation in a civilized world," she did *not* say that the United States would not tolerate an Iraqi invasion of Kuwait.

The following day, Glaspie delivered a copy of Tutwiler's remarks and an announcement of the refueling exercises to the Iraqi Foreign Ministry. She returned to her office and was summoned back a half-hour later by Deputy Foreign Minister Nizar Hamdoon. To her surprise, she was taken immediately to the presidential palace to meet Saddam, whom she had never met privately. She arrived without a note-taker and without fresh instructions from Washington.

The contents of the conversation between the Iraqi president and the American ambassador are a matter of dispute. In testimony before the Senate Foreign Relations Committee on March 20, 1991, Glaspie called an Iraqi transcript of the meeting "fabrication" and "disinformation," adding that the most significant inaccuracies involved three key exchanges that were either omitted or edited. But aides to Secretary of State Baker and other senior administration officials who have seen her classified report on the meeting have said privately that although there are a few omissions and distortions, the two versions are not dramatically different.

The refueling exercises with the UAE had caught Saddam's attention. Holding the American statements in his hand when Glaspie arrived, he used the meeting to protest the exercises. He also described an American conspiracy against him, complained of what he called an official American media campaign to discredit his country, and warned the United States not to oppose his goal of getting economic concessions from Kuwait and the UAE, which he accused of robbing him of oil revenues by producing more than their OPEC quotas. Clearly misreading what would be the U.S. response to his impending invasion, he told Glaspie that the United States should thank Iraq for stopping Iran's aggression during the war, because Washington could never fight such a war to defend its friends in the region. American society would not tolerate massive casualties, he explained.

Both Saddam and Glaspie sent mixed signals in the conversation. He characterized the feud with his neighbors as an inter-Arab dispute that must be solved through negotiations—"in an Arab context and through direct bilateral relations," according to the Iraqi transcript. At one point, he left the room to take a call from Egyptian President Mubarak, which gave Glaspie the chance to jot down a few notes on the conversation on the back of an envelope. When Saddam returned, he told her the Kuwaitis had agreed to meet an Iraqi delegation for a protocol meeting in Saudi Arabia to resolve the crisis, to be followed by a meeting in Baghdad. "We are not going to do anything from our side until we meet with them," he assured her, according to the transcript. "If we see that there is hope when we meet, then nothing will happen." During her congressional testimony in March 1991, Glaspie stated that his assurances were even stronger. She quoted him as saying he had told Mubarak, and she should tell President Bush, "that he would not solve his problems with Kuwait by violence, period. He would not do it."

On the other hand, Saddam openly suggested in his meeting with Glaspie that he would use terrorism to curb any effort by the United States to try to keep him from his goals. "If you resort to pressure and coercion, we too shall resort to pressure and the use of force," he said, according to the Iraqi transcript. "We know that you can hurt us. We are not threatening you, but we too are capable of causing you harm. Each can cause harm according to its size. We cannot get to you in the U.S. Perhaps some Arab individuals can get to you." At another point, he warned her that Iraq must not feel trapped. "If we are unable to find a way out, then naturally Iraq will not accept death," he added, according to the Iraqi transcript. Even then, he tempered the warning by telling her his message was one of "good news," and that is how Glaspie interpreted it.

In her remarks to Saddam, Glaspie expressed Washington's "concern" about Iraq's military buildup at the Kuwait border and Saddam's recent threatening remarks and asked him for an explanation. She made clear that she had received instructions from Washington to "ask you, in the spirit of friendship—not in the spirit of confrontation—about your intentions." She tried to convince Saddam that there was no American conspiracy against him. "President Bush is an intelligent man," she said. "He is not going to declare an economic war against Iraq." She noted her "direct instruction from the President personally to deepen and expand the scope of relations with Iraq." She was also quoted as saying, "We take no position on inter-Arab disputes, like your border dispute with Kuwait." In her 1991 testimony before the Senate Foreign Relations Committee, Glaspie said that in her discussion of the American position on border disputes, the rest of her remarks were left out. She maintained that she emphasized several times to Saddam "that we would insist on settlements being made in a nonviolent manner, not by threats, not by intimidation, and certainly not by aggression."

On July 25, the same day as Glaspie's meeting with Saddam Hussein, the State Department made a formal recommendation that the Pentagon send the aircraft carrier USS *Independence* and its battle group from the Indian Ocean to the mouth of the Gulf as a signal to Saddam that the United States would not tolerate an invasion of Kuwait. The Joint Chiefs of Staff, with the support of the Pentagon, resisted, arguing that such a move would have little more than symbolic value if Saddam attacked, and that the *Independence* would have to stop at the American naval base at Diego Garcia in the Indian Ocean for additional training first. By the time the National Security Council overruled the Pentagon and sent the *Independence* and its warships into the Gulf as Iraqi troops were poised to cross the border, it was too late to have an impact.

After Glaspie sent the State Department a classified report of her meeting with Saddam, Bush instructed her to go back to him the following day with another mixed message. The United States was concerned about Iraq's threats to use force against its neighbors, which was unacceptable, the presidential message said. But, it stressed, Washington wants to have better relations with the Iraqi government. On July 26, Glaspie delivered that message to Tariq Aziz. "The intent of our message was to reassure Saddam that although we were very concerned, that moderate behavior would be rewarded," said one senior official who saw the message. "It was very cryptic."

Glaspie's cable describing her meeting with Saddam was also sent to the American embassy in Kuwait. Ambassador W. Nathaniel Howell and Barbara Bodine, the chargé d'affaires, were alarmed by what they interpreted as Saddam's threatening stance and Glaspie's weak reply. They drafted a long cable, entitled, KUWAIT: WHAT'S AT STAKE, that laid out probable scenarios. They predicted that the Iraqis would move troops across the border, but even they did not foresee a total invasion.

Two days before the August 2 invasion, Assistant Secretary of State John Kelly relayed to Congress essentially the same message that Margaret Tutwiler had uttered from the podium and Ambassador Glaspie had delivered to Saddam a few days earlier. "We have no defense-treaty relationships with any of the [Gulf] countries. We have historically avoided taking a position on border disputes, or on internal OPEC deliberations, but we have certainly, as have all administrations, resoundingly called for the peaceful settlement of disputes and differences in the region." While "profoundly concerned" about Iraq and its military buildup, the Bush administration was firmly opposed to sanctions against Iraq, he added. "We believe that what you need are devices that allow you to modulate policies toward countries, not a meat-axe approach," he said. Later, senior administration officials acknowledged that the main reason they opposed sanctions was that the initiative came from Congress.

~

In the weeks after the invasion, American policymakers argued about whether Saddam would have changed his war plans if the United States had taken a harder line. Some said that if the administration had sent stronger signals, it would later have been accused of pushing Saddam into extreme actions. Glaspie, who became the scapegoat for a failed policy, was not allowed to return to Baghdad and was stuck behind a desk at the State Department. Secretary Baker, meanwhile, termed "absolutely ludicrous" the congressional criticism that the administration's signals led Iraq to believe the United States would not object to an invasion. But he also scrambled to distance himself from the instructions that his department had sent to Glaspie. His testy response to a television interviewer on NBC's "Meet the Press" was typical of his efforts to evade responsibility for the failed policy. "There are probably 312,000 cables or so that go out under my name as Secretary of State," he said, implying that he could not read all of them.

When Glaspie, who had been barred from talking to the press or the Congress about her conversation with Saddam, was finally allowed to tell her side of the story, she maintained that she meticulously followed instructions from Washington. But an exchange between Glaspie and Representative Lee H. Hamilton, Democrat of Indiana, in a hearing before the House Foreign Affairs Committee on March 21, 1991, revealed the weakness of those instructions. "Did you ever tell Saddam Hussein, 'Mr. President, if you go across that line into Kuwait, we're going to fight.'?" She replied, "I did not." In that case, Hamilton asked, why should Saddam have been frightened? "I told him we would defend our vital interests . . . ," Glaspie explained. "It would have been absolutely wrong for me, without consulting with the President, to inform anybody of a change in our policy."

~

Four days after the invasion of Kuwait, Saddam, misreading the American response to his actions, received Joseph C. Wilson IV, the American chargé d'affaires, at the presidential palace. He wanted to assure the American envoy that despite his seizure of Kuwait, he had no designs on Saudi Arabia and that Baghdad's relationship with Washington was unchanged. Noting that the United States bought oil from Iraq, he said, "We are familiar with the declarations that have been made. Your interests are your trade and the continuation of oil supplies to you. What then is the threat that makes you contemplate military action in which you shall be defeated? And I will tell you how you shall be defeated." At one point, he echoed what Saadoun Hammadi had told George Shultz in 1983—that Iraq could be a more reliable ally than Saudi Arabia for the United States because it had more power. But the best illustration of Saddam's misunderstanding of change in the administration's attitude came in an aside to Wilson about the emir of Kuwait. "By the way," said Saddam, as if it were business as usual, "say hello to President Bush. And tell him that Jaber and his clique are finished; they're history. The Sabah family are has-beens."

~ 9 ~

The Regional Superpower

I think your excellency will agree that the time has come when it is desirable to reaffirm the existing frontier between Iraq and Kuwait.

> —Letter from Iraqi Prime Minister Nuri al-Said
> to Sheik Ahmad al-Jaber al-Sabah,
> emir of Kuwait, July 21, 1932

If Iraq wants to be important, it's important because it's proved to be a stable factor in the area. The Iraqi people want the good life. They have fought courageously to protect their country. They would not be in a position to support any adventurous policies. We would like to live in peace within our borders. Within our borders. We have mountains, hills, valleys, water. Iraq has everything it needs.

> —Iraqi Foreign Minister Tariq Aziz, in a 1984 interview

~ The Spoils of War

The images that best captured the mood of the Iraqi regime in 1988 at the end of its eight-year war with Iran were two identical, rather grotesque monuments that sat in a huge field at the entrance and exit of a parade ground in the heart of Baghdad. Each of the "Victory Arches" consisted of two disembodied bronze forearms holding long, thin crossed swords. Iraqi flags were set into the point where the swords crossed. They were 131 feet tall—taller than the Lincoln or Jefferson memorial and almost as tall as the Arc de Triomphe in Paris. Saddam Hussein himself conceived the idea for the monuments, which were executed from plaster casts of his own forearms and hands, even down to his fingerprints and hair follicles. The swords of the monuments were forged with steel from melted-down weapons of Iraqi "martyrs" who died in the course of the Iran-Iraq war—not unlike the tankards and beakers that the Allies crafted from the war debris of World War II.

Perhaps what was most interesting about the Victory Arches was the bright-green helmets—5,000 of them in all—that spilled out from nets attached to each arm. They were taken from the bodies of dead Iranian soldiers, and many of them were riddled with shrapnel and bullet holes. Some of the helmets were cemented into the parade route under the arches. When I saw them, I couldn't help but think of the pyramid of skulls that Hulagu Khan built when he seized Baghdad in the thirteenth century.

In his 1991 monograph on the Victory Arches, *The Monument*, Samir al-Khalil said that no Iraqi foundry was big enough to make the arms. They had to be cast at the Morris Singer foundry in Britain, the largest professional art foundry in the world and the one that cast the sculptures of Henry Moore. The bronze arms were transported to Iraq in pieces in a truck convoy. "To look at the helmets in the knowledge that their scratches, dents and bullet holes were made by real bullets, that actual skulls may have exploded inside, is just as mesmerizing as the knowledge that these are not anybody's arms, but the President's own," al-Khalil wrote. "Or, for that matter, that not any old steel was used in the sword blades, but only that taken from Iraqi 'martyrs.' "

Saddam intended the monuments to be understood as symbols of renewed imperial ambitions, of Iraq's power and defiance. On August 8, 1989, the day the arches were inaugurated, he rode under them as though they were the gateways to the recovery of past greatness for the future of Iraq. Iraqi television showed him astride a white stallion, just as Hussein, grandson of the Prophet Mohammad, had ridden on a white horse when he was martyred in A.D. 680 at the battle of Karbala. Leading the parade, Saddam wore a white jacket with gold epaulets and an elaborate white helmet with a white ostrich feather—the same garb that Iraq's kings had worn during official ceremonies before the monarchy was overthrown in 1958. No matter that Saddam had opposed the monarchy as a young man; he now wanted to be king. And not just an ordinary king, but a king who lived by the sword, as glorious as the ancient kings of Babylon. A huge poster of Saddam as a helmeted soldier at the battlefront was wheeled behind him. To evoke the imagery of ancient Babylon, a miniature ziggurat and an Ishtar Gate were positioned on the parade grounds.

The arches unintentionally exposed the flaws in Saddam's vision, flaws that led his country to destruction. The arches revealed a soaring, warlike vision far beyond the resources of a debt-ridden nation of 18 million people. Despite the xenophobic message of the monuments, they could be erected only with foreign help and borrowed money. In the end, they were not only monuments to Saddam's unrestrained ego and craving for grandeur, but also an illustration of the gap between what was coveted and what was possible.

~ Iraq Victorious

Saddam Hussein's invasion of Kuwait on August 2, 1990, was not the result of a single event. Rather, it resulted from the convergence of a number of developments and circumstances over a period of months in the aftermath of the Iran-Iraq war. First, Saddam believed that seizing Kuwait would provide a quick fix to his postwar economic problems. Second, it was the fulfillment of his dream of turning Iraq into a naval power. Third, it would teach the Kuwaitis and the rest of the world a lesson for conspiring to steal from him what he believed was his rightful position as the most important military and political force in the Middle East.

Saddam believed that the grueling war with Iran was fought not for Iraq alone. By stopping Khomeini's fundamentalist revolution at Iran's border, he thought he had fought for the whole Arab nation and promoted global stability in the process. The world—particularly his Arab brothers, he felt—owed him something in return.

At the end of the war between Iraq and Iran, neither country had achieved its war goals. But in the eyes of much of the world, Iraq emerged as the clear winner. Because of Iran's refusal to accept a cease-fire for so many years, most of the world was on Iraq's side and was slow to realize that the end of the war created a military imbalance and a political vacuum that put Iraq in a new position of power and influence. The war left the ayatollahs in Tehran physically and economically devastated and politically humiliated. The Iranian Army's collapse in the face of relentless Iraqi firepower, and Khomeini's stunning decision to make peace, left Iraq with a small piece of Iranian territory, 65,000 prisoners of war, huge caches of captured military equipment, and the ability to play a new, assertive role in the Middle East. When Khomeini died on June 3, 1989, Iran's attention was diverted by an internal struggle between militancy and pragmatism. The more repressive Iraqi regime, on the other hand, did not have to worry about internal dissent.

The Iran-Iraq war had sidetracked Saddam from his vision of making Iraq a great regional power. During the war, he had been forced to put off development projects, curb his ambitions, and moderate his rhetoric. Now that it was over, he could revive the "national charter" for the Arab world that he first proposed in 1980, which had rejected the military presence of the superpowers in the region and charted a course of regional nonalignment. He was well positioned to launch his campaign. The war had given him the opportunity to develop his military industry and helped him put one million men under arms.

After the war, Iraq's military development continued apace. With the help of Egypt and Argentina, Iraq was able to develop new, longer-range Scud missiles. In December 1989, General Hussein Kamel al-Majid announced that Iraq had developed a medium-range, surface-to-surface missile with a range—he exaggerated—of at least 1,240 miles. At the same time, he boasted that he had successfully completed a test launch of the first stage of a three-stage, 48-ton rocket capable of putting a satellite into space. The Iraqi press heralded the announcement, saying that Iraq was the first Arab nation to have launched such a satellite into orbit. Although Western intelligence officials believed Iraq may have overblown its achievement, the U.S. Defense Intelligence Agency confirmed the launch.

Iraqi newspapers were filled with self-congratulation, as Iraq began to portray itself as a new superpower. The satellite launch "rectified" the Arab-Israeli military and strategic balance, the English-language *Baghdad Observer* boasted. Other announcements claimed that the acquisition of advanced missiles and satellites proved that Iraq was no longer a Third World backwater. The new arsenal made the country unique in the Arab world and gave it the firepower to pose a major threat to Israel. It was this same impulse—the development of weapons and space technology bigger and better than what the rest of the Arab world possessed—that motivated Saddam to try to build a giant artillery gun that would have been more than twice the caliber of the 16-inch guns on American battleships and capable of firing nuclear or chemical shells for hundreds of miles.

At home, the regime did not have to worry about dissenting voices. The use of chemical weapons against Iraq's Kurdish civilians and their massive relocation in 1988 had quieted Kurdish opposition. Saddam could point to small measures taken ostensibly to open up his repressive political system. On April 1, 1989, for example, Iraq held national elections for deputies for its new 250-member National Assembly. By Western standards, the election was a joke because the only candidates were Baath Party members in good standing. The regime portrayed the election as an exercise in democracy and liberalization after the long war. According to Saddam, the assembly was supposed to endorse a new constitution establishing a multiparty system that might even lead to presidential elections.

~ What's Wrong with this Picture?

After the Iran-Iraq cease-fire, Baghdad overnight was forced to confront issues that had long seemed irrelevant: the need to reorient its economy, reintegrate its massive armed forces into civilian life, and forge new relationships with other countries.

Iraq was intent on an ambitious reconstruction program. Throughout the war, the regime had promised its people a peace dividend, vowing that the financial sacrifices they were forced to make would end suddenly once the conflict was over. Peace would bring an earthly paradise of jobs, access to consumer goods, a lifting of wartime restrictions (such as a ban on foreign travel), and development of the country's infrastructure. Saddam ordered up more and more projects, plunging his country further into debt. He drew up plans for $30 billion to $35 billion worth of projects such as a Baghdad subway station, an airport in Mosul, six-lane highways to Jordan and Turkey—even a factory to make a million tires a year. But the country did not have the money to bankroll the new prosperity. To continue its war with Iran, Iraq had relied on roughly $40 billion in interest-free "loans" and grants from the rich Gulf states—which it expected to be forgiven. Iraq also owed as much as $35 billion to Europe, Japan, and the United States in loans that it would have to pay back in increasingly scarce hard currency, and about $7 billion to $8 billion to the Soviet bloc.

The payoff did not materialize. On the contrary, everyday life became worse. Measures initiated during the war to loosen restrictions on private investment attracted speculators interested in quick returns but few investors willing to gamble on long-term projects that could activate the economy. One way the regime dealt with the cash-flow problem was simply to print more money. In 1990, inflation was running at 40 percent or higher, in part because of the removal of price controls on imports. Particularly hard hit were those Iraqis on fixed incomes, including the massive civil-servant class, whose salaries had remained static throughout most of the war.

When travel restrictions were eased after the war, Iraqis visited Kuwait and saw the luxuries that oil money could buy. They arrived on weekends with hard currency to buy food unavailable in Iraqi markets. Some foodstuffs were so scarce that when Iraq held the Arab summit in Baghdad in May 1990, it was forced to truck in meat and fresh fruits and vegetables from Kuwait. Even in the strictly controlled Iraqi news media, there were letters from Iraqis complaining that although goods were plentiful in private markets at exorbitant prices beyond the reach of most ordinary citizens, the shelves in the state-controlled supermarkets were empty. To dampen domestic grumbling, Iraq continued to spend a disproportionate amount of its precious foreign exchange on consumer imports. To encourage the imports, the regime allowed the flourishing of a black market that dramatized the worthlessness of the Iraqi dinar. Kuwaitis, meanwhile, took advantage of the deteriorating economic situation in Iraq. With the Kuwaiti dinar worth several times more than its official value on the Iraqi black market, rich Kuwaitis began to buy huge tracts of Iraqi real estate, prompting Saddam's regime in 1989 to ban real estate purchases by foreigners.

Rather than develop a comprehensive, rational plan of reconstruction, Saddam created an atmosphere of artificial movement. Eager for a physical display of Iraqi power after the war, he invested in the showplace reconstruction of parts of Basra, Iraq's second-largest city and its main outlet to the Gulf, and its southern port at Fao—projects that did not generate revenue.

Newspapers and television programs showed the same images of reconstruction, the same buildings, and probably the same cranes, over and over. Saddam also pumped huge sums into white-elephant projects: monuments like the Victory Arches and the reconstruction of ancient sites such as Babylon. He also began to build a monstrous palace for himself in the heart of Baghdad. Iraqi television aired interminable footage of Saddam meeting with engineers and architects, studying the maquette, and examining the builders' progress—down to the design of the main gates. Watching the program on Iraqi television beamed into Kuwait City, Kuwaiti officials bristled at where their money had gone.

To make matters worse, reconstruction took second place to defense purchases and development of Iraq's high-tech military-industrial complex. There seemed to be no restrictions on the money poured into the Ministry of Industry and Military Industrialization, run by Saddam's son-in-law, Hussein Kamel al-Majid. From 1988 to 1992, Iraq budgeted $5 billion a year—40 percent of its total oil revenues in 1988 and 1989—for defense, but only half that amount for reconstruction.

Instead of growth, there was fast-growing unemployment. Iraq was able to demobilize only 200,000 to 300,000 of its troops in the first year after its cease-fire with Iran. Because of the huge numbers of women and foreigners in the labor force and a no-growth economy, veterans could not be reintegrated into civilian life, and the demobilization ended. The Iraqis began to resent the Egyptian and Sudanese expatriate workers who entered the country without visas or work permits and held jobs as if it were still wartime. In November and December 1989, there were spontaneous fights between Egyptian workers and unemployed Iraqi veterans. Thousands of Egyptians left Iraq, some of them in coffins. By the end of 1989, Saddam needed to do something drastic to occupy the Army he had built so assiduously.

A steady decline in oil prices in 1988 canceled the effect of Iraq's increased postwar oil exports of 2.2 million barrels a day. Iraq emerged from the war with Iran with $80 billion in debts—about one and a half times its gross national product. Debt-service payments to foreign creditors alone totaled $6 to $7 billion annually. By the end of 1988, Iraq's cash-flow problem became so serious that it defaulted on loan payments to the United States, Canada, Australia, and Britain. Western banks began to turn down Iraqi requests for credit. France—Iraq's main Western supplier of weapons and military equipment—suspended arms sales to Baghdad in early 1990 after the regime defaulted on its $4.5 billion debt. France also refused to reschedule loans or give Iraq parts for its Mirage fighters because of the arrearages. Even some Eastern European countries would no longer cooperate with Baghdad. The Iraqis could not understand what was happening. At one point, the ministries stopped answering telexes from frustrated commercial creditors demanding to know when the payments would come.

Saddam Hussein was unwilling to manage his debt according to traditional banking procedures. Paranoid about financial disclosure and adamant that the country not be seen as a weak Third World country, he refused to renegotiate his debts through multilateral institutions such as the Paris Club and the International Monetary Fund. Saddam insisted on cutting separate deals with each of his creditors in the hope that he would receive better terms from some. Rather than paying off principal, he rolled over the loans, demanding new credit along the way. By the time Saddam invaded Kuwait, according to international bankers, Iraq owed Western creditors $10 billion more than at the end of the Iran-Iraq war.

There were several reasons for Saddam's obstinacy. First, despite his near-total ignorance of economics, he tried to run his economy the way he had run the war with Iran: by himself, without much input from experts. Foreign banks had extended credit throughout the war with Iran and, with a few exceptions, his rich Arab brothers had provided the cash he needed, Saddam reasoned, so why should the situation be different now? In 1989, he dismissed the governor of Iraq's Central Bank when he tried to restrict military spending. According to Arab bankers, Saddam established an economic office within the presidency in which he began to function as the country's chief financial officer, personally deciding which creditors would get paid in foreign currency. In October 1989, Iraq announced the dismissal of Finance Minister Hikmat Mukhaylif, after he apparently pressed Saddam to consolidate Iraq's debt and was linked to allegations of violations of American banking laws.

A second reason for Saddam's obstinacy was that a secret society like Iraq bred resistance to financial disclosure. Rescheduling Iraq's debt through international bodies would have required the disclosure of intricate and perhaps embarrassing financial details. Perhaps the corruption of family members such as Saddam's son Uday would be exposed. Disclosure would have put Iraq in the same category as the debt-ridden developing nations, a concept that ran counter to Saddam's vision of Iraq's rightful place in the world as a great nation. Finally, mere settling of the debt issue would not have resolved Saddam's massive economic problems. Saddam needed vast infusions of money to rebuild the country. Invading Kuwait became the way to get it.

~ First Signs of Adventurism

Saddam Hussein's frustrations at home did not stop him from meddling abroad. No longer did the Iran-Iraq war constrain him from saying and doing what he liked in the Middle East, and he felt no need to curb his pursuit of one of his most basic goals: expanding his influence in the region to the point where he could set its agenda.

In addition, at a time when the U.S.-PLO dialogue was going nowhere and the Arab world seemed to have lost the momentum to push the Palestinian cause forward, Saddam went on the offensive. In an effort to build support in the Arab street and to become the champion of the Palestinians, he reverted to the harsh rhetoric of the prewar days, once again articulating a belligerent stance toward Israel and a policy aimed at pushing foreign forces out of the region. He solidified ties with the PLO and encouraged its leaders to regard Baghdad as its base. Yassir Arafat began to spend more time in Iraq, and he flew around to Arab capitals in a private Iraqi jet. Saddam seemed to believe in his own rhetoric—that he somehow had a mission to speak for the Palestinians. Other Arab leaders regarded the embrace of the PLO as purely tactical maneuvering to bolster his position in the Arab world.

Peace with Iran also gave Saddam an opportunity to take revenge against Syria, which had supported Iran in the border war. At the end of the Iran-Iraq war, Syria had more than 25,000 troops in central and northern Lebanon and 7,000 troops and military advisers in West Beirut. Saddam gave money, communications systems, weapons, and logistical support to anti-Syrian Christian groups in Lebanon led by General Michel Aoun. At the Arab summit in Casablanca in May 1989, Tariq Aziz lobbied hard, but unsuccessfully, to persuade Arab leaders to end Syria's hegemony over Lebanon. The debate became so acrimonious that Aziz at one point addressed his Syrian counterpart, Farouk al-Sharaa, as "the honorable minister, the demagogue, and the liar," participants said. Al-Sharaa responded by describing Aziz as "his excellency, the minister and terrorist." But Saddam overreached. Aoun, his Lebanese client, was a former ally of the Israelis, and despised in much of the Arab world. With Syria so well entrenched in Lebanon, there was little Saddam could do to help Aoun win.

Saddam regarded with dismay the events in the Soviet Union and the Soviet "new thinking" in foreign affairs. Moscow, which supplied Iraq with the bulk of its weaponry, was becoming less interested in costly regional entanglements, and Saddam was concerned about the impact on Iraq of the Soviet decline. When Soviet Foreign Minister Eduard A. Shevardnadze visited Baghdad in February 1989, Saddam praised the Soviets as Baghdad's main ally and friend and urged them to take a more active role in the region.

Saddam was slow to understand how the end of the Cold War might affect the Middle East, and how it might motivate even Moscow to turn against him because it needed Washington's friendship even more. He was also baffled by the democracy movements that swept through Eastern Europe. It couldn't happen in Iraq, he insisted. When a senior Bulgarian delegation visited Baghdad in May 1990, Saddam was "very interested in what was happening in the Soviet Union and Eastern Europe and insisted that none of these negative things could happen to him," according to a Soviet official familiar with the meeting. In an interview with French television on July 8, 1990, Saddam said, "When you direct your media against an Eastern European country, it collapses within a week. But Western media have been trying to harm Iraq for a year, and we will give you another year. You will find that the Iraqi people are adhering to and believing in their march; they believe in, respect, and will not abandon their leadership." During his meeting with Ambassador April Glaspie two weeks later, Saddam charged that the United States assumed that Iraq "was in a situation similar to that of Poland, Romania, or Czechoslovakia," and would similarly collapse.

Like other Arab leaders, Saddam was displeased with Moscow's moves to establish ties with Israel after so many years of unswerving military and financial support for the Arab states and the PLO. He also paid lip service to the concerns of other Arab leaders about Moscow's intentions to allow large numbers of Jews to emigrate to Israel. Although he mentioned the subject only in passing in discussions with the Soviets, they said, he publicly expressed grave concern that the new immigrants would settle in the occupied territories and force Palestinians off the land.

Saddam now began to see the United States as the only remaining superpower. Unlike Syria's Hafez al-Assad, his archenemy, who concluded that the best way to survive was to seek a closer relationship with the United States, Saddam saw himself as a regional leader able to challenge Washington. On February 19, 1989, he created the Arab Cooperation Council, which grew out of his wartime alliance with Jordan, Egypt, and Yemen. The organization was intended to isolate Syria and to challenge the Gulf Cooperation Council (GCC), the Saudi-led alliance of six oil-rich Gulf countries established in the early days of the Iran-Iraq war. The GCC had excluded both belligerents, and when the war was over, Iraq was not invited to join. Iraq also signed bilateral nonaggression pacts with Bahrain and Saudi Arabia in early 1989— ostensibly to ease fears among Gulf Arab states about Iraq's regional ambitions in the aftermath of its war with Iran.

~ The Whims of the Colonialists

In addition to money, there was another, equally important impediment preventing Iraq from finally achieving what Saddam Hussein felt was his rightful place in the world. With only 26 miles of Gulf shoreline and no port directly on the Gulf, Iraq had always felt cheated, suffocated. Kuwait, on the other hand, had a shoreline of 310 miles. Iraq had always felt—despite its substantial resources of oil and water, and 18 million people—"like a man with huge lungs but a tiny windpipe," according to historian Phebe Marr.

It was unacceptable to Saddam that a country as great as Iraq did not have a long coastline. Over and over he talked about the necessity of building a Navy and becoming a seafaring power. Iraq's isolation from the sea was a cruel accident of history, he believed, and one that had to be rectified—a theme he continued to dwell on after his invasion of Kuwait. "Is it possible for a civilization which is 6,000 years old to have been isolated from the sea?" he asked in a speech on November 3, 1990. "A part of Iraq's land was cut off by English scissors."

Although successive Iraqi regimes had longed for more access to the sea, it was Saddam who acted on the desire. Having failed to gain complete control of the Shatt al-Arab waterway that divided Iran and Iraq and flowed into the Gulf, he now decided to try again. The pipelines that transported his oil had made him dependent on his neighbors. He wanted a deepwater port and a sea outlet for his oil exports.

Despite the cease-fire in the Iran-Iraq war, the Shatt remained closed to traffic and Basra was left half-destroyed. The waterway was blocked with years of silt and unexploded mines, and to restore it to working condition would have been a major undertaking. The only way for Iraq to get a port was to dredge the Khor Abdullah channel, the narrow waterway that curved around the Kuwaiti islands of Bubiyan and Warba along Kuwait's coast and led to the Iraqi port and naval base of Umm Qasr. Possession of these islands would also have given Saddam the opportunity to develop a blue-water, or deep-sea, Navy, a goal that had been thwarted by the Iran-Iraq war. The core of his new Navy—four frigates and six corvettes, bought from Italy at a cost of $2.6 billion—had been rusting in Italian and Egyptian ports since the early days of the war. Saddam had recently spent nearly $300,000 to refurbish his $19 million private yacht—with its dozen suites, board room, and gold fixtures. But he had no place to put his Navy and no place to sail his yacht.

~

Iraq's border dispute with Kuwait was rooted in the origins of Kuwait and Iraq as nations. Historically, the desert was much like the high seas, where nomads roamed at will. The only borders were shadowy lines of tribal jurisdiction, and the only signs of organized authority were concentrated at the ports and the oases.

The European concept of territorial sovereignty did not exist. The Arabian tribesman owed his personal loyalty to his family, his tribe, or his sheik, not to an abstract nation-state. For Saddam Hussein, as for many other Arab Gulf leaders, official boundaries meant little. They were lines that British imperialists drew in the sand and did not reflect the aspirations of the Iraqi people. But after having recognized Kuwait throughout his rule, relying on its largess throughout the war with Iran, and honoring its ruler when the war was over, Saddam developed a complicated argument stating that he had a legitimate territorial claim on the emirate.

Before oil was discovered in the mid-twentieth century, Kuwait was little more than one of a string of British trading posts stretching from India to Arabia. It was a poor, obscure port that became the feudal domain of the Bedouin nomadic Sabah clan as early as 1752. Kuwait was never occupied or conquered by the Turks, and Ottoman Turkey never established complete sovereignty over Kuwait as it did over Iraq. But foreign powers, including the British, did recognize Turkish sovereignty, and the Turks did hold a vague suzerainty over Kuwait in the second part of the nineteenth century and up to World War I. The Turks treated Kuwait as a semiautonomous province and the Sabahs as Ottoman vassals. In 1871, the Turks loosely attached Kuwait to the southern Iraqi province of Basra and turned over Kuwait's administration to the Basra governor. Despite the tenuous character of Turkish control, it was this connection to Basra that Saddam parlayed into a claim over all of Kuwait. For its part, the Sabah family alternately sought the protection of the Turks or the British whenever it was in trouble.

In 1896, two Sabah brothers, Mohammad and Jarrah al-Sabah, took control of the sheikdom. But one night, their half-brother, Mubarak, and his sons staged a raid against the rulers, killing them both and seizing control of the city-state. In 1899, in exchange for £15,000, Mubarak al-Sabah secretly agreed to make Kuwait a British protectorate. When Turkey and Britain went to war in 1914, the Sabahs fought on the British side. The British and Turks had agreed on the borders for Kuwait that year, but the treaty was never ratified.

Eight years later, in a British Army tent in the Arabian desert, the border between Iraq and Kuwait was determined. There, at the 1922 conference at the Gulf port of Uqair, Sir Percy Cox, Britain's representative in Baghdad, drew the borders of Saudi Arabia, Iraq, and Kuwait. Lieutenant Harold Dickson, the British military attaché in the region, described Sir Percy in his memoirs as a "sphinx-like" character who spoke poor Arabic and was determined to serve British interests at the expense of the Arabs.

The major dispute at Uqair was over Saudi Arabia's borders with Iraq and Kuwait, and it took considerable coaxing to get Abdul Aziz ibn Saud, soon to become the king of Saudi Arabia, to the conference. Iraq sent only a junior political officer, Sabih Beg, who said little. Kuwait sent a British major who said nothing. Although scant attention was paid to the border between Iraq and Kuwait, the negotiations illustrated just how whimsically the colonialists treated national boundaries.

In the days before oil, what made territory valuable were the water wells, grazing grounds, and trade routes. Ibn Saud fought against fixed boundaries, which he considered arbitrary lines drawn on a piece of paper. To safeguard the rights of his tribes and prevent boundary disputes in the future, he fought for more flexible "tribal" boundaries with neutral zones.

But Sir Percy "lost all patience over what he called the childish attitude of ibn Saud in his tribal boundary idea," Dickson wrote. He called ibn Saud into his tent and presented him with a fait accompli. "It was astonishing to see the Sultan of Najd being reprimanded like a naughty schoolboy by H.M. High Commissioner and being told sharply that he, Sir Percy Cox, would himself decide on the type and general line of the frontier." Self-determination was not an idea expressed within the confines of the British tent.

Sir Percy took out a red pencil and a map of Arabia and carefully drew the borders of what became modern-day Iraq, Kuwait, and Saudi Arabia. To placate ibn Saud, he gave Saudi Arabia two-thirds of the territory claimed by Kuwait, pushing back its southern boundary 150 miles. He gave Iraq a large part of the territory claimed by Saudi Arabia. "He won the day . . . ," wrote Dickson, "but he grievously harmed a great reputation for fair dealing among the Arabs."

A few days later, when Kuwait's ruler, Sheik Ahmad al-Jaber al-Sabah, asked why most of his territory had been transferred to the Saudis without his knowledge, Sir Percy replied that not to have given in would have provoked a war. But even Sir Percy realized how meaningless his red pencil lines were. The sheik asked Sir Percy if the British would object if some day, after ibn Saud's death, he were to denounce the border and recover his lost territory. Sir Percy laughed and replied, "No! And may God bless your efforts."

When Iraq won its independence from Britain in 1932, the Kuwait-Iraq border was informally confirmed in an exchange of letters, although it was never formally demarcated.

Iraq's claims to Kuwait surfaced from time to time afterward. Sometimes Iraq called for complete annexation, sometimes for bits of territory—including Kuwait's northeastern coast, the Rumaila oil field on the Kuwait–Iraq border, and the strategic islands of Bubiyan and Warba, the uninhabited swampy outgrowths of the Tigris and Euphrates delta that blocked Iraq's direct access to the sea. Warba was nothing more than a large mound of earth. In fact, it disappeared at high tide. Bubiyan, linked to the Kuwaiti mainland by bridge, had only a few small military posts built during the Iran-Iraq war and served mainly as a refuge for migrating birds. But it had extraordinary strategic importance to the Kuwaitis, who considered it a "dagger" into the heart of Kuwait City.

In 1937, Iraq's King Ghazi called for Kuwait's annexation. A fervent nationalist who became an outspoken critic of British rule, he portrayed Kuwaiti leaders as British pawns and even massed troops near the border. The Sabah family and its British protectors blocked the move, and the claim died when Ghazi was killed in a car accident.

~

The dress rehearsal for Saddam Hussein's invasion of Kuwait came in 1961. The marker was laid by Major General Abd al-Karim Qassim, then the dictator-president of Iraq, whom Saddam later tried to assassinate. On June 19, 1961, Kuwait became independent from Britain, and British troops withdrew from their military garrisons. Qassim, rattled by the fact that Kuwait was now an independent state, and intent on deflecting attention from problems at home, laid claim to the emirate. Kuwait constituted "an integral part of Iraq," he said, adding that Britain had "declared an oil well a state." He referred to the nineteenth-century dispute, when the Ottomans had appointed the sheik of Kuwait a *qaimakam*, or local leader, and put the country under the authority of Iraq's Basra province.

Even though there was no evidence of a troop buildup in 1961, rumors of an impending Iraqi invasion prompted the ruler of Kuwait to invoke its defense pact with Britain, which rushed in a contingent of troops from Kenya the next day and deployed RAF forces and eventually a full regiment. Two weeks later, over Iraqi opposition, Kuwait was admitted into the Arab League and appealed for Arab help. By October 1961, a 3,000-man army of Saudi, Egyptian, Syrian, and Jordanian troops was positioned inside Kuwait, and British troops withdrew. Qassim backed off, and the adventure was such a disaster that it isolated him among other Arab leaders and paved the way for his eventual political demise.

After the 1963 revolution that briefly brought the Baath Socialist Party to power, Iraq officially acknowledged the existence of an independent Kuwait. In exchange, Kuwait gave Iraq an $85 million "loan." This kind of "checkbook diplomacy" was the only way Kuwait could get security. Although Iraq vaguely accepted the border, it remained unfixed. A treaty was negotiated but never ratified.

At various times, Iraq used a number of pretexts to make incursions into Kuwait. During a period of heightened hostility between Baghdad and Tehran in 1969, for example, the emir of Kuwait allowed Iraq temporarily to station its troops on the Kuwaiti side of the border. Four years later, Iraq massed troops on the border and tried to occupy the Kuwaiti police station at al-Samitah. In negotiations that followed, Iraq reiterated its claims to Bubiyan and Warba. After Iraq signed its Treaty of Friendship with the Soviet Union in 1972, the Soviets wanted to bring larger ships into the port of Umm Qasr. The Iraqis again asked for Bubiyan and Warba, but the Kuwaitis, fearful of both Iraqi and Soviet expansionism, refused. "We got into lengthy discussions," said Kuwait's ambassador to Washington, Saud Nasir al-Sabah, who was involved in the dispute as an official in the legal department in the Ministry of Foreign Affairs. "We told the Iraqis that in the spirit of friendship and brotherly Arab neighborliness, we will dredge Warba." The Iraqis, he said, never responded.

When Iraq invaded Iran in September 1980, the claims resurfaced. Saddam argued that Iraq needed the islands to prevent Iran from occupying them first. He asked for a long-term lease. But the Kuwaitis did not trust him. Give him a lease and he'll stay forever, they said among themselves.

~ The Deception Odyssey

After the Iran-Iraq war ended in August 1988, both Iraq and Kuwait let only a few months go by before they both—each in its own way—raised the border issue. The first sign of trouble came in February 1989, in a visit to Baghdad by Kuwait's crown prince, Sheik Saad al-Abdullah al-Sabah. Both sides said they were eager to resolve the matter of the border. Kuwait had never taken Iraq's war debt off its books; it wanted drilling rights for the Rumaila oil field since Iraq's war with Iran was over. It had plans to build a new city for 100,000 people on the Subiya Peninsula across from Bubiyan island and to build a resort on the island itself. Iraq's idea of a border agreement meant gaining control over both Bubiyan and Warba. Saddam was spending $1 billion to develop the ports of Umm Qasr and Khor Zubair, and he did not like the idea that Kuwait controlled his access to the sea.

During the visit, Saddam rather rudely sent the crown prince on a sightseeing tour, told him he had no intention of paying back the billions the Kuwaitis had lent him during the Iran-Iraq war, and demanded rights to the two disputed islands. Iraqi newspapers claimed that Iraq wanted to settle the border issue and "put an end to blackmail," and Saddam was quoted as telling the crown prince that Iraq was more eager than Kuwait to settle the dispute "in a brotherly spirit." Privately, each side accused the other of obstructionism. It was, said Abdullah Bishara, the Kuwaiti head of the Gulf Cooperation Council, "the beginning of the deception odyssey."

Despite a series of meetings in the months that followed, the matter mysteriously lost its urgency. Perhaps the two sides merely took a break between rounds. In September 1989, the emir of Kuwait made his first trip to Iraq in a decade in order to receive the Rafadin Medal, Iraq's highest honor. He was greeted at the airport with a 21-gun salute and a double embrace by Saddam. The Iraqi news media referred to him as a "brave Arab leader." The emir did not speak directly about the border issue, but instead suggested taking the matter to the International Court of Justice.

Iraq dismissed Kuwait's offer, and Saddam found another way to both intimidate Kuwait and promote Iraq's centrality in the Arab world. On February 19, 1990, at a meeting of prime ministers of the Arab Cooperation Council in Cairo to mark the organization's first anniversary, he began to signal larger ambitions in the Gulf. He stunned the group when he demanded that the United States, which had operated in the region for more than 40 years, withdraw its military presence from the Gulf, arguing that it was no longer needed in peacetime. The United States had no more than a handful of vessels in the Gulf; the move was a blatant attempt to pick a fight with Washington. Disturbed by Saddam's remarks and his lobbying for intelligence-sharing and military cooperation among the group's members, Egyptian President Hosni Mubarak concluded the anniversary celebration a day early.

At the Arab Cooperation Council summit meeting in Amman five days later, Saddam repeated his call for the United States to leave the Gulf, adding that the Soviets had vanished as a world power and left the region with a too-powerful United States. He speculated that it would take five years to correct that imbalance with the rise of Japan and the Europeans. "If Arabs are not careful, they will see the Gulf governed by U.S. will," eventually putting the United States in a position to fix oil prices, he warned. Some policymakers in Washington were alarmed, but not enough to adjust American policy.

Saddam also was convinced that now that the United States had what he called a "free hand" in the Middle East, Israel was beginning to plot a military strike against him. The Iraqi media began to speak of a Zionist-inspired media campaign that was to lay the groundwork for an Israeli attack similar to the bombing of Iraq's Osirak nuclear reactor in 1981. Saddam's continuing paranoia about Israel was illustrated in the Bazoft affair.

Farzad Bazoft, an Iranian-born journalist on assignment for the London *Observer*, was caught trying to investigate a mysterious explosion at an Iraqi military complex south of Baghdad that, according to some reports, killed as many as 700 people. An odd character who was behind in his rent payments in London and had spent 18 months in a British prison in 1981 for trying to rob a building-society office, Bazoft reportedly took photographs and collected samples of soil and debris, hoping to have them tested in Britain for nuclear or chemical components. The Iraqis accused him of spying for Israel and put him in solitary confinement for six months in Abu Gharib prison, outside Baghdad. Under duress, perhaps under torture, he confessed on Iraqi television that he was a spy for Israel. Despite Britain's pleas for clemency (Bazoft held British residency), he was hanged in public in March 1990. "I always liked Iraq and its people," he said in his final words dictated to a British diplomat. "Everyone makes a mistake and I made one too." British Prime Minister Margaret Thatcher denounced the hanging as "an act of barbarism." Iraqi officials countered that such a negative reaction constituted interference in Iraq's internal affairs. "Thatcher wanted him alive," remarked Iraqi Information Minister Latif Nassif Jassim, a close aide to Saddam. "We sent him in a box."

The other Arab states were reluctant to condemn Iraq for the execution. King Hussein defended the action; King Fahd invited Saddam to Saudi Arabia the day after Bazoft was hanged. The Arab Cooperation Council echoed

Iraq's denunciation of Western criticism, and the Arab League branded Britain's response "unfair."

Bazoft's memory lived on in Baghdad after the invasion of Kuwait. "Remember what we did to Bazoft," became a line used frequently by Ministry of Information officials when they felt a journalist was becoming too demanding. The line was said in jest, but the message was clear. After the allies attacked Iraq in 1991, the allusion to Bazoft became more sinister. When a four-man crew from CBS News was seized by Iraqi soldiers, the journalists were accused of being spies. After the crew was freed, Peter Bluff, the CBS producer, said that at one point their captors remarked that he was British. On the trip from Basra to Baghdad, he recalled, one of them "kept leaning forward and whispering in my ear, 'Bazoft,' and then they'd have a conversation which I didn't understand, except the name kept popping up."

Saddam became more belligerent in a speech on April 2, 1990. Convinced that another Middle East war was inevitable, he vowed to retaliate with chemical weapons if Israel attacked Iraqi military installations. "By God, we will make the fire eat up half of Israel if it tries to do anything against Iraq," he said. He boasted that Iraq possessed the same advanced binary chemical weapons that the Soviet Union and the United States had in their arsenals. "Whoever threatens us with the atomic bomb, we will annihilate him with the dual chemical," he said. Saddam may have intended the speech as a message of deterrence, but because of its ominous rhetoric, it was widely interpreted as a concrete threat to Israel.

Alarmed, Israel's Foreign Ministry called on the world community to prevent Saddam from pursuing his "irresponsible designs." The U.S. State Department called the statements "inflammatory, irresponsible, and outrageous." On April 9, Saddam clarified the speech, stressing that Iraqi weapons would be used in self-defense only. But the speech received tremendous Arab applause, resonating throughout the Middle East. Saddam had stood up to Israel at a time of stalemate in the Arab-Israeli peace process, growing militancy among Palestinians, and deep malaise among many Arabs who saw themselves as abandoned by the Eastern bloc, ignored by the West, and helpless to confront Israel. He criticized Western intentions in the region at a time when the U.S.–PLO dialogue had faltered. By portraying himself as the champion of the Arabs, he began to emerge as the new Arab hero. Not surprisingly, the news media in Jordan, which had become Iraq's strongest Arab ally, lauded Saddam's position. "Hussein awakened the desire in every Arab soul for a glorious Arab stand," said the Jordanian newspaper al-Destour. "His combative tone awakened every Arab's longing to respond to his nation's enemies with language not used for a long time." But the Gulf states also heaped praise on Saddam. The response of the Bahraini newspaper Akbar al-Khalij was typical. "Iraq's statement is a declaration of Arab capability to confront Israel and its aggression," it said.

Meanwhile, Iraq's economic situation had become increasingly desperate. As oil prices dropped from $20 to $14 a barrel between January and June 1990, Saddam pressured the rich Gulf Arabs to "forgive" the $40 billion they had "loaned" him during the war, to make outright grants, and to invest in his economy. The ruling Sabahs of Kuwait humiliated him by refusing to bankroll his economy, as they had during the war, and by brushing off his claims to bits of Kuwaiti territory that would have given him greater access to the sea. Saddam repeated the demands he had made of Kuwait the previous year—this time, more forcefully and openly—and added territorial claims. He also charged that Kuwait and the United Arab Emirates were exceeding their quotas set by the Organization of Petroleum Exporting Countries (OPEC), and that higher production was driving down oil prices.

Saddam touched a raw nerve, openly articulating what a number of other oil producers—including Saudi Arabia, Iran, Oman, and Bahrain—had been whispering in private. The UAE, a loose federation that had no control over its individual members, had been overproducing for more than two years. Kuwait's overall production in 1989 averaged 1.8 million barrels a day, more than twice its quota. As Kuwait's oil minister, Sheik Ali al-Khalifa al-Sabah had alienated most of OPEC with his open disregard of quotas. In an address to the National Press Club in Washington three months after the invasion of Kuwait, Sheik Ali justified his stance, saying that of OPEC's 13 members, ten were cheating. "Those who could, did," he said. "Those who couldn't, complained."

Iraq made still another accusation, asserting that Kuwait had stolen oil from the Rumaila oil field, one of the largest oil reservoirs in the world, while Iraq was diverted by the war with Iran. Most of the 50-mile-long, banana-shaped pool of oil sat in Iraqi territory, but two miles of its southern tip jutted into Kuwait. Iraq demanded adjustments in its border with Kuwait so that the entire oil field would come under Iraqi control. It also handed the Kuwaitis a bill for $2.4 billion for what it claimed was lost revenue because of their exploitation of the field.

Before the Iran-Iraq war, Iraq, which had consistently refused to negotiate an agreement with Kuwait on the use of Rumaila, had drawn significant amounts of oil from it. But the war made Iraq's oil reservoirs vulnerable to Iranian attack. Iraq closed its operations at Rumaila and laid thousands of mines. For its part, Kuwait increased its production from that field, in part to sell oil for Iraq's war effort. When Iraq began to drill again in the field after the war, it accused Kuwait of using advanced equipment to siphon oil from the Iraqi side of the field. The Kuwaitis denied the charge, but many oil experts agreed that it was true.

All these developments came together in a vast conspiracy theory that Saddam had conceived years before. Over the years, he wove in new elements until he constructed a rigid argument that convinced him that the world was out to get him. On the eve of the Iran-Iraq war in 1980, the theory went, Iraq was both economically and diplomatically at the height of its power. The regime had championed the Arab world's opposition to the Camp David peace accords. At home, Iraq's treasury was full, its development programs booming. Then the war broke out—Saddam said it was Iran's fault—and the world did little to stop it. Countries continued to sell arms to Iran. The secret American arms sales to Tehran at a time when the Reagan administration professed support for Iraq proved the cynicism and duplicity of the Americans. Still, Saddam the Arab savior fought on for the whole Arab nation. He deserved something in return. He began to believe there were three solutions to his problem: a dramatic increase in oil prices, territorial concessions from Kuwait, and an ambitious "Marshall Plan" for rebuilding Iraq. But help was not forthcoming. In the postwar era, he said, the world would not tolerate a powerful Iraq. In Saddam's eyes, there was a vast American- and Zionist-inspired plot to rob him of his destiny.

Accordingly, Saddam said, the West launched a three-pronged attack against him. Economically, it tried to burden Iraq with so much debt that it could not recover from the Iran-Iraq war. The West—through its lackeys, Kuwait and the United Arab Emirates—flooded the market with cheap oil to prevent Iraq from amassing much-needed hard currency. Militarily, the West collaborated to try to prohibit technology transfers and the purchase of advanced weapons that Iraq needed to confront Israel in the post–Cold War era. Politically, both the United States and Israel conducted a smear campaign, attacking Iraq for its treatment of the Kurds and its use of chemical weapons. The United States even sent missions to the Middle East and secret cables to various American embassies to enlist the help of other Arab states to keep Iraq weak, he said. As proof, the Iraqis produced a "top-secret" memo from Kuwait's director of national security, Brigadier General Fahd Ahmad al-Fahd, to the minister of the interior, Sheik Salem al-Sabah al-Salem al-Sabah, claiming that the CIA had agreed on the importance of damaging Iraq's economy in order to force Iraq to agree to a border agreement with Kuwait. The CIA called the document crude Iraqi disinformation.

~

With the staunch support of Jordan, the two Yemens, Libya, and the PLO, Saddam Hussein had begun to eclipse both Egypt's Mubarak and Saudi Arabia's Fahd as the leader who set the political agenda for the region. In preparation for the May 1990 Arab League summit in Baghdad, Iraq publicized details of a State Department memorandum that had been circulated to American embassies in the Arab world. The memo was innocuous enough—it instructed U.S. diplomats to advise the conference participants that if they resorted to inflammatory attacks on the United States, they risked damaging their relationships with Washington. For Saddam, the memo was further confirmation of the conspiracy against him.

Initially, Saddam intended to use the summit as a vehicle to boost his status as the Arab world's most vociferous opponent of Israel and of Soviet Jewish emigration to Israel. But on May 30 he turned the attention of the summit to his own problems. He told an emergency closed meeting of the Arab League that oil overproduction by both Kuwait and the United Arab Emirates had destroyed the OPEC quota system and cost his country $14 billion. "We cannot tolerate this type of economic warfare," he warned.

On a tour of the Gulf in late June, Iraqi Deputy Prime Minister Saadoun Hammadi went to Kuwait and demanded a dramatic increase in oil prices and an immediate $10 billion from the Sabahs. The Kuwaitis knew that if they gave $10 billion in 1990, they would have to give it every year. Kuwait's ambassador to Washington, Sheik Saud Nasir al-Sabah, recalled the meeting: "The emir said to him, 'We are going through an economic crisis. The price of oil is down. We have an internal economic problem with our stock market. We are willing to make available to you immediately $600 million to rebuild the Fao area." According to the Kuwaiti version, the emir promised to help in specific reconstruction projects in the subsequent two years, but only if Kuwait could ultimately decide how the money was spent. He agreed to forgive Iraq's debt to Kuwait on the condition that Iraq agree to reschedule the rest of its foreign debt according to established financial practices.

But the gravity of the matter seemed to elude the emir. He told his Iraqi guest that Sheik Ali al-Khalifa al-Sabah, by then minister of finance, would get in touch with his Iraqi counterpart sometime in the future, a gesture that the Iraqis interpreted as a brush-off. Hammadi left abruptly without accepting or declining the offer.

On July 17, in a televised speech marking the 22nd anniversary of the Iraqi revolution, Saddam Hussein for the first time publicly accused Arab oil-exporting countries of trying to strangle his economy and threatened to use force against them. Without mentioning Kuwait and the United Arab Emirates by name, he accused them of plotting with the United States to flood the market with cheap oil, repeating the charge that Iraq had lost $14 billion a year because of their connivance. Elaborating on his conspiracy theory, he asserted that Iraq had sacrificed "the flower of its youth" on the battlefield with Iran so that the treasuries of certain unnamed Arab states "could become ever more crammed with money." Instead of rewarding Iraq as their savior, he complained, "they plunged a poisoned dagger in our back." If diplomacy failed to resolve the crisis, he warned, Iraq "will remember the proverb that cutting necks is better than cutting livelihoods. If words cannot provide its people with protection, then action will have to be taken."

The next day, a letter that Tariq Aziz had delivered to the Arab League accusing Kuwait of border violations was made public. The letter said that

Kuwait had built "military installations, border posts, oil installations, and farms" on Iraqi territory and had stolen $2.4 billion of oil from the Rumaila oil field. In tones usually reserved for Israel, it called such action "tantamount to military aggression." He mentioned Kuwait and the United Arab Emirates by name, accusing them of participating in an "imperialist plan" to depress oil prices.

Aziz's aggressive tone was undercut by his humiliating appeal for help. He found himself in the uncomfortable position of asking for an Arab Marshall Plan for Iraq. "Iraq sacrificed this debt many times over from its own resources throughout the destructive war and offered rivers of blood from the flower of its youth in defense of the nation's territory and its honor, dignity and wealth ...," Aziz argued. "Doesn't the nationalist logic and security, if we take the American precedent as an example, impel these states to cancel this claim on Iraq and furthermore to organize an Arab plan similar to the Marshall Plan to compensate Iraq for what it lost in the war?"

Kuwait dispatched delegations of ministers to nearly all the Arab countries and wrote a letter to the Arab League claiming "astonishment and surprise" and "indignation" at what it called the "baseless" allegations by "sisterly Iraq."

Paradoxically, by now Saddam had become not only the main arbiter of OPEC oil prices but also the OPEC policeman, successfully challenging Saudi Arabia's leadership in setting oil policy. At a meeting in Geneva on July 25, Saddam forced Kuwait and the UAE to reduce production and pressured OPEC to raise prices, although not nearly as much as he would have liked. On July 27, OPEC agreed to raise its target oil price by $3, to $21 a barrel. In pushing up oil prices, Saddam achieved some of what he said he wanted. It was not enough.

As tensions rose, Iraq began to move troops to its southern border and to focus exclusively on Kuwait. Because of their shared border, Kuwait was an easier target than the UAE, which had never been an enemy of Iraq. Further, on July 23, the U.S. Air Force, in response to the Iraqi threats, began modest, emergency refueling exercises with the United Arab Emirates, involving two American aerial tankers and an American cargo transport plane. The Bush administration announced that the exercises were conducted at the UAE's request; the UAE, afraid that this disclosure would enrage Saddam even more, denied that it was carrying out joint maneuvers and insisted that the United States was merely engaged in technical training. Pentagon officials suggested to Kuwait's ambassador in Washington that if Kuwait wanted U.S. military cooperation, Washington would be happy to oblige. But the ambassador could not convince the emir or the crown prince, and the offer was turned down. By the following week, Iraq had openly moved 30,000, then 100,000, troops to its border with the emirate.

∼ The Jiddah Debacle

On July 31, King Fahd invited Kuwait's crown prince, Sheik Saad al-Abdullah al-Sabah, and Izzat Ibrahim, officially Iraq's second-in-command, to the Saudi seaside city of Jiddah to discuss the dispute. Ibrahim, a quiet survivor who had been one of Saddam's coconspirators before the 1968 Baath Party takeover, was so little trusted at home that he tape-recorded the conversations. Visibly nervous, he read from a prepared text. He repeated Iraq's demands. The Kuwaitis came up with a feeble reply that they believed would defuse the tension—a list of their own demands, including the redeployment of troops away from the border and an end to hostile propaganda. In addition, according to Kuwaiti Foreign Minister Sheik Sabah al-Ahmad al-Sabah, in an interview shortly after the invasion with the Egyptian magazine *al-Mussawar*, "Iraq asked us to drop the debt and we did not object. Iraq asked for Bubiyan island. We agreed to give them Warba island." Sheik Saad presented the paper to Ibrahim, who told him bluntly that he had no authority to negotiate, only to communicate the demands. After 90 minutes, Ibrahim announced, "The meeting is over. Nothing is negotiable." He added that he had a bad headache and wanted to be alone.

Although the talks collapsed, King Fahd believed he had convinced the two sides to meet again in Baghdad a week later. He brought them together for a lavish Lebanese-style meal in the guest palace in Jiddah. "All was correct," said one Kuwaiti participant. "We talked about nothing, about palm dates and horses." But as Iraqi and Kuwaiti ministers were dining, Iraq's troops were loading their vehicles and assembling their weapons. The Kuwaitis left Jiddah at 6 P.M. on Wednesday; eight hours later, the first Iraqi troops crossed the border.

On the night of August 1, foreign diplomats in Baghdad gathered in the al-Rasheed Hotel for a reception hosted by the Chinese. The talk was about the failed Jiddah discussions. The consensus was that if the Iraqis were to move, they would only cross the border. "No one," said one ambassador in Baghdad, "hallucinated that Saddam would go all the way."

∼

Saddam Hussein's historical claims to Kuwait sounded particularly absurd to Turkey's president, Turgut Ozal. Shortly after the August 2 invasion, Iraq's First Deputy Prime Minister, Taha Yassin Ramadan, visited Turkey to plead Iraq's case. As Ozal told a group of journalists over breakfast in Washington a few weeks after the invasion, "He explained to me, he said, 'Basra province at the time of the Ottoman period had Kuwait, and that is the historical evidence.' " To Ozal's ears, such an argument was nonsense. Until World War I, the Ottoman Turks controlled much of the Middle East, although their claim of sovereignty over Kuwait was never recognized. "I almost said that the whole of Iraq belonged to us, including Kuwait," Ozal said, smiling. "This is history, you see."

~ 10 ~
The Invasion of Kuwait

The Revolutionary Command Council has decided to respond to the request made by Kuwait's free provisional government . . . We will withdraw when the situation becomes stable and when Kuwait's free provisional government asks us to do so. This may not exceed a few days or a few weeks. . . . We will make of the glorious Iraq and the dear Kuwait a graveyard for all those who may be tempted to launch aggression and who are moved by the desire to invade and betray.

> —Iraq's Revolutionary Command Council, announcing the invasion of Kuwait on Baghdad Radio, August 2, 1990

This will not stand.

> —George Bush on the White House lawn, August 5, 1990

~ The Invasion of Kuwait

At 2 A.M. on Thursday, August 2, 1990, Iraq crossed the line that British colonialists had drawn in the sand nearly 70 years earlier. One hundred twenty thousand of Saddam Hussein's battle-hardened soldiers moved in waves across the border into Kuwait. They came in columns of tanks, in armored personnel carriers, in trucks and vans, supported by helicopter gunships overhead and fuel and water tankers behind. The thunder of 1,000 Soviet-made T-72 tanks and as many as 900 armored fighting vehicles rent the quiet of the flat, dusty scrubland of southeastern Iraq as they overwhelmed the desert emirate. The war machines hurtled down a six-lane highway built by the oil riches of Kuwait's ruling family and across the desert toward the capital city

80 miles away, setting off alarms in listening posts in the Gulf and in capitals around the world.

The invasion was not a surgical strike against key Kuwaiti installations, but a relentless and undisguised onslaught of military power. With its Army of one million men, Baghdad had the means to easily overwhelm Kuwaiti forces. Iraq had more than 700 combat aircraft; up to 5,500 Soviet, Chinese, and British battle tanks; more than 8,000 armored personnel carriers and infantry fighting vehicles; and 160 armed helicopters. Still stung by their failure to achieve an expected early victory in Iran a decade earlier, the Iraqis were taking no chances. The forces sent into Kuwait were far larger than what would have been needed to occupy the country. So massive was the assault that Saddam Hussein was quickly able to feel confident of victory. He sent reinforcements in rickety buses left over from war days with Iran.

A special operations division with helicopter-borne troops moved across the western part of Iraq's border with Kuwait, followed by an assault of three infantry divisions in trucks and armored personnel carriers. The first Iraqi units occupied the small extension of the Rumaila oil field that spilled over from Iraq into Kuwaiti territory. Other soldiers seized Bubiyan island, the tiny but strategic land mass that Saddam had long coveted because it blocked Iraq's access to the sea. It took the Iraqis little more than an hour to reach the capital at Kuwait City.

Initially, the Sabahs were so blind to Iraq's intentions that when Kuwait's ambassador to Washington, Sheik Saud Nasir al-Sabah, urgently called his Foreign Ministry with American intelligence reports of the first troop movements toward the border, he was told that his information was wrong. His superiors accused him of panicking and, even worse, of catching a bad case of clientitis. In Kuwait City, meanwhile, Crown Prince Sheik Saad al-Abdullah al-Sabah called the American Embassy for immediate help to stop the invasion, but he insisted that the request "not be made public or treated as official." He called back an hour later to make the request official, and, if need be, public; before the United States could reply, the crown prince had rushed to Dasman Palace, the royal residence on the shore of the Gulf, to save the emir from death or capture. As the Iraqi attackers bombed the main airport, the key ministries, and the country's main military airbase, the emir and his family rushed to find an escape route. They fled the palace to the Saudi desert in a caravan of bullet-proof Mercedes limousines—leaving behind their wives, their children, and their people.

At 6 A.M., four hours into the invasion, Iraqi tanks and artillery attacked Dasman Palace. Dasman, which means "place of plenty," was less a grand palace than an old villa, the centerpiece of a walled compound that had been completed in 1930 by the emir's father, Sheik Ahmad al-Jaber al-Sabah. Set back from the main Gulf Road that faces the sea, the compound included other villas for the emir's vast family, a mosque, a garden, and a military barracks. The emir had substantially bolstered security around the palace after an Iranian-inspired assassination attempt in May 1985. Still, the compound continued to be a place of tranquillity, a quiet reminder of what Kuwait was before the oil boom of the 1960s and 1970s.

Fifty Iraqi tanks surrounded Dasman Palace and the nearby American Embassy. Other troops attacked by helicopter. Because of poor planning or an unwillingness to take risks, the troops moved in slowly and were left unsupported for several hours. The emir's private guard fought back desperately, took a number of Iraqi soldiers captive, and held on for about two hours, using artillery, machine guns, and bazookas. But the Iraqis needed the palace to consolidate power quickly by either driving out or destroying the Sabah clan. As Iraqi jets flew overhead, the Iraqis finished their assault, bombing the palace throughout the first day and leaving it a burnt-out shell.

The emir's younger half-brother, Sheik Fahd al-Ahmad al-Sabah—the popular head of Kuwait's Olympic Committee and a former commander of a paratroop regiment who had fought in Lebanon in the 1960s on the side of the Palestinians—stayed behind and was killed. A heroic version of the story was told this way by a 21-year-old Iraqi soldier named Jassim who deserted to Turkey after the assault: "He personally killed several soldiers around me and he inspired his men to keep up their defense. But they had no chance—we were too many. When the Sheik was shot, many of the Iraqis cheered. An officer ordered the Sheik's body to be put in front of a tank and run over."

~

In the days before the invasion, according to Egypt's President Hosni Mubarak and Saudi Arabia's King Fahd, Saddam Hussein had given his word that he would not invade Kuwait. He had told the American ambassador to Baghdad, April Glaspie, that he would not resort to force as long as negotiations were proceeding to resolve a recently renewed border dispute with Kuwait. In conversations with Jordan's King Hussein, Yemen's President Ali Abdullah Saleh, and PLO leader Yassir Arafat, he had stressed the seriousness of the matter but had given no clue to his intentions. They, in turn, had passed on assurances to the emir. King Hussein twice telephoned President Bush—on July 28 and again on July 30—to assure him that Saddam would not resort to the use of military force. In the Arab world, a person's word determines one's standing. No Arab leader could believe that another would lie to him about a matter so grave.

On the recommendation of Arab leaders who advised against provoking Saddam and who hoped against mounting odds that appeasement could still work, Kuwait did not position troops at the Iraqi border. Instead, it took its sentries off alert status. Some foreign diplomats, concerned by the massive buildup of Iraqi troops on the border, called Kuwait's Civil Defense Ministry in the days before the Iraqi invasion in case it became necessary to evacuate foreigners, but they were told that key officials were on vacation and they should call back in three weeks.

Both the Kuwaitis and the Saudis were convinced that the Iraqi troop buildup was a bluff. On the night of July 27, an American reconnaissance satellite detected Iraqi trucks transporting fuel, water, ammunition, and other supplies from Baghdad and Basra toward the troops massed at the border. The Bush administration informed the Saudi and Kuwaiti ambassadors in Washington of the intelligence reports and called the buildup "ominous." But the Saudis advised the United States to play down the troop buildup, "so that it wouldn't become a self-fulfilling prophecy," recalled Prince Bandar bin Sultan, the Saudi ambassador to Washington. The Kuwaitis, meanwhile, ever suspicious of American intentions, thought that the United States was exaggerating the threat as a pretext for increasing its military presence in the Gulf.

Four days before the invasion, the Bush administration went back to the two ambassadors, telling them that Iraq's forces were now in battle formation and had been issued ammunition. This time, King Fahd telephoned Saddam and sent his foreign minister to Baghdad, but Saddam assured them that his troops were merely conducting seasonal exercises. The Saudis relayed that message to the White House and the Pentagon, advising the United States to sit tight. A full-scale invasion was simply not one of the scenarios. The Kuwaitis had supported Saddam during his long war with Iran. If there were a military move, they reasoned, it would be a brief border crossing, a scare tactic to get the Kuwaitis to bend to Iraqi demands—nothing out of the ordinary in a region where most borders were either contrived or disputed. They felt so safe that much of the emirate—including much of the military establishment and diplomatic corps—had left for vacations abroad. Soviet ambassador Victor Posuvaliuk paid a call on Iraq's foreign minister, Tariq Aziz, on July 29 and asked him if he could depart for his annual leave. "Sure," Aziz replied, smiling. So he left, as had his British and Canadian colleagues.

Even if the United States had correctly analyzed the intelligence reports on Iraq's military buildup, it could have done little except threaten Saddam with military action, a strategy that was anathema to the Saudis, the Kuwaitis, and the Egyptians, who pleaded for silence and discouraged any American military response. Saddam was still regarded as a brother, however wayward. Only after the invasion did the Gulf states conclude that they faced a threat so large that they would need to invite in outsiders to protect them, and that Saddam might be completely out of control.

~

An old Arab proverb advises: "Show your enemy your sword and your gold." Kuwait certainly had the money to buy off its enemies, but not the military force to confront them. The country was ill-prepared to resist the invasion. Kuwait was 1/25 the size of Iraq, with about one-ninth of its population. On paper, its military consisted of 20,000 troops, but the actual number was closer to 16,000. Only a minority were Kuwaitis, and most of those were officers. There was a draft, but exemptions were easy to obtain. Some of the troops were part of expert combat-capable battalions, but many—too many—were ill-trained Bedouins who were not Kuwaiti citizens. The military also included Britons, Jordanians, Palestinians, and Egyptians seconded from their own services or working on contract. For nearly a decade, Kuwait's defensive structure had been geared toward dealing with a threat from Iran, particularly Iranian aircraft and missiles, which had successfully attacked Kuwait during the Iran-Iraq war. The military conducted only infrequent exercises, and there was virtually no coordination among the services.

Like the other Gulf states, Kuwait was the victim of the "glitter factor" in its arms purchases. From 1977 to 1987, the emirate spent $2.2 billion for arms, by no means a massive sum. But it bought the weaponry piecemeal, gobbling sophisticated systems from whatever willing sellers it could find, with little regard for military strategy or use. Sales pitches were often made to the politicians in the capital, not to the defense ministers and commanders who would have to use the weapons.

In 1988, Kuwait concluded a $1.8 billion deal to buy 40 F-18 aircraft from the United States, a flashy onetime purchase that nearly matched its entire military expenditure for the previous decade. The emirate said it needed the sophisticated planes for its air defense against threats in the region. It was just plain luck that none of them were delivered by the time Iraq invaded, or they might have fallen into Iraqi hands. Of the 245 tanks the Kuwaitis owned on paper, only about 90 were operational; the rest were in storage, in training, or undergoing repairs. Their armored fighting vehicles were a bad mix from the inventories of a number of countries. The Kuwaiti artillery was grossly underarmed and far from combat ready. Despite the sophistication of the antitank weapons, they were an awkward mixture of Soviet, French, and American equipment, each requiring different training systems. The Kuwaiti air defense system, too, was poorly integrated; the emirate had bought Soviet ground-to-air missiles even though they couldn't use them with the rest of their air defense; they had trouble supporting and running their more than 20 French-made Mirages, the best planes in their Air Force. "It was," said Anthony H. Cordesman, an expert on modern warfare, "a mixture of leftovers, a dog's breakfast."

~

Within Kuwait, the initial reaction to the invasion was one of disbelief. Although the emirate was by far the most democratic of the Arab Gulf states, its news media were censored, so there had been no mention of Iraq's massive border buildup in the newspapers or on radio or television in the weeks beforehand. Some people learned about it, however, from the BBC, the Voice of America, and CNN, which was beamed into the country via satellite, and from official Iraqi television, which was within range of Kuwait City.

At 4:05 A.M. on August 2, Stephanie McGehee, an American freelance photographer, and Kathy-Lynn McGregor, a Canadian executive with a Kuwaiti hotel, were awakened by the sound of distant explosions. The two women ran to the balcony of their seaside apartment. "The sea was like glass, first light, peaceful, birds singing, no cars on the road," they wrote in a diary. "The explosions had been distant, no sign of the source, no smoke—nothing. We didn't feel threatened at that moment, so we went back to bed."

By 5 A.M., the women were awakened again by gunshots, and they realized the Iraqis were coming. Their balcony gave them a front-row seat: "We saw busloads of soldiers—so much activity. Our first thought was that these were Kuwaiti soldiers. . . . It was soon clear that these were not Kuwaitis, as they started shooting at cars that refused to stop at the checkpoint. We saw them running on the streets in front of us firing machine guns. Chaos in the streets. . . . We knew the Iraqi soldiers had been massing on our borders. We knew what kind of man Saddam was, yet we never, ever thought he would dare invade us."

Kuwaitis and those foreign workers with no access to outside news woke up the morning of the invasion in complete ignorance of what was happening. Many headed off to their jobs as usual, not realizing that the makeshift checkpoints at various intersections were manned by Iraqi, not Kuwaiti, soldiers. Later, panicked Kuwaitis abandoned their cars at roadblocks and fled on foot. Others watched from their rooftops what they thought was pure spectacle, a fantastic air show of low-flying Iraqi helicopter gunships and artillery.

"Everyone went to the streets and to the roofs to watch," recalled Abbas al-Muallah, a 53-year-old retired Kuwaiti civil aircraft expert who fled with his family to Saudi Arabia three months after the invasion. "Everyone thought it was a joke. Everyone thought it was the Iraqis showing off. It was only in the late afternoon that we started realizing what had happened, that we were losing our country."

A communiqué broadcast simultaneously on Iraqi radio and television and on a Kuwaiti radio station stated that Saddam had moved in his tanks and troops to support a coup by young Kuwaiti revolutionaries opposed to the Sabah family. It said that the new government had dismissed the emir, and it promised free, honest elections. One of the final messages broadcast by Kuwaitis before the Iraqis gained full control of the airwaves was a pathetic plea from a commentator for other Arab nations to "rush, rush to our help."

At the Kuwaiti military compound near the southern border, the minister of foreign affairs, the minister of planning, and other senior officials stood by helplessly, watching as tiny blips—representing the Iraqi military—on a state-of-the-art electronic tracking system filled the screen and swarmed across the map of Kuwait throughout the morning. As the Iraqis moved in, the ministers retreated to a police station on the Kuwait-Saudi border, where they monitored the fighting from their car phones. At 11 A.M., they received a call from the military compound that Kuwait was lost. "The message was, 'Say goodbye to Kuwait. We've run out of ammunition,' " recalled Abdullah Bishara, the Kuwaiti who heads the Gulf Cooperation Council. "From that moment on, we became witnesses to our destruction. Everyone was trying to find his own survival route. It was total disarray. We were outgunned, outmanned, outmaneuvered, outflanked, outarmed. Too many outs."

Twelve hours after Saddam began his attack, he controlled the airport, the central bank, the radio and television stations, and all key government buildings. The Iraqi occupiers set up their headquarters at the Sheraton Hotel, evacuating the guests and moving them to a park across the street, where they were ordered to lie face-down. Drunk with victory, the invaders waved Iraqi flags as they raced their cars through deserted streets. By the evening of August 3, Iraq firmly controlled Kuwaiti television, announcing in a communiqué that "the national power" had decided to leave the country and promising a "new era of democracy" for Kuwait. The so-called Kuwaiti announcer spoke with an Iraqi accent and did not know how to wear the *gutra*, the traditional Kuwaiti headdress.

~ Washington Wakes Up

In Washington, it was just another sweltering August night. Only three people were on duty in the Situation Room of the White House. Dinner hour had passed and they were working through a routine night shift in the highly secure conference room in the basement of the West Wing that served as President Bush's electronic lifeline to the Pentagon, the CIA, and the State Department.

By the afternoon before the invasion, U.S. satellite photos showed that Iraqi soldiers, part of a formation of 100,000, had begun loading their weapons and assembling and moving their forces, and the Pentagon's top generals had met to consider a top-secret cable indicating that Iraq had an actual invasion force assembled and ready to attack. The CIA estimated that there was more than a 50 percent chance of an invasion but assumed that at most Saddam would take Kuwait's two strategic islands and the Kuwaiti side of the Rumaila oil field. No alarms were sounded. Hindered by their policy of accommodating Saddam, and lulled by assurances from Arab leaders, the president and his aides had let down their guard.

George Bush was in the White House, but his attention was focused far from the Gulf—on grueling negotiations with Congress over the federal budget. The White House had an inkling of what was happening in Kuwait by about 6:30 that evening—1:30 A.M. in Baghdad—half an hour before the first Iraqi troops crossed the border. Brent Scowcroft, the austere but likable military intellectual from Utah who served as national security adviser, took Richard N. Haass, his deputy for the Middle East, into the Oval Office to see the president. There was no hard evidence yet of an invasion, just sketchy reports of military movements.

At 6:45 P.M., Robert M. Kimmitt, the under secretary of state for political affairs, contacted Secretary of State James A. Baker III in the remote Siberian city of Irkutsk. Kimmitt told him in elliptical language over an unsecure phone line that the CIA had concluded that the situation on the Iraq-Kuwait border was "far more serious than we had been led elsewhere to believe." The secretary relayed the news to his fishing buddy, Soviet Foreign Minister Eduard A. Shevardnadze. The two officials had developed the most trusting relationship in the history of Soviet-American diplomacy. Shevardnadze was visibly shaken. "Our experts say that cannot happen," he said.

At 8:40 P.M., Kimmitt telephoned Scowcroft to tell him that Iraqi forces had just crossed the Kuwaiti border and had taken some border positions. Scowcroft seemed taken aback. He said he had just spoken to William H. Webster, director of the Central Intelligence Agency, who had not indicated that anything was happening on the ground.

The United States—and the rest of the world—probably could have lived with a partial invasion of Kuwait that could then have been sorted out later among the two countries and their Arab neighbors. Only a few days earlier, for example, Scowcroft had talked about Iraq's military buildup and the possibility of an attack. He said that the administration would not be surprised if Iraq launched a limited strike against Kuwait and seized the two islands and the oil field that jutted from Iraq across the Kuwaiti border. If that happened, he added, "There's not much we can do."

Other senior aides were caught off guard. Robert M. Gates, the former CIA official who served as Scowcroft's deputy, had taken off for a hiking trip in Washington state. General Colin Powell, chairman of the Joint Chiefs of Staff, was getting ready to go on vacation. Secretary of Defense Dick Cheney was planning to accompany George Bush to Aspen, Colorado, where the president was scheduled to give a speech the following day on the future of America's defense. Then Cheney, too, would go on vacation.

Soon after the invasion began, intelligence reports pointing to a massive military operation in Kuwait began pouring into the Situation Room. At 4 A.M., Scowcroft lay down on the couch in his office and took a short nap while the Treasury Department drafted an executive order to freeze Kuwaiti and Iraqi assets in the United States, estimated at $30 billion. Forty-five minutes later, he took the order to the president, who signed it in bed. Forty-five minutes after that, Bush was in his private study, watching the latest television reports. Britain and France quickly joined the United States in freezing Kuwaiti and Iraqi assets.

In those early hours, it was largely a political operation, but by the next morning, military leaders were making preparations to give the president options for sending troops to the Middle East.

~ The Middle East Reacts

Most Arab capitals responded initially to Iraq's invasion of Kuwait with private shock—and public silence. They ignored Kuwait's public cries for help and urged the United States to stay out of the crisis and allow Arab diplomacy to work.

In Cairo on August 2, aides awoke President Hosni Mubarak at dawn with the news that Saddam Hussein had crossed the border. "I woke up and I couldn't believe what was going on," Mubarak later told reporters. "I was dazed." When Mubarak had traveled to Baghdad to confront Saddam face-to-face with evidence of his military buildup in the days before the invasion, Saddam had denied the reports, the Egyptian leader said. "He told me these were just routine movements and that the troops were 80 kilometers away from the border. And then I asked him another question: Did he intend to attack Kuwait? And he told me no."

To calm the waters just before the invasion, Mubarak had called Saddam a "man of peace" and characterized the trouble between Iraq and Kuwait as "a cloud that will pass with the wind." A sadder, wiser Mubarak acknowledged afterward that he should have trusted the evidence on the ground rather than the word of Saddam. "If someone is planning an invasion, he would not tell the others about it because this will spoil everything," he said.

At almost the same time that Mubarak was told, aides woke Saudi Arabia's King Fahd in Riyadh. "Are you sure?" the king asked, stunned by the action by the Arab leader he had supported, bankrolled, and defended throughout his war with Iran. Saddam had assured the Saudi monarch that the troop buildup was simply "very normal movements and normal training of the Iraqi Army," the king later told reporters. He, too, felt betrayed. "It is only natural that we believe a head of state," Fahd said. "We are supposed to believe a president."

Fahd tried to phone Saddam five times that day but was told that the Iraqi leader was not within range of a telephone. When Saddam finally called back in the afternoon, he was lighthearted and confident. "My brother, don't worry about this," he told Fahd. "It's not a big deal." Fahd pressed Saddam to withdraw his troops to the border area, promising that if the troops were out, he would go to Baghdad, convince the emir to go as well, and find "an Arab solution" to the crisis.

On August 6, Saddam denied that he ever promised not to invade. "There were rumors that Saddam Hussein promised certain Arab officials that he would not resort to force in any way, shape, form, or under any circumstances against Kuwait . . . ," Saddam told Joseph C. Wilson IV, the American chargé d'affaires in Baghdad, in a private meeting. "I gave no such guarantee to any Arab."

From Jordan, King Hussein, who had become Saddam's closest ally in the Arab world, phoned Tariq Aziz and later spoke to Saddam himself. King Hussein had also supported Iraq throughout its eight-year war with Iran, allowing vital supplies to pass overland to the Jordanian port of Aqaba on the Red Sea when Iraq lost its access to the Gulf. Saddam gave Jordan $50 million a year in outright aid; Jordan imported more than 80 percent of its oil from Iraq on easy barter terms; tens of thousands of Jordanians, many of Palestinian origin, were employed in Iraq, sending $800 million in remittances back home every year. Jordanian exports to Iraq totaled $500 million annually, and 45 percent of the traffic through Aqaba was Iraqi-related.

In Middle Eastern style, King Hussein tried to open the bazaar, to get serious bargaining started. But he was powerless to make threats, and Saddam Hussein was not in the mood to negotiate. To complicate matters, King Hussein's own agenda was murky. Washington's longtime friend, the quintessential Arab moderate in the eyes of the West, he became an apologist for Saddam. Even after the invasion, he called the Iraqi leader "a person to be trusted and dealt with . . . an Arab patriot in the eyes of many."

On the day of the invasion, the Jordanian monarch flew to the Egyptian port of Alexandria to meet Mubarak, who argued that they had to find a "face-saver"—a dignified way out that would not leave Saddam empty-handed. King Hussein stressed that they had to avoid a condemnation of Saddam by the Arab League, whose foreign ministers were meeting on other matters in Cairo. Mubarak spoke with the Kuwaiti emir, Saudi Arabia's King Fahd, Syria's President Hafez al-Assad, and Yemen's President Ali Abdullah Saleh, expressing the hope that the Arabs could keep the crisis "in the family" and find a way to reason with Saddam. He convinced Fahd, "with great difficulty," he said later, to postpone a potentially divisive vote by the 21-member Arab League for at least one day.

That same day, Israel publicly denounced the invasion. But privately, some Israeli officials expressed satisfaction that their assessment of Saddam as a regional menace had been confirmed. The official Saudi Press Agency expressed only "deep concern"; Mubarak's press secretary announced that the Egyptian president "has been following the situation." In Damascus, a spokesman for Assad said only that the Syrian president was consulting with Mubarak about "what useful moves could be undertaken concerning these dangerous developments." Algeria, which tended to side with Iraq, issued a statement through an unnamed Foreign Ministry spokesman, who expressed "deep pain and concern" and warned of "increased dangers of foreign intervention in the region." An official Libyan statement echoed that sentiment, saying, "Foreign intervention by imperialist powers is something which we utterly reject." Yassir Arafat, meanwhile, flew to Baghdad the day after the invasion and was seen on television throughout the Arab world embracing Saddam.

The Arab League met for a full day without agreeing on a joint declaration of concern. In one of the first public statements to come out of the Arab world, Clovis Maksoud, the veteran Arab League representative to the United Nations, explained in New York that member countries "don't think it is advisable . . . to render moral judgment" against Iraq because such condemnation could harm the league's potential role as a mediator. The Arab foreign ministers squabbled for two days before passing a resolution condemning the invasion of Kuwait—and even then, Iraq, Jordan, Libya, Algeria, Sudan, Yemen, Mauritania, and the PLO either voted against the resolution or abstained.

On the morning of the invasion, Jalal Talabani, the Iraqi Kurdish leader whose supporters were gassed by Iraqi troops in 1988, was awakened by a neighbor at his Damascus home. Just the night before, Talabani later said, he had warned dinner guests that an invasion was coming, "if not tomorrow, then in the coming days." Unlike most of the world, Talabani said the news delighted him. "I was very glad when I heard about it," he recalled. "I said to myself that this has been Saddam's biggest mistake, and it will lead him to his grave."

~ Do We Send Troops?

Washington never enjoyed particularly close relations with Kuwait. Because of its large, noncitizen Palestinian population, the emirate took a shrill, anti-American line on the Arab-Israeli conflict. In 1983, it had refused to accredit a career Foreign Service officer, Brandon H. Grove, Jr., as ambassador because he had served as consul general in Jerusalem, even though the United States did not recognize Jerusalem as Israel's capital. For several decades, Kuwait had been the only Gulf country that maintained diplomatic relations with Moscow and had even bought Soviet weapons. In January 1987, at the height of the "tanker war" in the Gulf, the emirate skillfully played Moscow and Washington off against each other to convince both countries to escort its tankers through the Gulf. The Reagan administration, concerned about an increased Soviet presence in the Gulf, had no choice but to accept, even though Kuwait refused to allow the U.S. Navy any onshore facilities.

Had it not been for the American Navy's reflagging and escorting of Kuwaiti oil tankers during the war between Iran and Iraq, many Americans probably would never have known of Kuwait's existence until Saddam's invasion. The emirate was less a country than the largest shopping mall in the Gulf, it was often said—a sanitized, futuristic bazaar of glass and concrete built on sand with a flag and a seat at the United Nations. Rich Kuwaitis bought their jewelry at Harry Winston and their couturier clothes on the rue du Faubourg St.-Honoré in Paris. They had their teeth capped in London and vacationed in summer homes in Marbella and Beverly Hills. The ultra-modern shopping centers in Kuwait City were open day and night, over-flowing with extravagant consumer goods—Japanese cellular telephones, Swedish mink, French luggage, Russian caviar. Kuwait's per capita income was one of the highest in the world. Perhaps the single best symbol of what oil wealth had done to Kuwait—little more than a Bedouin trading post before oil was discovered—was the $400 million conference center built for a meeting of the Islamic Conference Organization in 1987. It covered nearly 100 acres and included an elaborate shopping mall and lavish housing for the dele-gates—even a custom-made bed for the six-foot, eight-inch-tall President of Senegal.

The Kuwaitis were, and still are, the best businessmen of the Arab world, and the country was driven by a capitalistic business ethic of profit and loss—with the emphasis on profit. For years, the sheikdom had invested most of its money abroad—in American resorts, British banks, even a 14 percent share of Daimler-Benz stock. By 1988, the country earned more money from its overseas investments than from its oil, and, as a result, became the only oil-producing country in the world that did not have to worry much about fluctuating oil prices. The government had cleverly invested "downstream" by buying Gulf Oil's European refining operations and 4,700 retail gas stations spread from Italy to Denmark. More important, it had invested "upstream" as well, signing oil exploration contracts with countries as far-flung as China and Gabon—an ingenious way to make money on oil outside the constraints of OPEC. On the eve of the invasion, the country's overseas investments totaled $100 billion, those of individual Kuwaitis $50 billion more.

Most Americans could not relate to Kuwait's wealth, its social customs, and its political system. Even with falling oil prices, Kuwait spawned bil-lionaires, and even ordinary people became millionaires many times over.

The emir was a delicate, aloof, unexceptional monarch, not a heroic desert warrior. He had married about 70 times, and there was no official count of how many children he had fathered. Family members and other officials defended the practice, arguing that he adhered strictly to the Islamic practice of never keeping more than four wives at a time. Although he cul-tivated the image of a hoarder of billions who chose to live austerely, going to sleep early and rising before dawn to tend the roses in the palace garden, he made sure that hundreds of members of his vast family were installed in every government ministry and that they profited from most business ventures.

Despite its reputation as the most open society in the Gulf, Kuwait could hardly have been called democratic by any Western standard. It suspended its Parliament in 1986 and replaced it in June 1990 with a National Assembly with considerably fewer powers and less independence. Women were not allowed to vote, political parties were forbidden, and the press was censored. Slavery was still common in Kuwait and other parts of the Gulf well into the 1930s, and stories about the physical abuse and even rape of foreign servants—especially women from East Asia and the subcontinent—were common. Only those Kuwaitis whose ancestors had lived in the emirate in 1921 were made full citizens with all rights and privileges. Others enjoyed limited citizenship, and a third class had no citizenship at all. No matter how long foreigners lived in Kuwait, they could never acquire the right to buy a house, a piece of property, or more than a minor share in a business.

Kuwait knew that it had a perception problem. After the invasion, a group of influential Kuwaiti exiles organized a private group in Washington to publicize its plight. Called Citizens for a Free Kuwait, the group was funded largely by the Kuwaiti emirate-in-exile. The group hired the high-powered public-relations firm of Hill & Knowlton to improve Kuwait's image in the mind of America. In the three and a half months following the invasion of Kuwait, the public-relations firm received $5.6 million for its lobbying, one of the highest sums a public-relations firm has ever been paid for a contract for such a short period of time.

~

When President Bush convened his senior advisers at 8 A.M. on August 3, the key issue was Iraq's aggression, not America's relationship with Kuwait. As Bush and the others sat around the table in the White House Cabinet Room, they abandoned the premise that had guided American policy toward Iraq in recent years: that Saddam was a pragmatic, moderate leader with whom the United States could do business. They agreed that if the American military were going to move, it had to do so quickly and with maximum possible strength. Although there was some hesitation among American military leaders, General Powell was certain that the United States would send troops.

At that first meeting, Powell offered Bush the Pentagon's initial assessment of the military choices open to him. The strategy, if an attack were ordered, would be to carry out massive bombardments of targets in Iraq and on Iraqi military units maneuvering outside Kuwait City. But the president could also order a massive deployment aimed first at protecting Saudi Arabia and then at giving the United States a military springboard for a land attack on Iraq if Bush chose that course.

Powell, whose mistrust of vague political goals and small-scale military operations was born of his experience in the Vietnam war, wanted to be sure that the political decision to send soldiers was made forcefully and clearly before the first troop transports left. He also made certain that Bush knew from the outset that the risks were extraordinary: American forces would be extremely vulnerable to Iraqi attack; they might have to fight in 100-degree-plus heat; America might not tolerate images of its young men killed or wounded by Iraq's arsenal of poison-gas weapons. He was also determined not to be trapped with insufficient force on the ground if the political will for war was sapped at home.

But Bush's key advisers were divided on what Saddam Hussein's next move might be. CIA Director Webster had not predicted the invasion, and he was eager not to be accused again of underestimating Saddam. He said that the Iraqis would invade Saudi Arabia next, a view supported by some of the generals in the Joint Chiefs and their staff. Over the next few days, Webster's warnings became increasingly shrill; at one point, he telephoned Bush to insist that an invasion of Saudi Arabia was imminent.

Powell was more skeptical. He saw that Iraqi troops were moving south toward Saudi Arabia, but he thought it might be a feint, not a preparation for an invasion. Iraq's historic problems with Kuwait and its recent threats were well known, but Iraq had never threatened the Saudis; indeed, the two countries had taken the same side against Kuwait in recent OPEC meetings. But Powell did not want to take chances. He was a politician almost as much as he was a soldier. He saw that Saddam's action might be likened to Hitler's invasion of Central Europe in the 1930s—an aggressive dictatorship determined to swallow its neighbors while the rest of the world dithered about what to do. Armed with maps, charts, and satellite photographs, he painted a chilling picture of how easily and quickly Iraq had overrun Kuwait. Crucial Saudi pipelines and refineries were less than 100 miles south across the desert from Kuwait, and one major offshore Saudi oil field, Safaniya, was only about 40 miles from the border. Saddam had nothing to stop him if he wanted to continue his march.

～ The Saudi Embrace

Unlike Kuwait, Saudi Arabia was an important country in the mind of America. The United States had built its oil wells. When Richard Nixon was in the White House and Shah Mohammad Reza Pahlevi was still on the Peacock Throne in Iran, Washington based its policy in the Gulf on Saudi Arabia and Iran—rich, territorially large monarchies that would act as two pillars of stability and buffers against the Soviets. When Ayatollah Khomeini established an anti-American Islamic republic in Iran in 1979, Saudi Arabia became all the more important to U.S. interests.

On the second day of the invasion, American intelligence alerted the Saudis that Saddam was moving three divisions of soldiers, as well as ground-to-ground missiles and other equipment, toward Saudi Arabia. Saudi Arabia had a ground force of only 40,000 men and 250 tanks, plus a 35,000-man National Guard. Its arsenal included about 140 modern combat aircraft, backed up by an air defense that included roughly 800 surface-to-air missiles and five American AWACS early-warning aircraft. The Saudi military could never have withstood an Iraqi onslaught.

The Saudi armed forces, National Guard, and internal-security forces were organized under separate commands, each with its own function. The stovepipe structure was designed to prevent any branch from becoming too powerful, but it hindered coordination and efficiency. Another problem with the Saudi military was that Saudis saw themselves as dashing warriors, not cooks or bottle scrubbers or mechanics. Much of the maintenance of Saudi equipment was done by Yemenis. Prince Bandar bin Sultan, the Saudi ambassador to Washington, for example, had been a fighter pilot, not a drill sergeant, and the hero of the Saudi press for most of 1985 was Prince Sultan Salman al-Saud, a nephew of King Fahd who was the first Arab to fly in space.

As far back as 1945, King Abdul Aziz ibn Saud of Saudi Arabia had told Franklin Roosevelt, who had pledged to come to the king's defense, never to send any troops to the kingdom. Even if the United States could get permission from the Saudis to station troops in Saudi Arabia, the task of moving them to the region and supporting them in alien territory for an unknown period was daunting. Powell's fear was that the first American troops to arrive could be slaughtered because it would take so long to move in tanks and other protective weaponry.

In Aspen, where he met with British Prime Minister Margaret Thatcher on the day of the invasion, President Bush spoke to King Fahd by telephone, but both leaders danced around the sensitive subject of sending in American troops. Bush knew that there would have to be a military response, but he and his aides were not at all sure of Saudi resolve. For his part, King Fahd was concerned that the United States might not have the stomach or the staying power. Fahd was still haunted by the memory of the 1979 Iranian revolution—when Jimmy Carter sent a squadron of F-15s to Saudi Arabia and announced when they were in midair that they had been sent unarmed—and by the memory of the withdrawal of American forces from Beirut four months after a suicide truck bomb blew up the Marine barracks in 1983, leaving 241 American servicemen dead.

What convinced the Saudis of their vulnerability was a concrete example of Iraqi aggression against them. Sometime on August 3, a contingent of Iraqi troops briefly moved six miles into the kingdom, in violation of a non-aggression pact that Saddam and Fahd had signed in 1989. On the way out, the Iraqis blew up a bridge that spanned the Saudi-Kuwait border. Suddenly, the Iraqi invasion was no longer an abstract problem for an Arab neighbor, but an immediate threat to Saudi sovereignty.

The incursion prompted Fahd to launch his own telephone diplomacy, and he activated one of the two hotlines that the Saudi and Iraqi armed forces had installed six years earlier during the Iran-Iraq war. The Saudi chief of staff, General Mohammad al-Hammad, quickly telephoned his Iraqi counterpart, Lieutenant General Nizar al-Khazraji, after the first incursion into Saudi territory. The Iraqi commander apologized and assured al-Hammad that the border crossing had been a mistake. A reassuring telex from the Iraqis was transmitted to the Saudi command center. "If one Iraqi soldier puts his finger across your border, we will cut off his arm," it said. Six hours later, a second incursion occurred at a different location; this time, a junior officer said on the hotline that no one in authority was available but that someone would call back. The return call never came. Six hours after that, the Iraqis moved in a third time. When al-Hammad called, no one answered. The Saudis concluded that an invasion was imminent, and that they needed American help.

By the time Bush and Fahd spoke by telephone on August 5, Fahd was willing to listen to American proposals for the deployment of troops. Bush dispatched Dick Cheney to present the American evidence. The American defense secretary took off for Jiddah without knowing Fahd's intentions. Even if he did let in U.S. troops, would there be limits on numbers and impossible constraints?

On the evening of August 6, in the royal palace in Jiddah, King Fahd sipped tea and listened intently as Cheney and General H. Norman Schwarz-kopf, the U.S. commander in the Middle East, gave a two-hour presentation of intelligence data on the Iraqi buildup on the Saudi border. The king needed no persuading. He turned to his ministers, and one by one they gave their consent. "I never dreamt that we would have to ask foreign forces to come to help us against an Arab brother," Prince Bandar, who sat in on the meeting, quoted Fahd as saying. "But Saddam did the unthinkable and therefore we have to do the unthinkable. I have to put the safety and protection of my people first."

A rare glimpse into the basic enmity between the Saudis and the Kuwaitis came that evening. After the American presentation, the king turned to his brother, Crown Prince Abdullah, and said rapidly in Arabic, "The Kuwaitis waited too long. As a result, there is no longer a Kuwait." The crown prince disagreed, arguing that Kuwait still existed. But Fahd replied with bitterness. "Yes," he said, "and the entire nation is living in our hotel rooms."

On August 7, five days after the invasion, Bush ordered an initial contingent of American combat troops and warplanes to Saudi Arabia, launching Operation Desert Shield. At first, that meant sending some 200,000 troops, enough to defend Saudi Arabia and to provide an offensive option.

~ The United Nations and Direct Dial

The Iraqi invasion of Kuwait came at a moment of inflated expectations and unexplored political potential, a moment of uncertainty as the Cold War was declared over. For the first time since the end of World War II, both the United States and the Soviet Union responded swiftly to condemn and punish an aggressor. The response reflected more than the extraordinary changes that had taken place in the world in the previous year. It was also a sign of a new, more pragmatic Soviet approach toward foreign policy.

Iraq had been Moscow's strongest link to the Gulf. But Moscow's economy was crumbling, and it needed Western aid more than it needed Baghdad. The Soviet Foreign Minister, Eduard A. Shevardnadze, agreed to freeze all Soviet military deliveries to Iraq. This pivotal decision was the first signal of what became an unprecedented new alliance between Washington and Moscow. On August 4, Shevardnadze joined Secretary Baker at an airport in Moscow to issue a joint statement condemning the aggression and urging a global ban on arms deliveries to Iraq. Although the initial decisions to cooperate were a product, in part, of the close personal relationship between Baker and Shevardnadze, the cooperation survived even the later tensions that developed over Soviet efforts to suppress Baltic separatism, and the resignation of Shevardnadze as foreign minister.

In hours after the invasion and over the coming days, the United States also began rallying the international alliance that stood against Saddam Hussein. President Bush moved swiftly to control the international response by seizing the initiative. He used two instruments—the United Nations and the telephone—to forge arrangements that to his credit were marked by flexibility and compromise.

The United Nations track served three purposes: It bought the administration time while the lengthy process of deploying men and matériel unfolded; it kept open the possibility of a political solution; and it gave a cover of international legitimacy to an American-driven policy.

Suddenly, the superpowers rediscovered the United Nations, with its rusty but still functioning machinery ready and waiting for such a moment. Shortly after the first Iraqi troops crossed the Kuwaiti border, the chief American envoy to the United Nations, Thomas R. Pickering, called for the Security Council to condemn the invasion. Washington and Moscow worked hand in hand in a joint exercise in superpower crisis management. Negotiating through the night of August 2, by 6 A.M. a group of sleepy, disheveled diplomats passed a strong resolution condemning the invasion, demanding a complete withdrawal to international borders, and threatening global economic sanctions if Iraq did not pull out.

Bush had another item on his agenda after the invasion. He wanted to get to the rest of the key players around the world before Saddam reached them. So he did what he liked to do best. He picked up the phone. Bush used an imperial sort of diplomacy that cut out all the middlemen—the ambassadors, the under secretaries, the desk officers—leaving them wandering around the corridors of government wondering what was happening above their pay grade. He had long been the butt of jokes inside the Washington Beltway for his telephone diplomacy. Bush had schmoozed by phone with Soviet President Mikhail S. Gorbachev about the outcome of Nicaragua's presidential election and phoned Pope John Paul II to thank him for his help in resolving the crisis in Panama. Occasionally the approach backfired, however. Bush once was snookered by a group of Iranians who convinced him that their president, Ali Akbar Hashemi Rafsanjani, wanted to talk to him. The call was put through to the White House and Bush actually thought he was talking to the Iranian president—until the translators who were monitoring the call realized that Bush was talking to an impostor.

But following the invasion, Bush's direct-dial relationship with many of the world's leaders proved useful. While flying out to Colorado on Air Force One to meet Margaret Thatcher on the day of the invasion, Bush spoke with King Hussein and Hosni Mubarak. Both pressed for accommodation, pleading with Bush to give them more time to find an Arab diplomatic solution to the crisis. Longtime allies of Iraq, they were convinced they could persuade Saddam to pull back his troops, at least to the border area. Saddam was not suicidal, they argued, and would listen to reason once they explained what the consequences of a prolonged occupation would be.

In the next two weeks, Bush telephoned a score of foreign leaders, some of them several times, in an effort to get them to join in strangling Iraq economically through sanctions and contributing troops or money to the multinational military force converging on the Gulf. On Saturday, August 4, he reluctantly left the tennis court at Camp David during a match with Chris Evert and Pam Shriver to take a call from the German chancellor, Helmut Kohl, who told him that the European community would join the United States in boycotting Iraqi oil. And he got up at 2:30 one morning to telephone French President François Mitterrand and Egypt's Mubarak to talk about sanctions and troop movements.

The rest of the world was receptive to the global approach. Britain, just as eager to move forcefully against Saddam, endorsed Washington's decision to send troops and quickly committed forces of its own. France, Iraq's closest ally in the West for a decade and a half, was willing to abandon its relationship in the face of Saddam's aggression. In one crucial phone call, Bush convinced Japan's Prime Minister, Toshiki Kaifu, to join the boycott of Iraqi oil—a particularly bitter decision, since Japan imported 12 percent of its oil from Iraq and Kuwait. Bush had to contact Turkey's president, Turgut Ozal, three times before convincing him to shut down the oil pipeline that ran from Iraq through his country. Worried about possible Iraqi retaliation and the loss of revenue, Ozal made up his mind after the United States convinced the Kuwaitis to promise economic aid and worked out a formula by which Turkey stored but did not ship Iraqi oil.

The maneuvering paid off. On August 6, the U.N. Security Council voted overwhelmingly to impose a worldwide embargo on trade with Iraq—the first time in United Nations history such sweeping sanctions were adopted.

Bush's most frustrating calls were the ones to his longtime friend King Hussein. Bush tried, without success, to convince the monarch to abandon Saddam, proving the limits of personal diplomacy. Bush had better luck with Syria's Hafez al-Assad, who had strategic reasons for aligning himself with an adversary like the United States. The two men had never spoken before. Syria was on the State Department's list of countries supporting terrorism, and Washington still had some sanctions in place. No matter. Bush told Assad on August 12 that he welcomed his support for the global blockade and for the international military coalition that was shaping up in the Gulf. Assad had little to lose and much to gain. Said one White House official of this uneasy alliance of convenience, "The two of them found a court they could play ball on."

The only call Israel received on the day of the invasion was from an aide to Under Secretary Robert Kimmitt who telephoned the Israeli Embassy in Washington with word that the invasion had begun. The message was nothing more than one in a series of pro forma telephone calls that the aide made to a number of embassies. The United States feared that Israel would be drawn into the conflict, a move that could break up the still-fragile coalition Bush was trying to build. But after nearly two years of personal animosity and distrust between the leaders of the two countries, Bush would not talk to Israeli Prime Minister Yitzhak Shamir about the crisis in the Gulf until the first Scud missiles fell on Tel Aviv.

~ The Iraqis Dig In

From the outset, the Iraqi invasion was colored by the distortions of truth and the manipulation of history that pervaded Saddam's rule of Iraq. Even as Saddam's troops stormed Kuwait City, Mohammad al-Mashat, Iraq's ambassador to Washington, baldly denied that Iraq had invaded. "The events currently occurring in Kuwait are an internal affair with which Iraq has no relation," he told reporters. In Baghdad, on the morning of the invasion, Tariq Aziz summoned in one by one the most senior diplomats of the United States, the Soviet Union, Britain, France, and China to explain why Iraq had invaded. In calm tones, he told them that the talks with the Kuwaitis in Jiddah had failed and that Iraq had sent in troops in response to an appeal by "young revolutionaries" in Kuwait who had asked for help. Iraq would withdraw once calm was restored and the new government was secure, he promised. Joseph C. Wilson IV, the American chargé d'affaires, was called in first. He told Aziz dryly, "One failed session does not a negotiation make."

None of the envoys bought the clumsy Iraqi explanation. No new government of Kuwaitis stepped forward; Kuwaiti citizens did not collaborate with their occupiers. Yet in a meeting with Wilson in Baghdad four days after the invasion, Saddam said three times that Iraq's invasion was intended solely as a show of support for the mythical revolutionaries. Baghdad announced it was setting up a new Kuwaiti Army in which 100,000 Iraqis had volunteered to serve. It also created a puppet regime that it insisted consisted of nine Kuwaiti officers, headed by an unknown, unseen Kuwaiti named Colonel Ala Hussein Ali.

Saddam had clearly misread Kuwait. He had seen the difficult process of the Kuwaitis' attempt to democratize and interpreted the calls for liberalization as opposition to the ruling Sabahs. When some Kuwaitis held pro-democracy demonstrations in May 1990 to protest the government's refusal to allow a free parliament, Saddam had encouraged them with financial support. He may have deluded himself into believing that the fissures were wide enough to crack the Kuwaiti system when he invaded.

To perpetuate the myth of the Kuwaiti invitation, Saddam bused in Iraqi civilians, many of them from Basra, and dressed them up as Kuwaitis. These Iraqis donned the traditional Kuwaiti white robe and headdress and participated in looting the country. Like the Iraqi television commentators, the occupiers did not know how to drape their *gutras*. Some even used the traditional headdresses to wipe sweat off their faces, a gesture a real Kuwaiti would never make.

On August 8, Saddam abandoned the cover story that he had invaded Kuwait to help its "revolution," dropped all hints of a military pullout, and annexed the country. Twenty days later, a northern strip of Kuwaiti territory was renamed Saddamiyat al-Mitlaa, in honor of Saddam, and incorporated into Basra; the rest of the country was made the nineteenth province of Iraq. Kuwait City, the capital, was renamed Kadhima, the city's pre–World War I name when both Kuwait and Iraq were controlled by the Ottoman Empire. Ali Hassan al-Majid, an Iraqi colonel and one of Saddam's cousins, was given the ambitious portfolio of prime minister, commander-in-chief, minister of defense, and minister of interior of occupied Kuwait. Al-Majid, who held the job until the country was pacified three months later, was best known as the leader of the military and chemical-weapons assault on Halabja in March 1988 and had supervised the forced relocation of tens of thousands of Kurds.

A few weeks later, the territory that had been Kuwait had been devastated. But the country continued to function from abroad as a kind of corporation-in-exile. Because Kuwait's assets had been frozen so quickly, the Iraqis were denied access to them. Kuwait continued to run its business empire from London. It set up a government in a Saudi Arabian hotel, headquartered its national airline in Cairo, and kept open its embassies. Kuwaitis hid computer disks containing the country's birth records by burying them, later smuggling them out and depositing them with the United Nations. The Kuwait Petroleum Corporation located its clients by turning to its holiday greeting card lists.

Initially, most Arab states had serious misgivings about Saudi Arabia's invitation of hundreds of thousands of American and other foreign "infidels" onto the land of the holiest shrines in Islam. Few Arab regimes felt strong enough to withstand the religious and nationalistic passions that could be stirred up against them if they welcomed the imperialist presence in their midst. When the United States asked Hosni Mubarak to send troops to Saudi Arabia, he said he would do it only if other Arab countries did the same. "I'm not going to help foreign troops, but I will help Arab troops," he declared.

A number of Arab leaders launched their own diplomacy, rushing emissaries to Baghdad to reason with Saddam and receiving the Iraqi emissaries Saddam dispatched throughout the Middle East. But the only subject Saddam wanted to talk about was his right to Kuwait, and both King Fahd and Mubarak concluded that the only response Saddam would understand was force, not talk. When it became clear that a massive Western military presence was not only inevitable but also necessary for Saudi Arabia's defense, Fahd and Mubarak crafted a strategy of damage control. They realized that a confrontation between the American superpower and its allies on one side and Iraq on the other would stir up sympathy for Saddam and expose Saudi Arabia to the charge that it was nothing more than an American puppet. They knew they had to be part of any military buildup.

"The choice before us is clear," Mubarak told an emergency session of the Arab League on August 9. "An Arab act that will preserve higher Arab interests or a foreign intervention in which we will have no say or control." The prospects for cooperation looked dim, and participants reported that at one point, the Iraqis at the official luncheon threw plates of food at the Kuwaitis. At another point, Kuwaiti Foreign Minister Sheik Sabah al-Ahmad al-Sabah, overcome by the pressure, fainted.

Under Mubarak's leadership, 12 of the organization's 21 members voted to honor the United Nations economic embargo on Iraq, endorsed the Saudi invitation to American troops, and broke ranks with tradition by agreeing to commit troops to an all-Arab force in Saudi Arabia. Algeria and Yemen abstained; Jordan, Sudan, and Mauritania expressed reservations and did not vote; but only Iraq, Libya, and the PLO voted against the measure. Despite the nay-sayers, the vote was a watershed, the first time in three decades that the Arab League agreed to join outside powers to fight against one of its own.

~ 11 ~

The Drift to War

Regrettably, ladies and gentlemen, I heard nothing today that—in over six hours, I heard nothing that suggested to me any Iraqi flexibility whatsoever on complying with the United Nations Security Council resolutions.

—Secretary of State James A. Baker III on January 9, 1991, following his meeting with Iraqi Foreign Minister Tariq Aziz

We shall not accept to be treated as a nation as underdogs . . . We have prepared ourselves for the worst from the very beginning.

—Tariq Aziz at a news conference following his meeting with Secretary Baker

~ Mutual Misunderstanding

In the fall of 1990, the crisis in the Gulf settled into an uncomfortable second stage: stalemate. The Bush administration faced the task of executing its policy and somehow keeping up the momentum. The strategy was based on the assumption that Saddam Hussein would blink, and from the beginning, President Bush had no intention of giving in. A partial withdrawal or an incomplete solution was unacceptable. The Iraqi leader had to be convinced that he had two choices. If he stayed in Kuwait, he would risk a war and perhaps his overthrow. If he withdrew, he could survive.

For his part, Saddam was waiting to see if the international coalition would unravel and if the American president would back down. Throughout the next five and a half months, he gave no serious indication that he would relinquish the emirate he had occupied and annexed. From time to time there were occasional vague hints of interest in a deal, but nothing that clearly stated a recognition that Kuwait did not belong to Iraq or an intention to withdraw.

George Bush and Saddam Hussein never understood each other. The two men came from different worlds, and when they spoke of diplomacy and of war, they were speaking different languages. Bush was a patrician product of private schools and country clubs, a firm believer in face-to-face diplomacy. A World War II veteran whose view of the world was shaped by the Cold War, he kept a copy of Martin Gilbert's *The Second World War* aboard Air Force One—and he reacted emotionally to Saddam and his aggression. If he could only get his message through to Saddam, thought Bush, he was certain he could sway him. If Bush was the blue-chip warrior, Saddam was the guerrilla. Raised in an environment of poverty and suspicion, Saddam saw Bush as the leader of a global conspiracy determined to destroy him. He was a man who had learned no lessons, who had fought a brutal eight-year war, and who seemed to be ready to fight another.

Both men believed they were engaged in a clear contest between right and wrong. They played a game of public diplomacy that was designed as much for their respective audiences back home as it was for each other. Saddam was Hitler, worse than Hitler, Bush charged, using a model that was understandable to the American people, if not altogether accurate. Saddam threw the epithet back at Bush. Each called the other a liar. They tried to intimidate each other by talking at length about the strength of their military machines and the death and destruction they could cause. Both knew how to dominate—and manipulate—the media to get their messages across—Bush with his frequent news conferences and speeches, Saddam with his rambling interviews to assorted Western television reporters. Both visited their troops at the front and aired the visits on television back home; both taped messages for each other's domestic audiences.

On August 12, ten days after the invasion, Saddam unveiled what he portrayed as a peace plan. He offered to work out "the formulation of arrangements for the situation in Kuwait," but he linked it to the immediate and unconditional Israeli pullout from the Arab-occupied territories in Palestine, Syria, and Lebanon; the withdrawal of Syria from Lebanon; and withdrawal of the last Iranian and Iraqi troops from each other's territory. The rhetoric caught fire in pockets of the Arab world and was repeated by Saddam and his lieutenants in the months ahead. But it was neither credible nor workable as a basis for a dialogue with the West—and, in the end, it did nothing to forestall war.

Throughout his political career, Saddam had paid little attention to the Palestinian struggle. His newfound commitment to the fate of these Arabs was transparently opportunistic, a smokescreen for his real ambition of acquiring territory and money. Arab leaders aligned against him saw through the strategy. On January 17, 1991, Egypt's foreign minister, Esmat Abdel

Meguid, revealed that in 26 private diplomatic contacts Hosni Mubarak had had with Saddam since the summer of 1990, the Iraqi leader did not mention his concern for the Palestinians until nearly four months into the Gulf crisis.

Three days after unveiling his peace plan, Saddam made a remarkable peace overture to Iran, proving once again that he was not a merchant skilled in the art of negotiation. "Dear Brother President," Saddam wrote to Ali Akbar Hashemi Rafsanjani, "everything you wanted . . . has been realized." He added that he looked forward to "a new life in which cooperation prevails under the shadow of Islamic principles and that each of us respects the rights of the other and keeps away those fishing in muddy waters on our shores." With that letter, Saddam gave up all of his important demands of the Iran-Iraq war: He agreed to accept the 1975 agreement (dividing the Shatt al-Arab waterway) that he had publicly torn up a decade before; he offered to withdraw all remaining Iraqi troops from Iranian territory and to begin an exchange of the remaining prisoners of war.

In making such an overture, Saddam was thinking primarily of his own survival. He needed to free up troops who were guarding the eastern border with Iran; he also hoped to enlist Iran's help in circumventing the global trade embargo against him. With a new gunfight brewing on a new front, he believed he had no choice but to withdraw from the old one. Instead of negotiating with the Iranians, he raised his hands and surrendered.

But in the weeks ahead, Saddam proved that he had nothing but contempt for the norms of international behavior, making up the rules as he went along. On August 19, he ordered all Western foreign nationals in Kuwait to assemble in three hotels in Kuwait City. Hundreds of French, British, American, Australian, Belgian, Dutch, German, Scandinavian, Italian, and Japanese nationals were rounded up and transported to Iraq for "relocation" to strategic military and industrial sites to act as shields against potential U.S. bombing. Saddam conveniently forgot the outrage he had expressed after Iran seized the U.S. Embassy in Tehran in November 1979 and held Americans hostage for 444 days. In those days, it suited his interests to condemn Iran as the international outlaw.

There was no ideological rationale or standard of treatment behind the hostages' detention. Saddam tried to explain to his people—and to the world—that his hostage-taking was an act of peace. But there were different categories of hostages. The first category included those Westerners taken from Kuwait and dispersed as human shields—some were treated fairly well, but others were mistreated by sadistic guards and put on diets of stale bread and water. Another category included men who had been living in Iraq but were prevented from leaving the country. They could wander relatively freely around Baghdad, shopping for food and visiting other hostage groups. When some of them turned up at the Interior Ministry, however, to help their wives and children obtain exit visas, they were arrested and deployed as human shields.

Using foreigners as guest-hostages was nothing new for Saddam. I remember attending a three-hour press conference in Baghdad in 1983, when a group of Iranian refugees was presented to us. Although both the Iranians and their Iraqi hosts agreed that they were seeking to escape Ayatollah Khomeini's brand of repression, it became painfully clear as they talked that their destination was Paris, not Baghdad. In trying to escape through Turkey, they had taken a wrong turn and ended up in the Iraqi capital instead. Jamshid Izadi, one of the refugees and a former journalist with the Iranian magazine, *Bamdad*, spoke English and was able to communicate directly with the Western reporters. He made a mockery of the carefully-staged presentation of his Iraqi hosts. "I am a guest of the Iraqi government," he said. "I am awaiting an answer from the authorities on my visa to Paris." I never knew what became of him.

∼ The Waiting Game

Iraq's invasion of Kuwait presented the world community with both an opportunity and a burden: the opportunity to impose sanctions globally and the concomitant burden of patience. At the United Nations, the United States spearheaded a series of punitive sanctions against Iraq. On August 25, the Security Council gave the world's navies the right to enforce the embargo. It was the first time in the U.N.'s 45-year history that such sweeping military authority had been conferred without a United Nations flag or command, the most stringent peacetime blockade in modern history.

Some members of the coalition were convinced that sanctions would work. Turkey's president, Turgut Ozal, told President Bush that sanctions would bring Saddam to his knees within a month. The Egyptians, particularly Foreign Minister Meguid, thought it would take two months at the most. If the United States wanted to keep the coalition together, it would have to exhaust the sanctions route. Initially, there were also high hopes in the administration—particularly among Secretary Baker, National Security Adviser Brent Scowcroft, and Robert Gates, his deputy—that sanctions, backed by the threat of force, would force Saddam to bend. By mid-October, two months after the embargo was imposed, Baker was boasting to the Senate Foreign Relations Committee that the political and economic isolation of Iraq had been achieved. He urged the world to have patience as sanctions tightened on Baghdad. CIA Director William H. Webster reinforced this view when he told the National Council on World Affairs Organizations in Washington on October 25 that the sanctions had cut off 98 percent of Iraq's oil exports and perhaps as much as 95 percent of its imports.

There was more to making the sanctions work than verbal arm-twisting and sweet-talking. The policy was backed by cold cash. Those countries that went along with the policy were rewarded; those that did not were penalized. Saudi Arabia, for example, made it clear that in the future it would subsidize only those countries that supported the anti-Iraq coalition. The Saudis ousted Jordanian and Yemeni diplomats in a blunt show of displeasure with their governments' support for Baghdad. The Saudis also cut off their oil supply to Jordan, and hinted to Japan, Germany, and South Korea that their chances of winning business contracts in the kingdom when the crisis was over could hinge on their active support for coalition forces. The Kuwaiti government-in-exile began to grant contracts for rebuilding the emirate to companies in countries that were on its side.

Gathering the coalition together and keeping it intact while the American-driven strategy unfolded also meant that Secretary of State Baker had to hit the road. Between August 2 and January 15, he undertook ten foreign missions, traveled more than 100,000 miles, and held more than 200 meetings with foreign leaders, sometimes hopscotching to three or four capitals in a single day. On some of the stops, Baker became a global fund-raiser, persuading and cajoling a disparate group of allies to put money into the coalition and the countries whose economies had been hardest hit by the crisis. Congress was especially peeved that Germany and Japan, which boasted the world's most robust economies, were not contributing more. By mid-September, Saudi Arabia, Kuwait, and other Gulf states had pledged about $12 billion for 1990; Japan, $4 billion; the European Community, about $2 billion; and West Germany, about $1.8 billion. Washington had to make a number of subsequent solicitations as the crisis dragged on, and even after the war was over, some of the donors were reluctant to hand over the money they had pledged. Asking for money was not a role Baker the patrician assumed easily. On September 5, reporters traveling on his Air Force jet gave him a gag present: a pewter mug inscribed NOTHING LESS THAN A BILLION, PLEASE. The secretary was not amused.

Baker had to ensure the cooperation of Syria, which agreed to send 15,000 paratroopers to the multinational force. U.S.–Syrian relations had been uneasy for years, largely because of Syria's support of terrorism. Syria's president, Hafez al-Assad, might be just as brutal as Saddam, but his country's participation was considered crucial political cover for other Arab states aligned with the West, particularly Egypt and Morocco. To cement Syria's participation in the coalition, Baker in September made the first visit of a U.S. secretary of state to Damascus in several years. More important, Bush in late November became the first American president to meet with Assad in 13 years.

Baker also wanted to make sure that the allies read from the American-penned script: It's the world against Saddam. If the American people were to rally behind the show of force in the Gulf, the argument continued, then other countries had to be on the front lines beside the United States. Countries with far greater vested interests in the crisis—and far stronger economies—at least had to be shown bearing the financial burden, if not also the human sacrifice.

~ Losing Momentum

October brought an unwelcome surprise to the coalition allied against Iraq. On October 8, Israeli police killed at least 19 Palestinians and wounded more than 100 others in a rock-throwing spree on the Temple Mount in Jerusalem, the third-holiest site in Islam after the shrines in Mecca and Medina. The death toll was the highest in a single incident in the three-year-old anti-Israeli *intifadeh* in the occupied territories, and Jerusalem's bloodiest day since Israel captured the city's eastern sector in the 1967 war. Suddenly, the attention of the world shifted from Saddam's seizure of Kuwait to the plight of the Palestinians. The Temple Mount violence also gave legitimacy and urgency to Saddam's demand for a comprehensive Middle East peace settlement that included resolution of the Palestinian-Israeli dispute. At the United Nations, the coalition threatened to break up over resolutions condemning Israel and demanding an official Security Council investigation. The United States felt it had to protect Israel from more strident condemnation; on the other hand, it could not afford to alienate Arabs in the coalition.

At one point during the Security Council debate, Baker received word that France's chief delegate, Pierre-Louis Blanc, was willing to give Secretary-General Javier Perez de Cuéllar a broader mandate in the crisis than the Americans wanted. Already suspicious of the French agenda, Baker summoned France's ambassador to Washington, Jacques Andreani, to the State Department. "Mr. Ambassador, I want to tell you we are leading to a major confrontation," Baker said, his face red with anger. According to his close aides, he accused the French of reneging on a pledge to support the American version of the resolution and of helping Saddam Hussein by distracting attention from the Gulf crisis. Sounding like a teacher threatening to take a recalcitrant student to the principal's office, Baker said that he would call Andreani's boss, Foreign Minister Roland Dumas, and that President Bush would call French President François Mitterrand to straighten things out. On October 11, Bush telephoned Mitterrand and urged him to back the American version of the Temple Mount resolution in order not to split the anti-Iraq alliance. The two presidents penciled in final changes on the phone. The resolution that emerged condemned Israel for the killings, but in language that was not as harsh as some countries would have liked.

As the international campaign to intensify pressure on Saddam sputtered, there was time for reflection on how the sanctions were working. The conclusion: better than expected but not well enough. There was increasing sentiment that although sanctions were a necessary component in convincing Saddam to withdraw, they probably could not do the job within a time frame acceptable to the Bush administration and some of its allies.

The administration believed that sanctions could not continue indefinitely because the coalition, already showing strains, would crack if the crisis dragged on. The longer Saddam held the world at bay, it felt, the more he would enhance his standing in the Arab world. Moreover, the opening for fighting a desert war under conditions of maximum advantage to the coalition was limited to the period between January and March—after the new deployment of American troops was in place, before the Muslim fasting period of Ramadan, and during the season when desert temperatures were coolest and sandstorms weakest.

By mid-October, there was a sense in Washington that the policy was drifting. There were no fresh ideas and Saddam had not budged. In this stagnant atmosphere, peace feelers toward Baghdad began to blossom. Both Paris and Moscow tried and failed to get negotiations started, and their efforts caused consternation among Bush and his aides. With their history of close ties to Baghdad, the French and the Soviets were still suspected of trying to position themselves favorably for the post-crisis Arab world.

Soviet leader Mikhail S. Gorbachev sent Yevgeny M. Primakov—a Kremlin political insider and a veteran Arabist who had known Saddam for 20 years—on two missions to Baghdad to meet the Iraqi leader and determine whether there was a peaceful way to end the crisis. Afterward, the Bush administration warily welcomed Primakov to Washington for talks. The Soviet official told Dennis B. Ross, director of the State Department's Policy Planning Staff, that Saddam wanted and needed a face-saving way out. To that end, Primakov laid out a package of concessions. He suggested that in exchange for an agreement to withdraw from Kuwait, Moscow was prepared to offer Saddam an international conference on the Palestinian issue, control over the two strategic Kuwaiti islands and the part of the Rumaila oil field on Kuwaiti territory, and perhaps even a referendum to determine Kuwait's political future. Ross rejected the deal, calling it totally unacceptable because it would reward Saddam for aggression.

Members of the administration did not want to be seen as negotiating with Saddam before he withdrew unconditionally from Kuwait. They feared that the Iraqi leader—who insisted he would fight to the death for Kuwait— would play for time by trying to split the alliance with specious peace overtures. By the time Primakov met with Bush, the Soviet proposal had become decidedly more modest.

Questions were also raised about Saudi Arabia's staying power after Defense Minister Prince Sultan bin Abdul Aziz publicly suggested in October that if Iraq withdrew from Kuwait, Riyadh would not oppose Iraq's legitimate claims against the emirate, even if they involved territorial concessions. Prince Sultan's remarks were a public admission of the animosity many senior Saudi officials felt toward the Kuwaitis, and they reflected the sort of partial solution that the Bush administration dreaded. After the Americans made their displeasure known, the Saudis quickly backed off from the remarks and denied that their resolve was weakening.

Throughout the early months of the crisis, the administration had a difficult domestic problem as well: It was unable to succinctly articulate its Gulf policy and often came up with contradictory explanations. Political strategists within the administration were acutely aware of flubbing the public-relations, public-diplomacy angle. Vietnam had taught the United States that an American war could not be won if it did not enjoy public support, and Bush could not hope to rally that support if he could not offer a compelling rationale for why American men and women should die.

America was in the Gulf for one reason and only one reason, said Senate Minority Leader Robert Dole during the budget debate in October: "O-I-L." Early on in the crisis, Bush himself had cited the "O"-word, arguing in a speech to Defense Department employees on August 15 that "our jobs, our way of life, our own freedom, and the freedom of friendly countries around the world would all suffer if control of the world's great oil reserves fell into the hands of that one man, Saddam Hussein." As time went on, Bush eschewed that rationale. To cite oil as the reason for going to war was politically incorrect. It reminded Americans that there was no effective U.S. energy policy. And it smacked of crass consumerism rather than high-minded principles. By mid-October, Bush picked up a new theme, declaring that "the fight isn't about oil; the fight is about naked aggression." But it was difficult to defend the policy in terms of curbing aggression. After all, for the first year and a half of the Bush presidency, it supported a policy in Cambodia that envisioned a government in which the Khmer Rouge—held responsible for killing more than a million Cambodians in the 1970s—would share power. And the administration continued a relationship with China despite its terrible human-rights abuses in Tibet.

Other high-minded themes were also invoked. One day Bush and his top officials condemned Saddam's hostage-taking; the next day they focused their ire on Saddam's treatment of American diplomats who were made virtual prisoners in the American Embassy in Kuwait. On November 13, Baker shifted back to the theme of American self-interest, linking the administration's decision to send hundreds of thousands of troops to the Gulf to the well-being of the American economy. "If you want to sum it up in one word, it's jobs," he said.

After New Zealand's former prime minister, David Lange, visited Iraq in November to win the release of some of his countrymen who were held hostage, he pointed to the duplicity of the American policy. "Isn't it a little odd to point a quarter of a million troops in the direction of Iraq, when [the United States] just in the last few years walloped Libya, invaded Grenada, stoushed Panama? You name it, they've been there. Isn't it a bit odd that Liberia is an abattoir of carnage and human suffering and we don't even pass a U.N. resolution about it?"

Fighting to restore or extend democracy—a surefire argument that had a special claim on American hearts and minds—would not work in the case of Kuwait, which had been ruled by a tightly controlled family oligarchy since the mid-eighteenth century. There was no guarantee that the Sabahs would share power or open up the political process if their country's sovereignty were restored.

By Thanksgiving, Bush found a rationale for the American military build-up that both he and the American people felt comfortable with. When a poll showed that the American public was concerned about Saddam's preoccupation with acquiring a nuclear weapon, Bush called attention to this threat, adding that Saddam must be stopped.

∿ Doubling the Troops

As the diplomacy continued, so did the troop buildup. Operation Desert Shield was already the largest American deployment of troops overseas since the Vietnam war and the most intense airlift since World War II. Instead of backing down in the face of massive force, economic strangulation, and George Bush's increasingly shrill rhetoric, Saddam dug in. Drawing on eight years of experience in fighting the more populous Iranian military, Iraqi combat engineers built a modern-day version of Verdun, the World War I French battlefield where more than a million men were killed and wounded in brutal trench warfare. They erected miles of tank traps, enormous sand barriers, trenches filled with flammable substances, mine fields, and barbed wire. The front lines were backed up with tanks, mortar, and artillery emplacements. Saddam Hussein's goal was to draw his enemies into a land war that they would discover was too costly in terms of casualties.

Saddam also upped the ante by increasing his troop strength on the southern front. If more than 200,000 American troops had not altered Saddam's behavior, Bush wondered, would more than twice that number do it? The administration had begun offensive military planning in September, and on October 30, Bush secretly approved a timetable for launching an air war in January and a ground war a month afterward. As part of that strategy, Bush decided to double the number of American forces in Saudi Arabia. At the same time, the administration began to press Security Council members for a resolution authorizing the use of force to oust Iraq militarily from Kuwait.

On November 8, Bush announced the massive new deployment, a move that dramatically shifted the operation from a defensive phase. Bush explained that the increase was necessary to guarantee that the military coalition "has an adequate offensive military option." The initial deployment had been sold to the American public and the world as purely defensive, and the president's remarks said clearly for the first time that American troops might initiate an attack against Iraq. "This was a clear dividing point," one senior administration official acknowledged. "We had to stop Saddam from setting the agenda. The sanctions were irrelevant because if they didn't affect him personally, they didn't affect his calculus. We went to an overt offensive posture based on military force from a defensive posture of containment to deter further aggression with sanctions."

The president obviously knew that his decision had domestic political ramifications. He had deliberately kept it secret until two days after the elections. The firestorm that followed—both among the American public and in Congress—unnerved the administration. Polls showed most Americans favored the continuation of pressure through economic sanctions. The White House had not devised a strategy to keep Congress satisfactorily informed of the new deployment of troops. Only an hour before the buildup was announced, Defense Secretary Dick Cheney phoned Senator Sam Nunn, the Georgia Democrat who chaired the Senate Armed Services Committee, with the news. "I was not consulted," Nunn snapped later. "I was informed."

A formidable power on Capitol Hill, Nunn immediately arranged for public hearings before his committee that greatly accelerated and set the tone for a national debate on the crisis. Among the first witnesses were influential former chairmen of the Joint Chiefs of Staff and former defense secretaries, who paraded in front of television cameras to urge that sanctions be given more time to work.

James Baker's trip to the Gulf in early November highlighted the administration's political dilemma. Donning khakis and cowboy boots, he flew an hour by military helicopter from Bahrain, then drove by sand-encrusted Jeep to a dune overlooking a flat plain in Saudi Arabia. Ahead—in straight rows on three sides—4,200 soldiers of the U.S. Army's First Cavalry Division were waiting for him in the hot sun. They complained that they were tired of waiting, that they wanted to complete their mission and go home. They asked him to sample their prepackaged ready-to-eat meals and hot drinking water. From there, Baker traveled to the hilltop resort of Taif, an hour away, where the emir of Kuwait and his retinue were living in comfortable exile, ordering room service and enjoying air-conditioned suites at the Sheraton Hotel. The lobby was filled with seemingly able-bodied Kuwaiti men, part of the Kuwaiti diaspora. In fact, about 75 percent of the Kuwaiti population of 800,000 had left their country before and during the invasion, some of them biding their time in the clubs of London and the discotheques of Cairo until it was safe to go home again. Over and over, reporters traveling with Baker asked the touchy question that no administration official seemed to be able to answer: Should Americans endure harsh desert conditions and perhaps fight and die to liberate Kuwait if the Kuwaitis themselves were unwilling to make the same sacrifice? Shortly after the Baker visit, American commanders escorted journalists to watch Kuwaiti troops-in-exile training for battle.

~ The Use of Force

With Secretary Baker in the lead, the Bush administration set out to secure the Security Council's blessing for using force against Iraq. The allies had long been urging that the crisis not be allowed to degenerate into a strictly U.S.–Iraq confrontation, and a resolution would keep the international coalition together and perhaps send a powerful new message to Saddam about global resolve. In the United States, it would become harder for Congress to oppose the use of force if the United Nations had already approved such a move.

The resolution, known as 678, was the result of a global road show by Baker that took him to such far-flung capitals as Bogotá, Colombia, and Sanaa, Yemen, to meet with the leadership of the other Security Council members while Bush worked the phones back home. It was a return to nineteenth-century, face-to-face diplomacy. Baker and Bush wanted to cut out the middlemen and make sure that their messages got through straight, with no coloration. Baker had been exasperated by what he perceived as "out of control" delegates at the United Nations who had personal agendas that sometimes were out of sync with the deals he had cut directly with the delegates' foreign ministers. There would be no misunderstanding this time, as Bush and Baker launched a full-scale carrot-and-stick campaign. The administration wooed the Soviets by encouraging the Saudis to give $1 billion in aid to help Moscow through the winter. Washington promised its own credit guarantees to the Soviets. Bush also stated explicitly for the first time that Moscow should and would play an important role in the Middle East process, a policy change that previous American presidents had resisted. The Chinese were told that if they did not veto the resolution, their foreign minister would be welcomed at the White House after a year and a half of diplomatic isolation following the Tiananmen Square massacre.

Bush and Baker suggested not so subtly to the smaller members of the Security Council that their relationship with the United States would suffer if they voted the wrong way. When the delegate from Yemen—the only Arab member on the council and one of Iraq's strongest defenders—was applauded by supporters after he explained in the council chamber why his country voted against the resolution, Baker made good on the threat. "I hope he enjoyed that applause, because this will turn out to be the most expensive vote he ever cast," Baker said to his delegation. The message was relayed to the Yemenis, and the Bush administration abruptly ended a program of more than $70 million in foreign aid and did not include Yemen in the 1992 U.S. budget request. So dogged were Bush and Baker in their lobbying that at one point, Bush even tracked down Malaysia's prime minister, Mahathir Mohammad, in a Tokyo restaurant to push him into convincing his foreign minister to visit the United States and listen to Baker's arguments.

At first, the resolution authorizing force presented special problems for Moscow. The Soviets, increasingly consumed with internal unrest, were anxious about armed conflict in the Gulf. Still humiliated by their unsuccessful war in Afghanistan and their forced retreat from Eastern Europe, and struggling with a deteriorating economy and political turmoil, the Soviets had made it clear that they would send no troops to the Gulf, even in a symbolic gesture of solidarity with the coalition. The Soviet military, which was re-emerging as an influential force in the central government, was uneasy about jettisoning a long-standing relationship with Iraq. Asked about the prospect of force in the Gulf on November 8, 1990, as he began talks with Baker, who was testing support for the resolution, Eduard Shevardnadze said simply, "It is undesirable." This was not what the United States wanted to hear. War in the Gulf would be difficult, but to have ally Moscow turn active opponent would be excruciating.

On the afternoon of November 8, Baker and Dennis Ross sat at a glass-topped table across from Mikhail Gorbachev and Shevardnadze in the library of the Soviet leader's country house. The day was cold and clear and they had a superb view of the rolling lawn that runs along the Moscow River. It was a privileged place: Few foreign officials had ever been invited to the secluded dacha 30 minutes from downtown Moscow. Before they sat down to talk, Baker did not know whether Gorbachev would side with Shevardnadze (who supported the American position) or with his Middle East envoy, Yevgeny M. Primakov (who shared the reluctance of many members of the Soviet military command to abandon Moscow's ties with Baghdad). But the Soviet leader was fed up with Saddam. Despite their 1972 Treaty of Friendship, even Moscow had been unsuccessful in getting through to him.

The conversation became an open, almost freewheeling, two-and-a-half-hour exchange of the military options. Gorbachev concluded that Saddam would never leave Kuwait unless he felt truly threatened by force. At one critical moment, he looked at Baker and said, "You understand now, if we pass a resolution authorizing force, and if Saddam does not move, you will have to use force. If you do it, you have to use it. Are you ready to do that now?" Baker replied yes, that President Bush was ready to do that. Later, at a joint press conference back in Moscow, Shevardnadze, after some persistent questioning by reporters, disclosed the policy change, saying that while Moscow preferred a political solution, the use of force "could not be ruled out. . . . A situation may arise which will call for such a solution."

Gorbachev favored the passage of two Security Council resolutions. The first would authorize force and be conditioned on a second resolution—to be approved after another lengthy round of diplomacy—that would give the actual go-ahead for war on January 31. Baker wanted one resolution that authorized force without a deadline. If there had to be a date, he said, it should be earlier, and he suggested January 1. During a 23-nation arms control summit meeting in Paris on November 19 and 20, Gorbachev told Bush that he would accept the American notion of one resolution on the use of force, but that it had to be two-tiered: It had to include a "pause for peace" to enable a period of vigorous new diplomatic activity before military action could occur. The two sides compromised on a deadline of January 15.

By journey's end, Baker knew he had the votes to ensure that the resolution would pass in the Security Council with a comfortable margin. But he continued his obsessive diplomacy, reverting to his role as a political campaign chairman, personally soliciting every vote. On November 28, the night before Security Council members cast their ballots, he met for two hours with Shevardnadze at the Soviet Embassy on Manhattan's East Side. And at midnight, having gone without sleep for two nights, he conferred briefly in his Waldorf-Astoria Hotel suite with Chinese Foreign Minister Qian Qichen, who had just arrived from Beijing. In a vain effort to get the support of the nay-sayers, Baker even spent 90 minutes with Isidoro Malmierca Peoli, the foreign minister of Cuba, at the United Nations, the highest-level public meeting between the two countries since Fidel Castro came to power in 1959.

On November 29, 1990, the Security Council passed Resolution 678 by a margin of 12 to 2. Yemen and Cuba voted against it; China abstained. It was the first time the body had approved the use of force since the Korean war in 1950.

～ Last-Ditch Diplomacy

The evening of November 29, Baker and the foreign ministers of France, Britain, China, and the Soviet Union sat around a table in Baker's suite at the Waldorf and savored their victory. They agreed to make one last effort to open a dialogue with Saddam Hussein, promising that any effort would be coordinated with the group as a whole. The next morning, however, Bush dropped a diplomatic bombshell. At a White House news conference, he announced that he was inviting Iraqi Foreign Minister Tariq Aziz to meet him in Washington and offered to send Baker to Baghdad anytime between December 15 and the January 15 United Nations deadline. Not only that, the ambassadors of the Arab countries involved in the coalition would sit in on the Washington meeting. The decision was made by Bush himself, with the counsel of only a handful of top advisers. No foreign leader knew of the plan.

Other members of the international coalition were stunned. Why was the United States acting on its own at this late date? they wanted to know. It reminded them of other defining moments in the crisis when the United States had made important decisions that they learned about only after they were made public: Baker's announcement on a Sunday television talk show in August that the United States had decided it had the authority unilaterally to interdict Iraqi commerce at sea, for example, and his proposal in testimony before Congress the following month for a "new regional security structure" for the Gulf that would be similar to NATO.

The Bush decision was made primarily with an eye toward domestic politics—particularly to convince Congress and the American people that the president had done everything in his power to avoid war. But there was another reason for the unusual offer of exchange visits, one that stemmed from Bush's personal approach to diplomacy. He couldn't just pick up the phone and call Saddam, but somehow he had to get his message through—himself. None of the public diplomacy via CNN, none of the diplomatic emissaries to Baghdad had gotten his message across. A close aide to Baker was more blunt—and more honest: "The gesture protected you against all the critics, all the Arab experts, who would have said after the war started, 'If you had only met. If you had only talked. You were so stupid. You don't know the Arabs.'"

Saddam agreed to the meetings, saying he would receive Baker in Baghdad—but only on January 12, three days before the United Nations deadline. It was a shrewd tactical move. Moving from Bush's offer to talk to actual talks became an international spectacle as the two sides jockeyed over dates. Bush rejected Saddam's choice of January 12, in effect backing off his initial offer, contending that it was too close to the United Nations deadline.

The Iraqi leader tried another tactic. In the months following the invasion of Kuwait, he had whimsically released some of his foreign hostages—handing them out like candy to an odd parade of visiting dignitaries—Reverend Jesse Jackson, former British Prime Minister Edward Heath, former American heavyweight boxing champion Muhammad Ali, former West German Chancellor Willy Brandt, former Texas Governor John B. Connally, former Japanese Prime Minister Yasuhiro Nakasone, right-wing French politician Jean-Marie Le Pen, former U.S. Attorney General Ramsey Clark, Swedish Foreign Ministry envoy Peter Osvald, Austrian President Kurt Waldheim. On December 6, Saddam announced that he would release the remaining 2,000 foreign hostages as a gesture of peace, "with our apologies for all harm." He finally became convinced that these individuals—many of them held at strategic Iraqi sites as human shields against a U.S.-led attack—would not deter the Americans and might actually provide the pretext for a military assault.

He calculated that by appeasing other nations on the hostage issue, he would prevent or at least stall the coalition from going to war. In an interview with CNN's Peter Arnett on January 28, 1991, just 11 days after the war started, Saddam expressed annoyance with what he called hypocritical Western politicians who convinced him that letting the hostages go would keep peace.

~ Endgame

At 11 A.M. on January 9, after an awkward handshake for the benefit of photographers, Tariq Aziz and James Baker sat across from each other at a makeshift conference table cobbled together from catering trestles in the windowless Salon des Nations in Geneva's Intercontinental Hotel. In many ways the two officials were very much alike: cool, pragmatic men who measured their words, avoided emotional outbursts, and kept their feelings private. Their loyalty to their respective presidents was rock solid—the product of relationships that went back decades.

For months, PLO Chairman Yassir Arafat and Jordan's King Hussein had tried to convince Washington that Saddam was ready for a compromise but that no one wanted to listen to him. But if there had been any thoughts that Saddam might relinquish Kuwait without a fight, they were dispelled by the marathon Geneva meeting between Baker and Aziz. To the end, Saddam proved that he was the outlaw willing to shoot it out, not the merchant ready to deal. Baker arrived with the weight of 12 U.N. Security Council resolutions and a 28-country military coalition behind him; Aziz arrived both empty-handed and handcuffed. To ensure that Aziz did no freelance negotiating, Saddam's half-brother Barzan was seated to his right and Saddam's personal interpreter to his left.

In their six hours and 27 minutes together, Baker and Aziz talked past each other. The tone of the meeting was set early on, when Baker passed him a sealed manila envelope carrying a letter—an original plus a copy for Aziz—from George Bush to Saddam Hussein that clearly explained the American position. Aziz spent six minutes reading the copy of the letter slowly, carefully. The letter began, "We stand today at the brink of war between Iraq and the world." If Iraq complied fully with the Security Council resolutions, it continued, "Iraq will gain the opportunity to rejoin the international community. More immediately, the Iraqi military establishment will escape destruction." If Iraq resorted to the use of chemical or biological warfare, terrorism, or the destruction of Kuwait's oil facilities, on the other hand, "you and your country will pay a terrible price."

Aziz handed the letter back to Baker and said, "I am sorry, I cannot receive this letter. The language in this letter is not compatible with language between heads of state." Baker did not take back the letter. Instead, he left both the original and the copy in the middle of the table. They sat there throughout the talks, a visible reminder of the chasm between the two sides.

Aziz recited Iraq's familiar litany of grievances: that after the Iran-Iraq war ended, the United States, Kuwait, and Israel had conspired in an economic war to deprive his country of its rightful place in the world. As evidence, he cited the American decision to suspend the U.S. Department of Agriculture's credit guarantees, the curbs on the export of American technology, and the overproduction of oil by some countries in the OPEC cartel. Aziz did not want to talk about Kuwait. In fact, he never once mentioned Kuwait. Instead, he spoke at length about the Palestinian issue and the need for a resolution of that crisis. Aziz also openly blamed the Soviet Union for Iraq's plight. "We don't have a patron anymore," Aziz complained. "If we still had the Soviets as our patron, none of this would have happened. They would have vetoed every U.N. resolution."

Baker told Aziz that Iraq had made a series of "miscalculations" but should not miscalculate again. He laid out the reasons why Iraq should comply with the United Nations resolutions and bluntly told Aziz why he should not look forward to war. "I owe it to you, out of respect, to tell you what the consequences will be," Baker said. Referring to Iraq's long war with Iran, he said, "Don't think if war comes, this will be parallel to your previous experience. . . . Understand what you're up against. You won't define the terms of a war."

But Aziz coolly informed Baker that the allies would not win, echoing Saddam's misguided thinking. "Your Arab allies will desert you," he predicted. "Your alliance will crumble and you will be left lost in the desert. You don't know the desert because you have never ridden on a horse or a camel."

As Aziz continued his performance, he sounded almost rehearsed. "He seemed to have instructions to be friendly, to be professional, but not to give an inch," recalled Robert M. Kimmitt, under secretary of state for political affairs. At one point, Aziz insisted that Saddam had made it clear to Arab leaders—he mentioned King Hussein by name—that the Iraqis had only said they would not use force against Kuwait as long as negotiations continued. Sandra Charles, a White House specialist on the Middle East, quickly intervened, saying that King Hussein had assured President Bush twice in the days before the invasion that Saddam would not invade. Only once did Baker nearly lose his temper. When Aziz asserted that Iraq had invaded Kuwait because Iraq felt threatened, Baker snapped, "That's ridiculous."

Just as there were moments of tension, there were flashes of humor as well. At one point, Baker surveyed the dozens of bottles of mineral water laid out for the delegations on the conference table and said, "In my next life, I will go into the business of bottling water." At another point, Aziz lit one of his Cuban cigars, and in an aside remarked that wisdom comes only to those over the age of 40. When Dennis Ross, director of the State Department's Policy Planning Staff, interjected a comment on a complicated point, Aziz asked him how old he was. "I am two years past the point of gaining wisdom," Ross said, to laughter on both sides.

At the end of the meeting, Baker asked Aziz if he was sure that he did not want to accept the letter from Bush. "I'm sure," said the foreign minister. Baker asked him whether he wanted to meet the press first. Aziz replied that Baker could go first.

Then the delegations—nine members on each side—shook hands as they did at the start, one by one. Charles stopped to talk with Iraqi Deputy Foreign Minister Nizar Hamdoon, whom she had known well when he was ambassador to Washington. "I guess this is goodbye," she said. "God bless you." There was a sense of finality about the encounter. Hamdoon replied, "I wish you all the best. I guess this is the last time."

Aziz watched Baker's news conference live from his hotel suite. Their talks had gone on much longer than anticipated, raising hopes that some last-minute resolution had been found. But both men acknowledged that was not so. "Regrettably, ladies and gentlemen, I heard nothing today that—in over six hours, I heard nothing that suggested to me any Iraqi flexibility whatsoever on complying with the United Nations Security Council resolutions," Baker said in his briefing. Aziz echoed those words: "The tone of his language was diplomatic and polite. I reciprocated. But the substance was full of threats. And I told him, also in substance, we will not yield to threats."

In Washington, as the talks went on for so long, Bush was calm, even upbeat. Meeting with a group of congressional leaders, he left the room to take a call from Baker when the talks broke for lunch. When Bush returned, the expression on his face had changed dramatically. He was grim, deflated. "No progress," he told participants in the meeting. When asked why the meeting had gone on for so long, he replied, "History."

The die was cast. In a news conference later in the day, the president was asked why Baker did not meet face-to-face with Saddam in Baghdad. He did not mention the fact that he had initially offered Saddam until January 15 to meet, and instead blamed Saddam for not being flexible on dates. "Because he's had every opportunity, and he keeps stiff-arming," Bush said. "We finally said, 'This is the last step.' " On the plane from Geneva to Riyadh—where he briefed Saudi leaders—Baker paid Aziz a compliment of sorts. "I think the minister did a very good job with an extraordinarily bad brief," he said.

The end of the American diplomatic exercise unleashed a flurry of diplomacy by last-minute peacemakers—the French, the Germans, the Algerians, the Jordanians, the Soviets, the Scandinavians, even the Zambians—all of whom got nowhere. Three days after the Baker-Aziz meeting, Congress authorized the use of force against Iraq, essentially by endorsing Security

Council Resolution 678. The Senate passed the resolution by a scant five votes, but it gave the president the mandate he felt he needed and cleared away the last major obstacle to war.

It was left to Secretary-General Javier Perez de Cuéllar to make the final peace overture. Reluctantly, he flew to Baghdad, and on January 13, two days before the deadline, he met with Saddam. In their two-and-a-half-hour meeting, Saddam gave no sign of flexibility. Perez de Cuéllar, a former Peruvian diplomat who ordinarily took great pains to hide his pessimistic side, did not disguise his disappointment this time. Visibly exhausted, he said he could report no progress on persuading Iraq to withdraw from Kuwait. During a brief exchange with reporters, the secretary-general was asked if there would be war. "Only God knows," he said.

Saddam told Arab journalists later that he had informed the secretary-general that Kuwait was "now a symbol," more than just a part of Iraq. "We won't surrender. We want Palestine and won't give it up," he insisted. As the January 15 deadline came and went, there was acknowledgment in Washington that the administration simply didn't understand Saddam. But then, neither did the rest of the world.

~

At 10:30 A.M. on Tuesday, January 15, George Bush sat in the Oval Office surrounded by his closest aides. He was about to sign a national security directive authorizing the attack unless there was a last-minute diplomatic breakthrough, but there was no particular sense of drama. Bush had already made peace with his decision during a 12-day retreat at Camp David over Christmas and New Year's. "I have resolved all moral questions in my mind," he had told his White House staff. "This is black and white, good versus evil." A headline in the pro-Iraqi al-Rai, Jordan's largest-circulation daily, made the same point, just the other way around: "We fight with the sword of God. The U.S. fights with the sword of Satan." Bush polled foreign leaders— including Mikhail Gorbachev—aides, lawmakers, and friends, and then decided that he had no choice but to go to war.

After signing the document, Bush instructed Secretary of Defense Cheney to execute the order subject only to revocation from the president should Saddam begin to withdraw before the end of January 16. The mood in the Oval Office that day was that this was another step in a long continuum. "There was a certain inevitability to the process by then, more than that it was a historic moment," said one senior U.S. official who was present. "The decision had been made and it was simply a question of getting it down on paper, of codifying it" said another participant. "When the president signed it, he just handed it to Brent [Scowcroft] and put the pen back in his pocket."

Bush left the date open in case Saddam Hussein had a last-minute change of heart. The next morning, the president ordered the war to begin.

~ 12 ~

The Degradation of Iraq

I must also declare to you, dear brothers, that the fighters at the front who are preparing to destroy the arrogance of infidels, deviants, and hypocrites will not be dissuaded from this role by the minor difficulties of daily life. They realize that these difficulties are temporary, and that once the emergency situation is over, the bright sun we have been waiting for will rise.

—Saddam Hussein at a joint meeting of the Revolutionary Command Council and the Council of Ministers, January 2, 1991

The husband of a neighbor of mine was a police officer. He was taken away by the Iraqis. The next day, the doorbell rang. His wife saw on her doorstep what she presumed to be the fingernails and the eyeballs of her husband.

—Barbara Bodine, American chargé d'affaires in Kuwait

~ Disintegration of the Dream

When Saddam Hussein invaded Kuwait, he broke promises—promises to his own people, to his Arab brothers, and to the rest of the world. He had promised his people a better life after the long war with Iran, a peace dividend, a return to the prewar era that had begun to bring them bridges, roads, schools, hospitals, factories, acres of farmland, and the tractors and fertilizer to work them. More important, he had promised them stability. Instead, he handed them food rationing, bread lines, unemployment, more military service, a worthless currency, and an all-out war that destroyed their country, crushed their spirit, and unleashed waves of violence in the Shiite towns and cities of the south and the mountains of the Kurdish north.

Saddam had promised his Arab brothers that Iraq would lead them into a new era of greatness, a post-Cold War era of independence from both superpowers. The Arab world would develop a weapons capability that could compete with Israel, he said. Instead, his military adventure deeply split the Arab world and pitted Arab against Arab on the battlefield. He linked withdrawal from Kuwait to a resolution of the Palestinian crisis, but then dropped that demand in a desperate move to guarantee his survival in the face of defeat. Over and over, Saddam had protested that Iraq was not a Third World country, but a United Nations survey of damage to the country conducted when the war was over called the results of the allied bombing "nearly apocalyptic," returning Iraq to a "pre-industrial age."

Saddam Hussein had presented himself to the world as a mature statesman and a reliable trading partner. He insisted he was no longer a leader who funded, armed, and housed terrorists or who rejected peace with Israel. In the end, he proved that he was a global pariah who broke the rules of international law—invading and annexing a neighbor; seizing thousands of Kuwaiti and other foreign hostages; imprisoning, torturing, and executing civilians in Kuwait; causing what may have been the largest oil spill ever recorded; setting ablaze hundreds of Kuwaiti oil wells. His vision of greatness was artificial. What he knew best was the use of force.

Not only had Saddam degraded Iraqi society, he had degraded the Iraqi soul. Despite the official rhetoric that his regime would survive, even thrive, the people no longer believed him. After more than two decades of Baath Party rule, they saw for themselves that the system was empty. What struck me about Baghdad during my visit in January 1991, just days before war broke out, was how little talk there was about the lofty goals of Baath Party socialism that had been the ideological foundation of the regime for more than 22 years. The Party saw its task as the creation of the new Iraqi man—disciplined, uncorrupted, and committed to a romantic blend of Arab nationalism and a tame socialism that was more nationalistic than Marxist. But what ostensibly provided the ideological glue for the regime was a vague, artificial, secular hybrid that never resonated among the Iraqi people in the same way, say, that religion did among the people of Iran. By the beginning of 1991, the Party principles were largely forgotten, overtaken by a fierce pragmatism based on survival.

The invasion of Kuwait accelerated the process of corrosion of Party ideals that had begun several years earlier. Certainly, as an organizing principle, the Party structure still worked. On the eve of war, the Party carried out the country's food-rationing system, bused in women and children for daily "spontaneous" demonstrations in front of the American Embassy, mobilized the masses for civil-defense exercises, and continued to penetrate all segments of Iraqi life—from schools and neighborhoods to unions and the military. But people couldn't eat ideology, and ideology couldn't run their cars and factories after the United Nations imposed—and enforced—a global embargo on Iraq. In an atmosphere in which the price of eggs rose 500 percent in the five months after the August invasion of Kuwait and rationing tickets bought less and less flour, sugar, tea, and rice (when they were available at all), the rhetoric had to be adjusted.

In a speech ten days after the invasion of Kuwait, Saddam told Iraqi families to cut their meat consumption in half and buy less rice, bread, and clothing. The government issued a strict warning that people who hoarded food for profit would be executed, but the edict was widely ignored and never enforced. Any ordinary Iraqi who had enough space in the cellar felt encouraged to hoard, and many admitted openly that they were stockpiling one to two months' worth of food and emergency items in anticipation of war. At first the regime refused to call the measures rationing. Naji al-Hadithi, the elegantly dressed, Western-educated director general of the Information Ministry, and a fierce defender of even the most absurd excesses of the regime, described the system as the "rationalization of consumption." Some of the deprivations were even heralded as positive developments. At one point, Saddam told his people to refrain from smoking, because, he said, it was not good for their health. He didn't mention the shortage of tobacco.

As the months passed, the regime's call for collective sacrifice became louder. Saddam acknowledged that the embargo was strangling Iraq's economy, but he told his people to accept deprivation as the means to preserve Iraq's dignity—its freedom, he said, from a master who would impose slavery on them. "Yes, the siege is effective because we were not isolated from the world in the past; we were part of it, selling to it and buying from it. But if the choice is either to keep our dignity, holy places, sovereignty, and our national and pan-Arab rights intact while the siege continues or to lose everything and have the siege lifted, then we prefer that the siege remains. . . . If the siege remains for a period of time, the Iraqis will adjust."

Not many Iraqis were listening. Their dreams were easy to interpret: They wanted peace, stability, and a better life for their children. During the war with Iran, Iraqis were generously compensated when their sons and husbands and fathers died. But the mood in Baghdad at the beginning of 1991 was that there would be no compensation if war came again, and that one had to take what one could get—now. The Iraqi people were also taught from the time they were children that Kuwait once had been part of Iraq, and Saddam falsely inflated their hopes and corrupted their sense of reality when he told them they had a right to be there. They were cut off, isolated, and humiliated. "Survival of the fittest" began to replace "collective sacrifice for the good of the nation." That attitude grew even stronger after Iraq lost the war, when the dissatisfaction with the regime Saddam had built burst into the open.

Iraq under Saddam had always succeeded in ruthlessly suppressing even the slightest hint of unrest. But after the invasion of Kuwait, the regime introduced a new level of flexibility to keep private grumbling from exploding into public protest. In the months after the invasion, the regime's pragmatism became transparent. Its priority was to ensure that Iraqis enjoyed a minimum standard of living, and it shut its eyes to violations of the rules—particularly in the capital, where the look of prosperity and the support of the people were most important to the longevity of the regime. The government closed the traditional tea houses of Baghdad, one of the main sources of amusement, but the grumbling became so loud that it opened them up again—and provided them with adequate supplies of scarce tea and sugar to give the look of abundance. The sweet shops were closed and opened again at Christmas. Similarly, the protests of taxi drivers became so forceful that only six days after Saddam introduced a stringent and unpopular system of gas rationing in October of 1990, he called the whole thing off, fired the oil minister, Isham Abdel-Rahim al-Chalabi—a competent, Western-educated technocrat—and replaced him with his own son-in-law, Hussein Kamel.

In a controlled environment such as Iraq, the only way to track the degradation of the regime's ideals was through isolated anecdotes. But each anecdote was a hole punched into the system, as with any totalitarian regime. To prevent foreigners from getting to know Iraqis, for example, there was a long-standing, unspoken rule that prevented them from hiring the same taxi driver from their hotels for more than a day or two. After the invasion of Kuwait, however, the regime allowed taxi drivers to work for weeks with the same foreign journalists, and the official "minders" from the Ministry of Information tried to convince journalists to hire their cousins and uncles. Even more important, the descent of hundreds of foreign journalists on Baghdad following the invasion overwhelmed the Ministry of Information staffers, whose jobs were to accompany them on every official appointment and visit they conducted. In one case, when the official Information Ministry guide assigned to go with me to an appointment did not turn up, a ministry official appointed my taxi driver as guide. No matter that he didn't have the rigorous ideological training of the ministry guides. No matter that his loyalty to the regime hadn't been tested. There was a shortage of guides, and the driver spoke English.

"You can be the guide," the ministry official said.

"I can't be the guide," the driver protested.

"Yes, you can," said the official.

"Give me a paper, a paper that officially says I am a guide," the driver demanded.

"There is no time. Just go, go. And do the translating, too."

So the driver, a charming, out-of-work sales manager for a construction firm, was elevated to the post of Ministry of Information guide for a day.

But isolated examples of chaos did not mean more freedom. While hosting Western journalists in Baghdad in the months before the war, Iraqi officials forbade them access to Kuwait. On a visit to Amman in October 1990, when First Deputy Prime Minister, Taha Yassin Ramadan was asked by a British journalist whether Western journalists would be allowed to see Kuwait for themselves, he evoked a common Arabic expression for stopping someone by force. "Kuwait is none of your affair," he answered curtly, "and we will cut off the legs of anybody who should enter Kuwait illegally."

More dramatic than the breakdown of rigid control was the corruption that crept into the country on the eve of war. A decade earlier, it would have been unthinkable for an average Iraqi to offer to change dinars for hard currency. The prison sentence would have been too long. As late as 1990, it often was not easy to find an Iraqi willing to risk the penalty for changing money. An American college student friend of mine who hitchhiked through Iraq in April 1990 went from shop to shop on Rashid Street, one of Baghdad's main thoroughfares, in search of a shopkeeper willing to change a few dollars for him at a better-than-official rate. One shopkeeper, an optician, told him frankly, "Look, for such a small amount of money, go to the bank. Don't risk getting arrested." But on the eve of war, Iraqis were desperate for dollars. The offers to change money came from all sides and with persistence—from taxi drivers, hotel maintenance men, shopkeepers. The fear of getting caught and punished had lifted.

In the face of war, the regime also had to bend the rules concerning the importation of consumer goods. Government officials, saying that they represented the Ministry of Trade, visited a number of Western corporations doing business in Baghdad and told them that all import restrictions and taxes would be waived if the businesses would help smuggle in food, spare parts, machinery, and other consumer items.

Even the Iraqi armed forces—whose loyalty to the regime was guaranteed by layers of Party apparatchiks and security officers among the military ranks—were touched by corruption. Officially, the regime treated the Iraqi military as the fittest class. The Army—particularly the elite Republican Guards—received perquisites not enjoyed by the general public, a signal to Washington that Saddam was willing to sacrifice his people to try to keep his Army as satisfied as possible. But the degradation penetrated deep into the military, and in the end, the troops did not have the will to fight.

One Army reservist, who had been a communications specialist for most of the Iran-Iraq war, spent much of his time devising ways to avoid reporting for active duty so that he could earn money as a taxi driver. First he paid off his commander so that he could delay reporting. His next move would be to report for duty with his cousin, a senior military officer, he said, to convince his superiors to exempt him from service altogether. Other reservists gave gifts to their commanders to obtain assignments closer to Baghdad, where they could try to find part-time work.

The retention of Kuwait remained more important than the well-being of the civilian population. In November, the trade minister, Mohammad Mahdi Salih, openly admitted that soldiers at the front were allotted a greater per capita share of food than the general public. Shortly after the New Year, Saddam tried to lift the morale of his military by decreeing a pay raise of 50 dinars a month for every enlisted man and officer, "to improve their purchasing power and raise their income because of the expenses they have to meet," according to the English-language *Baghdad Observer*. The decision came after grousing surfaced over the transportation costs reservists had to pay to get to and from the front. The average Iraqi soldier earned only about 100 dinars a month, and in many cases, transportation costs ate up 40 dinars for each trip back and forth to their units. However, in another concrete sign that Iraq's young men were not eager to fight another war for Saddam, as many as 20 percent of the reservists called up for active duty simply did not show up at the regional centers where they were required to report daily. In January 1991, when the draft age was suddenly lowered a year and 17-year-olds were ordered to report for duty, even fewer young men appeared, and Army teams began conducting door-to-door searches looking for draft dodgers.

~ In Praise of Self-Reliance

To counter the unrelenting deterioration of the country, the Iraqi regime began broadcasting claims of great new discoveries. Information is a most precious commodity in the Middle East, particularly in secretive societies like Iraq where the government controlled the news media and the distinction was blurred between rumor and fact. There had never been any rules in Saddam's campaign of media guerrilla warfare, and he did not seem to care that the claims of greatness did not match up with the reality.

At a time when the regime was promoting self-sufficiency in agriculture to offset the embargo, the country's farmers were discouraged by the lack of rain. So, to boost morale, Iraqi television announced that the country had succeeded in making artificial rain by seeding the clouds with chemicals. The report assured the population that the chemicals used in the operation were locally manufactured and would have no negative environmental impact. Then, to prove that the regime was continuing to make advances in its military technology—and could compete with American-made AWACs surveillance planes—on January 3, 1991, the government announced the launching of the Adnan-2, a "new generation" plane for advanced surveillance and early warning. The plane was little more than French radar mounted on a Soviet plane, but in the public announcements, the plane became yet another symbol of Saddam's military might. "The president stood behind the project right from the time when it was a mere idea in the mind of Military Industrialization," the official media declared.

A seminar sponsored by the Ministry of Agriculture and Irrigation urged a program to develop the use of maize as a food for people, not just animals, as was the custom in Iraq. The State Enterprise for Paper Industry announced its success in removing ink from scrap paper so that it could be turned into a white paste and recycled into school notebooks and typing paper. The Ministry of Health unveiled plans to find herbal substitutes for imported medicines. As the months passed, medications—from sophisticated anticancer drugs to garden-variety antibiotics—became more scarce. Hospitals in Baghdad ran out of polio, tetanus, and DPT vaccines for infants, and as supplies of baby formula dwindled, mothers began to feed rice water to their babies.

In schools throughout Iraq, children were told to sacrifice for war. On a cold, rainy morning at the Dijla Elementary School in the heart of Baghdad, children play-acted a farming sequence in which they planted wheat in response to the global economic embargo. They were lectured on how to curb their appetites so that there would be enough bread and milk for all. As part of their Thursday-morning outdoor military drill, they chanted their loyalty to Saddam, their "father-leader," and hurled insults at George Bush. Dressed in their Pioneer scout uniforms, they shivered and goose-stepped in the muddy courtyard as the flag was raised. Punching the air with their fists, the Pioneers chanted, "We shall give our souls for you, President Saddam." It was the same sort of performance I witnessed when I visited the same school, for years a showplace for foreign visitors, six years earlier. Then, however, the object of their vitriol had been Ayatollah Ruhollah Khomeini.

To emphasize the readiness of her charges, the physical-education teacher, a fashionably dressed woman of about 35, pulled out a Kalashnikov, pointed it skyward, and fired off three shots. When I asked whether the children, who ranged in age from 6 to 11, were frightened by the loud bangs, the schoolmistress, Nazbat Ismail, laughed. "Ha!" she told me, "if they are afraid of these small bullets, how will they be brave when Bush threatens to kill our children?" The lesson of the exercise at the school was clear, if crude: Our president is good, the American president is bad, and we want you to know it.

~ The Rape of Kuwait

One of the pillars of the Baath Party was to prevent and weed out corruption at all costs. Loyalty was the exclusive domain of the state, and corruption created a competing attachment to material goods. But the invasion of Kuwait caused a breakdown of military discipline, as soldiers used the occupation of the country for their own personal gain. The degradation of the ideals of the Iraqi system was most obvious in Iraqi actions inside the emirate.

The invasion quickly took on the appearance of a nationwide robbery, as the Iraqi occupiers systematically looted and destroyed the country. Troops emptied the gold bazaar and the automobile showrooms, the supermarkets and the ultramodern shopping centers. They stripped private homes, government ministries, museums, schools, office buildings, apartment complexes, and military camps, filling trucks with Islamic artifacts, furniture, typewriters, carpets, computers, desks, chairs, facsimile machines, photocopiers, filing cabinets, even kitchen sinks. They took CAT-scan equipment, X-ray and dialysis machines, and medicines from the hospitals. They dismantled the country piece by piece—traffic lights, lampposts, seats from the national football stadium, motors from pleasure boats, carousels and miniature trains from the amusement park, tires and tape decks from cars, marble panels from the new Ministry of Communications building, drainage pipes and cement blocks from construction sites. They loaded their war booty into trucks and hauled it up the main highway to Baghdad.

Iraqi soldiers viewed the massive looting of Kuwait not only as a means to enrich the state but also to help themselves. The elite Republican Guards benefited more from the looting than did the Army regulars, and infantry soldiers complained bitterly about the inequity of distribution of the spoils of war. In many cases, the occupying soldiers' greed got in the way of their duty. Soldiers released detained Kuwaitis in exchange for payoffs, particularly television sets and VCRs. A 23-year-old Kuwaiti who was arrested at a checkpoint and held for ten days said that he was offered his freedom in exchange for a television, a VCR, and videocassettes, according to a 1990 Amnesty International report on atrocities in the country. He was later told to bring perfume, a suitcase, and a car tire as well. A 17-year-old Kuwaiti was offered his freedom in exchange for an Indian or Filipino woman, the report said. Members of the Kuwaiti resistance told a particularly cruel story of a six-year-old girl taken hostage by Iraqi troops who demanded money and a car as ransom. The parents delivered the ransom, and when they went to a police station to pick up their daughter, the Iraqi soldiers shot her dead in their presence.

On another level, the invasion of Kuwait dramatically revealed the brutal nature of the Iraqi regime. The terror in Kuwait was a repetition of the terror that had existed in Iraq since the Baath Party took power in 1968. In Iraq, however, many of the stories went untold, because the witnesses to terror—even those safe in exile—were frightened of retaliation against their families in Iraq. Even after the invasion of Kuwait, Iraqis in exile remained reluctant to tell their stories. But the Kuwaitis had not yet been beaten down by the terror, and as soon as they left the country, their stories began to spill out.

When liberation came in late February 1991, the full horror of the occupation was revealed.

In the first flush of the invasion, responding to armed attacks by Kuwaiti and other Arab resisters, the Iraqis arbitrarily arrested and detained thousands of Kuwaiti civilians and military personnel, Iraqi exiles, and other foreigners. At first the arrests took place in the streets, then in private homes. Hundreds of unarmed civilians, including children, were tortured, hundreds of others executed. The mutilated bodies that were delivered to Kuwait's medical centers testified to the brutality of the occupiers: Some of the victims were burned by acid or acetylene torches; others had their ears or noses cut off and eyes gouged out or holes drilled through their heads, shoulders, and kneecaps. One woman was beaten and shot three times in the chest before her skull was sawed off. The tortures sounded particularly gruesome to the outside world, but they were no different from the tortures described for years in various human-rights reports on Iraq.

Iraqi military cars and trucks patrolled neighborhoods in search of anyone who might have worked for the Kuwaiti armed forces, police, or security forces, and thousands of Kuwaitis "disappeared" into makeshift prisons in Kuwait City or were sent to Iraq. "People could not move about freely, even to carry out essential tasks, for fear of being arrested or killed or of disappearing," said an October 23 memorandum by the Kuwaiti Red Crescent, the equivalent of the Red Cross. "Raids on homes became a daily occurrence, which people could expect at any time. . . . Young men were shot near their homes and in front of their families." What made the atmosphere so frightening was that there were no rules, no defined limits of behavior. "The arrests, interrogation, torture, punishments and killings were carried out in an arbitrary and whimsical manner, decided upon by intelligence agents and others in the occupying forces," the memo said.

Just as Saddam had tried to homogenize his own people, he also tried to "Iraqize" Kuwait. Iraqi soldiers forced Kuwaiti citizens to assume Iraqi identity papers and to replace car license plates with Iraqi versions. Kuwaiti shopkeepers were forced to accept the Iraqi dinar—a weak currency worth ten percent of the rock-strong Kuwaiti dinar on the free market—as if it were Kuwaiti money. The Iraqis also renamed many of the Kuwaiti streets and public buildings, particularly those referring to the emir and his family. The only problem was that when Iraqi troops stopped Kuwaiti civilians and asked them for directions, the responses no longer made any sense.

Kuwaitis were beaten and tortured for raising the Kuwaiti flag, for violating the curfew, for refusing to take down pictures of the emir and replace them with portraits of Saddam, for possessing firearms, for providing medical treatment to suspected resistance members, for preventing the removal of medical equipment from hospitals. The death penalty was announced for hoarding food for commercial purposes and for harboring Westerners. Thousands of agents of Iraq's secret police set up detention centers in sport clubs, schools, private homes, ministry buildings, the law and literature departments of Kuwait University, even Dasman Palace, the emir's residence. Those detained were forced to make confessions and to provide detailed information about their families, including their political activities. Iraqi forces at all levels—ordinary soldiers, senior officers, intelligence and security agents— were involved in torture.

Two groups of detainees were especially singled out for torture: actual or suspected members of the Kuwaiti armed forces or security apparatus and people suspected of being involved in the resistance—men, women, and in some cases, teenagers. The treatment of women was particularly heinous when judged by the standards of Islamic law. Rape was the favored method of torture for them. Some victims hid signs of their torture. As was the case in Iraq, those prisoners who were visibly mutilated had a more difficult time obtaining release, and they sometimes were executed simply because their bodies were so broken. The Iraqi regime wanted no visible evidence of the brutality.

One particularly chilling story came from Deborah Hadi, an American woman who met her Kuwaiti husband at the University of Louisville and had spent the last 12 years living in Kuwait. Testifying before the House Human Rights Caucus on October 10, 1990, she told American congressmen what she saw and heard after the invasion of Kuwait. "I saw an Iraqi soldier raping a woman and a young girl," she said. "The soldiers forced the woman's husband to watch, and when they had finished, they shot him. . . . I watched them take boys from the ages of 16 to 20 who they said were in the resistance, put the boys on their knees with their hands handcuffed. The soldiers held their eyes open and put lit cigarettes into them, to reveal information about the resistance. I saw the Iraqi soldiers take one man from the resistance, pull his pants down, and force a broken Coke bottle up his backside in order to get information from him. They then shot him. Iraqi soldiers would come to our home to ask for water and at that time I would have to hide in the closet, sometimes for hours, because they said they would kill the whole family for harboring Americans. . . . We took our cousin, who was in labor, to Sabah Maternity Hospital. Upon our arrival, we saw a Kuwaiti woman at the front door—in hysterics, because she was in labor and they would not allow her to enter. When she continued to scream, they put a bayonet through her stomach."

As in Iraq, some families of the execution victims were billed for the bullets. Several weeks after the invasion, some soldiers began to charge families for the right to bury their dead. It also became more difficult to bury the bodies. The Iraqis had stolen the digging equipment used for burials, even the burial shrouds.

On November 12, 1990, when a British journalist asked Saddam Hussein about the atrocities in Kuwait, he replied, "I have not heard of any such acts. It is possible that in the same way that the Western media is trying to fill the minds of people everywhere, every day, with lies about the situation . . . some false reports may come out of Kuwait."

～ The Hundred-Hour Ground War

Six months and two weeks after the invasion of Kuwait, the crisis in the Gulf entered a new phase. The United States prepared to expand the air war and attack the Iraqi Army on the ground as Saddam Hussein, with the help of the Soviets, scrambled to find a face-saving way to retreat.

Night after night, allied planes and missiles relentlessly pounded Saddam's troops and systematically destroyed his country's military infrastructure. In one month of war—the most intense aerial bombardment in military history—the allied coalition flew about 100,000 sorties, an average of one bombing mission a minute. The allies demolished most of Iraq's strategic sites, including command-and-control centers, factories, ministries, Baath Party headquarters, bridges, power stations, and various other targets. They also destroyed the bulk of Saddam's tanks, armor, and artillery; demoralized his Army; and terrorized his people. Every night, the people of Baghdad ran to civilian shelters, but every morning, despite what the allies claimed were assiduous efforts to limit "collateral damage," more civilians were dead. An Iraqi man quoted by the Reuters news agency in a February 14 dispatch could have been speaking for the Iraqi nation when he said, "The Americans inflicted more damage on our country in two hours than the Iranians did in eight years."

The first hint that Saddam Hussein was wavering in his determination to hold onto Kuwait came four weeks into the air war and shortly after the allies proved that even large numbers of civilian deaths would not deter them from continuing. At 4 A.M. on February 13, two U.S. Stealth bombers targeted a reinforced shelter in the middle-class, residential Amiriya district of southwest Baghdad, believing it to be a recently activated alternate command-and-control post. The Iraqis claimed that it was a civilian shelter, and, indeed, there were more than 400 civilians, including women and children, in the building that night. An Iraqi military communiqué described the bombing as "a premeditated plan to target civilians," and officials in Jordan, Algeria, Tunisia, and Yemen condemned the attack. Television footage showed the bodies of scores of men, women, and children burned beyond recognition while family members stood by helplessly, weeping with rage and sorrow. For the first time, the war's horror was brought home to the world. Following a month of sanitized war coverage filtered through allied censors and Iraqi propaganda, the meaning of the military jargon of "sorties flown" and "targets neutralized" became concrete.

American officials said that their decision to bomb the building had been based on intelligence information of military activity, including military communications emanating from the building, the presence of military trucks and limousines belonging to the Iraqi leadership, a security fence around the perimeter of the shelter, and camouflage markings on its roof. "We missed this one," Lieutenant General Thomas W. Kelly, director of operations for the Joint Chiefs of Staff, admitted to reporters. American officials could not explain why U.S. intelligence had failed to mention large numbers of civilians entering the building. The bombing raised the first serious questions about "collateral" damage in the war. Kelly, as well as other allied officials, expressed remorse, but he insisted it was all Saddam's fault, suggesting that he had callously put civilians in harm's way.

Whether Saddam was shaken into submission by the bombing of the shelter or whether it was coincidental, two days afterward, on February 15, 1991, his Revolutionary Command Council abruptly uttered the two magic words: *withdrawal* and *Kuwait*. For months, Saddam had vowed he would never give up Kuwait, and the volte-face came with no explanation. In a CNN interview the previous October, for example, he had said that for Iraq to give up Kuwait would be comparable to the United States giving up Hawaii. At other times, he had likened Iraq to a mother and Kuwait to the baby at her breast. Just weeks earlier, he had told U.N. Secretary-General Perez de Cuéllar that even to say the word *withdrawal* would create "the psychological conditions for enemy victory."

That was before defeat seemed certain, before Saddam Hussein's survival seemed in doubt. The outlaw was still incapable of making the concessions needed to open the bazaar. Saddam had surrounded the word *withdrawal* with a flurry of conditions—not only old conditions that the U.S.-led coalition had already rejected, but new ones as well. Among these conditions were abolition of 11 of the 12 U.N. Security Council resolutions dealing with Iraq's invasion of Kuwait; withdrawal by the allies of all troops and matériel from the region within one month of a cease-fire; withdrawal by Israel from all occupied territories; and a future government in Kuwait "in accordance with a genuine democratic practice and not on the basis of the rights acquired by the Sabah family."

The proposal, Bush told reporters, was nothing but "a cruel hoax." French President François Mitterrand called it "the diplomacy of propaganda"; Egyptian Foreign Minister Esmat Abdel Meguid called it "an insincere offer." Reaction in Iraq was much different. Jubilant Iraqi soldiers and civilians took to the streets of Baghdad and celebrated what they believed was the war's end, firing into the air machine guns, pistols, rifles, even antiaircraft weapons. Jordan and the PLO hailed the proposal.

The Iraqi move signaled an opening for negotiation, and Soviet President Mikhail S. Gorbachev seized it. In an apparent effort to improve his image in the Arab world and demonstrate that his country had a foreign policy independent of Washington, he came up with a peace proposal of his own on February 18. Bush expressed "appreciation" for Gorbachev's efforts but declared that the initial Soviet plan "falls well short of what would be required." Meanwhile, Tariq Aziz shuttled back and forth from Baghdad to Moscow via Tehran in a whirlwind, eleventh-hour diplomatic marathon. On February 21, Moscow announced that Iraq had agreed to a proposal for a "full and unconditional withdrawal" from Kuwait that could end the war. But this seven-point plan still fell short of fulfilling the demands of the 12 Security Council resolutions passed since the Iraqi invasion, and Bush rejected it.

On February 22, after consulting with his coalition partners, President Bush set a deadline of noon the next day for Iraq to begin its withdrawal from Kuwait or risk a ground war that would augment the air campaign. Under Bush's terms, the Iraqis would have to depart so quickly that they would have to abandon much of their equipment. Despite the odds, Gorbachev played out his peace initiative until the last moment, frantically telephoning one head of state after another in a vain effort to forestall the ground war. Less than an hour before Bush's deadline, Gorbachev called and asked Bush to consider merging their two plans and to delay the ground war for two days. Bush politely refused. As the deadline passed, the people of Baghdad waited. "I don't care what happens tonight," a man pulling a bucket of water up a pulley told ABC News. "I just want water for my family." His comment spoke volumes about the goals of the Iraqi people. They wanted peace and stability, not grandiose schemes or foreign adventures.

~

The monthlong allied air campaign had achieved its objective: It broke the fighting capability and spirit of the Iraqi Army. The stated objective of the second phase of the war was to send in ground troops to retake Kuwait. But there was an unspoken objective as well: the degradation of Iraq's military machine, the foundation of Saddam's power, so that the state he had built would be weakened forever. Saddam thought that his Army would successfully withstand any direct frontal attack. Indeed, the initial offensive plan that General H. Norman Schwarzkopf, the allied commander, presented was an unimaginative, head-on assault that Dick Cheney and Colin Powell rejected. So Schwarzkopf sent up a new plan that envisioned a flanking attack around Iraq's front line. "First we are going to cut it off," said General Powell of the more imaginative plan to encircle and isolate the Iraqi Army, "and then we are going to kill it."

When no withdrawal came, the allies launched the ground offensive on schedule. The allied counterattack against Iraqi troops in and around Kuwait was fought according to a military catechism that detailed precisely how to fight and decisively win a war. Known as the AirLand Battle Doctrine, the plan called for swift, massive armored attacks supported by aerial bombing. The goal was not simply to push Iraqi forces out of Kuwait, however. The American doctrine contemplated no return to the "status quo antebellum." When an enemy attacked, the doctrine stated, it set up a new status quo, and the purpose of fighting back was to impose terms chosen by the victor. The allies did not know what to expect from the Iraqi side, and the strategy was aimed at confronting a number of war scenarios. The only major ground battle of the war had been the battle of the abandoned Saudi city of Khafji— an attack that was believed to have been planned by Saddam himself. It taught the allies two lessons about the Iraqi president: He was not a military strategist, but he was willing to sacrifice his soldiers in a battle he knew he could not win. What the allies did not know was whether Saddam's soldiers were prepared to be sacrificed.

In Kuwait, Saddam used the same strategy that had served him well in the Iran-Iraq war: a dug-in and fortified three-tier defensive system that put his poorest troops on the front lines, most of them just inside Kuwait's 138-mile border with Saudi Arabia. Tactical reserves were placed farther back in Kuwait. His best-trained and most-disciplined units, the Republican Guards, were positioned to the north—where, he calculated, they could be used to counterattack an allied advance.

The allied forces were fully prepared to encounter stiff resistance, including the use of chemical weapons. American intelligence reports indicated that Saddam had ordered his troops to fire chemical weapons as soon as enemy ground troops advanced. Concern that he would unleash his stocks of mustard and nerve gas had slowed the allies' preparedness and required months of drill. Troops went into battle with their bulky protective suits, gloves, boots, and antidote syringes.

The allies launched their first attack over a 300-mile area with more than 200,000 troops. But several days before the attack they had shifted the bulk of their heavy armored forces—more than 150,000 American, British, and French troops—as far as 300 miles to the west along the Saudi-Iraqi border. Schwarzkopf also put an amphibious unit of about 18,000 Marines as a decoy in the Gulf to deceive the Iraqis with the threat of a coastal landing.

At 4 A.M. Gulf time on February 24, U.S. Marines and Saudi troops broke through the Iraqi lines into Kuwait. Half an hour into the ground war, the shape of the battle became clear; resistance was light and the enemy quick to surrender. The VII Corps to the west "leapfrogged" by air and ground into Iraq. It was a logistical tour de force, requiring enormous forward-based refueling and supply stations to be set up deep in the Iraqi desert. The allies achieved their military objectives for the first day of the ground war: Heavy armored columns advanced 20 miles into Kuwait, while American airborne and tank units led by the French Foreign Legion advanced 70 miles into Iraq. The 101st Airborne Division swiftly moved north to the Tigris-Euphrates Valley only 100 miles from Baghdad. The VII Corps and allied forces led ground assaults into Kuwait and into Iraq, where, 15 miles west of Basra, they smashed units of the Republican Guard in the largest armored encounter since the Battle of the Bulge.

Anticipation of an amphibious Marine assault kept Iraqi troops pinned down in Kuwait, but the assault never came. Instead, the broad flanking maneuver trapped the Iraqi forces in an Arabian Dunkirk.

As the allied forces moved up the coastal road toward Kuwait City, the Iraqi front lines disintegrated. In wave after wave, they surrendered to the allies, abandoning their posts en masse—the same way small units had done when faced with Iranian invaders in the early years of the Iran-Iraq war. Some soldiers begged for mercy, while others kissed the hands of the allied soldiers who met them. Still others were reported to have been executed, shot, or decapitated by their officers as they tried to flee. The Iraqi force was hollow, intimidated, and, in the end, apparently abandoned by some of its own officers. Saddam's military machine had turned brittle. His soldiers had believed in the war against Iran and fought it as a struggle for survival. But they were not willing to die for Kuwait. More than 5,000 Iraqis surrendered to the allies on the first day, hundreds of them raising white flags before the allied forces even reached their positions. Others surrendered with copies of the Koran held over their heads. The allied forces described many of the deserting and surrendering troops as hungry and lice-ridden.

In explaining the large numbers of Iraqi defectors, Prince Khalid bin Sultan, the Saudi general who headed the coalition Arab forces, summed up the problem in a briefing with reporters. "I'm not underestimating the Iraqi soldiers' ability and professionalism in fighting," he said. "As a matter of fact, they are good. But there is one thing they are lacking, that they don't believe in what they are fighting for right now."

In Kuwait itself, American Marines stopped short of entering Kuwait City in a diplomatic gesture that gave the Arab forces the glory of liberating the capital. Columns of Kuwaiti and Saudi tanks and personnel carriers rumbled up the broad boulevards of Kuwait City, past barbed wire and bunkers, burnt-out tanks and wrecked cars, and freed the battered capital. The city exploded in a collective outburst as thousands of jubilant, flag-waving Kuwaitis swarmed into the streets to embrace their liberators. The Kuwaitis flashed the V sign and chanted slogans in praise of George Bush.

The liberation also brought revenge. Kuwaitis burned and shredded the portraits of Saddam and the Iraqi flags that had been hung throughout the emirate. Bands of young, armed men set up roadblocks and roamed the streets looking for Iraqis and their collaborators. In some cases, Kuwaiti vigilantes used the same methods of torture and execution as had their captors. According to Middle East Watch, Kuwaiti military or resistance factions seeking vengeance killed at least 10 people and abducted or imprisoned about 2,000 in the month after liberation. Kuwaiti soldiers and resistance fighters conducted house-to-house searches in the capital's main Palestinian neighborhood looking for suspected collaborators, and doctors at the city's largest hospital reported treating dozens of Palestinians who had been beaten, stabbed, and in some cases shot by Kuwaitis.

As the Iraqi soldiers fled, they torched 600 of the country's 950 oil wells, creating towering fires and choking black smoke that dimmed the sun all the way from northern Saudi Arabia to central Iran, produced soot-contaminated "black rain," and threatened to change the weather patterns of the entire Gulf region. Unexploded mines littered beaches and the highway to Baghdad; food, water, medical supplies, and gasoline were scarce; and much of the emirate was without electricity and phone service. Before leaving, the Iraqis shelled hotels and government buildings, and burned the National Assembly headquarters. Much of the emir's Dasman Palace was destroyed, its rooms gutted, its hallways smeared with human excrement. The main airport and the port facilities were largely intact, however; backup generators provided some electricity and the roads were in fairly good condition.

As the extent of the destruction of Iraq's armed forces became apparent, little by little the Iraqis backed down. On February 26, Saddam went on Baghdad Radio to declare a moral victory and a unilateral withdrawal. As he began to speak, an air-raid siren was heard in the background. The speech was reminiscent of the moment in mid-1982 when Iran had pushed back his Army and he had retreated—a unilateral withdrawal in the name of peace.

The move was not enough for Washington. Bush called Saddam's speech an "outrage" and warned that only Iraqi soldiers who laid down their arms and equipment would be safe from attack. The American president, with the backing of the Security Council, continued to insist that Saddam accept all 12 U.N. resolutions—including one that declared his annexation null and void and another that called for war reparations when the fighting finally ended. As White House spokesman Marlin Fitzwater explained, no one wanted a repeat of the battle of Khafji, when Iraqi troops pointed the turrets of their tanks backward—a gesture of surrender—then drove up to the Saudi lines and opened fire. The goal was an unambiguous, humiliating defeat for Saddam Hussein, one that threatened to strip him of both his power and his dignity.

On February 26, thousands of Iraqi soldiers tried to flee along the road north of Kuwait City in more than 1,000 vehicles—including tanks, armored personnel carriers, trucks, even buses, police cars, ambulances, and cars stolen from Kuwait. They left with the booty they had stolen—jewelry, VCRs, gold watches, perfume, silverware, clothing, even toys. But the mile-long convoy was trapped between U.S. armored forces to the north and Marines to the south. Instead of letting them go home, the allies mowed them down, mercilessly bombing, strafing, and shelling the panicked soldiers. One American pilot later described the attack as "shooting fish in a barrel"; another likened it to a turkey shoot.

Weeks later, bodies were still trapped in the burned-out, tangled web of twisted, scorched metal that was left behind. No one seemed willing to dispose of the Iraqi bodies, the wreckage, or the unexploded mines that littered the highway north toward Basra. Many of the bodies were left to scavenging desert dogs and buzzards.

∽

In a brief televised address to the nation on February 27, President Bush suddenly ordered a cease-fire in the war that had begun 43 days earlier, declaring Kuwait liberated and the Iraqi enemy defeated. "Seven months ago, America and the world drew a line in the sand," the president said from the Oval Office. "We declared that the aggression against Kuwait would not stand, and tonight America and the world have kept their word. This is not a time of euphoria, certainly not a time to boast, but a time of pride." General Schwarzkopf, meanwhile, when asked what he thought of Saddam as a military strategist, summed it up in the first word of his answer: "Ha!" he exclaimed. "As far as Saddam Hussein being a great military strategist, he is neither a strategist, nor is he schooled in the operational arts, nor is he a tactician, nor is he a general, nor is he a soldier. Other than that, he's a great military man."

The ground war ended exactly 100 hours after it had begun. Allied forces occupied 15 percent of Iraq's territory, more than three times the area of Kuwait. Military analysts calculated that Bush had called for a cease-fire in order to leave some of the Iraqi military intact. The conventional wisdom—or perhaps the wishful thinking—in some quarters of the Bush administration was that the people would rise up to overthrow Saddam and perhaps join with the remnants of the Army to restore order to the country.

From then on, Saddam made one concession after another. On the day of Bush's speech, Tariq Aziz dispatched a letter to the Security Council, saying that Iraq would comply with all 12 U.N. resolutions. Saddam then accepted Bush's demand for a meeting of military commanders to discuss allied terms for a permanent cease-fire. He abandoned his demand that withdrawal from Kuwait be linked to a resolution of the Palestinian problem. On March 5, Baghdad Radio announced that Iraq had agreed to void the annexation of Kuwait and return seized Kuwaiti assets, including gold, currency, airliners, and the contents of Kuwait's art museum. The Iraqis also agreed to release all allied prisoners of war.

On March 3, General Schwarzkopf and Saudi Arabian Prince Khalid bin Sultan met with Iraqi military commanders in a tent at a captured Iraqi airfield in Safwan, about three miles north of the Kuwait-Iraq border, to arrange for a cease-fire. Schwarzkopf said that allied troops would retreat from Iraq only upon the signing of a formal cease-fire, not before.

As the temporary cease-fire took hold, there were still a number of mysteries about the war. One was the number of casualties Iraq suffered. Even with the cease-fire, the Americans stubbornly refused to divulge details of human losses—both military and civilian—on the Iraqi side. Independent military analysts such as Trevor Dupuy estimated that there had been between 100,000 and 120,000 Iraqi military casualties—among them 25,000 to 40,000 dead—as well as countless civilian casualties. More than 60,000 Iraqis were taken prisoner. Unofficially, some American commanders put the number of Iraqi war dead as high as 100,000; other military analysts said that the number could be as low as 10,000. On the American side, at the war's end, there were only about 125 combat deaths, about 100 noncombat deaths, and about 350 wounded. The other countries in the allied coalition suffered even fewer casualties.

Another great mystery was why Saddam never carried out his threat to use chemical weapons. Allied commanders had a number of theories, but no concrete answers. One theory was that the Iraqi artillery—the primary delivery system for chemical-weapons shells—may have been too badly damaged for the Iraqis to launch the attacks. Another theory was that the chemical weapons had lost their potency during several months of storage at the battlefront. There had also been a potential problem of winds blowing in the wrong direction. And the Iraqi commanders may have taken seriously the allied threat that if they used chemical weapons, each of them would be held personally responsible—a burden they may not have wanted to bear. Finally, the ground war came and went so quickly that perhaps the Iraqis never had an opportunity to use these weapons. But that still did not explain why so few chemicals were found in the Kuwaiti theater of operations. Perhaps Saddam actually feared that the United States would retaliate with a nuclear weapon. Not even Saddam's own hardened bunkers could survive a nuclear attack.

~ Postwar Iraq

When the war was over, the Middle East began to look much as it had before Saddam Hussein invaded Kuwait on August 2. A tour of the region in March 1991 by Secretary of State James Baker quickly revealed that no country was eager to dramatically shift its long-term policies and embrace new positions. There was little reason to hope for a breakthrough in the intractable Arab-Israeli dispute, a redistribution of wealth between the rich and poor nations of the Middle East, or a curb on the size of armies and arms purchases in the region.

The primary difference was that the military machine Saddam had built was broken as a threat to his neighbors. Billions of dollars worth of Iraqi weaponry was destroyed. The Army's cohesiveness, command-and-control, logistics, and morale were degraded, and his eight elite Republican Guard divisions were significantly diminished. But Saddam possessed a large Army with considerable amounts of equipment useful for imposing internal security. He had retained an estimated 25 to 27 divisions—between 300,000 and 500,000 men—considerably more than the 200,000 men he had under arms when he invaded Iran in 1980. The allies destroyed only a fraction of Iraq's 160 helicopters, only about 100 of more than 800 aircraft. More than 120 of his best warplanes were stowed in Iran—although the Iranians later confiscated them. Saddam still controlled a substantial number of tanks, armored carriers, and artillery—a greater number than American military authorities had initially estimated at the end of the war. Although Saddam had lost most of his Scud missile launchers, these could be replaced, and he was thought to retain at least a hundred of the missiles, which were small enough to hide easily. He had many of his chemical-weapons stocks, and the allies were unable to ascertain what had happened to the fissionable material that could be used for production of a nuclear weapon.

Meanwhile, Kuwait was put under at least three months of martial law. A new tone of disrespect for the ruling al-Sabah family crept into the voices of the Kuwaiti people, who blamed the emir openly for abandoning them in a time of crisis and for refusing to return until opulent accommodations were ready for him. In the weeks following liberation, there was deep resentment among Kuwaitis that the top priority for the emir seemed to be the renovation of one of his palaces—with the help of the U.S. Army Corps of Engineers— not the restoration of basic services such as water and electricity. Despite promises of democratization, the Sabahs showed little enthusiasm for granting even limited political freedoms. President Bush was reluctant to ease the emir toward democracy, because, his aides said, he did not want to interfere in the country's internal affairs. But in a symbolic gesture that assured Kuwaitis that prosperity was on the way, the ruling family quickly reopened the banks and introduced a new currency.

The Iraqis would not enjoy the same prospects for economic recovery. When the war ended, they were still subject to Saddam's brutal rule, and more time would be needed to assess the full extent of the war's effect on a profoundly shaken Iraqi society.

Before the war, Baghdad had been one of the most modern cities in the Middle East. Weeks after the cease-fire, however, there was still no tap water, no electricity, no heat, no telephones or telex, no traffic lights, no postal service, no working toilets for the capital's four million inhabitants. Gasoline was still rarely available, and when it was, hundreds of cars lined up. Because of the loss of power, Baghdad's 250 waste-treatment facilities did not function, and the capital was transformed into a giant, open sewer, as raw sewage poured into the Tigris River. Huge mounds of trash and human waste clogged the streets.

With shortages of medicine and equipment, medical care was almost nonexistent, and people who needed emergency surgery had to be turned away from hospitals, which were operating without heat, refrigeration, and electricity. Diarrheal diseases and other medical problems were widely reported in both Baghdad and Basra because of the lack of fresh water—a particular hazard to children. A United Nations report warned that the country could face epidemics and famine without massive and immediate help in agriculture, food, water, sanitation, and health—prompting the Security Council effectively to lift its embargo on food supplies to Iraq and ease restrictions on critical humanitarian shipments.

It was impossible for outsiders to assess the physical damage to Iraq. In Baghdad, some neighborhoods were left untouched; others were completely destroyed. Dozens of bombed bridges crumpled into the Tigris and Euphrates rivers, stark reminders of the extent of the allied attacks. Ordinary Iraqis tried to get on with their lives. Vendors took to the streets selling dates, cabbages, spices, onions, candies, nuts, oranges. Candles, batteries, and gas lanterns were available only at vastly inflated prices.

The regime announced, then suddenly canceled, plans to reopen schools and universities. Women held vigils in the bus stations of Baghdad, waiting for their sons and husbands to come home. Thousands of deserters refused to heed Saddam's offer of amnesty and his promise of higher pay. Some soldiers spoke openly of their hatred of the leader who, even in defeat, insisted they had won the war. For the first time in Saddam's presidency, his portraits were openly defaced and torn down. In Basra, opponents of the regime scrawled, DOWN, DOWN WITH SADDAM on the sides of buildings.

In a dramatic sign that Saddam was losing control of his people, opponents of the regime took to the streets and battled government forces in the Shiite south and the Kurdish north. In a series of spontaneous revolts in a dozen cities, Shiites killed government officials and suspected collaborators. Not since the 1920–21 revolt for independence against the British mandate in Iraq—which took British troops a year to crush—had Shiite opposition to the central authority in Baghdad been so widespread. In the north, lightly armed Kurdish guerrillas seized huge areas, and by the end of March, they controlled most of Kurdistan—about one-seventh of Iraq's territory. So confident were the Kurds of victory that Massoud Barzani, one of the leaders of the two main Kurdish rebel groups, invited the entire Iraqi opposition to set up a provisional government in liberated Kurdistan.

But hopes that Saddam would fall quickly were dashed as he successfully fought back. The Iraqi leader was well aware of the magnitude of the revolt and appealed to his people's longing for stability and patriotic instincts. "Is it democracy and patriotism to break Iraq up into sects and ethnic communities fighting among themselves?" he asked in an address to the nation broadcast on Baghdad Radio in mid-March. "Is it patriotism and democracy for a single Iraq to be turned into factions and clans, as happened in Lebanon?" He reminded Iraqis that their country had been poor and backward before he became president in 1979, adding that it was the Baath Party that had ushered in modernization and prosperity. What he did not mention was that it had been the Party's totalitarian rule and military aggression that had caused such devastation and despair.

Saddam moved swiftly to put down the civil war, ordering in his Republican Guards. They moved first to suppress the Shiites, indiscriminately attacking civilian neighborhoods. Witnesses described the brutality of the Republican Guards in putting down unrest: strafing crowds of civilians, dousing the wounded with gasoline and setting them on fire, and publicly hanging captives as lessons to would-be plotters. Instead of hiding the ruthlessness of the regime's response, Saddam was eager to flaunt it, as he had done repeatedly in the past, and journalists were taken on official tours of pacified cities. In the Shiite holy city of Karbala, they witnessed the destruction—houses demolished, government buildings burned and looted, and mosques damaged by artillery and gunfire. Some of the victims' bodies had been left unburied—testaments to the extent of the regime's insensitivity.

When the south was pacified, the regime turned to the Kurds, attacking them with tanks, artillery, and rocket-firing helicopter gunships. Washington had warned the Iraqis not to use its fixed-wing aircraft against the rebels—and had shot down two of them to drive home the point. But the allies did not prohibit the use of helicopter gunships, in part because General Schwarzkopf had been "suckered," he said, into permitting their use for transportation. So the regime turned the gunships against the Kurds.

The Iraqi leader also moved to consolidate what was left of his Army and security apparatus, while simultaneously trying to convince his people that the survival of the Iraqi nation-state was at stake. On March 6, he named his cousin Ali Hassan al-Majid as minister of the interior—responsible for the country's overlapping security forces. Al-Majid had ordered the gassing and massive relocation of the Kurds in 1988 and had been assigned to maintain order in Kuwait in 1990 during the first three months of Iraqi occupation. On March 16, Saddam appeared on television in military uniform and promised broad political reforms that he said would transform Iraq into a multiparty democracy. He also pledged to create a new constitution, cabinet, and parliament, although he did not say when these reforms would come. A week later, he shuffled his cabinet, relinquishing his own post as prime minister to Saadoun Hammadi, a Shiite who was one of his deputy prime ministers. Tariq Aziz, a Christian who was foreign minister, and Latif Nassif Jassim, the information minister, lost their portfolios, although Aziz retained the title of deputy prime minister. Ahmad Hussein Khudayer, Saddam's chief of staff relatively unknown outside Iraq, was named foreign minister.

By the beginning of April, the Army appeared to have crushed the rebellion. In the south, fighting subsided; in the north, the Kurdish uprising collapsed as the Army massacred thousands, including women and children, and the guerrillas abandoned the major cities they had captured. Fearing reprisals against themselves and their families, over two million Kurds tried to flee—some of them on foot—across the border into Turkey and Iran. They no longer praised President Bush as their liberator, but cursed him for having encouraged them to revolt and then refusing to come to their aid.

∼ A State Without Saddam?

It never was any secret that the U.S. administration favored an Iraq without Saddam Hussein, a leader Bush had called worse than Hitler. On February 7, 1991, in testimony before the Senate Foreign Relations Committee, Secretary of State Baker said that the United States would undertake no rebuilding or reconstruction of Iraq as long as the current leadership remained in power. Bush saw Iraq as ripe for popular upheaval. He talked about the people of Iraq as if they understood democracy, and he referred to the Romanians' overthrow and execution of longtime dictator Nicolae Ceausescu in 1989. On February 15, in the midst of the air barrage, Bush called on the Iraqi people to revolt against Saddam. There were two ways for the bloodshed to stop, he had said to employees of Raytheon, the firm that manufactured the Patriot missiles. One way was for Saddam to comply with the United Nations resolutions. The other was "for the Iraqi military and the Iraqi people to take matters into their own hands and force Saddam Hussein, the dictator, to step aside and then comply with the United Nations resolutions and rejoin the family of peace-loving nations." The administration also sent signals about war reparations, suggesting that the bill would be lower if Saddam were no longer in power.

By mid-March, however, still awaiting the formal cease-fire, Bush insisted that the United States was "not in there trying to impose a solution on Iraq." More than 100,000 American troops—and token British and French contingents—still were in Iraq while the rest of the country was swept up in civil war. The United States lacked a clear mandate for military intervention in Iraq's unrest, and Bush and his military commanders worried about the perception that the foreign troops had the look of an army of occupation. Throughout March, tens of thousands of Iraqi civilians poured into the small villages on the southern banks of the Euphrates and the rural desert communities in Iraqi territory still controlled by the allied forces. The Americans found themselves in the uncomfortable position of having to supply food and emergency medical care to waves of civilians wounded in the pitched battles with the Iraqi Army. Under international law, the United States was required to provide minimum services for people in the area it controlled, and there was deep concern in the Pentagon that if American troops did not pull out, they would soon have to provide shelter, schools, hospitals, and political asylum.

Domestic and international pressure was mounting for the United States to withdraw as quickly as possible. But even as some American troops were returning home, Colin Powell told reporters that the United States would keep a military contingent in southern Iraq "for some months to come" to enforce unfulfilled provisions of the United Nations cease-fire agreement and prevent Iraq from quelling nationwide unrest with chemical weapons and air strikes. The United States had crossed the threshold into the postwar phase, but it did not seem to know what to do next.

Bush had made the Gulf war a litmus test for "the new world order," basing his policy in part on a commitment to the principle of self-determination. He had aggressively used the tools of diplomacy—particularly marathon telephone conversations with world leaders and the machinery of the United Nations—to assemble and hold together an unwieldy international coalition. But Bush was unwilling to continue that strategy as a way to keep Saddam from massacring his own people. The administration decided that the prevention of Iraq's dismemberment and a speedy withdrawal of American troops were more important than self-determination. The United States and the rest of the coalition took no action against Saddam in the first month of the civil war. Only in mid-April, as each day some 1,000 Kurdish refugees lay dying from hunger, exposure, and disease, did the United States, Britain, and France order their troops to create sanctuaries in northern Iraq.

Iraq's Arab neighbors did not want to see the installation of a Shiite-dominated Islamic regime in Baghdad. Nor did they look favorably on the disintegration of the Iraqi nation along sectarian and ethnic lines. Far better would be a coalition of the military and the Baath Party.

When asked in a CNN interview aired on February 23 what the new Iraq would look like, Turkey's president, Turgut Ozal said, "We would like to see a democratic Iraq. You see, there isn't democracy in the Western standard in the Middle East except Turkey." Ozal said he was not asking for a "Western standard democracy," but he noted that the kings, sheiks, and emirs were more democratic than Saddam Hussein. However, in a joint news conference with President Bush during a visit to Washington a month later, Ozal urged the world to keep out. "I think it would be better if everybody stayed out and let the Iraqi people decide what they want to do," he said. And when a flood of Kurds moved toward the Turkish border, Ankara announced that it would not allow masses of refugees to enter Turkey's largely Kurdish southeastern region. Kuwait, for its part, closed its borders to Iraqis and other non-Kuwaitis seeking to enter from Iraq.

Saudi Arabia's King Fahd predicted at one point that a government would "emerge in Baghdad with a national and Islamic stature" that would have good relations with the kingdom. The Saudis, with the acquiescence of the Americans, quietly assembled former Iraqi military and political officials to form a potential government-in-exile that could fill the vacuum in Baghdad if Saddam were ousted. In comments that seemed more like wishful thinking than a concrete plan, the Saudis said that the exile group might be able to lead an army of Iraqi deserters. But as Saddam held on, the Saudis seemed to lose their appetite for revolution. The Ministry of Information ordered Saudi newspapers to cease criticism of Saddam and to limit coverage of the Iraqi civil war. On April 3—for the first time since Iraq's invasion of Kuwait—Saudi newspapers carried no personal attacks on Saddam.

It was no accident that one of Egypt's senior foreign-policy decision-makers, Boutros Ghali, said at the end of the war that Egypt could coexist with Saddam, even cooperate with him. For Egypt, an Iraq with a weakened Saddam and an impotent military machine was preferable to an Iraqi military left partially intact, with or without Saddam. Even Israeli leaders stopped calling for Saddam's overthrow. Ghali knew, as did the Israelis, that capabilities create intentions, and that a military machine in Iraq could prove again to be a threat. But would it be in the interest of stability to totally destroy Saddam's Army? How else could any future regime maintain order?

The PLO, Morocco, Jordan, and Syria began to call for Arab unity and the healing of the war wounds. Even Jordan, which had supported Saddam throughout the Gulf crisis, called for political change in Iraq. "Ultimately," said Jordan's Crown Prince Hassan in an interview with CNN in late March, "one hopes that the situation will change to a participatory system." Syria's Hafez al-Assad, the clever merchant who knew how to play all sides, urged reconciliation but simultaneously promoted open rebellion against Saddam, throwing his support behind a wide variety of opposition leaders. In March, more than 20 Syrian-supported opposition groups met in Beirut—including liberal secularists, Shiite clerics, Communists, Kurds, and former Baath Party officials. Many professed a commitment to a federal system and to democratic principles, but they failed to agree on a plan of action, and no single Iraqi leader emerged as an alternative to Saddam.

Leaders in Iran, meanwhile, initially called for stability in Iraq. Then, in a dramatic policy shift, they openly supported the Iraqi rebellion and called for Saddam's ouster. Eager to see the withdrawal of foreign forces from the region, they were just as eager to avenge Saddam for the Iran-Iraq war. They continued to deny that they were trying to install an Islamic republic in

Baghdad, one of the main foreign-policy goals of the late Ayatollah Ruhollah Khomeini. But weapons, food, and medicine flowed across the long border with Iran, and armed personnel infiltrated into the Shiite cities of the south and the Kurdish areas of the north. Tehran announced in early April that it would welcome Kurdish refugees, and it asked international organizations to provide financial assistance. Still, there was deep concern even in Tehran that Iraq would crumble, and at one point, Iran's president, Ali Akbar Hashemi Rafsanjani, urged the Iraqi people to avoid factionalism at all costs.

~

On April 3, the U.N. Security Council overwhelmingly passed Resolution 687, which would end the Gulf war and progressively lift most sanctions against Iraq if Saddam agreed to accept a series of stringent financial and military conditions. According to the 4,000-word document—the longest resolution in the Security Council's history—the Iraqi regime would have to pay billions of dollars in war reparations, accept the internationally recognized border with Kuwait, renounce terrorism, relinquish its weapons of mass destruction, and pledge never to acquire such armaments again.

Three days later, Iraq agreed to the terms of the resolution. But it was in no position to pay compensation for damage caused by the war with Kuwait. The Iraqi regime still owed about $80 billion in foreign debts accrued before the war; it would have to import even more food than before and probably would have to bear most of the cost of its own reconstruction. There were no reliable estimates of how long it would take before Iraqi oil production would return to the prewar levels of three million barrels a day. But no matter how badly the allies had degraded it, Iraq was not a backward agricultural society; it was a modern, industrialized country with 70 percent of its population in cities. It would continue to enjoy vast water resources from the Tigris and Euphrates rivers. And Iraq would still have the second-largest oil reserves in the world.

~

Could Iraq ever be democratic? Democracy had never been part of the agenda—not for the Iraqis, not even for George Bush, despite his wishful thinking about the success of a popular revolt. The Iraqi opposition remained disorganized, bereft of a credible leader. The postwar revolt had followed the old ethnic and religious divisions, as the Shiite majority and the Kurdish minority—both groups still largely excluded from power—demanded more freedom and representation.

In many respects, the vision of the new Iraq was to be found in the old. Not one nation favored the dismemberment of Iraq or the alteration of its borders. There were increasing fears among the coalition members that Iraq would be thrust back into a climate of political instability similar to the 1930s, when a new government appeared every 10 to 12 months until a frustrated military stepped in and took over. If history were to be a guide, the only way for Iraq's Sunni minority to keep power and hold the country together was through strong, forceful rule. Democratization would require power sharing, which was anathema to Saddam. Even if Saddam were overthrown, there was no evidence to indicate that a future regime would be more representative and less repressive—although it was unlikely that any new leader could be as brutal as he. Despite Saddam's efforts over the years to force Iraq into homogeneity, the deep religious and ethnic splits remained. Democratization would be a messy process, and neither the United States nor Baghdad's neighbors seemed willing to sacrifice Iraq's stability for self-determination. It seemed as if the only questions in their minds were whether Saddam would continue to rule or whether a new tyrant would emerge, and whether he would be more of a merchant than an outlaw.

Even some of Saddam's enemies—the Iraqi exiles who had opposed him for years and were ready to seize control in the event of his fall from power—did not foresee democratization in Iraq's immediate future. "We say that we are all angels and that the minute we get rid of Saddam Hussein all our problems will be solved," said Hani al-Fekaiki, a former minister in the Baath Party regime of 1963 and a leader of the Iraqi opposition. "When we talk about democracy, I don't know how mature we are. I don't know how willing we are to recognize others' beliefs. In 1963, when we came to power, we all talked about democracy and Arab unity and a sort of paradise for our people, a unique, ideal democratic government. And then we came in and you know what happened. We killed thousands of innocent people. We imprisoned thousands of innocent people. The roots of violence are in our nature, in our culture. It's not a matter of Saddam Hussein. We all have a little Saddam Hussein inside of us."

Appendix

The following texts are Iraqi versions of conversations between Saddam Hussein and American officials in 1990. In both cases, the texts are imperfect, but largely accurate, renderings of the conversations. They are perhaps as valuable in explaining Saddam's thinking both before and after the invasion of Kuwait as they are in providing glimpses into American foreign policy.

The text of the meeting between April C. Glaspie, the U.S. ambassador to Iraq, and Saddam Hussein on July 25, 1990, was released in Arabic by the Iraqi Foreign Ministry in Baghdad in September. Glaspie's remarks had been translated from English into Arabic. At the time, the State Department declined to comment on the accuracy of the transcript, although officials said privately that it was "essentially correct." In testimony before the Senate Foreign Relations Committee on March 20, 1991, Glaspie broke more than seven months of silence and spoke about the meeting for the first time. She characterized the transcript as "a heavily edited document, edited to the point of inaccuracy." At another point, she said that the transcript was "fabrication; it is disinformation. It's not a transcript. This is the kind of thing the Iraqi government has done for years, and not very subtly." On the following day, Richard A. Boucher, the deputy State Department spokesman, said that the transcript had been "heavily edited to the point of inaccuracy." Senior State Department officials who are familiar with the classified cable describing the content of the meeting that Glaspie sent back to the department have continued to say privately that although there are some omissions and variations in the Iraqi text in key areas, the two versions do not differ dramatically.

The irony of the transcript imbroglio is that Iraqi officials did not release it to embarrass Glaspie. Rather, they said they made it public to prove that Saddam was not, as Bush had called him, a liar for promising that he would not invade Kuwait. They assumed that the transcript would make clear that Saddam promised he would not invade Kuwait—only as long as negotiations were continuing.

The text of the meeting between American Chargé d'Affaires Joseph C. Wilson IV and Saddam Hussein on August 6, 1990, was also released in Arabic by the Iraqi Foreign Ministry. Wilson said that the Iraqi version is essentially accurate, but that some of his comments were omitted, others were added, and some of Saddam's comments were enhanced. He added, "I never said, 'I love life here.' " There was no visible tape recorder in the room during the meeting, he said.

Both the Glaspie and Wilson texts were independently translated into English.

Efforts were made through the Freedom of Information Act to obtain the texts of the cables sent to the State Department by Glaspie and Wilson after their meetings with Saddam, but these efforts were unsuccessful.

Text of the meeting between Iraqi President Saddam Hussein and United States Ambassador April C. Glaspie on July 25, 1990, as released by the government of Iraq:

SADDAM HUSSEIN: I asked for you today so that we could engage in a wide-ranging political discussion, which will amount to a message for President Bush.

You know that our relations with the United States were severed until 1984. You are aware of the circumstances of and the reasons for the break in relations. We made it clear to you that the decision to restore ties with the U.S. was actually made in 1980, about two months before the outbreak of the war between us and Iran. But once war had broken out, given the opportunity for misunderstanding, we were careful that our conduct in this and in all-important matters should not be misinterpreted by our counterparts, and we postponed the resumption of relations until the hoped-for day when the war would end. But the war dragged on for a long time. . . . So in affirming our commitment to the principle of nonalignment, we had to restore ties with the U.S. . . . This took place in 1984.

Naturally, the U.S. is not like England, for instance, whose relations with Arab countries of the Middle East, including Iraq, go back a long way. In addition, because relations between the two countries were broken off for the entire period from 1967 to 1984, clearly it was going to be difficult for the U.S. to fully understand many things about Iraq. We had hoped that under the new relationship, after we reestablished ties, we would help each other facilitate mutual understanding, because for our part as well, there is much that we do not know about the background for and the basis on which American decisions are made.

We had dealings with each other during the war and we engaged in a dialogue at those levels where an opportunity arose, the most important one at the foreign minister's level. We had hoped that the scope of mutual understanding would increase, as would the opportunities for cooperation that would be mutually beneficial for the Iraqi and American peoples—for the entire Arab nation, we hoped—whenever the parties concerned found this possible.

However, the relationship, while still new, suffered a number of traumas as it ran its course. The most important blow to the relationship was in 1986 (two years after the resumption of ties),[1] in the form of what came to be called Irangate. By coincidence, that year Iran occupied the Fao Peninsula.

It is only natural that as a relationship develops and the interests of the parties become more interdependent, it is possible to compensate for errors in the course of that relationship. However, when the interests at stake in that relationship are not very meaningful, and the relationship has not matured sufficiently to be conducive to mutual understanding, then any error, however small, could have a disproportionate impact on that relationship. Still, we accepted the apology of the American president (for Irangate) through his envoy to us.[2] We wiped the slate clean. One should not unearth the past unless other steps follow that serve as a reminder that the past error was no passing matter.

That was the tenor of our relationship. Nagging suspicions grew after we liberated the Fao Peninsula, propaganda got mixed up with politics, our suspicions surfaced anew, and a big question mark appeared as to what the United States was after, seeing as it wasn't happy with the results of the fighting through which we liberated our territory.

It was clear to us beyond any doubt that certain circles in the United States—we do not say that the president of the United States was involved, for we have no tangible proof of that—still there are cliques in the United States, some of which have links with information agencies, with the intelligence community, and with certain cliques in State—I can't say that it is the secretary of state—I do say that it became apparent to us that these circles were not happy that we had liberated our lands. Some of the cliques we mentioned began to compile a dossier on "Who will succeed Saddam Hussein?" Then contacts were made with some Gulf states in order to create fear of Iraq in these states. It was made known, or hinted at, that it was undesirable for the Gulf states to grant any economic aid to Iraq. We most certainly felt the impact of these activities.

Iraq came out of the war with about $40 billion in debt . . . not to mention the aid it received, which some Arab states still record as loans to Iraq, although they know, as you do, that if it were not for Iraq, neither these nor other sums would still have been in their hands, and the future of the region would have been different from what it is.

You, along with others, put together a Marshall Plan for your allies after the war. During the war you gave them generous aid. All this was given to them by American taxpayers.

Then we were confronted with the start of a policy that forced down the price of oil. America, which speaks of democracy, began to lose patience with the views of the other side. An information campaign was launched against Saddam Hussein by the official American Information Center.[3] The United States thought that Iraq was in a situation similar to that of Poland, Romania, or Czechoslovakia.

The campaign disturbed us, but not unduly. We hoped that, given enough time, several months in fact, American decision-makers could see for themselves whether the campaign was having the desired effect on the life of Iraqis, or quite a different one. We hoped that after this lengthy opportunity, American officials would be able to make better decisions concerning relations with Iraq.

It is widely acknowledged that relationships, even when they develop into some form of friendship, cannot be assumed to result in a convergence of views. . . . Americans know that even within the same leadership, one cannot assume that there will be consensus. However, when oil prices are forced down through a deliberate plan, without commercial or economic justification for the decline, then that amounts to another war on Iraq. War kills people through recourse to bloodshed, whereas economic war stifles their humanity after robbing them of the chance at life with dignity.

As you know, we gave rivers of blood in a war that lasted eight years, yet we did not relinquish our humanity, meaning Iraq's right to live with dignity. Accordingly, we categorically reject that anyone should injure the dignity of the Iraqi people or compromise their right to a happy, prosperous, and fulfilling life. (Our tolerance for this was already limited before the war; it is twice as limited now.)

Kuwait and the United Arab Emirates were the front for this policy aimed at humiliating Iraq and robbing it of the opportunity for a life of happiness, and yet you know that our relations with the Emirates and with Kuwait used to be good. In addition, while we were busy with the war,[4] the state of Kuwait was expanding at the expense of our territory.

You might say that this is just propaganda, in which case we refer you to a single document, called the "Patrol Line,"[5] which is the line of demarcation established by the Arab League, with the intention of keeping any military forces well clear of that line in 1961—that is, away from their side of the line.

Go and check for yourselves, go stand on the Kuwaiti side and see if you can't spot police stations, farms, and oil installations to a considerable depth from this line. All these facilities and installations were set up where none had existed before in order to confront Iraq with a fait accompli. This was going on while the Kuwaiti government enjoyed stability, whereas the government in Iraq kept changing—until well after 1968, for ten years after that date, we were busy with many things—once in the north,[6] then once again in the 1973 war, and there were many other things too that kept us busy. Then the war with Iran came along ten years ago.

We believe that the United States must understand that people who live in luxury and economic security can reach an understanding with the United States on what are legitimate joint interests. But the starved and the economically deprived cannot reach the same understanding.

We do not put up with threats from anyone because we do not threaten others. . . . Still, we say clearly that we hope the U.S. will not entertain any undue illusions, and that it will strive to make friends and not add to the ranks of its enemies.

I have seen American statements concerning its friends in the region . . . and I say that each party has the right to choose its friends in the region. . . . Everyone in the whole world has the right to choose its own friends. . . . We have nothing against that. . . . But you know that it was not the U.S. that protected its friends during the war with Iran. . . . I will say categorically that had the Iranians run amok in the region, the armies of the U.S. would not have been able to stop them except by using nuclear weapons.

That is not to belittle you, but it is a reflection of the facts of geography and the nature of American society, which has made the U.S. unable to bear the possibility of ten thousand dead in one battle.

You know that Iran did not agree to a cease-fire because America blew up a small oil platform after the Fao Peninsula was liberated. . . . Is this to be Iraq's reward for its contribution to stability in the region and for protecting the region from a flood that would have cast it up against, God knows, which shore?

What does it mean when America now says that we are committed to the defense of our friends, singly and collectively? It clearly means a blatant bias not for some alignment or against another, but simply a clear bias against Iraq at this stage. This position, in conjuction with other statements and maneuvers, amounts to clear encouragement for Kuwait and the Emirates not to respect Iraq's rights.

Let me be quite clear on this point: We shall obtain every single one of Iraq's rights mentioned in the memorandum.[7] This might not take place right away, after one month or even a year, but we will secure them all, because we are not the sort who will forgo our rights. . . . Kuwait and the Emirates have no historic rights, no legitimate basis, and no need to usurp our rights. If they are in need, so are we.

The U.S. should be attuned to this. It ought to demonstrate clearly that it desires the friendship of all who want to be its friends, and that it seeks the enmity of those who want to be its enemies . . . it ought not to make enemies of those who differ with it in their views of the Arab-Israeli conflict, or other issues.

We understand perfectly when America says that it wants to ensure the flow of oil. We understand when America says it wants ties of friendship with states in the region, that it wants to expand the scope of common interests in various fields. But what we cannot understand are the attempts to encourage some to do harm to Iraq.

The U.S. wants to secure the free flow of oil. . . . We know and understand this. America wants peace in the region. . . . So we hear. . . . We understand this.

Yet it must not resort to courses of action that it claims to find abhorrent—pressure tactics and saber-rattling. If you resort to pressure and coercion, we too shall resort to pressure and the use of force. We know that you can hurt us. We are not threatening you, but we too are capable of causing you harm. Each can cause harm according to its size.

We cannot get to you in the U.S. Perhaps some Arab individuals can get to you. You can reach Iraq with aircraft and missiles—we are aware of this fact—but do not drive us to the point where we shall cease to care!

When would we cease to care? When we sense that you want to humiliate us and to deprive Iraqis of the opportunity for a life of dignity and happiness. Death would be better than that. In that case, we would not care if you responded to each of our missiles with a hundred of your own, for without pride, life has no value.

It is out of the question that we should ask our people to bleed rivers of blood for eight years and then tell them that they now have to accept the aggression of Kuwait, the Emirates, the U.S., or Israel. We do not place all these countries on the same footing. In the first place, it pains us that matters between us, Kuwait, and the Emirates should come to such a point. The solution for it is to be found in the Arab context and through direct bilateral relations.

Nor do we regard America as an enemy. We put it among the ranks of those we would like to befriend. We tried to be friends, but it would appear from the repeated American statements, particularly last year, that it does not have proposals of friendship in mind. It is of course free to behave in this manner.

When we try to be friends, our notion of friendship entails dignity, freedom, the right to grasp our opportunities by virtue of our efforts, particularly those opportunities that do not injure friendship. We want to deal with others according to our stature, and to treat others according to their stature. We are not blind to the interests of others while we pursue our own interests. Others ought not to be blind to our interests while pursuing their interests.

What does the summoning of the Zionist minister of war[8] at this time to America mean? What do these inflammatory statements that have been coming out of Israel in the past three or four days mean, and the talk of an increasing probability that war is at hand?

We do not want war, because we know what war means. Do not push us to the point where we find war to be the sole avenue to a life of dignity for us and happiness for those of us who survive. We know that the U.S. has nuclear bombs. But we are determined either to live in dignity or all die together. I do not believe there is an honorable man anywhere on this planet who does not understand this.

We are not asking you to solve our problems. I told you that we Arabs will solve our problems among ourselves. But do not encourage some people to get too big for their boots, for no good reason.

Do not believe that those who befriend Iraq will lose. In my opinion, the Arabs cannot fault the American president for anything he has done, except perhaps his decision to suspend the dialogue with the PLO was the wrong decision. That decision appears to have been some sort of concession to Zionist pressure, perhaps a tactical retreat before the Zionist mobilization, after which he may return to the offensive. We hope that the conclusion we just drew is the right one—yet we still say it was the wrong decision.

You shower the usurper with your economic and political favors, with arms and with praise in the media. I wait for the day when, for every three words of praise for the usurper, you will have just one kind word for the Arabs. When will humanity have its day in the form of a just American decision, which will give the same weight to the human rights of 200 million people as it does to the human rights of three million Jews?

We want friendship, but we are not running after it. . . . We do our duty. . . . We will not be victimized by anyone. . . . If we find that there is a determination to cause us injury, we will resist. . . . That is a human right, regardless of whether the injury comes from America, the Emirates, Kuwait, or Israel.

Of course, I do not place all these states on the same footing. Israel has usurped Arab land. America is supporting it. But the Emirates and Kuwait are not. They are Arabs after all. Yet when they insist on weakening Iraq, they are helping our enemies—under those conditions, Iraq has a right to defend itself.

In 1974, I met the son of Mullah Mustafa Barzani.[9] His name was Idriss, and he was sitting right where you are. He came to ask me to postpone the implementation of autonomy for Iraqi Kurdistan as had been agreed in the declaration of March 11, 1970. I said to him, "We are determined to live up to our commitments, and we expect you to live up to yours."

When I sensed that Barzani had evil intentions, I told him, "Give my regards to your father, and tell him this is what Saddam has to say." I then spoke to him about the balance of power, citing facts and figures, just as I did in my open letter to the Iranians during the war.[10] I summarized these matters by saying, "If there is war, we will win." I asked him, "Do you know why? For all the reasons I just gave you, plus a political one. You are relying on the dispute between us and Iran (the Shah). But Iran's dispute with Iraq is over its ambition to get half of the Shatt al-Arab. If we had the option of keeping all of Iraq, including the Shatt al-Arab, all being well, we would not relinquish sovereignty over the Shatt al-Arab. However, if we were to find ourselves in a corner faced with the choice of either giving up half of the Shatt al-Arab or the whole of Iraq, we would give up the Shatt al-Arab in order to keep the whole of Iraq in the shape we want.

We hope that you will not bring matters to a point where we have to bear this wisdom in mind in our relations with Iran. Afterward we were to give up half of the Shatt al-Arab, and Barzani was to die and be buried outside of Iraq, having lost his battle.

The only barrier to better relations between us and Iran at this point is the Shatt al-Arab. Whenever we are confronted with a choice between dignity and honor for Iraq or the Shatt al-Arab, our negotiating position will be based on that word of wisdom from 1974. At that point, many will lose their historic opportunities, just as Barzani lost his.

Convey my regards to President Bush.

I hope that he will look into this matter himself, and not leave it in the hands of the clique in the State Department—that does not include the secretary of state and Kelly,[11] whom I met along with his wife, and with whom I have spoken.

APRIL C. GLASPIE: I thank you, Mr. President, and it is a great pleasure for a diplomat to meet and talk directly with the president. I clearly understand your message. We studied history at school. They taught us to say freedom or death. I think you know well that we as a people have had our experience with the colonialists.

Mr. President, you mentioned many things during this meeting on which I cannot comment on behalf of my government. But with your permission, I will comment on two points. You spoke of friendship and I believe it was clear from the letters sent by our president to you on the occasion of your National Day that he emphasizes. . . . (interrupted)

SADDAM: He was kind and his expressions met with our appreciation and respect.

GLASPIE: As you know, he instructed the U.S. administration to categorically reject the proposal to impose trade sanctions.

SADDAM (smiling): There is nothing left for us to buy from America, except wheat. Because every time we want to buy something, they say it is forbidden.

I am afraid that one day you will say, "You can make gunpowder out of wheat."

GLASPIE: I have a direct instruction from the president personally to deepen and expand the scope of relations with Iraq.

SADDAM: But how? We too have this desire. But matters are running contrary to this desire.

GLASPIE: The more we talk, the less likely that becomes. For example, you mentioned the article published by the American Information Agency,[12] which was truly unfortunate. I have presented a formal apology for it.

SADDAM: You adopted a noble position. We are Arabs. It is enough for us that the person concerned should say, "I am sorry. I made a mistake." Then we carry on. But as a rule, the media did not let up. And it is full of stories. If the stories were true, no one would get upset. But we understand the persistence on this course, that there is a determination [to harm relations].[13]

GLASPIE: I saw the Diane Sawyer program on ABC. And what happened in that program was cheap and unjust.[14] It is a true picture of what happens in the American media—even to American politicians themselves. These are the methods the Western media employs. I am pleased that you add your voice to the diplomats who stand up to the media. Because your appearance in the media, even for five minutes, would help us to make the American people understand Iraq. This would increase mutual understanding. If the American president had control of the media, his job would be much easier.

Mr. President, not only do I want to say that President Bush wants better and deeper relations with Iraq, but he also wants "a historic" Iraqi contribution to peace and prosperity in the Middle East. President Bush is an intelligent man. He is not going to declare an economic war against Iraq.

You are right. It is true as you said that we do not want higher prices for oil. But I would ask you to contemplate the desirability of oil not being overpriced.

SADDAM: We do not want very high prices for oil. Let me point out that in 1974 I gave Tariq Aziz the idea for an article he wrote severely criticizing the policy of overpricing oil. It was the first article by an Arab to express this view.

TARIQ AZIZ: Our policy in OPEC opposes sudden jumps in oil prices.

SADDAM: However, $25 a barrel is not a high price.

GLASPIE: We have many Americans who would like to see the price go above $25 because they come from oil-producing states.

SADDAM: The price at this stage has dropped to $12 a barrel, and a reduction in the modest Iraqi budget of $6 billion to $7 billion is a disaster.

GLASPIE: I think I understand this. I have lived here for years. I admire your extraordinary efforts to rebuild your country. I know you need funds. We understand that and our opinion is that you should have the opportunity to rebuild your country. But we have no opinion on inter-Arab disputes, like your border dispute with Kuwait.[15]

I served in the American Embassy in Kuwait during the late sixties. Our instructions during this period were that we had nothing to do with this issue and that America had nothing to do with it. James Baker has directed our official spokesman to reemphasize this instruction. We hope you can solve this problem using any suitable methods via Klibi[16] or via President Mubarak. All that we hope is that these issues are solved quickly.[17] Nevertheless, may I ask you to see how the issue appears to us?

My assessment after 25 years of service in this area is that your objective must have strong backing from your Arab brothers. I now speak of oil. But you, Mr. President, have fought through a horrific and painful war. Frankly, we cannot help but see that you have deployed large units in the south. Normally that would not be any of our business. But when this is seen in the context of what you said on the anniversary of the Revolution; when we read the details in the two letters of the Foreign Minister; and when we examine the Iraqi point of view that the measures taken by the UAE and Kuwait are, in the final analysis, tantamount to military aggression against Iraq, then it is reasonable for me at the least to be concerned. And for this reason, I received an instruction to ask you, in the spirit of friendship—not in the spirit of confrontation—about your intentions.

I have simply described the concern of my government. I do not mean that the situation is a simple situation. But our concern is a simple one.

SADDAM: We do not ask anyone not to be concerned when peace is at issue. This is a noble human feeling that we all feel. It is natural for you as a superpower to be concerned. But what we ask is that you should not express your concern in such a way as to make an aggressor believe that he is getting support for his aggression.That is what we mean.

We want to find a solution that is fair to us but that does not deprive others of their rights. But at the same time, we want the others to know that our patience is running out regarding their actions, which are having a negative impact even on the milk our children drink, and the pensions of the widows who lost their husbands during the war, and the pensions of the orphans who lost their parents during the war.

As a country, we have the right to prosper. We have lost so many opportunities. Others should value Iraq's role in protecting them. Even this Iraqi (the president means the interpreter) feels bitter like all other Iraqis. We do not intend to commit aggression but we do not accept aggression from others either. We sent them envoys and handwritten letters. We tried everything. We asked the Custodian of the Two Shrines—King Fahd—to hold a quadripartite summit, but he suggested a meeting at the level of the oil ministers. We agreed. And as you know, the oil ministers[18] met in Jiddah. They reached an agreement that fell short of the mark, but we agreed.

Only two days after the meeting, the Kuwaiti oil minister made a statement that contradicted the agreement. We also discussed the issue during the Baghdad summit.[19] After we had finished all the tasks on the agenda, I told the Arab kings and presidents that some brothers were waging an economic war against us, that not all wars are fought with arms, and that we regarded this kind of war as a military action against us. Because if the capabilities of our Army are lowered then, if Iran renewed the war, it could achieve goals that it had been unable to achieve before. And if we lowered the standard of our defenses, then this could encourage Israel to attack us. I said that in front of the Arab kings and presidents. Only I did not mention Kuwait and the UAE by name, because they were my guests.

Earlier, I had sent them envoys reminding them that our war had also amounted to their defense. Therefore, the aid they gave us should not be regarded as a debt. We did more than the U.S. would have done against someone who encroached on its rights.

I explored the same topic with a number of other Arab states. I communicated with brother King Fahd a number of times through envoys, and over the telephone. I talked with brother King Hussein and with Sheik Zaid[20] after the conclusion of the summit. I walked the sheik to his plane when he was leaving Mosul. He told me—just wait until I get to the Emirates. But after he reached his destination, the statements that were issued from there were very bad; not from him, but from his minister of oil.[21]

Also, after the Jiddah agreement, we received intelligence that they were talking of sticking to the agreement only for two months. Then they would wiggle out of the agreement. Now tell us: If the American president found himself in this situation, what would he do? I said it was very difficult for me to talk about these issues in public. But we must tell the Iraqi people, who face economic difficulties, who is responsible for that.

[Saddam apparently leaves to take a phone call from Egyptian President Hosni Mubarak. Parts of text omitted.[22]]

GLASPIE: I spent four beautiful years in Egypt.

SADDAM: The Egyptian people are kind and good and of noble lineage. The people who have oil should help the Egyptian people, but unfortunately they are stingy beyond belief. It is painful to admit it, but some of them are disliked by Arabs because of their stinginess.

GLASPIE: Mr. President, it is a matter of concern and it would be helpful to us if you could give us an assessment of the effort made by your Arab brothers and whether they have achieved anything.

SADDAM: On this matter we have made a breakthrough. We agreed with President Mubarak that the prime minister of Kuwait[23] would meet with the deputy chairman of our Revolutionary Command Council[24] in Saudi Arabia, because the Saudis initiated contact with us. President Mubarak's efforts were in the same vein. He just telephoned me a short while ago to say the Kuwaitis have agreed to that suggestion.

GLASPIE: Congratulations.

SADDAM: A protocol meeting will be held in Saudi Arabia. Then the meeting will reconvene in Baghdad for in-depth discussions directly between the Kuwaiti and Iraqi delegates. We hope we will reach some result. We hope that the long-range view and real interests will overcome Kuwaiti stinginess.

GLASPIE: May I ask you when you expect Sheik Saad to come to Baghdad?

SADDAM: It should be on Saturday or on Monday at the latest, according to what President Mubarak has told me. I told brother Mubarak that the agreement should be in Baghdad on Saturday or Sunday. You know, of course, that we have an inside track to brother Mubarak.

GLASPIE: This is good news. Congratulations.

SADDAM: Brother Mubarak told me that the Kuwaitis were scared. They said troops were only 20 kilometers north of the Arab League line (the Kuwaiti border). I said to him that regardless of what is there, whether they are police, border guards, or Army, and regardless of how many are there, and what they are doing, reassure the Kuwaitis. We are not going to do anything from our side until we meet with them. If we see that there is hope when we meet, then nothing will happen. But if we are unable to find a way out, then naturally Iraq will not accept death. . . . And yet wisdom is above everything else. There, you now have good news.

Tariq Aziz: This is a scoop.

Glaspie: I had planned to go to the U.S. next Monday. I hope to meet with President Bush in Washington next week. I thought of postponing my trip because of the difficulties we had begun to face. But now I will fly on Monday.

~ Notes

1. Words and phrases in parentheses reflect parentheses in original Arabic text.
2. Richard W. Murphy, then the assistant secretary of state for Near Eastern and South Asian Affairs
3. The Voice of America
4. The Iran-Iraq war
5. The line of demarcation between Iraq and Kuwait established by the Arab League
6. Government suppression of Kurdish unrest
7. The memorandum submitted by Iraq to the Arab League on the disputes with Kuwait, July 18, 1990
8. Israeli Defense Minister Moshe Arens met with Defense Secretary Dick Cheney in Washington on July 21, 1990.
9. The founder of the Kurdish Democratic Party, and hero of Kurdish independence
10. Five open letters were sent from Saddam Hussein to Iran on Iraq's intentions during the Iran-Iraq war
11. John H. Kelly, assistant secretary of state for Near Eastern and South Asian Affairs
12. The Voice of America
13. Words and phrases in brackets reflect an effort by the translator to make the translation smoother.
14. In testimony before the Senate Foreign Relations Committee on March 20, 1991, Glaspie said that her criticism was directed at the heavily edited version of the interview as shown on Iraqi television. Glaspie claimed that "the Iraqis had cut out everything which involved her [Diane Sawyer] asking a hard question and Saddam Hussein unable to give a good answer."
15. In her testimony on March 20, Ambassador Glaspie said that some of her remarks on the border issue were omitted from the Iraqi transcript. She acknowledged that she made the statement on border disputes, but that she also had said, "But we insist that you settle your disputes with Kuwait nonviolently." At another point in her testimony, she said that the Iraqi account omitted the first half of the sentence on border disputes, in which she said she emphasized "that we would insist on settlements

being made in a non-violent manner, not by threats, not by intimidation, and certainly not by aggression."
16. Secretary-General of the Arab League, Chadli Klibi
17. The official policy formulation is that the United States takes no position on inter-Arab disputes, except that they be resolved peacefully. This is the formulation that Glaspie expressed over and over to diplomats in her embassy, and she used the word *peacefully* in her exchange, according to State Department officials familiar with her written version of the meeting.
18. The oil ministers of Iraq, Kuwait, United Arab Emirates, Qatar, and Saudi Arabia
19. Arab League summit held in Baghdad on May 29–30, 1990
20. The ruler of the United Arab Emirates
21. Man bin-Said
22. In her March 20 testimony, Ambassador Glaspie said that during her conversation with Saddam, he left the room to take a telephone call from Mubarak. When he returned, she said that he told her that "he and Mubarak wanted me to inform President Bush that he would not solve his problems with Kuwait by violence, period. He would not do it. He would take advantage of the Arab diplomatic framework which President Mubarak and King Fahd had set up. That's what he would do." At another point in her testimony, she said that when the Iraqi president returned, "He mused about what Egyptian foreign policy should be. That of course is not in there." At that time Saddam "didn't want to insult President Mubarak, so of course he edited it out."
23. Sheik Saad al-Abdullah al-Sabah
24. Izzat Ibrahim

Text of the meeting between Iraqi President Saddam Hussein and American Chargé d'Affaires Joseph C. Wilson IV on August 6, 1990, as released by the government of Iraq:

SADDAM HUSSEIN: What is the news on the political and diplomatic fronts?

JOSEPH C. WILSON IV: Your minister[1] has more information through CNN than I do.

SADDAM: I sent for you so that we may examine the latest developments since our meeting with the ambassador.[2] Since that meeting, the talks between us and the previous government of Kuwait broke down, and whatever happened, happened.

WILSON: The minister informed me early on.

SADDAM: I have been informed about the American position in detail. We understand that up to now, whenever something of this sort happens, whether it is in the Arab world, Europe, Asia, or Latin America, the United States adopts a position. We are not surprised that the United States should condemn an action of this sort, especially as it had no part in it. But I wanted to say that the U.S. should not rush headlong, under the influence of bad advice, into some action that might get it into a tight position.

I say this because it is in our nature, regardless of our convictions or those of the other side, to do what we think is necessary [to prevent][3] the damage that may result from present or future developments.

You have no doubt seen our letters to Iran during the war which included a sincere appraisal of the present and the future, freely given.[4] Because these letters were extremely frank, the Iranians thought they were a tactical ploy. In fact, we said everything that was on our minds, because we wanted peace and we were pained by the continuation of the war. You know the result. Had Iran accepted the advice we offered, what happened would not have happened, perhaps the worst of which was that the war went on for so long.

I shall talk of the relationship between Iraq and the United States in the light of the developments, and what the future will hold if the U.S. were to take the wrong course of action.

To begin with, I would like to discuss three points that I will relate to each other in the course of my presentation.

Kuwait was and still is a state with unfixed borders—that is, a state without borders. Until 1961 it was not a state in the opinion of many people. Then certain events took place during the time of Abd al-Karim Qassim,[5] who issued a presidential decree appointing the ruler[6] of Kuwait a provincial governor[7] under Basra, making Kuwait a province[8] of Basra.

Why did this take place in 1961? Abd al-Karim Qassim and all Iraqis knew very well that Kuwait was part of Iraq and that the ruler of Kuwait was really a provincial governor who received a salary from the ruler of Basra in the Ottoman era. That situation continued until 1912. Then World War I came along and a new situation resulted. So, up to now Kuwait was a state but it had no borders. Not to quibble over fine points, the internal developments that took place in Kuwait and Iraq's entry[9] should not be taken as a standard for action throughout the Arab world.

As to the second point (Iraq and Saudi Arabia),[10] you are aware that we have had very good relations with Saudi Arabia from 1975 on, which were progressing in a satisfactory way until August 2.

There was ongoing mutual confidence and coordination on all levels until August 2. To the best of our knowledge and judging by declared U.S. policy—assuming that U.S. policy does not go beyond the declared policy and is essentially the same as that policy—we do not find that good relations between Iraq and Saudi Arabia are detrimental to U.S. interests. If this observation is correct—that good relations between Iraq and Saudi Arabia will not harm U.S. interests, but have been a factor of stability in the region—then meddling in that relationship will be greatly detrimental to the security of the region and to U.S. interests.

Judging by this, we fail to understand the significance of the sudden about-face represented in the statement that the Americans are concerned about Saudi Arabia in light of Iraq's strength and all the talk and the great number of statements that it will be Saudi Arabia's turn after Kuwait.

We don't know if your intention in anticipating events is to drive Saudi Arabia into taking action against Iraq that will lead to an Iraqi reaction. Perhaps your aim is to provoke.

Kuwait was part of Iraq, and instead of taking the right action, it took the wrong action.

You know that we were the first to propose a security agreement with Saudi Arabia that stipulated nonintervention in each other's internal affairs and no recourse to the use of force. We signed that. We offered it to Kuwait, which refused to sign such an agreement with us; it would seem that Kuwait was taking advice from the West, perhaps from Britain.

As you know, some Western circles were very uncomfortable with and skeptical of the notion of treaties of nonaggression and nonintervention in each other's internal affairs, as though the situation were comparable to that between Britain and France. We thank God that Kuwait did not sign such an agreement with us. I was delighted that no such agreement existed when we decided to support the revolutionary faction in Kuwait; because had such a treaty existed, we would not have acted as we did.

The Saudis are our brothers; they helped us in the war. At their initiative we secured an oil pipeline, and they gave us financial aid in the form of grants and not loans, some of which we did not even request but which came at their initiative. Things took their natural course. They are our brothers—unless you should spoil things between us and incite them against us—in which case each will have the right to defend its legitimate interests.

Therefore, if you are concerned about Saudi Arabia, there is no objective reason for your concern. If, on the other hand, you are trying to appear to be concerned in order to create anxiety among the Saudis, then that is a different matter.

We say the same thing to our Saudi brothers. We are prepared to provide any guarantees that may be required to alleviate their anxiety and give them peace of mind. On the contrary, we feel that it is our duty to defend Saudi Arabia if their security is threatened by a foreign power. We Arabs can make peace among ourselves overnight, but then relations between us can collapse overnight. So far we have not felt any anxiety on their part. At any rate, the

Saudis have had a guarantee from the beginning, and we are true to our word and are careful to respect it.

This leads us to the third point I want to make. There were rumors that Saddam Hussein promised certain Arab officials that he would not resort to force in any way, shape, or form or under any circumstances against Kuwait. We have also learned in one way or another that certain Arab officials have led the Americans to this conclusion. I do not want the Americans to form the impression that we have no regard for our credibility.

I gave no such guarantee to any Arab. What happened is that some officials among our Arab brothers had discussed with me the existence of Iraqi force concentrations toward Kuwait. They told me that the Kuwaitis were anxious and scared. I told them that I would promise not to take any military action before the meeting in Jiddah[11] took place. And that is what happened. There was no military action, in whole or in part, prior to that meeting. But, since we were expecting a serious result from the Jiddah meeting, we did not make the decision until the vice-president[12] returned to tell us what the Kuwaiti position actually was.

Then there are those who interpret the speed with which the operation took place as an indication that it was premeditated prior to the Jiddah meeting. Yes, such a possibility was contemplated prior to the Jiddah meeting in accordance with the patriotic movement in Kuwait. However, it was not the first priority, nor the one that guided our actions; rather, the premise on which we based our calculations was that we should regain our rights through negotiations. Furthermore, don't forget that we are Arabs, so it is only natural that if we are wronged by whomever it may be, we are in a position to seek a link with the opposition, just as the Kuwaitis or others are in a position to establish contacts with the Iraqi opposition if [someone] wrongs them.

When our vital interests were exposed to certain and premeditated danger and all other means to find a solution failed, we used military force. I address my question here to the president of the United States and to American officials: Where is the danger to American interests, both inside and outside Kuwait?

You know that Iraqi oil has been sold to you ever since we came to power, although relations were severed at the time. The volume of trade increased following the restoration of relations in 1984 and up to the time you decided to embargo Iraqi oil. You were importing about a third of our exports. This came about not at the initiative of the technicians or market preferences but as a result of a political decision.

We are familiar with the declarations that have been made. Your interests are your trade and the continuation of oil supplies to you. What then is the threat that makes you contemplate military action in which you shall be defeated? And I will tell you how you shall be defeated.

You are a great power, and we know that you can hurt us, as I told the ambassador. But you will lose the region afterward. You would not get us to kneel down even if you were to use all your weapons.

You can destroy our scientific, technical, economic, and oil facilities. But the more you destroy, the more difficult it will become for you. After that, we will not hesitate to attack your interests in the region. We even attacked Kuwait once it became clear to us that [we had to choose between] the conspiracy and its dangerous consequences or a proud, peaceful, and capable Iraq.

Do not place us in such a position once again. When we see that we are denied life's opportunities, we shall deny them to others. I know that you are a great power and can inflict injury and destruction, but no one except God can crush man.

But why do you seek our enmity? You made grievous errors when you weakened your friends to the point that they lost their influence in the eyes of their people. I urge you to allow your friends room to maneuver and the opportunity to reshape their personalities so as to become more acceptable in the eyes of their people.

You speak of Iraq's tendency to commit aggression. If Iraq is aggressive, why were you engaged in a dialogue with Iraq while it was at war with Iran? Do you like aggression? If you are referring to the statement of last April 2, you know that we did not issue such a statement before, during, or after the war.[13]

Why did I make such a statement? Certain Western and American cliques were setting the stage for Israeli aggression against us. The statement was necessary to forestall a stupid action against us. We believe this serves peace better than silence, which would not deter Israel from taking a stupid action against us, forcing us to retaliate.

You recall that during the war, we were under constant bombardment from Iran against Baghdad for a year. Then when we obtained rockets, we did not use them, but threatened Iran that we would use them.

Had Iran listened to our advice, we would not have used them. Praise be to God that so far Israel has listened to us. Is that better for peace? Baghdad can take many rockets, but Israel's cities cannot. So we are happy that such a thing has not happened.

Who loves peace? The party who is pleased that nothing has happened or the one who wants to strike?

In brief, if what the American president wants is the same as his declared policy concerning American interests in the area as we spoke of them, it is our opinion that escalation, tension, and military action go against those interests. However, if there are other American interests of which we are not aware, other than what we mentioned, then that is another matter.

In any event, we do want stability. We want peace. But we hate submission and shall not accept it. We hate hunger, because our people went hungry for a thousand years, and we shall not go back to that. We look to a future characterized by honor and legitimate human endeavor, including developed and good relations with the United States of America if it so wishes.

That is my new message, which I would like to relay to President Bush.

WILSON: Thank you, Mr. President. I shall certainly relay it to my government. I shall first relay your words by telephone upon my arrival at the embassy, then I shall relay them in writing.

You justly observed that this is a critical period not only for Iraqi-U.S. relations but also for stability in the region and the world.

SADDAM: Why critical to the world?

WILSON: There is anxiety and instability in world markets.

SADDAM: You knew that. We accepted $25 per barrel, and now, had it not been for your embargo, the price would have gone down to $21 per barrel, more or less.

However, when there is a sudden embargo on five million barrels, anxiety arises. We are committed to the OPEC decision of $21 per barrel. . . . Perhaps others, the merchants, will benefit, but not the American people. We have a strong case. A small part of Iraq,[14] instead of respecting greater Iraq and its interests, was encouraged by some to play a conspiratorial role against the economy of Iraq so as to destroy our economy. We defended ourselves without detriment to any other party, such as the United States.

WILSON: I sense that I touched a raw nerve. Actually what I meant to say was that in these difficult and perilous times, it is in my view absolutely essential to keep an avenue of communication open between us in order to avoid incidents and miscalculations. That is the only way that we can keep this tense and emotional situation [from getting] worse.

I therefore welcome this opportunity to relay this message. I would like to make a couple of observations, and to go back and explore some of the points you raised. I shall convey the reply of my president to you and to the minister.

In the first part of your message, you mentioned that Kuwait is a part of Iraq.

SADDAM: That is historically accurate. In saying this, we are affirming that Kuwait should have cooperated with Iraq, not conspired against it. Yet Kuwait's paranoia made it conspire against Iraq.

That is the special relationship between Iraq and Kuwait that should have guided its actions. That relationship does not exist with all the other countries, such as Egypt and Saudi Arabia, which have the best of relations with Iraq.

WILSON: It is very important that I understand the precise nature of this relationship.

SADDAM: The nature of this relationship is determined by the relationship between the peoples of the two countries. Neither I nor the Americans nor the Soviets nor anyone else determines them. We are of the opinion that it should be based on shared fraternity and mutual respect.

WILSON: Is that what was missing in the relationship with Kuwait?

SADDAM: Yes, especially in recent months. I kept running after Jaber[15] so that we could determine where the border should be, and he kept saying, "No, leave it to others." We have documents to substantiate that. We were perplexed by what was happening, then it turned out that he was conspiring against us.

WILSON: Thank you. The second point you raised had to do with your brotherly relations with Saudi Arabia, and you mentioned your nonaggression pact with Saudi Arabia. I wish to convey to you the concern of my government regarding Iraq's intentions now. I feel that you have addressed that concern in a general way, but permit me. . . .

SADDAM: What would it take to put your concerns to rest?

WILSON: I don't know, but I will ask my president. But I do know that you are a clear and frank person. [If] you were to give me your assurances that under current circumstances—as of now we have not witnessed any military action on the part of the United States or Saudi Arabia—under these circumstances I would like to ask for assurances from you that you have no intention of taking any military action against Saudi Arabia.

SADDAM: You may convey my assurances to Saudi Arabia and to everyone in the Middle East. We shall not attack anyone who does not attack us. We shall not harm anyone who does not harm us. Anyone who solicits our friendship shall find us more eager for friendship than he is. This is not an agenda to suit the needs of the hour as some imagine but one due to humanitarian considerations and in the interests of our people.

As for Saudi Arabia, such a question never even occurred to me. Relations between us are strong, unless you have something that we do not know. It is only natural that King Fahd should receive Jaber and the crown prince of Kuwait,[16] when he calls on him. That does not bother us. What would bother us is if they were to permit some action against Iraq from Saudi Arabia.

By the way, say hello to President Bush. And tell him that Jaber and his clique are finished. They're history. The Sabah family are has-beens.

It is legitimate for one to be concerned about one's interests. We would like to know precisely what the legitimate interests of the United States are, and how to reassure the United States about those interests.

I say this not as a tactical ploy because you have imposed an embargo against us—I was careful to wait until after your embargo before I saw you, nor am I trying here and now to get the embargo lifted, or expecting the United States to be in favor of what has taken place—but in order to understand what legitimate U.S. interests are and to advise the United States not to get carried away to the point that it becomes difficult for it to retreat from a position.

WILSON: I shall convey this to my government. I came here with three things on my mind that reflect the concerns of my government. First, there is the nature of the invasion, and you know the position of my government on this point very well. Second, your intentions toward Saudi Arabia, which you have answered. The third point concerns the safety of American citizens, particularly allowing U.S. citizens to leave. You know that Americans are very sensitive about being prevented from leaving. This also concerns Americans in Kuwait, regardless of any withdrawal.

SADDAM: How can you say that there has been no withdrawal, and then say something altogether different?

WILSON: I saw three convoys from Basra,[17] and informed Washington of that.

SADDAM: It took our forces three days to enter Kuwait, so the withdrawal cannot be completed in one day. The withdrawal of forces depends on the international climate. We shall not leave Kuwait a delectable morsel to be swallowed up by anyone, even if we have to fight the whole world.

If the threat to Kuwait increases, we shall double the forces there. The size of our forces will be adapted to fit the size of the threat. When the threat ceases to exist, all forces will be withdrawn. We do not want Kuwait to become another Lebanon. I do not think that it is in [anyone's] interest for Iraqi forces to withdraw in a hurry, which would leave Kuwait to the warring factions.

The provisional government[18] was advised to form various militias; we advised them that the Popular Army would suffice.

As to the Americans in Kuwait and Iraq, there is a ban on travel that applied to everyone, Iraqis and foreigners, in Iraq and Kuwait. Your sources know that our Army there has been extremely disciplined toward foreigners. Yet the communiqué issued by the Kuwaiti government permits them to travel to Iraq, and over here security clearly reigns.

WILSON: May I ask you directly: When will you allow American citizens, both residents and visitors, to leave?

SADDAM: Rather, when shall we allow foreigners in general to leave?

WILSON: I do not permit myself to talk on behalf of others.

SADDAM: I wanted to make it clear that this restriction does not apply only to the Americans. In due course we will inform you.

WILSON: Please allow me to ask you that you study this question urgently because it is a highly emotional and sensitive issue both for our government and our people.

SADDAM: We understand that and we also understand the humanitarian aspect.

WILSON: Finally, I would like to say two things. You have pointed to the good behavior of Iraqi troops, and your minister[19] and your deputy minister[20] also assured me of this and I think this is expected. Let me draw your attention, and this is an important point, to the fact that last night the house of the counselor of our Embassy in Kuwait was broken into by some Iraqi soldiers. This contradicts the policy that you have stated, and I add that it is also a violation of diplomatic immunity. I would not have said this if you had not brought up the matter.

SADDAM: Yesterday I met with some of our officers and they told me about some elements—Asians, Saudis, and others—who were breaching security in some warehouses. Anyway, if the Iraqi Army had done this, we would acknowledge it and assure you that it was a mistake and we would take measures to punish those involved. This behavior is against our policy.

WILSON: Last point. During these difficult days, especially on the safety of the American citizens. . . .

SADDAM: Do you plan to attack us and for that you want to remove your citizens?

WILSON: No. But it is my duty to give them the freedom to decide to leave. I personally will stay, and I love life here. I would like to say also that during the crisis the doors were always open to me and to my colleagues in the Foreign Ministry from 8 A.M. to 4 P.M. and I appreciate that. I appreciate your wish to meet with me and to reassure me on the fate of our citizens in Kuwait.

SADDAM: Rest assured.

WILSON: I would like to assure you of my professionalism as minister. Dialogue is the lifeline for diplomats and politicians.

SADDAM: It is natural that you assure me of the good intentions of your colleagues, but you must assure me of your effort to carry my letter to President Bush.

～ Notes

1. Tariq Aziz
2. April C. Glaspie
3. Words and phrases in brackets reflect an effort by the translator to make the translation smoother.
4. Five open letters were sent from Saddam Hussein to Iran on Iraq's intentions during the Iran-Iraq war.
5. Former Iraqi leader, 1958–63
6. In Arabic, *hakim*
7. In Arabic, *qaimmaqam*
8. In Arabic, *qada*
9. The invasion of Kuwait
10. Words and phrases in parentheses reflect parentheses in original Arabic text.
11. The meeting between the prime minister of Kuwait and the deputy chairman of the Revolutionary Command Council of Iraq on July 31–August 1, 1990, in Jiddah, Saudi Arabia
12. Taha Muhieddin Marouf
13. The Iran-Iraq war
14. Kuwait
15. Kuwaiti Emir Sheik Jaber al-Ahmad al-Sabah
16. Sheik Saad al-Abdullah al-Sabah
17. These convoys appeared to be part of an Iraqi withdrawal from Kuwait after the initial invasion.
18. The government set up in Kuwait under Iraqi control following the August 2, 1990, invasion
19. Tariq Aziz
20. Nizar Hamdoon

A Chronology of Events

~ Time Line

636: The greatest battle ever fought between Persians and Arabs takes place on plains of Qadisiyah in southern Iraq.

1534: Ottoman Turks conquer Baghdad.

1752: Sabah dynasty established in region of present-day Kuwait under Sheik Sabah bin Jabir al-Sabah; area loosely controlled by the Ottoman Turkish Empire.

1871: Sheik Abdullah ibn Sabah al-Sabah accepts status as subprovincial governor within the Basra province of the Ottoman Turkish Empire.

1899: Sheik Mubarak ibn Sabah al-Sabah signs "exclusive agreement" with Britain; treaty was never ratified.

1913: British-Ottoman treaty recognizes Kuwait as an autonomous district of the Ottoman Empire with special ties to Britain; treaty was never ratified.

1916: Sykes-Picot Agreement between Britain and France delineates future control of the Middle East between the two countries.

October 3, 1918: Ottoman rule over Arabs ends.

April 25, 1920: Iraq is made Class A mandate entrusted to British.

August 27, 1921: British install Faisal as first king of Iraq.

April 1923: Britain, as mandatory power for Iraq, approves Protocol of Uqair, which establishes borders among Iraq, Kuwait, and Saudi Arabia.

October 13, 1932: Iraq gains independence.

April 28, 1937: Saddam Hussein is born in village near Tikrit.

April 1, 1941: Rashid Ali coup.

July 14, 1958: Coup led by General Abd al-Karim Qassim. Nationalist military officers overthrow pro-Western, Hashemite monarchy; Qassim becomes prime minister and commander-in-chief.

October 7, 1959: Qassim survives assassination attempt by Baathists, one of whom is Saddam Hussein.

June 19, 1961: Kuwait becomes independent.

June 25, 1961: Iraq's revolutionary prime minister, Abd al-Karim Qassim, claims sovereignty over Kuwait; further action is forestalled by rapid deployment of British forces, later replaced by an Arab League force.

February 8, 1963: First Baathist regime replaces Qassim. Baathists implicitly recognize independence of Kuwait but reserve position on boundaries.

November 18, 1963: Abd al-Salaam Arif overthrows the Baath Party regime in a bloodless coup.

October 1964: Saddam is imprisoned and spends two years at the central prison in Baghdad after a failed coup attempt.

June 5, 1967: Six-Day war with Israel begins, resulting in a military defeat for the Arab forces.

June 6, 1967: Iraq severs relations with the United States with the onset of the Six-Day war.

July 17, 1968: Baath Party comes to power for the second time in Iraq; Ahmad Hasan al-Bakr becomes president and commander-in-chief of the army; Saddam Hussein becomes deputy chairman of the ruling Revolutionary Command Council.

February 1969: War with Kurds intensifies.

March 11, 1970: Baath Party reaches autonomy agreement with the Kurds.

April 9, 1972: Soviet Premier Aleksei Kosygin signs 15-year Soviet-Iraqi Treaty of Friendship and Cooperation with Baghdad.

June 1, 1972: Iraq Petroleum Company (IPC) is nationalized.

March 20, 1973: Incursion and brief occupation by Iraqi forces of al-Samitah, a Kuwaiti border post.

April 28, 1973: Iraq reasserts claim to two Kuwaiti islands, Warba and Bubiyan, which control Iraqi access to the Gulf.

October 6, 1973: October war breaks out between Arabs and Israelis; oil embargo follows.

March 9, 1974: Kurdish autonomy accords collapse and full-scale fighting breaks out; hundreds of thousands of Iraqi Kurds flee to Iran.

March 6, 1975: Iran and Iraq sign the Algiers agreement, under which Iran agrees to end its support of the Kurds and Iraq gives up half of the Shatt al-Arab waterway.

September 17, 1978: The United States, Egypt, and Israel sign the Camp David Peace accords, producing peace between Egypt and Israel.

October 6, 1978: Ayatollah Ruhollah Khomeini, expelled from Iraq, arrives in France.

January 16, 1979: The Shah of Iran, Mohammad Reza Pahlevi, flees Iran.

February 1, 1979: Ayatollah Khomeini returns triumphantly to Iran; ten days later, he proclaims an Islamic republic.

July 17, 1979: Saddam Hussein becomes president, chairman of the Revolutionary Command Council, and commander-in-chief of the armed forces.

September 17, 1980: Saddam abrogates 1975 Algiers agreement and declares Iraqi sovereignty over the Shatt al-Arab waterway.

September 22, 1980: Iraq invades Iran.

June 7, 1981: Israeli warplanes destroy Iraq's Osirak nuclear facility.

June 6, 1982: Israel invades Lebanon.

November 26, 1984: The United States and Iraq resume diplomatic relations.

February 9, 1986: Iranians capture Iraq's Fao Peninsula.

May 17, 1987: Iraqi warplane attacks USS *Stark*, killing 37 American sailors.

March 28, 1988: Iraqi Army attacks Kurds with chemical weapons.

August 20, 1988: Cease-fire is announced in the Iran-Iraq war.

June 3, 1989: Ayatollah Ruhollah Khomeini dies.

September 1989: The Kuwaiti Emir makes his first trip in a decade to Iraq to receive the Rafadin Medal, Iraq's highest honor.

February 19, 1990: Saddam, in a speech to the Arab Cooperation Council, says that the United States should remove its military presence from the Gulf.

March 15, 1990: Iraqis hang journalist Farzad Bazoft; Britain recalls its ambassador.

April 2, 1990: Saddam Hussein announces that if Iraq is attacked by Israel, he will "burn half of Israel" with chemical weapons.

July 17, 1990: Saddam publicly accuses some oil-producing states of trying to strangle his economy by overproducing oil and keeping world prices low and implicitly threatens to use force against them.

July 18, 1990: Iraqi Foreign Minister Tariq Aziz accuses Kuwait of border violations and stealing Iraqi oil.

July 24, 1990: Iraq deploys tens of thousands of troops to the Kuwaiti border; American warships in the area are put on alert.

August 1, 1990: Talks between Iraq and Kuwait in Jiddah, Saudi Arabia, break down.

August 2, 1990: Iraq invades Kuwait at 2 A.M.; the emir flees to Saudi Arabia and sets up a government-in-exile; the United States, Britain, and France freeze assets of Iraq and Kuwait; United Nations Security Council condemns invasion, passing Resolution 660, calling for immediate, unconditional withdrawal of Iraqi troops from Kuwait.

August 6, 1990: Security Council passes Resolution 661, ordering a global embargo of trade with Iraq; the Saudi government agrees to permit the deployment of American and foreign troops on Saudi soil.

August 7, 1990: U.S. President George Bush orders combat troops, ships, and warplanes to Saudi Arabia, beginning Operation Desert Shield.

August 8, 1990: Iraq annexes Kuwait; other oil-producing nations indicate they will step up production to make up for embargoed Iraqi and Kuwaiti oil.

August 9, 1990: Security Council passes Resolution 662, declaring Iraqi annexation of Kuwait as "null and void."

August 10, 1990: Arab leaders meet in Cairo, where 12 of 21 Arab League members vote to honor the United Nations embargo, endorse the Saudi invitation to American troops, and agree to commit troops to an all-Arab military force to join Americans and other nations in defense of Saudi Arabia.

August 12, 1990: Saddam Hussein announces peace plan linking an Iraqi withdrawal from Kuwait to an Israeli withdrawal from the occupied territories and a Syrian withdrawal from Lebanon.

August 15, 1990: Saddam agrees to all Iranian demands to settle Iran-Iraq war.

August 17, 1990: Iraq says it will hold Westerners at civil and military installations as human shields against attack.

August 18, 1990: Security Council passes Resolution 664, demanding the immediate release of foreigners from Iraq and Kuwait.

August 24, 1990: Iraqi troops surround the embassies of several Western countries in Kuwait City and cut off electricity and water to those inside.

August 25, 1990: Security Council passes Resolution 665, authorizing the use of force by Western navies to enforce sanctions.

August 28, 1990: Iraq renames a northern strip of Kuwaiti territory Saddamiyat al-Mitlaa, in honor of Saddam, and incorporates it into Basra; the rest of Kuwait is made the nineteenth province of Iraq.

September 9, 1990: President George Bush and Soviet President Mikhail S. Gorbachev hold a summit meeting in Helsinki, Finland, where they declare unconditional support for international sanctions against Iraq.

September 13, 1990: Security Council passes Resolution 666, reaffirming Iraqi responsibility for the safety and well-being of foreign nationals and specifying guidelines for the delivery of food and medical supplies.

September 16, 1990: Security Council passes Resolution 667, condemning Iraqi aggression against diplomats and diplomatic compounds in Kuwait.

September 22, 1990: Saudi Arabia ends oil supplies to Jordan, orders Jordanian and Yemeni diplomats to leave the kingdom.

September 24, 1990: Security Council passes Resolution 669, emphasizing that only a special United Nations sanctions committee can approve the shipment of food, medicine, and other humanitarian aid shipments to Iraq or occupied Kuwait.

September 25, 1990: Security Council passes Resolution 670, expanding the economic embargo to include air traffic in or out of Iraq and Kuwait, except for humanitarian aid authorized by the special sanctions committee.

October 29, 1990: Security Council passes Resolution 674, demanding that Iraq cease the mistreatment of Kuwaiti and other foreign nationals.

November 28, 1990: Security Council passes Resolution 677, condemning Iraq's attempts to change Kuwait's demographic composition.

November 29, 1990: Security Council passes Resolution 678, authorizing the use of force against Iraq if it does not withdraw from Kuwait by January 15.

December 6, 1990: Saddam announces release of all foreign hostages.

January 9, 1991: U.S. Secretary of State James A. Baker III and Iraq's Foreign Minister Tariq Aziz meet for talks in Geneva to avert war but fail to find peaceful solution.

January 12, 1991: U.S. Congress votes to give the president the authority to go to war to liberate Kuwait from Iraqi occupation.

January 15, 1991: Security Council deadline for Iraqi withdrawal from Kuwait expires at midnight.

January 17, 1991: American and allied air forces begin bombing Baghdad less than 19 hours after the United Nations–mandated deadline.

January 18, 1991: Iraq hits Israel with at least eight Scud missiles.

January 20, 1991: Patriot rockets shoot down two Iraqi missiles as they approach Dhahran, Saudi Arabia.

January 22, 1991: An Iraqi Scud missile eludes the Patriot air-defense system and strikes Tel Aviv, leaving three people dead and at least 70 injured; Iraq begins setting Kuwaiti oil facilities ablaze.

January 23, 1991: After some 12,000 sorties, General Colin L. Powell, chairman of the U.S. Joint Chiefs of Staff, announces that allied forces have achieved air superiority.

January 25, 1991: American military officials announce that Iraq has sabotaged Kuwait's main supertanker loading pier, dumping millions of gallons of crude oil into the Gulf.

January 30, 1991: The first major ground battle of the war is fought in and around the frontier port of Khafji in the northeast corner of Saudi Arabia; U.S. General H. Norman Schwarzkopf says that the allies have achieved air supremacy over Iraqi skies, and that allied forces have destroyed all of Iraq's nuclear reactors, half of its biological-warfare plants, and chemical storage and production sites.

January 31, 1991: Saudi forces recapture the town of Khafji near the Saudi-Kuwaiti border after more than 30 hours of fighting against Iraqi forces.

February 4, 1991: Iranian President Ali Akbar Hashemi Rafsanjani makes a surprise offer to hold direct talks with both Iraq and the United States to try to end the Gulf war.

February 15, 1991: Iraq offers a plan for withdrawal from Kuwait, but it adds new conditions and President Bush dismisses it as "a cruel hoax."

February 18, 1991: In Moscow, President Gorbachev presents Iraqi Foreign Minister Aziz with a last-ditch effort to end the war.

February 19, 1991: Bush rejects Soviet plan, saying it "falls well short" of Security Council requirements for ending the war.

February 22, 1991: Bush and the allies give Iraq until 8 P.M. Gulf time on February 23 to begin withdrawing from Kuwait or face a ground campaign.

February 24, 1991: Allied forces launch ground offensive; more than 300 attack helicopters from the 101st Airborne Division move deep into Iraq in the largest helicopter assault in military history.

February 26, 1991: Iraq scores its most devastating Scud attack of the war when a missile explodes in the air and hits a U.S. barracks in Dhahran, Saudi Arabia, killing 28 soldiers and injuring at least 89; with its forces surrounded, Iraq announces it is withdrawing from Kuwait, but Bush says war will continue.

February 27, 1991: George Bush declares victory over Iraq and announces Kuwait's liberation; orders allied combat suspended at midnight, Washington time.

February 28, 1991: Saddam Hussein orders his troops to cease fire; he begins to repress unrest among the Shiites in the south and the Kurds in the north.

March 2, 1991: Security Council passes Resolution 686, formally offering to speed the flow of medicine to Iraq, while reaffirming the sanctions against Iraq; it also demands that Iraq accept liability under international law for damages incurred by Kuwait during the seven-month Iraqi occupation.

March 3, 1991: Allied and Iraqi commanders meet at an Iraqi airfield at Safwan to lay the groundwork for an official cease-fire.

March 4, 1991: Iraqis release first ten POWs, including six Americans; Kuwait's Crown Prince Sheik Saad al-Abdullah al-Sabah returns to Kuwait City for first time since invasion.

March 5, 1991: Iraq voids annexation of Kuwait and promises to return looted property; Iraq frees 35 more POWs, including 15 Americans; thousands of Iraqis flee growing anti-Saddam unrest.

March 8, 1991: Iraq frees over 1,000 Kuwaitis abducted as hostages, 40 foreign journalists, and two more American POWs; U.S. Secretary of State James A. Baker III meets with General H. Norman Schwarzkopf and Saudi leaders in Riyadh at start of his Gulf tour.

March 14, 1991: Sheik Jaber al-Ahmad al-Sabah, the Emir of Kuwait, arrives in Kuwait after seven and a half months in exile; Kurdish rebels claim control over wide areas of the Kurdish region in northern Iraq.

March 20, 1991: An American F-15 shoots down an Iraqi fighter-bomber over Iraq after it defied ban on Iraqi military flights.

March 22, 1991: Security Council lifts its embargo on food supplies to Iraq and eases restrictions on shipments of certain critical humanitarian goods including fuel for trucks and electrical generators.

March 23, 1991: Saddam reshuffles his cabinet as he struggles to maintain control in light of continued insurrection.

April 2, 1991: Iraq's Army appears to have crushed a month-long rebellion in the Shiite south and the Kurdish north.

April 3, 1991: Security Council passes resolution 687, offering to end the Gulf war and progressively lift most sanctions against Iraq if Saddam accepts a series of stringent military and financial conditions.

April 6, 1991: Iraq accepts the United Nations cease-fire.

Bibliography

∼ Books

Abu Jaber, Kamel S. *The Arab Baath Socialist Party: History, Ideology, and Organization.* Syracuse, N.Y.: Syracuse University Press, 1966.

Abu-Hakima, Ahmad Mustafa. *The Modern History of Kuwait 1750–1965.* Montreal: McGill University Press, 1982.

Ajami, Fouad. *The Arab Predicament: Arab Political Thought and Practice Since 1967.* Cambridge: Cambridge University Press, 1981.

Al-Ebraheem, Hassan A. *Kuwait: A Political Study.* Kuwait: Kuwait University, 1975.

Al-Khalil, Samir. *The Monument: Art, Vulgarity and Responsibility in Iraq.* Los Angeles and Berkeley: University of California Press, 1991.

——— . *Republic of Fear: The Politics of Modern Iraq.* Los Angeles and Berkeley: University of California Press, 1989.

Amnesty International. *Amnesty International 1990 Report.* New York: Amnesty International Publications, 1990.

——— . *Amnesty International 1990 Report on Kuwait.* New York: Amnesty International Publications, 1990.

——— . *Iraq: Evidence of Torture.* London: Amnesty International Publications, 1981.

Axelgard, Frederick W. *A New Iraq?* The Washington Papers, no. 133, The Center for Strategic and International Studies. New York: Praeger, 1988.

Bakhash, Shaul. *The Reign of the Ayatollahs: Iran and the Islamic Revolution.* New York: Basic Books, 1989.

Baram, Amatzia. *Culture, History and Ideology in the Formation of Ba'thist Iraq, 1968–89.* New York: St. Martin's Press, 1991.

Batatu, Hanna. *The Old Social Classes and the Revolutionary Movements of Iraq: A Study of Iraq's Old Landed and Commercial Classes and of Its Communists, Ba'thists, and Free Officers.* Princeton: Princeton University Press, 1978.

Bulloch, John, and Harvey Morris. *Saddam's War.* London: Faber and Faber, 1991.

Chubin, Shahram, and Charles Tripp. *Iran and Iraq at War.* Boulder, Colo.: Westview Press, 1988.

Cordesman, Anthony H. *The Iran-Iraq War and Western Security, 1984–87.* New York: Jane's, 1987.

———. and Abraham R. Wagner. *The Lessons of Modern War,* volume II: *The Iran-Iraq War.* Boulder, Colo.: Westview Press, 1990.

Crystal, Jill. *Oil and Politics in the Gulf: Rulers and Merchants in Kuwait and Qatar.* Cambridge: Cambridge University Press, 1990.

Dann, Uriel. *Iraq Under Qassem.* Tel Aviv: Praeger, 1969.

Devlin, John F. *The Baath Party: A History from Its Origins to 1966.* Stanford, Calif.: Hoover Institution Press, 1976.

Dickson, H.R.P. *Kuwait and Her Neighbors.* London: Allen and Unwin, 1956.

Friedman, Thomas L. *From Beirut to Jerusalem.* New York: Farrar, Straus and Giroux, 1989.

Ghareeb, Edmund. *The Kurdish Question in Iraq.* Syracuse, N.Y.: Syracuse University Press, 1981.

Held, Colbert C. *Middle East Patterns: Places, Peoples, and Politics.* Boulder, Colo.: Westview Press, 1989.

Helms, Christine Moss. *Iraq: Eastern Flank of the Arab World.* Washington, D.C.: The Brookings Institution, 1984.

Iskander, Amir. *Saddam Hussein: le militant, le penseur et l'homme.* Paris: Hachette Réalités, 1980.

Joyner, Christopher C., ed. *The Gulf War: Lessons for Strategy, Law and Diplomacy.* Westport, Ct.: Greenwood Press, 1990.

Karsh, Efraim, ed. *The Iran-Iraq War: Impact and Implications*. New York: St. Martin's Press, 1989.

Khadduri, Majid. *The Gulf War: The Origins and Implications of the Iraq-Iran Conflict*. New York: Oxford University Press, 1988.

——— . *Socialist Iraq: A Study in Iraqi Politics Since 1968*. Washington, D.C.: The Middle East Institute, 1978.

——— . *Independent Iraq: A Study in Iraqi Politics from 1932 to 1958*. 2d ed. London: Oxford University Press, 1960.

——— . *Republican Iraq: A Study in Iraqi Politics Since the Revolution of 1958*. London: Oxford University Press, 1969.

Lamb, David. *The Arabs: Journeys Beyond the Mirage*. New York: Random House, 1987.

Litwak, Robert. *Security in the Persian Gulf: Sources of Inter-State Conflict*. Montclair, N.J.: Allan Held, Osmun and Co., for The International Institute for Strategic Studies, 1981.

Longrigg, Stephen Hemsley. *Iraq, 1900 to 1950: A Political, Social and Economic History*. London: Oxford University Press, 1953.

——— . and Frank Stoakes. *Iraq*. New York: Praeger, 1958.

Marr, Phebe. *The Modern History of Iraq*. Boulder, Colo.: Westview Press, 1985.

Matar, Fuad. *Saddam Hussein: The Man, the Cause and the Future*. London: Third World Center for Research and Publishing, 1981.

Metz, Helen Chapin, ed. *Iran: A Country Study*. Washington, D.C.: U.S. Government Printing Office, 1989.

——— . *Iraq: A Country Study*. Washington, D.C.: U.S. Government Printing Office, 1990.

Middle East Watch. *Human Rights in Iraq*. New Haven: Yale University Press, 1990.

Miller, Judith, and Laurie Mylroie. *Saddam Hussein and the Crisis in the Gulf*. New York: Times Books, 1990.

Niblock, Tim, ed. *Iraq: The Contemporary State*. London: Croom Helm, 1982.

Pelletiere, Stephen C., and Douglas V. Johnson II. *Lessons Learned: The Iran-Iraq War*. Carlisle Barracks, Pa.: Strategic Studies Institute, U.S. Army War College, 1991.

────· and Leif R. Rosenberger. *Iraqi Power and U.S. Security in the Middle East*. Carlisle Barracks, Pa.: Strategic Studies Institute, U.S. Army War College, 1990.

Penrose, Edith and E.F. *Iraq: International Relations and National Development*. London: Ernest Benn, 1978.

Rossi, Pierre. *Iraq the Land of the New River*. Paris: Les Editions J.A., 1980.

Roux, Georges. *Ancient Iraq*. Harmondsworth, England: Penguin Books, 1980.

Sawdayee, Max. *All Waiting to be Hanged: Iraq Post Six Day War Diary*. Tel Aviv: Levanda Press, 1974.

Seale, Patrick. *Asad: The Struggle for the Middle East*. Los Angeles and Berkeley: University of California Press, 1989.

Sluglett, Peter, and Marion Farouk-Sluglett. *Iraq Since 1958: From Revolution to Dictatorship*. London: Kegan Paul, 1988.

Stark, Freya. *Baghdad Sketches*. London: John Murray, 1937.

────· *Letters*, vol. 1: *The Furnace and the Cup 1914–30*. United Kingdom: Compton Russell, 1974.

────· *Letters*, vol. 2: *The Open Door 1930–35*. United Kingdom: Compton Russell, 1975.

U.S. Department of State. *Patterns of Global Terrorism: 1989*. Washington, D.C.: Department of State Publication, April 1990.

Weissman, Steve, and Herbert Krosney. *The Islamic Bomb: The Nuclear Threat to Israel and the Middle East*. New York: Times Books, 1981.

Winstone, H.V.F., and Zahra Freeth. *Kuwait: Prospect and Reality*. London: Allen and Unwin, 1972.

Young, Gavin. *Iraq: Land of Two Rivers*. London: St. James Place, 1980.

~ Articles

Ajami, Fouad. "The Summer of Arab Discontent," *Foreign Affairs* (1990), pp. 1–20.

────· "The End of Pan-Arabism," *Foreign Affairs* (Winter 1978–1979), p. 355.

Bakhash, Shaul. "How Saddam is Dividing the Arab World," *The New York Review of Books* (November 8, 1990), pp. 49–51.

Baram, Amatzia. "National Integration and Local Orientation in Iraq Under the Ba'ath," *The Jerusalem Journal of International Relations*, 9, no. 3 (1987), pp. 38–49.

————. "Qawmiyya and Wataniyya in Ba'athi Iraq: The Search for a New Balance," *Middle Eastern Studies*, 19, No. 2 (April 1983), pp. 188–200.

————. "Saddam Hussein: A Political Profile," *Jerusalem Quarterly*, no. 17 (Fall 1980) pp. 115–144.

Batatu, Hanna. "Iraq's Underground Shi'a Movements: Characteristics," *The Middle East Journal*, 35 (1981), pp. 578–94.

Carus, W. Seth. "Iraq's Economic and Military Vulnerabilities: How Vulnerable is Iraq's Military?" The Washington Institute for Near East Policy: *Policy Focus* (October 1990), pp. 1, 10–21.

Collins, John M. "Iraqi Options Early in the Persian Gulf Crisis," *CRS Report for Congress* (August 14, 1990), pp. 1–5.

Cordesman, Anthony H. "Iraq and the Issue of Arms Sales," *Royal United Services Institution Journal* (Forthcoming—Spring 1991).

Dawisha, Adeed I. "Iraq: The West's Opportunity," *Foreign Policy* (Winter 1980–81), pp. 134–53.

Eisenstadt, Mike. "The Sword of the Arabs: Iraq's Strategic Weapons," Washington Institute Policy Papers no. 21, The Washington Institute for Near East Policy, 1990.

Helms, Christine Moss. "Iraq: The Regional Power or Pariah?" *The World* (December 1988), pp. 124–29.

Marr, Phebe. "Domestic Politics and Saddam Hussein: Will He Last?" *Middle East Executive Reports* (September 1990), pp. 9, 18–20.

————. "Iraq in the '90s: Its Role in Regional Politics," *Middle East Executive Reports* (July 1990), pp. 9, 14–17.

————. "Iraq in the '90s: Growth Dependent on Oil Revenues, Debt, Spending Priorities," *Middle East Executive Reports* (June 1990), pp. 11–15.

————. "Iraq's Uncertain Future," 90, no. 592 *Current History* (January 1991), pp. 1–4, 39–42.

Mylroie, Laurie. "After the Guns Fell Silent: Iraq in the Middle East," *Middle East Journal*, 43, no. 1 (Winter 1989), pp. 51–67.

————. "The Baghdad Alternative," *Orbis* (Summer 1988), pp. 339–54.

Sciolino, Elaine. "Iran's Durable Revolution," *Foreign Affairs* (Spring 1983), pp. 893–920.

Farouk-Sluglett, Marion, and Peter Sluglett, "Iraq Since 1986: The Strengthening of Saddam." *The Middle East Report* (November–December 1990), pp.19–24.

Timmerman, Kenneth R. "The BNL Blunder: How U.S. Policy Allowed a Bank in Atlanta to Help Finance Saddam Hussein's War Machine," Simon Wiesenthal Center, *Middle East Defense News* (1990), pp. 1–39.

Acknowledgments

This book is a product of both passion and folly, and I could not have written it without the help, encouragement, and friendship of a number of wonderful people.

I first want to thank a handful of scholars who encouraged me to go forward with a project that was a popular, rather than a scholarly treatment of a complicated slice of history. Phebe Marr—scholar, political analyst, role model, neighbor, and friend—has studied Iraq and its people for 35 years. A senior fellow at the National Defense University, Phebe is in a class by herself, and her generosity knows no bounds. She turned over her library to me, read most of the chapters of this book, made time for me despite her own deadlines, and spent long evenings sharing her stories and her analysis. Shaul Bakhash, author and professor of history at George Mason University, also read many of the chapters. He helped me to conceptualize the book with his patient observations and his brilliant analysis. His pursuit of excellence is an inspiration. Amatzia Baram, professor of history at Haifa University, knows Iraq and its history as if he had lived there all his life. A wonderful raconteur, he pulled me out of the quicksand of Iraqi history, told me stories, and made me laugh. Alfred B. Prados, a specialist on Middle East affairs at the Congressional Research Service, says he has "a wastebasket of a mind"; in reality, he is a human encyclopedia of the history of Iraq and its place in the region. Modest and self-effacing, Al patiently and tirelessly answered my endless stream of questions, filling me with bits of history and lore along the way.

I am also indebted to my colleagues: Carol Giacomo, whose insights, editing, and friendship got me through difficult moments; Andrew Rosenthal, who spent long hours sharing information about White House decision-making and Iraq's weapons buildup and reading and editing the early chapters of the book; John H. Cushman, Jr., who helped me through the technical apects of Iraq's military buildup and the conduct of the war; Robert Pear, who painstakingly read the manuscript, offering a combination of textual criticism and his usual kindness; Patrick Tyler, who offered camaraderie, support, and humor in Baghdad before the war. I also want to thank Howell Raines, the Washington bureau chief of *The New York Times*, and Philip Taubman, his deputy, for their understanding along the way. When the text of chapter one mysteriously disappeared from my computer's hard drive and backup system, Earl Smith and Von Aulston of the bureau's technology department worked tirelessly until they found it. Craig Whitney, London Bureau Chief of *The New York Times*, and his staff, offered hospitality and good will during my trip to London.

Other people spent considerable time reading parts of the manuscript and offering valuable suggestions. They include Anthony H. Cordesman, J.C. Hurewitz, Hermann F. Eilts, William C. Triplett, Peter Galbraith, Mark Charney, Michael Wines, Robin Toner, Lin and Carlos Widmann, John Arundel, and Ethan Schwartz. Adam Bellow, whose command of literature and history is breathtaking, urged me to think about the material in new ways. Leonard S. Spector, W. Seth Carus, and Janne E. Nolan saved me from making countless errors in the chapter on Iraq's arms buildup.

I am grateful to Monica Borkowski, an extraordinary researcher, for her assistance in researching the manuscript and for her friendship. Her positive attitude was contagious. Throughout the process, Charlotte Sheedy, my agent, handled all the technical and financial matters and logistical problems with her usual professionalism, offering much-appreciated guidance at crucial moments. Roger Scholl, my editor, devoted an extraordinary amount of time and effort to the project. Patricia Mann, a student at George Washington University, conducted interviews and did valuable research. She gave up evenings and weekends, and cheerfully filled in wherever she was needed. Despite tight deadlines, Kathleen Brandes copyedited the manuscript with precision and skill. Joe Marquette, a wonderful photographer, located and helped select photographs. Jenab Tutunji translated the Arabic texts of the meetings that Saddam held with April C. Glaspie, and with Joseph C. Wilson IV. Joyce Seltzer, as always, offered her friendship and advice. John L. Esposito and Youssef Ibrahim were compassionate during very bleak moments. Christine Rourke and Betsy Folkins, the librarians at the Middle East Institute, were extremely generous in making research material available.

In a sense, to undertake this project in such a short time with two daughters under the age of two was sheer folly. My mother, Jeannette Sciolino, and my mother-in-law, Sondra Brown, came through for me and helped with the children at difficult times in the writing process. I also thank Elma Sumondong, our babysitter, for the love and affection she showered on our girls.

I want to give a special thanks to Sören Kern, a student at Georgetown University who literally lived with this book during the months of writing, spending most of his free time doing research. Sören had once hitchhiked through Iraq, and he has a deep passion for its people and its culture. His precision, doggedness, and creative instincts were stunning.

Finally, and most important, this book would not have been written without my husband, Andrew Plump. Andy supported me in my decision to undertake this project, knowing that it would totally disrupt our lives for six months. He convinced me to stick with it at a moment when I was ready to drop it, and he responded to my ill-temper and fatigue with his usual grace under pressure. He read, edited, and helped rewrite the manuscript, over and over, with his lawyer's eye for detail and analysis. He sacrificed nights and weekends to the project, and was, for much of the time, both mother and father to our daughters, Alessandra and Gabriela.

This book is for him.

Washington, April 19, 1991

Index

Call of Islam Party,
  repression of, 93
Camp David Accords, 200,
  Iraq's position on, 131–32
Camp David Peace Accords, 297
Carter, Jimmy,
  relations with Iraq during presidency,
  162
CBS News,
  reports death of Khairallah, 76
Censorship,
  journalists expelled from postwar Iraq,
  13
  of publications in modern Iraq, 53
Central Intelligence Agency (CIA), 169,
  200, 230,
  operations in Iraq, 160–61, 162
Charles, Sandra, 242–43
Chemical Weapons, 258, 262,
  developed by Iraq, 149–151
  used on Kurds, 186
Cheney, Dick, 212, 236, 244,
  trip to Saudi Arabia, 220
Clark, Ramsey, 240
Cold War, 13
Connally, John B., 240
Corruption,
  in Iraq on eve of war, 249–50

Diplomacy,
  between Iraq and US, 11
  talks between U.S. and Iraq, 271–95
Dole, Robert J., 91, 175–176, 234
Dumas, Roland, 232

Egypt, 14,
  in Arab-Israeli conflict, 131
  relations with Israel, 134
  sends 40,000 troops, 25
  support of U.S. military involvement
  in Gulf, 126
Ellerkmann, Richard,
  as German ambassador to Iraq, 24

Fahd, King, 207–8, 268, 281,
  reaction to invasion, 213
Fairbanks, Richard M. III, 167, 169
Faisal, King
  as Iraq's first king, 44, 45
Faisal II,
  as infant successor to Ghazi's throne,
  46
Fascell, Dante, 177
Federation of Iraqi Women, 40–41, 67
Fitzwater, Marlin,
  announces commencement of war, 27
France,
  arms negotiations with Iraq, 147–48
  arms sales to Iraq, 141, 147–49
  as coalition partner, 148–49

Gates, Robert M., 212, 230
Ghazi, King,
  as successor to Faisal's throne, 46
Gilder, Joshua R., 177
Glaspie, April C., 207,
  interview with Saddam, 179–80
  as ambassador to Iraq, 177–81
  as diplomatic liaison pre-Gulf War, 175
  at hearing before House Foreign Affairs
  Committee, 182
  meeting with Saddam, 32, 271–84
  negotiations with Saddam, 33
  testimony before Senate, 271
  transcript imbroglio, 271–72
Gorbachev, Mikhail S., 233, 299, 300,
  U.N. Resolution 678, 238–39
Gulf Cooperation Council (GCC), 191
  and invasion of Kuwait, 211
Gulf War, 12, 13, 114,
  and environmental damage, 29–30
  and weapons used, 27–28
  estimated cost of, 155

Hadi, Deborah, 254
Hamdoon, Nizar, 33, 243,
  as Iraqi deputy foreign minister, 20
  effectiveness as ambassador to
  Washington, 165–66
  recounts Saddam's early leadership, 59
Hammadi, Saadoun, 75,
  as loyal follower of Saddam, 75
Hammurabi, 41–42
Heath, Edward, 240
Hill & Knowlton,
  as public relations firm, 70
Hitler, Adolph,
  as model for Iraqi nationalism, 46
Hostages, 234, 299,
  held during invasion of Kuwait, 229–30
  in Iran, 11
Howell, Nathaniel W., 181
Hussein, Barzan,
  career of, 72–73
Hussein, King, 207, 281,
  relations with Iraq following invasion,
  214
Hussein, Saddam,
  and activity before the Gulf War, 20
  and Baath Party, 14
  and his presidency, 49
  and his propoganda machine, 23
  and military strategy, 30
  and misreading of U.S. strategy, 33
  and propaganda about, 66–68
  animosity toward foreigners, 11
  arrested for murder, 58–59
  as leader of Baath party, 11
  as president, 55–56
  as successor to Nasser, 14
  as totalitarian ruler, 14